I0814064

Ethnicity, Identity, and the Development of Nationalism in Iran

Modern Intellectual and Political History of the Middle East
Mehrzad Boroujerdi, *Series Editor*

Other titles in Modern Intellectual and Political History of the Middle East

Becoming Turkish: Nationalist Reforms and Cultural Negotiations in Early Republican Turkey, 1923–1945
Hale Yilmaz

Class and Labor in Iran: Did the Revolution Matter?
Farhad Nomani and Sohrab Behdad

The Essentials of Ibāḍī Islam
Valerie J. Hoffman

Globalization and the Muslim World: Culture, Religion, and Modernity
Birgit Schaebler and Leif Stenberg, eds.

God and Juggernaut: Iran's Intellectual Encounter with Modernity
Farzin Vahdat

A Guerrilla Odyssey: Modernization, Secularism, Democracy, and the Fadai Period of National Liberation in Iran, 1971–1979
Peyman Vahabzadeh

International Politics of the Persian Gulf
Mehran Kamrava, ed.

Mirror for the Muslim Prince: Islam and the Theory of Statecraft
Mehrzad Boroujerdi, ed.

Pax Syriana: Elite Politics in Postwar Lebanon
Rola el-Husseini

Raging against the Machine: Political Opposition under Authoritarianism in Egypt
Holger Albrecht

Ethnicity, Identity, and the Development of Nationalism in Iran

DAVID N. YAGHOUBIAN

SYRACUSE UNIVERSITY PRESS

Syracuse, New York 13244-5290

First Edition 2014
14 15 16 17 18 19 6 5 4 3 2 1

∞ The paper used in this publication meets the minimum requirements of the American National Standard for Information Sciences—Permanence of Paper for Printed Library Materials, ANSI Z39.48-1992.

For a listing of books published and distributed by Syracuse University Press, visit www.SyracuseUniversityPress.syr.edu.

ISBN: 978-0-8156-3359-4 (cloth) 978-0-8156-5272-4 (e-book)

Library of Congress Cataloging-in-Publication Data

Yaghoubian, David N. (David Nejde), 1967–
Ethnicity, identity, and the development of nationalism in Iran / David N. Yaghoubian. — First edition.
pages cm. — (Modern intellectual and political history of the Middle East)
Includes bibliographical references and index.
ISBN 978-0-8156-3359-4 (cloth : alkaline paper) — ISBN 978-0-8156-5272-4 (e-book)
1. Armenians—Iran—Social conditions—20th century. 2. Armenians—Iran—Ethnic identity. 3. Armenians—Iran—Biography. 4. Armenians—Iran—Politics and government—20th century. 5. Nationalism—Iran—History—20th century. 6. Iran—Politics and government—1941–1979. 7. Iran—Ethnic relations—History—20th century. 8. Iran—History—20th century—Biography. I. Title.
DS269.A75Y24 2014
305.800955—dc23 2014011756

Manufactured in the United States of America

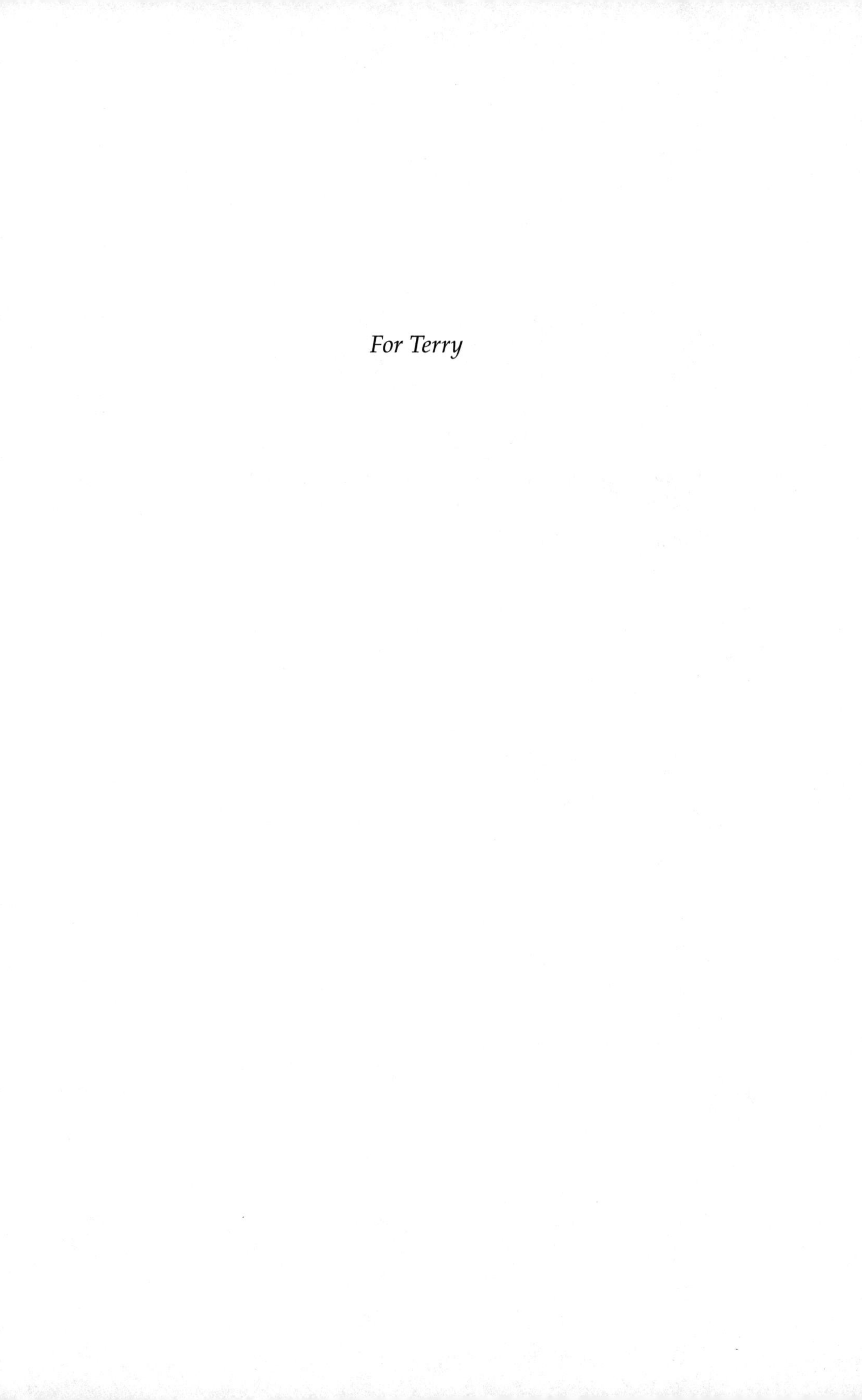

For Terry

David N. Yaghoubian is associate professor of history at California State University, San Bernardino. He is coeditor, with Edmund Burke III, of *Struggle and Survival in the Modern Middle East*, second edition (2006).

Contents

Illustrations

Preface

THROUGHOUT THE SUMMER OF 2008, in the waning months of the George W. Bush presidency, it was open to question whether the United States would launch military strikes against Iran to destroy its nuclear facilities. At the same time, the extent of covert activities within the Islamic Republic to create dissent and possibly topple the governing regime remained obscure. Speculation regarding a potential escalation of covert operations in Iran was fueled by revelations that Congress had appropriated hundreds of millions of dollars the previous year to destabilize the Iranian government, forge internal alliances, and gather intelligence for a potential attack. The expected returns for such an investment included the spawning of antigovernment separatist activity, ethnic insurgency, a "fifth column" of minorities or dissidents, and perhaps the initiation of a government crackdown that would legitimate American intervention to "protect" such groups. Nevertheless, no significant violence or uprising occurred in Iran, and the specter of attack and foreign meddling bolstered Iranian nationalism, if anything. This left few options for a US administration that had long eschewed diplomacy and worn its international alliances thin.

As public debate emerged regarding the potential benefits and perils of destabilizing the Iranian government or of bombing nuclear facilities and infrastructure while American military forces were burdened by commitments simultaneously in neighboring Iraq and Afghanistan, a general consensus developed among scholars of Iranian history and politics that the destabilization of Iran would not come about by means of agitation among the country's ethnic and religious minorities, whatever covert actions the United States might initiate. In a July 2008 *New Yorker* article by investigative journalist Seymour M. Hersh that attempted to plot congressional appropriations for covert operations and gauge the potential for military strikes in the waning months of the Bush administration, Professor Vali Nasr succinctly stated why the strategy of attempting to use ethnic minorities to undermine Iran's government was flawed: "Just because Lebanon, Iraq and Pakistan have ethnic problems, it does not mean that Iran is suffering from the same issue. Iran is an old country—like France and Germany—and its citizens are just as nationalistic. The U.S. is overestimating ethnic tension in Iran. You can always find some activist groups that will go and kill a policeman, but working with the minorities will backfire, and alienate the majority of the population."[1]

Although Nasr's juxtaposition of Iran to Lebanon, Iraq, and Pakistan is also applicable to neighboring Turkey and Afghanistan, where the status of minorities and issues of ethnicity and allegiance have arguably posed the greatest challenges to political stability and national cohesion, his observations regarding Iranian minorities and nationalism are spot-on and accord with the conclusions of other Iran specialists rendered since 2005.[2] And yet although such informed commentary attesting to the unique character of Iranian nationalism and the relative loyalty of Iranian minorities is not difficult to find, to date there has not been an in-depth study that explores the history of Iranian nationalism with the primary goal of illustrating and documenting its mass appeal and resonance within Iran's diverse population. How can we account for the allegiance inculcated via a Persian Islamic–oriented nationalism in a country that has only a 55 percent Persian-speaking majority and hosts substantial populations of linguistic minorities with historic and cultural ties to lands and peoples in bordering regions (Kurds, Baluchis, Azeris, Armenians, Arabs, Turkmen) as well as of religious minorities (Sunni Muslims, Christians, Zoroastrians, Jews)? How have modern Iranian regimes—whether royalist, secular nationalist, or Islamist in ideological orientation—sustained the loyalty of the nation's diverse population throughout wars, invasions, occupations, coups, and revolutions and in the face of persistent outside agitation? Inversely, how have Iranian minorities contributed to the development of Iranian nationalism and deepened their connections to the land and allegiance to political regimes by way of their participation and sacrifices in successive crises and upheavals? What makes Iran so different from its neighbors in this regard?

Certainly the process of arriving at a complex understanding of Iranian nationalism requires the deciphering of its various, often competing ideological strains, meanings, and functions within Iran's majority population of Persian-speaking Shi'a Muslims. Yet the diversity of Iranian society and the broad appeal of Iranian national identity to the country's minorities—who themselves use, shape, and sustain it—demands explication of the inclusive, collaborative characteristics that make Iranian nationalism so durable. This is why I argue that these questions cannot be answered by focusing solely on the dominant linguistic and religious majority, as the handful of existing studies on the subject attempt to do. This book demonstrates that vital insight can be gained into the appeal and durability of Iranian nationalism by understanding its evolution and functions within the country's minority communities and that such an approach is key to answering the most compelling questions about this phenomenon. A brief explanation of the relationship between my research agenda in this study, the Armenian Iranian minorities on which it is focused, and the paucity of works on the subject of Iranian nationalism necessarily brings us back to the subject of ill-conceived US-inspired covert activities to destabilize the Iranian government and the tensions between scholarship, ideology, and policy.

Any beginning student of Iranian political history will soon encounter Richard Cottam's prominent 1964 work *Nationalism in Iran.* Although the data on which the study is based were collected during the mid-1950s, Cottam's sound general observations regarding the historical development of Iranian nationalism and perhaps the dearth of English-language studies on the subject have kept the text in wide circulation and commonly referenced. A new conclusion appended to a 1979 reprint further extended the book's shelf life. Having originally traveled to Iran to gather data for his dissertation in 1951–52 as a Fulbright scholar, Cottam diverted from his research in June 1953 to take a position with the US Central Intelligence Agency (CIA) as an Iran specialist. By this time, Operation Ajax was well under way, rendering irrelevant any reservations the young scholar-turned-operative might have had regarding the covert plan to overthrow the government of Prime Minister Mohammad Mossadegh and the National Front, the progressive/secular nationalist umbrella. In the wake of the CIA-inspired coup of August 19, 1953, which resulted in Mossadegh's arrest and Shah Mohammad Reza Pahlavi's return as dictator, Cottam cultivated contacts and maintained close relationships with members of the National Front, arguing to his superiors that Ajax had been a mistake and that the United States should instead be supporting the shah's liberal opposition. Cottam was subsequently stationed at the American embassy in Tehran from 1956 to 1958, where undercover as a political officer for the State Department, he was tasked with monitoring the National Front and began covertly promoting its agenda. Following the exposure in 1958 of a coup plot by prominent progressive nationalists in which Cottam's own role remains unclear, Cottam resigned from the CIA and returned to academia. By way of a somewhat disillusioning career with the CIA, he had cultivated an appreciation for Iranian aspirations for sovereignty and a complex understanding of the intricacies of Iranian politics during the 1950s. He certainly had an expanded set of data and experiential knowledge to complete his book on Iranian nationalism in 1964, although the exact wellspring of his knowledge and research agenda would remain secret for almost two decades.[3]

The insights afforded by revelations of Cottam's personal experiences in Iranian politics, some of which came to light after the 1979 Iranian Revolution and others that followed his death in 1997, render *Nationalism in Iran* perhaps an even more compelling text in that one can account for Cottam's seeming obsession with the National Front and relatively boisterous—and arguably prophetic—condemnation of American policy, press coverage, and scholarship regarding Mossadegh and the shah. At the same time, these insights help explain why the bulk of the analysis is centered on national politics of the 1920s through the 1950s and why Cottam's coverage of minorities is thinly documented and based largely on logical yet untested and ultimately flawed assumptions. That Cottam considered Iranian minorities at all is laudable, especially as the text has remained the only English-language study on the subject of Iranian nationalism that does so. Yet without a lineage of subsequent analyses to test and refine this elementary and inherently cursory work, and in light of the clout Cottam developed as informal adviser to the Carter administration and in testimony before US Congress during the Iranian Revolution and Hostage Crisis, his conclusions have become canonized.[4] Although it is difficult to determine the extent to which Cottam's analysis on minorities is still influential in Iran policy formulation, if at all, it is perhaps not incidental that his study's flawed conclusions accord with the logic of aforementioned Bush administration assumptions regarding Iranian minority allegiances.

Cottam plotted the level of allegiance of Iranian minorities and their potential to accept Iranian national identity by way of the proximity of each group's linguistic and religious traditions to that of the Shiʿa Persian majority. Thus, primary loyalty to the Iranian nation would ultimately be based on the relative distance or propinquity of a minority group's religious traditions to Shiʿa Islam and of its traditional language to Persian. By this formulation, Cottam assumed that the factors working against the incorporation of Armenian minorities into the Iranian nation were much stronger than those facing the country's Kurds:

> Armenian history was long and proud and, unlike that of the Kurds, not an appendage of the Iranian past. Armenian culture, far richer than Kurdish, was more distinct from the Iranian. Although the Armenian, Kurdish, and Persian languages were all related, Armenian differed profoundly from the other two and was written in a different script from the Arabic used by both Iranians and Kurds. Finally, the Armenians were Christians, and the gulf between Iranian Moslems and Armenian Christians was certainly far greater than that separating the Iranian Shiʿite from the Kurdish Sunni. In addition, a larger proportion of the Armenian population than of the Kurdish was educated, had contact with the West, and was hence receptive to nationalism.[5]

By factoring religious and linguistic proximity with his own subjective comparisons of relative pride and cultural richness, Cottam assumed that Armenian receptivity to nationalism was inherently to *Armenian* nationalism and thus concluded that contemporary (i.e., 1950s) Iranian politics and international developments had "destroyed any possibility that Armenians might embrace Iranian nationalism." Accordingly, he foresaw "the arrival of the day in which Armenians and Iranians will understand that the loyalty Armenians have for Armenia is much too strong to allow fidelity to Iranian nationalism."[6]

Conceding the advantage afforded by twenty/twenty hindsight, it would be obvious to any informed observer of modern Iranian history or contemporary Iranian society that Cottam had things backward. Political and social developments in Iran and internationally in the intervening fifty years have proven exactly the inverse. Throughout the remaining decades of the Pahlavi regime, the Iranian Revolution, and Iran-Iraq War, the Armenian Iranian population deepened its fidelity to and stake in Iranian nationalism and almost universally chose not to immigrate to the neighboring Republic of Armenia following its independence in 1991. And yet, like Vali Nasr's integrally related point, given earlier, regarding the allegiance of Iranian minorities and Iranian nationalist sensibilities, such informed observations are essentially hearsay, without sustained analysis and documentation. Recognizing the value of Cottam's study as an essential if problematic seminal work, *Ethnicity, Identity, and the Development of Nationalism in Iran* draws from its framework and hypotheses regarding the Armenians of Iran to advance and refine our understanding of Iranian nationalism.

Because the parameters Cottam identified regarding the religious and linguistic proximity of Armenians were correct, and especially because his predictions at the time based on those factors turned out to be completely mistaken, Armenian Iranians are arguably the most important single group within Iran to study at present if one seeks to understand the mass appeal of Iranian nationalism and the dynamics of popular receptivity to it. Armenians do in fact hold deep attachments to their geographically adjacent, traditional homeland and have maintained a distinct language and religious faith that are central to their cultural identity. No other group of Iranians, save perhaps Iranian Jews, has remained as distant in linguistic and religious heritage to Iranian nationalism in any of its modern ideological orientations—monarchist, secular nationalist, Islamist, or Marxist. Illumination of the process by which Armenians have nevertheless acquired and maintained a strong sense of Iranian national identity uniquely enables us to examine the elemental functions and dynamics of nationalism in modern Iran.

Iranian allegiances are too complex to be plotted and too durable to be broken along ethnic lines. Only an analysis that explores the collaborative, dialogic characteristics that make Iranian nationalism appealing and functional to minorities and that documents the ways in which these minorities have used, shaped, and sustained it in their own lives is sufficient to illustrate this phenomenon. In a lighter frame, such an approach provides an opportunity to view the making of modern Iran and the epic events that distinguish its colorful history through the rich and unique lens of the minority experience.

Acknowledgments

DURING A FAMILY DINNER one night in the fall of 1979, which by default took place immediately after the evening news coverage of developments in Iran, I posed what I thought was a simple question to my parents. "Are we Iranian, Armenian, or American?" My father's affirmative response to that question marks the original inception of this study. I would therefore like to begin by recognizing the innumerable contributions that my parents, N. Jack Yaghoubian and Lynn Kreuzberger Yaghoubian, have made to the advent of this work and express my deep gratitude for their love and support.

This book is dedicated to Edmund "Terry" Burke III, whose riveting classes at the University of California (UC), Santa Cruz, inspired me to become a historian and whose seminal work on Middle Eastern social biographies laid the groundwork for this study. For his ongoing mentorship and continual inspiration, I am forever indebted.

I sincerely thank Ira Lapidus for his support throughout my graduate school years at UC Berkeley and for his interest in and guidance on my dissertation. I am also eternally grateful for the direction, patience, and encouragement of dissertation adviser Hamid Algar.

This study would not have been possible without the participation of the people who spoke with me at length about their lives and experiences, shared materials and insight, and offered support and assistance while I conducted interviews. My deepest appreciation extends to Sevak and Nella Saginian, Mara Setkhanian-Martin, Artavast and Lucik (Moradiance) Melikian, Vram Gorjian, Ruben Gorjian, Hagob and Arshalous

Hagobian, Nejde Hagobian, Arshak and Jennik Gorjian, Lilet Marzbetuny, and Zareh Marzbetuny.

Special thanks to Camron Amin, Houri Berberian, Jason Cohn, John Drabble, John Ely, Arash Khazeni, Michal Kohout, Afshin Marashi, Eric Massie, Michael Provence, Timothy Pytell, and Lynn Yaghoubian—each of whom generously took the time to read some or all of the manuscript and offer suggestions for improvement. My sincere thanks extend to Richard Allen, Pat Beaupre, Diane Clemens, Joyce Hanson, Jamal Nassar, Cheryl Riggs, Andy Steuer, and Chris Vaughan for the various ways in which their stalwart support contributed directly to the success of this project. Thanks also to copy editor Annie Barva.

I was fortunate to receive institutional support from the UC Berkeley Department of History and Center for Middle Eastern Studies, the California State University (CSU) San Bernardino Department of History, and the CSU San Bernardino College of Social and Behavioral Sciences. I am also thankful for the financial support provided by the Andrew W. Mellon Foundation, the CSU San Bernardino Office of Academic Research, the Mangassar M. Mangassarian Scholarship, and the Armenian Professional Society.

Finally, I am forever grateful to Mehrzad Boroujerdi for his interest in the manuscript and to Deanna McCay, Kelly Balenske, and Kay Steinmetz at Syracuse University Press for their expert assistance and guidance on the book.

Introduction

IN MAY 1927, the lands between the Caspian Sea and the Persian Gulf were officially named "Iran." Concomitantly, the heterogeneous population inhabiting the region—people of diverse ethnicities, languages, religions, and cultures—officially became "Iranians." Although the term *Iran* and individuals who considered themselves part of an "Iranian" political and cultural community already existed, arguably for centuries or even millennia before this date, the fledgling nation's parliamentary assembly (Majles), under the direction of the newly crowned dictator Reza Shah Pahlavi, enacted legislation to make this official, abstract distinction a reality for its diverse masses of new citizens. From Reza Shah's Motahed ul-Shekl Shodan-e Ahali-ye Iran (Promulgation of Uniformity for the People of Iran) of 1927[1] through the current efforts by the regime of the Islamic Republic of Iran, legal, educational, social, military, and economic programs to inculcate within the country's variegated population a sense of identification with and loyalty to the nation of Iran have continued.

It is a fact that in the course of the twentieth century Iranian nationalism shaped the lives, identities, and sentiments of tens of millions of people: Persian Muslims, non–Persian Muslims, non-Muslims, current nationals, and expatriates. It is also a fact that millions of people, in different senses and various instances, have considered themselves Iranian. Aside from these simple facts, we still know very little about when, why, and how the abstract concept of Iranian national identity was manifest among the mixed population of Iran. Although the historical narrative of Pahlavi decrees and national development efforts is well known, and the reorientation of the content and emphasis of national myths and history toward Islam and Shi'ism since the Iranian Revolution of 1978–79 has been given due attention, the process by which these projects and programs of Iranian elites intersected with the various projects, interests, and needs of individuals from this heterogeneous population to develop Iranian national identity and to shape and sustain Iranian nationalism has not yet been detailed.

As far as the development of Iranian nationalism has been pursued in the few English-language sources available on the subject, the questions and debates that have emerged mirror those current in the broad and abundant literature on and theories of nationalism and are as passionately contested. Is nationalism an ancient, primordial, organic sentiment? Or is nationalism a modern, rational construct of domestic and foreign intelligentsia imposed on populations in the nineteenth and twentieth centuries? Where is agency to be located in elite–nonelite interaction in the development of nationalism? How do we explain nonelite receptivity to and uses of the myths, symbols, maps, history, propaganda, and homogenizing programs developed by political elites and intelligentsia in the establishment and consolidation of nations? What is the role of ethnicity and religion in the development of nationalism and national identity? How do minorities experience and play a role in the development of nationalism? Why is nationalism so emotive? Perhaps most important, why are people motivated to kill others and sacrifice their own lives for nations? And what methods of documentation, scope of examination, and level of abstraction are necessary to effectively illustrate the dynamic process of the development of nationalism so that we can respond to these questions? The nascent study of Iranian nationalism has swiftly confronted the same questions and debates that have afflicted the general theories and narratives of nationalism as a phenomenon as well as the case studies of the development of nationalism focused on other nations.[2]

The similarities among the questions and debates that have emerged both in the large number of case studies and general theoretical works on nationalism and in the embryonic discourse on the development of nationalism in Iran are not surprising, for all of these works have neglected to investigate the impact, uses, and expressions of nationalism throughout the lives of individuals. Nationalism has the ability to create and destroy as it divides and brings together vast popular masses and physical spaces, and that is what interests us in its study. Yet this collective phenomenon resides within individuals who constitute its motivated masses around the world and is necessarily reliant on individual receptivity to it and expressions of it.

Nationalism and national identity, on whatever level of perception or study (as global phenomena, group sentiment, collective political identity, modern program and manipulation by elites, primordial ethnic identification, tool of the "subaltern," geographic project, etc.), are ultimately based in, sustained by, and demonstrated through the participation and activities of individuals. However educationally, genetically, economically, juridically, socially, militarily, cartographically, or otherwise imposed or inculcated, nationalism and national identity are manifest as thoughts, feelings, emotions, ideas, and sentiments experienced by individuals. Individuals of different classes, races, cultures, ethnicities, and religions are the producers, bearers, and interpreters of these collective, global phenomena. The sometimes unifying, powerful, destructive, and monolithic phenomenon of nationalism—which is more often expressed situationally and manifest in subtle and creative forms[3]—is constituted, shaped, and expressed around territories, economies, political ideologies, languages, and religions. Ultimately, however, nationalism is received and reconstituted in daily life by individual people whose lives are shaped by it in various ways as they use it in conjunction with religious, cultural, familial, urban, regional, and "team" forms of identity. Nationalism and national identity are fluid because of people's differing and ever-evolving needs, perceptions, classes, languages, and cultures as well as because of their dynamic expressions of the phenomena.[4] As they participate in or reject nationalism, individuals are what shape and define it and make it the powerful and dynamic force that it is.

Theories and case studies of nationalism that hinge on research and analysis of subjects such as economic systems, political parties, educational programs, military campaigns, cartography, religion, philology, and literature can broaden our understanding of nationalism's many interrelated components. Yet without sustained illustrations of individual experiences with nationalism, such research cannot detail how these components come together to be used, expressed, and reconstituted in people's lives. Therefore, they cannot answer the most compelling and persistent questions about this multifaceted phenomenon. Although several theorists of nationalism and scholars treating Iranian nationalism have commented on the importance of the individual experience to our historical and current understanding of the phenomenon,[5] research into the lives of individuals and their encounters with nationalism remains to be conducted. Why is that? Certainly, nationalism and national identity are abstract and complex subjects, leading some to deny the ability to answer the lingering questions they generate or to generalize about the process of their development in Iran or elsewhere.[6] It is my observation, however, based on my understanding of nationalism's critical underpinning in individual activity and expressions, that much of the conflicted discourse on the development of nationalism and our inability to answer its most compelling questions stem from essentially one methodological problem that can be remedied. Put simply, this problem is the lack of confluence between theories of nationalism and social biographical research. In the interests of advancing simultaneously the study of Iranian nationalism and our broader understanding of nationalism and national identity in general, this study demonstrates how theory and social biographical research can be brought together to document and interpret the many effects and uses of these phenomena.[7]

The core of this study examines how Iranian nationalism shaped the lives of Armenian minorities in Iran during the twentieth century and the variety of ways in which they participated in its development. Making use of oral historical and social biographical methodologies to investigate the lives of a selected group of heretofore unstudied Armenian Iranians—a truck driver, an army officer, a parliamentary representative and community organizer, a civil servant, and a scout leader—it explores the origins and character of Iranian nationalism as experienced and expressed by ethnic Armenians as well as the personal conflicts and paradoxes attendant upon their compound identities. Utilizing the stories and memories of individuals gathered in oral interviews, expanded with sources such as newspapers, documents, personal memorabilia, and photos, the study seeks to demonstrate how individuals encounter and use nationalism in the course of their lives, to detail the various roles and projects of elites and nonelites in the development of Iranian nationalism, and to exhibit the different loci of power in this dialogic process.[8]

By investigating the implications of the development of nationalism and its manifestations within the lives of this one group of Iranian citizens, this study's social biographical core begins the necessary work of detailing manifestations and forms of Iranian nationalism and national identity in people's lives. This core of data is then integrated into an analysis that brings together social biography and theory to enhance our understanding of the genesis and mechanisms of nationalism. By interweaving theoretical and social historical elements, this analysis seeks to bring into operation theories of nationalism while locating its conclusions within the current dialog on the development of nationalism and national identity. One of its fundamental goals is to demonstrate how theories of nationalism and historical research focusing on the lives of individuals can be brought together to answer pivotal recurring questions about how nationalism evolves, what broad forces and daily activities shape and sustain it, and the role of minorities in its development.

Thus, although the study is centered on the lives of individuals from a single Iranian minority group, it is not intended to be simply a history of the development of Iranian nationalism from the periphery or "the bottom up." Rather it is a study of how the "top" and "bottom" interact and negotiate as coparticipants in the creation of nationalism. It is not an attempt to simply deconstruct or debunk theories of nationalism and Iranian national identity by asserting that individual experiences deny the ability to generalize or theorize about the process. On the contrary, it endeavors to enrich our general understanding of the process by seeking to illustrate some of the many compelling theoretical interpretations available. Investigating the individual experience and bridging the gap between theory and the day-to-day realities of the people who constitute the nation are moves toward eventually being able to generalize about the broad phenomenon of nationalism and about the "Iranian" experience with it.

Like many of their newly proclaimed compatriots who by 1927 had also lived in the region with Persian Muslims for centuries—Turks, Arabs, Zoroastrians, Jews, Assyrians, Turkmen, Kurds, Lurs, Baluchis[9]—the

Armenians of Iran maintained close-knit communities and a distinct language and culture that stood apart from Persian or Iranian.[10] However, unlike most of these groups, Armenians maintained an ethnoreligious identification with their traditional homeland that makes them a particularly important minority group with which to begin detailing the development of Iranian national identity and refining theories of nationalism through social biographical research.

Armenians had lived for centuries within the borders of the land decreed Iran in 1927. Although Armenian lands in Anatolia and the Caucasus had been conquered by Persian dynasties as far back as the Achaemenids and their successors, the Parthians and Sassanians, Shah Abbas forcibly moved the first large Armenian population of 50,000 to the interior of the region in 1604.[11] After the commercial and artistic heyday of the New Julfan Armenian community in the seventeenth century, Armenians dispersed throughout the country. In the early nineteenth century, the Armenian population was concentrated in Tabriz, Isfahan, Shiraz, Maku, Koy, Urmia, and Hamadan and had grown to around 100,000.[12] Massacres of Armenians in the Ottoman Empire in the late nineteenth century and during World War I brought thousands more Armenians to Iran, where they found refuge.[13] In this period, Armenians were active in the region's politics and played a substantial role in the Constitutional Revolution of 1905–11. By the early 1920s, the country's roughly 120,000 Armenians could be found in every economic bracket and a multiplicity of occupations, from top administrative and military positions in the Qajar government to subsistence farming.[14]

Expressions of identification with the traditional Armenian homeland and Orthodox Church evident in the lives of many Armenians in diaspora—most concretely demonstrated in song, literature, artistic motifs, and the promotion of Armenian religious, cultural, and political organizations—have led theorists of nationalism and scholars of Iranian nationalism to generalize about the inability of Armenians in Iran and elsewhere to acquire any non-Armenian national identity. In such interpretations, Armenians are categorized as an "ancient" people with links to an historic homeland and a religiolinguistic heritage too strong to allow for another or even a mixed national identity.[15] Others dismiss the possibility of an Iranian national identity for the Armenians of Iran owing to international political events and primordial attachments.[16] Although I will state in advance of illustration that this study reveals just the opposite—that many Armenians have indeed developed a strong sense of Iranian identity and in fact have played an important role in the development of Iranian nationalism—these flawed interpretations help highlight the importance of considering Armenian experiences with and contributions to Iranian nationalism. It is my contention that illustrating the process by which Armenians of diverse backgrounds acquired and maintained Iranian national identity can tell us as much or more about the appeal of Iranian nationalism and the process by which it has been inculcated than a study of any other Iranian minority—or especially of the Persian Muslim majority—precisely *because* Armenians in Iran sustain unique traditions, attachments, and loyalties that differ from those of the majority and thus from the primary bases of both Persian monarchial and Shiʿa Islamic Iranian national myths. In short, I am arguing that of all Iranian ethnic and religious groups to study, Armenians enable the widest applicability of the study's theoretical findings and best underscore the effectiveness of sustained social biographical investigation.

To achieve these objectives, the study is divided into two parts, preceded by an analytical chapter concerned with locating this study and its methods in the current theoretical dialog on the development of nationalism and in the historiography on the development of Iranian nationalism. Through analysis of how nationalism and national identity have been thus far researched and defined, first in enduring general theoretical treatises on nationalism and second in studies of Iranian nationalism, chapter 1 demonstrates the need for confluence between theory and social biographical research in both subject areas and suggest the potentials for such a confluence.[17] It argues that social biographical research provides a key to elucidate the participation and collaboration of elites and nonelites in development of Iranian nationalism and to refine our understanding of the dialogic activity through which national identity is acquired and maintained.

The social biographical research presented in part I constitutes the core of the work. In its five chapters, we move away from theory to observe how religion, language, ethnicity, myth, memory, education, social networks, technology, geopolitics, governmental force, parentage, gender, personal initiative, desire, and historical circumstance intersect with nationalism in the lives of five individuals to produce multiple levels of national allegiance and compound forms of identity that, in turn, continue to shape and sustain nationalism.

Chapter 2 tells the story of Iskandar Khan Setkhanian (1865–1953), an Armenian Iranian descendant of longtime residents of Iranian Azerbaijan and participants in Qajar-era politics and culture, who rose to be the *amir tuman* (brigadier general) of the Cossack Brigade during the Constitutional Revolution of 1905–11. Focusing on Iskandar Khan's family and community ties, his military career, multinational allegiances, and activities during and after the Constitutional Revolution to illustrate the complexities of national identity, allegiance, and ethnicity during the period of change from the Qajar imperium to the Pahlavi national state, the chapter also details Iskandar Khan's personal experiences as his former Cossack subordinate, Reza Khan, rose to be shah of Iran and initiated his well-known programs of national development. Based on interviews with Setkhanian descendants and analysis of a rich family archive of rarely accessible Qajar *farman*s (edicts), photographs, letters, newspaper clippings, and other documents, supplemented with recent work on the Iranian Constitutional Revolution,[18] Iskandar Khan's social biography offers rich detail to illustrate the diversity of Armenian political allegiances at the turn of the twentieth century and changes brought by the Pahlavi regime. In addition, this chapter describes the long and for the most part prosperous history of Armenians in Iran and explores the unique position of one of the country's oldest ethnoreligious minorities in the nineteenth century.

Chapter 3 introduces Hagob Hagobian (1908–92), an Armenian Iranian of more humble origins who fled to Tabriz as a refugee orphaned by the intercommunal violence in the region of Urmia during World War I. Focusing on Hagobian's experiences as a long-distance truck driver in Iran during the late 1920s and 1930s, while exploring the role of the Armenian Iranian truck drivers' guild in both his career and in Reza Shah's nation-building efforts, this portrait illuminates how Iranian nationalism impacted Hagobian's life and what he, in turn, and his fellow Armenian Iranian truck drivers had to do with the process of its development. A close look at the role and functions of Hagob Hagobian's guild demonstrates how Iran's "late" infrastructural, economic, and bureaucratic development factored into the chronology of the emergence of national identity in Iran and how trucks and truck drivers were involved in the process. Based on oral interviews conducted with Hagobian, his coworkers, and his relatives, Hagobian's social biography is expanded with documents, photographs, and secondary sources on the Iranian guilds, infrastructure, cartography, and economy of the 1920s and 1930s. Interweaving the economic and political history of Iran from the 1920s through the 1940s with the story of Hagobian's life, this chapter shows how to some nonelite individuals the nation of Iran was not "imagined," but a traversed territory holding a diverse citizenry with which they continually interacted. Thus, Hagob Hagobian's social biography simultaneously informs our understanding of Pahlavi efforts to consolidate the nation and develop its economy and illustrates these efforts' impact on an individual's opportunities, decisions, memories, and layered identities.

Chapter 4 focuses on Sevak Saginian (1922–2003), a central figure in Armenian Iranian life from the late 1940s through the late 1970s. Son of Zohrab Saginian—a Dashnak revolutionary writer and publisher who was one of the two constitutionally required Armenian Iranian Majles representatives from 1921 to 1941—Sevak Saginian rose to serve in the same position from 1956 to 1978. Focusing on Saginian's family legacy of more than a century of Armenian Iranian military and political leadership, his activities in Tehran's Armenian Iranian community as a youth, his motivations and activities in cofounding the Anjoman-e Parvaresh-e Afkar-e Javanan-e Aramene (Organization for Fostering the Thoughts of Armenian Youth, later to be known widely as "Ararat") in 1946, and his path to tenure as Armenian Iranian Majles representative, this portrait illustrates how Saginian became one of the primary intermediaries between Iran's Armenian community and the shah and details his efforts and maneuvers in this important role. Drawn from oral interviews with Sevak Saginian, his friends, and his family members as well as from documents, photographs, newspaper articles, and written memoirs, Saginian's social biography reveals fascinating details about Armenian Iranian community organizations, political and educational opportunities and strategies, and the role of elite Armenian Iranians in forging within their Armenian communities a sense of Iranian allegiance and identity. On another level, his experience reveals strategies employed by minority Majles members working under a dictatorship to get things accomplished for their constituents and the primary importance of loyalty in the totalitarian political framework of Pahlavi Iran.

The life of Lucik Moradiance (b. 1930), a female Armenian Iranian professional, is the subject of chapter 5. Concentrating on her experiences in Iranian primary, secondary, and university education from the mid-1930s through the 1950s and her entrance into the working establishment and Iranian civil service, this portrait of Moradiance helps us to better understand the role public education played in the development of Iranian nationalism and demonstrates the extent to which educational programs and opportunities shaped national identity. Composed from oral interviews with Lucik Moradiance, her relatives, and her friends and supplemented with documents, photographs, and secondary sources on Iranian education under the Pahlavis, this biography details one woman's personal experiences in the Iranian education system in the 1940s and 1950s and in her career as an engineering professional involved in the nation's petrochemical development in the 1960s and 1970s. In its detailed exploration, this social biography helps illuminate the complex links among gender, ethnicity, identity, and secular nationalism.

Chapter 6 examines the life of Nejde Hagobian (b. 1934), son of the first-generation Armenian Iranian truck driver Hagob Hagobian introduced in chapter 3. Centered on his childhood experiences and role in founding and leading the Armenian Iranian youth organization Ararat's mixed-gender scouting wing in the early 1950s, Nejde Hagobian's story describes how Armenian Iranian youth were able to create an organization that enabled public expression of their Armenian symbols, traditions, and values and how, paradoxically, this Armenian-exclusive organization was a primary vehicle through which many of them acquired a strong and sublime sense of Iranian nationalism. Further, it explains why and how the Pahlavi regime used the Armenian scouts as a model for its own latent scouting program and in its efforts to develop a sense of Iranian national identity among its entire population in the pivotal 1950s. Based on oral interviews with Nejde Hagobian and his fellow Ararat scouts, friends, and relatives as well as on documents, photographs, letters, newspaper articles, and memorabilia, this social biography uses his experiences and activities in Armenian Iranian scouting as a prism through which we can view how he and his fellow youth participated in the dialogic process of the development of Iranian nationalism while celebrating and sustaining their Armenian identity and how Hagobian's life and opportunities and those of his family members were shaped by a compound Armenian Iranian identity.

In part II, these social biographies are conflated with the theoretical definitions, questions, and debates about nationalism and national identity explored in chapter 1 to execute the study's primary goal of demonstrating the efficacy of such a confluence to the study of nationalism in Iran and elsewhere.

By bringing together oft-quoted and enduring works of nationalism and hitherto undocumented personal experiences with the phenomenon of nationalism, chapter 7 demonstrates the effectiveness of social biography in answering some of the field's most vexing questions and the promise of advancing the dialogue on nationalism. The analysis seeks to illuminate how social biography can inform prevailing theories of nationalism and how these theories in turn can help us better understand the impact of nationalism in people's lives. The intent here is not as much to challenge established wisdom on nationalism's development, but to understand the intricate dynamics of the process by factoring the uniqueness of the individual experience and of modern Iranian history into different theoretical models and paradigms.[19]

The study's conclusion serves as an epilogue to the biographies of Iskandar Khan Setkhanian, Hagob Hagobian, Sevak Saginian, Lucik Moradiance, and Nejde Hagobian, explaining how each of these individuals and their families eventually became citizens of the United States residing in southern California.[20] The conclusion also briefly applies and extends the historical and theoretical interpretations presented in chapter 7 to consider current governmental efforts to shape and sustain Iranian nationalism in the Islamic Republic of Iran and the circumstances that motivate Iran's Armenian minorities to continue to participate strategically in this ongoing process. This analysis underscores the complexities of the political and religious dialogue on nationalism in Iran today, depicting continuity and change in twentieth- and twenty-first-century strategies by Iranian governments to inculcate and sustain Iranian nationalism and national identity within the nation's heterogeneous population. By juxtaposing the scope and intent of government efforts with a look at the activities and strategies of Armenian Iranians currently residing in Iran, the study's conclusion illustrates further the mechanisms of dialogic power relationships in the creation and maintenance of nationalism. It also underscores the ongoing evolution of Iranian nationalism as a dynamic, collaborative, and negotiated process.

Ethnicity, Identity, and the Development of Nationalism in Iran

1

Nationalism, Theory, and Social Biography

THE PHOTO on the following page depicts an event that took place on October 26, 1953, at Amjadieh Stadium in Tehran, Iran. A parade to honor the thirty-fourth birthday of Shah Mohammad Reza Pahlavi is led by a group of Iranian scouts, bearing flags of the Iranian nation and their scouting organization as well as a large photograph of the shah (king) as a young scout. Initiating the shah's traditional participation in the annual event, a lone *sayar* (explorer scout) turns to salute the king where he sits in the stands with Parliament members, generals, ministers, and other high-ranking state officials. With this honorific cue, the shah rises to his feet, returns the salute, and remains standing in review as the Iranian scouts, athletes, students, and an assortment of representatives from social and cultural organizations from across the country march past to the cadence of the national military band.

To suggest that this event might have something to do with the nation and nationalism is patently obvious. Annual parades in packed sports complexes featuring athletic expositions, scouts marching and saluting, political elites gathering, state leaders reviewing their citizens, patriotic songs playing, and flags waving are so much the stuff of nationalism as to be almost cliché. Indeed, the event as depicted in the photograph—and as seen across the country in *akbar* newsreels (the Iranian adaptation of America's *Movietone* shorts) shown in Iranian theaters that week—suggests a complex linkage and interrelation with the phenomena of the nation and nationalism.

1. Fourth of Aban parade, 1953. Unknown photographer. Courtesy of the author.

But how can we ascertain specifically what this event has to do with nationalism? How would we research the meaning and uses of this event for its variety of elite and nonelite participants? How can we determine what functions it serves the Iranian nation-state and its impact on the citizens who are participating in it?

Students of nationalism in Iran and of nationalism as a global phenomenon continue to be faced with the same problems and questions that have been challenging the field of nationalism studies for decades. When and on what bases did the nation emerge? In what sense is national community felt and experienced? How is nationalism generated and sustained? Why are nations appealing? Where is agency to be located in the development of nations and nationalism? How and why do nations and nationalism inspire violence and self-sacrifice? In a field rent by differences of opinion regarding every category of topic, focus, and method, the diverse and interdisciplinary literature on nationalism at present nevertheless shows unanimous agreement on three basic points: (1) understanding nationalism is critically important to broadening our understanding of political and social movements of the past as well as of the present and the foreseeable future; (2) nationalism has generated a vast body of literature; and (3) despite this scholarly attention we still have more questions than we do answers about this global phenomenon—calling for a "reframing" or "rethinking" of nationalism as we begin the twenty-first century.[1] Aside from these three points, consensus on most issues related to the subject and its study is hard to find.[2] One issue is clear irrespective of scholarly approach: despite enthusiastic predictions of the demise of sovereign states and nationalism in the face of globalization, changing political, economic, and strategic realignments of the 1990s, and new communications technologies such as the Internet and social networking, nations and nationalism are not vanishing and remain deeply influential if not dominant in the contemporary organization of human life and politics. To quote Craig Calhoun, "nations [and nationalism] matter."[3]

Although some scholars of nationalism have argued that lack of advancement in our understanding of nationalism is the result of nations and nationalism having been "undertheorized" as subjects[4] and thus have called for a renewed theoretical discourse to answer these persistent, lingering questions, other scholars and I have observed that just the opposite is true: we have an abundant pool of theory to draw from to structure and clarify our broad questions about the development of nationalism and to ponder its sublime, moving qualities.[5] What we are lacking, however, is historical research that puts into operation and refines these speculative, hypothetical frameworks to the point where we can ascertain their validity or utility, respond to the questions they generate, and ultimately move on to approaching new questions and topics. Thus, although theories abound that can help us (a) speculate about the moment the photo at issue captures and (b) frame complex questions about the dimensions of Iranian nationalism it might depict, answering those questions and advancing our understanding of nationalism necessitates an approach that conjoins and operationalizes existing theory with a suitable historical research methodology. At the conclusion of his survey of contemporary theories of nationalism, Umut Ozkirimli similarly identifies the potentials of theoretically informed historical analyses to help refine theories of nationalism and break the analytical stalemate that characterizes current debates in nationalism studies:

> At present, the field is saturated with a vast number of abstract theoretical works, and individual histories with relatively little interaction between the two. Theorists of nationalism generally refrain from applying their ideas to particular nationalisms, contenting themselves with passing reference to a limited number of cases for illustrative purposes. Historians of nationalism, on the other hand, remain innocent of recent theoretical developments in the field, embracing, more often than not, descriptive narratives of particular nationalisms. What we need is to bring the two together and test our theoretical frameworks against historical evidence, reformulating and improving our initial assumptions as we go along, enriching our analyses with empirical insights based on "real life" cases.[6]

Using the photo of the shah's 1953 birthday rally as a common point of reference, this chapter is devoted to assessing prevalent theories of nationalism and their application in existing studies on Iranian nationalism, before introducing the methods and potentials of an approach that grounds theory in the "'real life' cases" illuminated by social biographical research.

To accomplish these tasks, I first introduce popular and enduring theories of nationalism that have been utilized in existing works on Iranian nationalism. I assess the theoretical contributions by Ernest Gellner, John Breuilly, Elie Kedourie, Eric Hobsbawm, and Benedict Anderson to determine what perspectives and frameworks they independently offer to assist in our interpretation of the birthday rally snapshot.[7] In addition to these popular modernist theories, I also introduce recent ethnosymbolic approaches to the study of nationalism, a trend pioneered by Anthony D. Smith.[8] My brief consideration of the strengths and limitations of these theories will generate a set of theoretical questions to be pursued in part II and reveal the theorists' own leads regarding how their hypotheses can be tested. With this theoretical background, I then introduce the handful of existing book-length contributions to the study of Iranian nationalism to examine the ways in which they have utilized theory in their work. Considering how these studies aid our effort to decipher the historical snapshot from 1953 will expand the set of questions to be addressed in part II and locate the present study and its approach within the field. Finally, I introduce methods of social biography to explain how this form of historical inquiry can be used to put theories of nationalism and national identity into operation and how the scope and uses of social biography can be broadened through engagement with theory. As parts I and II demonstrate, social biographical research is uniquely suited to elucidate the participation and collaboration of elites and nonelites in development of Iranian nationalism and to refine our understanding of the dialogic activity through which national identity is acquired and maintained.[9]

Enduring Theories of Nationalism

Ernest Gellner: High Culture and the Role of Mass Public Education

Ernest Gellner's contributions to the study of nationalism are varied, but none has so clearly detailed his theoretical positions or been as widely read as *Nations and Nationalism* (1983), a sententiously argued work that is one of the most widely cited and tacitly accepted theoretical considerations of nationalism available.[10] Gellner's basic argument is that nations and nationalism are modern phenomena that are a product of the Industrial Revolution, where the dislocation of agrarian, rural peoples of diverse backgrounds and their concentration in industrializing cities to feed the growing demands of capitalism necessitated a common culture and language, both written and spoken, to facilitate communication and social interaction. In the transition from horizontally structured "agro-literate" communities to vertically organized industrial societies, urban elites draw from "low" or folk cultures to create a "high," literate state culture, which is spread and sustained through standardized mass public education, a process that Gellner terms "exo-socialization."[11] In this way, a uniform "garden culture" of citizens is cultivated out of the diverse "wild cultures" prevalent in agroliterate societies.[12] Nationalism, which Gellner narrowly defines as "a political principle [that] holds that the political and national unit should be congruent," is an elite tool created to inculcate societal cohesion and loyalty to the state, which simultaneously satisfies the increasingly egalitarian aspirations of the populace.[13]

In Gellner's formulation, nations are the product of nationalism, whereas nationalism is "an effect of industrial social organization."[14] Although nations and nationalism are therefore wholly modern constructions in Gellner's view, he speculates that the language, myths, traditions, and histories that are selectively used to create and sustain them must be in some way drawn from preexisting folk cultures, or else they would have no resonance or appeal.[15]

Used independently as a resource to interpret the shah's 1953 birthday rally, Gellner's theory offers several compelling hypotheses. Through Gellner's lens, we can view the event as evidence of the attempt by the Iranian political elite to cultivate a high garden culture in order to promote social cohesion, patriotism, and loyalty to the state. The rapid movement from agroliterate society to industrialization and urbanization fostered under the Pahlavis might explain the receptivity of the nonelite participants in the birthday event, who can, in light of Gellner's theory, be understood to be increasingly aware of the egalitarianism that the political principle of nationalism brings. We can speculate that the symbolism, myths, and traditions that are a part of the king's annual birthday celebration are modern artifacts that draw from premodern, low cultures to give them meaning and resonance. Certainly, Gellner's theory suggests that sentiments of community and evidence of linguistic commonality in the event would be the product of the state's efforts in developing an effective, standardized system of mass education. But how would we be able to render a determination? Although elite programs of mass education might be a factor in the development of linguistic unity and loyalty evident in the outward appearance of this event, Gellner's insights on their own do not help us understand how and why, if at all, sublime sentiment and patriotism are inspired. Why and in what ways might such an event be meaningful to its elite as well as its nonelite participants? Where is agency to be located in an event that involves elites and nonelites equally? Is it sufficient or accurate to interpret the event as a demonstration of the successful development of an educationally sustained high culture in Pahlavi

Iran? What is the role of culture in the event's organization, rituals, and symbolism? What does this parade have to do with Iranian nationalism?

John Breuilly: Nationalism as Political Phenomenon

Another popular and enduring study of nationalism that focuses on and locates nationalism's origins in the modern national state is John Breuilly's *Nationalism and the State* (1994). Breuilly sees the modern, territorially bounded national state as the most prominent and important feature of nationalism,[16] both in terms of its role in shaping nationalism and, more importantly for Breuilly, in the sense that the modern national state and its power are the objectives of nationalism.[17] Arguing that features of nationalism such as culture, ideology, identity, and class should be secondary considerations before engaging in an analysis of the causative interrelationship between achieving and maintaining state power and nationalism, Breuilly seeks to create a typology of nationalisms to provide a viable and precise theoretical framework for initial classification and understanding of the phenomenon.[18]

Breuilly's reduction of his definition of nationalism to a political principle is motivated by his perception that theories of nationalism (such as those advanced by Anthony D. Smith, whom he specifically confronts) are vague and impractical. In this way, his definition of nationalism as a form of politics "avoids the danger of being too vague and all-embracing and, among other things, draws attention to the modernity of nationalism."[19] Moreover, in his quest for precision, Breuilly's rejection of culture, identity, and ideology in his definition and typology alleviates the necessity for research and debate about that which he perceives to be beyond rational analysis and the historian's explanatory powers.[20]

Thus, taking a strictly political view of nations and nationalism—in explicit debate with scholars such as Smith who emphasize ethnicity and nationalism—Breuilly defines nationalism as a modern political movement aspiring for or in command of state power, which legitimates itself using a "nationalist argument." This political doctrine asserts: "(*a*) There exists a nation with an explicit and peculiar character. (*b*) The interests and values of this nation take priority over all other interests and values.

(*c*) The nation must be as independent as possible. This usually requires the attainment of at least popular sovereignty."[21]

Further reducing his focus on nationalism as a form of politics to concentrate on "opposition politics," Breuilly divides nations into six basic classes in his typology. His classification is structured around the relationship between the existing state—which is divided into two categories as either a nation-state or a "non-nation-state"—and the nationalist movement, which is moving toward either separation or reform or unification.[22] His study generally goes on to test and rationalize this typology by drawing general examples and comparisons from the history of European and some non-Western nations. Breuilly's conclusion reframes his introductory overview, explaining that nationalism, "a peculiarly modern form of politics which can only be understood in relation to the way in which the modern state has developed,"[23] is a product of the interaction and friction generated out of the concurrent rise of capitalism and the modern absolutist state, which pitted a budding and increasingly alienated political community against monarchies. The ensuing movements and struggles for unification or separation, whether won by the monarchy or by its opposition, are, to Breuilly, the critical, defining moments of nationalism.

Clearly, then, Breuilly's *Nationalism and the State* suggests that an event such as the Iranian shah's birthday celebration is irrelevant to our understanding of nationalism and that its cultural symbols and subjective experiences are beyond rational analysis. The photograph would not assist in locating Iran within Breuilly's typology of nations because it does not depict the moment of state formation or the monarchy's nationalist argument. At best, it serves as evidence that nationalism *has occurred* insofar as state power is shown to exist, although the celebratory moment depicted is the antithesis of the opposition politics that for Breuilly is the crucible of nationalism.

Elie Kedourie and the Rise of Nationalism in Asia and Africa

Although reminiscent of the work of the two seminal political modernist theorists discussed thus far, Elie Kedourie's widely read and frequently cited collected work on nationalism, *Nationalism in Asia and Africa* (1970), offers unique frameworks and hypotheses extended beyond Europe to include Asia and Africa as well as an analytical focus on the role of colonialism in the global proliferation of nationalism.

In his lengthy introduction to this anthology, which brings together the primary writings of nationalists and national movements, Kedourie argues that nationalism, a European doctrine of the nineteenth century, spread to Africa and Asia through the colonial experience. In Kedourie's narrative, traditional African and Asian peoples became dislocated, disillusioned, and alienated, and their societies were "pulverized" by the combined effects of political domination, the world economy, and colonial education. With traditional political and religious ideals as well as indigenous institutions and leaders discredited, and after rejection from the Western culture they had studied, emulated, and learned to admire, alienated intellectuals and political activists turned to violence—melding messianic myth, indigenous cultural references, and the European doctrine of nationalism to create a political religion to articulate and fulfill their quest for distinct identity and political independence.

In Kedourie's analysis, colonial education was the crucible from which nationalism emerged in Asia and Africa. Offering literacy and often secular Orientalist teachings that juxtaposed the economic, cultural, and intellectual superiority of Europe and the strength of its political institutions—which were based on Enlightenment ideals of individualism, freedom, and the doctrine of nationalism—with the weakness of African and Asian societies and their glory days past, colonial education simultaneously generated disillusionment and feelings of "inadequacy" and "inferiority" among its pupils in regard to their traditional society and its modes of thought, along with an admiration and a willingness to somehow become a part of the powerful and dominant foreign society. The harsh realization that the colonial subject–student could never become a part of the dominant society was often learned through failed attempts at integration and equality in civil service and/or the experience of personal rebuff during educational sojourns in Europe; these experiences produced feelings of unfulfillment and disaffection that inevitably spawned what amounted to an identity crisis and resentful and violent sentiments.[24] This crisis led to a search for identity by the marginalized to answer the ubiquitous question "What am I?"[25] The new class of disaffected "marginal men" consisting of intellectuals, military-technical students, and civil servants frustrated in the concurrent process of societal decay, economic ruin, disillusionment, and colonial education rebuff formed the vanguard of anticolonial movements, almost universally turning to the formerly alien, "imported" concepts of nationalism and independence to articulate their grievances and give shape to their demands.[26] Kedourie explains, "Of the doctrines and ideologies spread through the colonial encounters, the imported concept of nationalism, or the ideology that the world is divided into unique nations which should have independence and [self-]sovereignty, appealed most to the marginal men in Asia and Africa."[27]

Despite the imitative nature of their activities in seeking European-style uniformity of belief and the artificiality of the histories and myths they created to define, legitimate, and reify their oppressed nation,[28] nationalists in Africa, the Middle East, and Asia effectively manipulated religious symbolism and played on popular millennial expectation to create a powerful postcolonial political religion and new communal identity.[29] Simultaneously introducing the works contained within his anthology and utilizing them to support his argument about the origins of nationalism in Asia and Africa, Kedourie draws from the nationalist writings of Ziya Gökalp, Adamantios Koraes, Marcus Garvey, Michel Aflaq, and Mohandas Gandhi to illustrate how the question "What am I?" is answered by synthesizing two products of European thought: basic nationalist doctrine and millennialism. Melding the doctrine of a world divided into distinct nations, each of which should be sovereign, with an invocation of the "dark gods" and rites of traditional society to imbue the political-nationalist message with indigenous essence and directive,[30] nationalist elites forged a secular, political millennialism that offered to the alienated and disoriented masses the hope that oppression and injustice would be swept away and be replaced by a dispensation of liberty, equality, and brotherly love.[31]

Kedourie does not approach the issue of agency directly, and as a result his analysis is somewhat conflicted. On one hand, he emphasizes the power of European thought and its disseminators, who, to aggregate Kedourie's operative terms, import an alien doctrine, which colonial subjects "take up," accept unquestioningly, and imitate. On the other hand,

Kedourie's analysis and the anthology's selected writings of nationalists such as Gökalp, Koraes, Garvey, Aflaq, and Gandhi illustrate clearly that it is the African and Asian nationalists and the masses that they inspire who are the announcers, foot soldiers, propagandists, and, by all definitions, executors of the nationalist revolution.[32] Still, it is clear that, for Kedourie, European thought and the residue of colonialism are the active ingredients: "Resentment and impatience, the depravity of the rich and the virtue of the poor, the guilt of Europe and the innocence of Asia and Africa, salvation through violence, the coming reign of universal love: these are the elements of the thought of Sultan Galiev and Li Ta-chao, of Ikki Kita, Michel Aflaq, and Frantz Fanon. This theory is now the most popular and influential one in Asia and Africa. It is Europe's gift to the world."[33]

Kedourie's theory of nationalism provides us with another compelling yet speculative framework through which to interpret the shah's 1953 birthday rally: that of the colonial legacy in Iran and the influence of European thought in the development of Iranian nationalism. In this context, we can infer that the display and usage of symbols of national sovereignty and community (flags, anthems, review of regional representatives) illustrate the Iranian political elites' adaptation and propagation of basic European nationalist doctrine, which first emerged in Iran during the Constitutional Revolution as European-educated "marginal men" rose in opposition to the Russian and British colonial powers and the Qajar regime, which had collectively "pulverized" traditional Iranian society in the nineteenth century. The overtly Western, secular orientation and style of the 1953 birthday parade for Iran's king can thus be seen as the product of the reconstitution of pulverized traditional collectivities in the form of a national community based on a secular, European model.

But is it sufficient to view this event and its display of Iranian nationalism as merely imitation? How can we be more precise in determining the extent of European influence in the event and in locating agency? What does such an event, imitative or not, mean to its Iranian participants, and why is it appealing to them? Why does the message of nationalist elites resonate with the nonelite masses? How do the perceptions and attitudes of elites and nonelites interact in the production of Iranian nationalism?

Although Iran's colonial experience and the influence of European thought might have had something to do with the secular-nationalist character of the event, this in no way explains why its nonelite participants might be receptive to its symbolism and imagery. A top-down, monologic, diffusionist theoretical hypothesis such as Kedourie's fails to account for the ways in which the perceptions, sentiments, and attitudes of nonelite participants such as the scouts interacted with the elites' nationalist message, however tainted or shaped by Orientalist knowledge that message may have been.[34] What did such an event mean to the marching scouts? How did they use it? What did this event mean to the elites in the stands? How did they use it?

Eric Hobsbawm and Invented Traditions

Eric Hobsbawm's contributions to the study of nationalism span two popular books: *The Invention of Tradition* (1983), which he coedited with Terrence Ranger, and *Nations and Nationalism since 1780: Programme, Myth, Reality* (1990).[35] Although it is not focused solely on nationalism, Hobsbawm's introduction to *The Invention of Tradition* explores aspects of nation building and rituals that are further elaborated upon in *Nations and Nationalism since 1780* and thus supports the latter work. Hobsbawm's combined work generates perhaps the most explicit call for social biographical research to advance our understanding of nationalism—a call achieved by way of masterful and often entertaining abstract illustration and matched by pragmatic methodological and research recommendations.

In a short introduction to the essays that compose *The Invention of Tradition*, Hobsbawm establishes working definitions and a typology of what he terms "invented traditions" and what he views as their relationship to the origins and development of nationalism. To paraphrase Hobsbawm's general thesis, invented traditions are practices of a ritual or symbolic nature that are created to inculcate values and behavioral norms through repetition and are often legitimated through the factitious assertion of continuity with a historic past.[36] To illustrate the concept, Hobsbawm distinguishes between custom, which is "what judges do," and the invented tradition of the judge's wig, robe, and ritualized practices of the courtroom. He similarly distinguishes convention and practical sense from invented traditions with the example of head protection. Wearing a helmet while engaged in military combat or while motorcycle riding can be considered conventional and practical, whereas the "traditional" helmet and pink attire of British fox hunters are invented.[37] Unlike custom and practical convention, which vary over time as pragmatism and technology drive change, invented tradition is invariant, imposing fixed practices and implying strict continuity and longevity. The process of inventing traditions is one of "formalization and ritualization, characterized by reference to the past, if only by imposing repetition."[38] Although invented traditions can be clearly observed when they are initiated in the recent past by a single source—such as the Boy Scout rituals of Baden Powell or the Nazi symbolism and ceremonials at Nuremberg—they become more challenging for the historian to trace and interpret when they incorporate symbols and rituals that have evolved informally or in private groups. The study of invented traditions becomes all the more challenging when it is recognized that they are not unique to the modern age in that their creation has occurred throughout history.[39]

Hobsbawm argues that invented traditions are evident throughout history, but that the invention of tradition happens more frequently when societies undergo rapid change that destabilizes the existing social order.[40] By deliberately supplanting and juxtaposing old ways and traditions with radical innovation, "the nineteenth-century liberal ideology of social change systematically failed to provide for the social authority ties taken for granted in earlier societies, and created voids which might have to be filled with invented practices."[41] Thus, the process of inventing traditions is progressive in that the more things change, the greater the impetus is to fill the void by, to paraphrase Hobsbawm, dressing up novelty as antiquity by drawing from ancient materials and concepts to construct invented traditions.[42]

These invented practices fall into three general yet intermingling types. The first type seeks to establish or symbolize social cohesion or community membership; the second legitimizes institutions, status, and the hierarchy of authority; and the third targets socialization, values, and the inculcation of belief systems and behavioral conventions.[43] Hobsbawm refers to socialist May Day, the ritual salute to the flag in American schools, and Swiss nationalists' use of folk song, sporting events, parades, and religious symbolism to further illustrate the concept of invented traditions, although not specifically associating his typology to these examples. In Hobsbawm's view, the study of invented traditions offers modern and contemporary historians insight into what he describes as

> that comparatively recent historical innovation, the "nation," with its associated phenomena: nationalism, the nation-state, national symbols, histories and the rest. All these rest on exercises in social engineering which are often deliberate and always innovative, if only because historical novelty implies innovation. Israeli and Palestinian nationalism or nations must be novel, whatever the historical continuities of Jews or Middle Eastern Muslims, since the very concept of territorial states of the currently standard type in their region was barely thought of a century ago, and hardly became a serious prospect before the end of World War I.[44]

Hence, despite the paradox that nations are claimed to be organic and rooted in history—the opposite of construction or novelty—we must not be misled. Although there may be undeniable historical continuity in claims to an Israeli or Palestinian or French nation, these concepts are nevertheless rife with constructed, invented components in Hobsbawm's view. Accordingly, "the national phenomenon cannot be adequately investigated without careful attention to the 'invention of tradition.'"[45]

Hobsbawm's theory offers several fascinating ways to interpret the shah's birthday rally, which fit the general illustration of the phenomenon of invented traditions on several levels as well as Hobsbawm's typology of purpose. At the point in time captured in the photo, in an era of tumult and change in Iranian history, the Pahlavi state seeks to fill the void created through the destruction of traditional social organization and ways of life with invented traditions that create new national bonds around old, immemorial concepts. Combining the power and historical legitimacy of ancient ritual (a review of subjects by the Persian monarch) with modern national symbolism and activities (the gathering of regional sports clubs, scouting troops, and student organizations in the nation's central sports stadium for a birthday celebration), the event itself can be interpreted as one layer of invented tradition. Within this invented tradition, others are evident. The Iranian tricolor adorned with the monarchial Shir-o Khorshid (Order of the Lion and the Sun) waving in the stands and carried on the field formalizes and ritualizes the timeless connections between the people, the nation, and the monarchy. The scouts marching with a large photograph of the shah himself as a young member of the organization Pishahangi-ye Iran (Scouting of Iran) demonstrate continuity and legitimacy in their own organization and reflect its linkage to the state. The national scouting organization is itself based on invented traditions such as oaths, salutes, rites of passage, and rank. Multiple layers of invented traditions can be located in this event that fit Hobsbawm's general illustration of the phenomenon.

Remarkably, even a cursory discussion of the shah's birthday rally is consistent with not one but all three categories of invented traditions that Hobsbawm delineates in his typology. (1) It seeks to promote social cohesion and symbolize community membership through gathering and recognition by the shah of regional sporting, scouting, and student organizations, each of which generates social cohesion and community membership further; (2) it legitimizes institutions, status, and the hierarchy of authority by symbolizing the power and authority of the Pahlavi regime and by locating this power vis-à-vis its elite participants in the stands and its nonelite participants on the field; and (3) it targets socialization, values, and the inculcation of belief systems and behavioral conventions by upholding the Iranian nation, the monarchy, and youth organizations that themselves promote values and socialization.[46] Yet although entirely consistent with Hobsbawm's theoretical typology of invented traditions in the 1983 collection, his next book, specifically focusing on nationalism, would assert the role of the social historian in ultimately determining the accuracy, utility, and applicability of his theories. Interestingly, this guidance is provided by way of Hobsbawm's own critique of Ernest Gellner's work, discussed earlier.

> If I have a major criticism of Gellner's work it is that his preferred perspective of modernization from above, makes it difficult to pay adequate

> attention to the view from below. The view from below, i.e. the nation as seen not by governments and the spokesmen and activists of nationalist (or non-nationalist) movements, but by the ordinary persons who are the objects of their action and propaganda, is exceedingly difficult to discover. Fortunately social historians have learned how to investigate the history of ideas, opinions and feelings at the sub-literary level, so that we are today less likely to confuse, as historians once habitually did, editorials in selected newspapers with public opinion.[47]

Expanding on his point that top-down studies of nations and nationalism must be complemented with studies from the bottom up that take ordinary people's concerns into account, Hobsbawm maintains that ideologies of states and political movements do not inform our understanding of how citizens feel; that it cannot be assumed that people place their national identity above other sources and objects of identification; and that national identification changes or shifts over time, even within brief periods. He concludes these introductory comments in *Nations and Nationalism since 1780* with the assertion that "this is the area of national studies in which thinking and research are most urgently needed today."[48]

Pending such research in parts I and II of my study, although we may speculate that the shah's birthday celebration in 1953 and some aspects of its symbolism and rituals fit Hobsbawm's typology of invented traditions and surmise that the screening of the event nationwide in movie theater news places Iran squarely in Hobsbawm's framework for understanding the evolution and diffusion of the concept of the nation through technology in the postwar era, this framework is insufficient in explaining why the event and its symbolism might be meaningful specifically to the scouts, athletes, and students who are participating. What is the role of ethnicity and language in the event's organization, symbolism, and appeal to these nonelites? In what ways does ethnicity relate to a sense of national community and identity? Beyond analyzing the event generally as invented tradition, how can we understand how the sublayers of invention—such as the scouts' rituals and activities—relate to the elites' nation-building efforts, if at all? The theoretical exchange between Hobsbawm and Gellner suggests that answers to these questions will come through an approach that combines research into elite activities and inventions with study into the activities, perceptions, and memories as well as the "hopes, needs, longings and interests of ordinary people."[49]

Benedict Anderson: The Nation as Imagined Community

Perhaps the most widely read and frequently quoted book on nationalism is *Imagined Communities* by Benedict Anderson, first published in 1983 and with new editions produced in 1991 and 2006.[50] All three of the most recent monographs on Iranian nationalism to be discussed later in this chapter reference Anderson's work and utilize his theory in various ways. Similar to Hobsbawm, Anderson combines Marxism, modernism, and postmodernism to pursue the origins, development, and character of nations and nationalism. His sociocultural approach to nations and nationalism is centered around the argument that the critical features of nations—which are artifacts of recent history—are the ways in which they are imagined by individual members, whose subjective perceptions (such as a sense of belonging, unity, or patriotism) collectively provide the nation with its community, meaning, strength, and positive and destructive potentials. Despite the fact that the majority of a nation's members will never meet or know one another, their imagined communion and commonalities are what define and sustain their nation.[51] In an effort to understand how and why collective imaginings of the nation lead to, among other things, individual members' willingness to kill and die for a nation, Anderson seeks to trace the origins and evolution of nationalism to examine the phenomenon and the resulting devotion and allegiance it produces.

To explain the resonance and strength of the national imagination, Anderson aligns nationalism with the cultural systems of religious community and dynastic realm, both of which were taken-for-granted concepts in their heyday akin to the way nations and nationality are today.[52] By aligning nationalism and its emergence with the large "self-evident" cultural systems of religion and kingship and their demise rather than with "self-consciously held political ideologies" such as Marxism, fascism, and liberalism, Anderson endeavors to show how nationalism acquired its appeal, durability, and worldwide acceptance. He finds that three critical factors contribute to the initial development of nationalism: the fragmentation of religious community, the decline of the dynastic realm, and changing cognitions of time.

In Europe, the Reformation led to the emergence of new Christian denominations while assaulting the concept of universality promoted by the Catholic Church. With this fragmentation of central religious community and its perceived omnipresence came a corresponding decline in the universal scriptural language (Latin) and a rise of vernacular languages. The idea that a single language offered access to the truth became outmoded.[53] The contemporaneous development of print capitalism and the beginnings of the bourgeois class had the effect of spreading a standardized vernacular language through a broadening base of readership, which, Anderson submits, led to the spread of a common vernacular language and progressively to a sense of community and shared identity.[54]

No less influential in shaping the imaginings of the masses toward a sense of distinct community was the decline of dynastic states from the seventeenth through the early twentieth centuries. Whereas the dynastic realm, Anderson explains, was divinely legitimized and defined at its center, with indistinct and porous borders encompassing heterogeneous populations of "subjects," the modern state is legally demarcated and evenly sovereign over its entire territory. This new foundation of state legitimacy was defined in terms of the nation, which is frequently coincident with linguistic patterning. Despite attempts by threatened dynasts to oppose awakening linguistic nationalist movements, the conceptual damage to their divine legitimacy and ubiquitous power had been done, and the nation became the only legitimate form of state.

According to Anderson's theory, changing comprehensions of time also played a role in priming the mass consciousness for nationalism. Premodern conceptions of time involved cyclical, millennial, or messianic expectation. There was "no conception of history as an endless chain of cause and effect or of radical separations between the past and present."[55] Cosmology and history were one. Thus, with the fragmentation of religious community and decline of dynastic realm, there also came a change in cognitions of time toward a calendared, linear present and future, which enabled the creation of a common historical past.[56]

The conjunction of the demise of these three cultural systems, in Anderson's view, led to the search for "a new way of linking fraternity, power and time meaningfully together."[57] Print capitalism and a revolution in printing and bookmaking offered both impetus to this search—as they hastened the demise of scriptural language and ushered in vernaculars—and solutions in that they enabled people to relate to and imagine a broader community.[58] In assembling related vernaculars and creating "mechanically reproduced print-languages capable of dissemination through markets," print capitalism enabled "unified fields of exchange and communication below Latin and above the spoken vernaculars."[59] Thus, the convergence of capitalism and a printing revolution at a time of change in large cultural systems set the stage for nationalism.[60] Concurrent growth in literacy, commerce, industry, communications, and bureaucracy during the nineteenth century created additional impetus for linguistic unification.[61]

To combat the rise of linguistic nationalist movements, Anderson explains, the remaining dynasties of eastern Europe and Asia pirated the modular concepts of nationalism and sought to impose what Hugh Seton-Watson terms "official nationalisms" over their restless linguistic minorities.[62] Conservative adaptations of the spontaneous nationalisms that preceded and motivated them, these official nationalisms, such as in the Austro-Hungarian and Ottoman Empires or czarist Russia, are "a reactionary, secondary modeling" of the modular concept of nationalism.[63] In the twentieth century, a wave of anti-imperial nationalist movements swept through former colonies of Asia and Africa, where, utilizing advances in communications technology such as television and radio to complement print, "the lessons of creole, vernacular and official nationalisms were copied, adapted and improved upon,"[64] and the nation became the basis for the remaining portion of humanity's communal imaginings.

Having sketched the process of social change and shifts in consciousness by which the nation came to be imagined "and, once imagined, modeled, adapted and transformed,"[65] Anderson finally returns to the question he poses in his introduction: Why are people attached to these "inventions of their imaginations" and "ready to die for these inventions?"[66] The answers, he says, are essentially familial love and "purity, through fatality": "Dying for one's country, which usually one does not choose, assumes a moral grandeur, which dying for the Labour Party, the American Medical Association, or perhaps even Amnesty International can not rival, for these are all bodies one can join or leave at easy will."[67] More than racism and xenophobia, Anderson asserts, nations, once established, inspire self-sacrificial love—evident through expressions in literature and visual and musical arts. Nationalist love is the result of a vocabulary of kinship or home to describe the nation (*watan, fatherland, homeland*), which implies a natural connection.[68] Like the family, whose pure and natural connection and boundless love generate impetus to sacrifice, the "national interest" can similarly inspire and demand self-sacrifice.[69] The devotion and self-sacrifice the nation inspires are underpinned by common language. Appearing ancient and primordial however modern it may be, language is the cement of the imagined community: "What the eye is to the lover—that particular, ordinary eye he or she is born with—language—whatever language history has made his or her mother-tongue—is to the patriot. Through that language, encountered at mother's knee and parted with only at the grave, pasts are restored, fellowships are imagined, and futures dreamed."[70]

Brilliantly articulated, Anderson's popular work offers us yet another speculative yet useful theoretical framework through which to view the origins of nations and nationalism.

Applying Anderson's contentions to the birthday rally on behalf of the Iranian king depicted in the photo yields still more hypotheses about how such an event relates to the development and sustenance of national community and identity. Having been pirated in its modular form by secular Iranian intellectuals to secure the country's territorial integrity and sovereignty at the turn of the century, by the mid–twentieth century nationalism has produced imagined interconnectivity between the event's participants, who together represent the national community. United by a common language spread through mechanically produced print and the state's educational efforts, the elite and nonelite participants in the rally are evidently expressing and feeling their horizontal comradeship and love of the family–nation that they constitute. The patriotism demonstrated by the marching scouts is a by-product of the natural connection they imagine between themselves, their fellow citizens, and the state—the preconditions for devotion and self-sacrifice. Indeed, a general application of Benedict Anderson's theory enables us to wax eloquent in speculation about the imagined bonds such an event represents and sustains.

But how can we specifically locate and describe the essence and appeal of this abstract community to its various participants and the role of language in its evolution? Although a public display in recognition of a leader's birthday might unite its participants through imagined national community, and language may be a possible component of this imagining, the conceptual insight Anderson's theory grants us does not answer the question of why the participants might feel bound to each other and the nation. How can we research the ways in which the uses and extent of communal imaginings intersect with the complex interconnectivities presented by the realities of daily life? What realities underpin the relationship between the state and its citizens as well as the interests of each? Does language play a specific role in the event's symbolism and organization? Where would we focus our research to acquire an understanding of the nature and wellspring of this love and devotion? How can we ground such a lofty account of the origins and character of nationalism? As Anthony D. Smith, to whose work I now turn, puts the problem succinctly, "How do we get from knowing and imagining the nation to feeling and loving it?"[71]

Anthony D. Smith and Ethnosymbolism

Perhaps the most prolific writer on the subject of ethnic and national identities over the past three decades has been Anthony D. Smith. A central participant in ongoing theoretical dialogue between nationalism studies specialists, Smith generally offers refined definitions of key operating terms (e.g., *nation, nationalism, national identity*), observations and criticisms regarding prevalent theories of nationalism and contemporary interpretive trends, and varying degrees of explication of his favored approach, ethnosymbolism, which arose out of his dissatisfaction with existing modernist, perennialist, and primordialist paradigms. Offering a "supplement and corrective" to existing paradigms, Smith and his fellow ethnosymbolists have evolved a new and promising approach rather than a theory.[72] Still a growing trend within the field, ethnosymbolism has attracted a sufficient number of adherents and generated enough literature to be self-sustaining independent of Smith, but he remains the movement's unofficial dean and leading evangelist.[73]

The ethnosymbolic approach focuses on subjective sociocultural and symbolic elements such as memory, myth, symbol, value, ritual, tradition, and sentiment in the persistence of *ethnies* (ethnic communities), the emergence and formation of nations, and the appeal of nationalism. In this way, ethnosymbolism seeks to illuminate the "inner worlds" of nationalism and ethnicity.[74] The ethnosymbolic approach can also be distinguished by an interest in long-term, multigenerational analysis in opposition to modernist reasoning for concentrating on the eighteenth-century through the present.[75] Only analyses that consider social and cultural patterns over *la longue durée* can hope to illuminate the complex relationship between the past and the present in the persistence of collective cultural identities and the ways in which earlier forms of collective identity—most importantly the *ethnie*—have influenced the evolution of nations. Smith and the ethnosymbolists thus posit nations and nationalism within a continuum of collective identities rather than solely as products of modernity.[76] In contrast to the modernists' generally elite-focused, "top-down" analyses, an ethnosymbolic approach seeks to understand the activities, beliefs, and attitudes of nonelites and the ways in which they influence and are mobilized by the nationalist intelligentsia.[77] Unlike modernists, Smith contends, "ethno-symbolists stress the relationship between various elites and the lower strata ('the people') they aim to represent. But this is not a one-way relationship. The non-elites, partly through their cultural traditions, and partly in consequence of their vernacular mobilization, influence the intelligentsia, political leaders, and bourgeoisie, by constraining their innovations within certain cultural parameters and by providing motifs and personnel for their cultural projects and political goals."[78] Thus, Smith further distinguishes ethnosymbolism from modernism by its emphasis on the dialogic nature of the relationship between elites and nonelites and their reciprocal roles in the development of nationalism.[79]

An ethnosymbolic reading of the snapshot from the shah's 1953 birthday parade draws our attention once again to the interactions and relationship between the elite spectators and the nonelite participants on the track, whose activities and attitudes simultaneously bolster and constrain the elites' cultural and political projects. What does the salute and following procession mean to the shah of Iran and provide to him and the elites surrounding him in the grandstands? What does the salute, adorned uniform, pomp, and circumstance mean to the lead scout and to those following behind, bearing the portrait of the young shah in his own scouting uniform? As a corrective to research guided by the modernist paradigm (illustrated in the works of Gellner, Hobsbawm, Breuilly, Kedourie, and Anderson), the ethnosymbolic approach calls for investigation into the memories, myths, symbols, values, traditions, and sentiments of the participating scouts, athletes, and student groups to understand the "inner world" of Iranian nationalism and ethnicity and in turn to shed light on the ways the elites utilize and are limited by these subjective and symbolic elements as they appropriate the past and connect it to the national present.

Smith's ethnosymbolic approach asserts a complex, dialogic relationship between the elites and nonelites in the creation and maintenance of nationalism, and it demands explication of the symbols, myths, memories, values, sentiments that constitute the "inner world" of nationalism and ethnicity for the nonelite strata. Well more than a decade into its formulation, what this promising and compelling approach has yet to identify or illustrate is the research path to these inner worlds and the view from below that is required to behold them. Indeed, Smith and the ethnosymbolists chart a clear directive for the focus of future research on ethnicity and nationalism, yet at present they do not offer guidance regarding the research methods and sources one would employ to document and interpret the sociocultural and symbolic elements that are central to the approach. Ethnosymbolism therefore draws our attention to the myths, symbols, memories, and sentiments that generate and are in turn created and sustained by the shah's Fourth of Aban parade, but it does not as yet suggest how to proceed to investigate them.

Our consideration of the theories of Ernest Gellner, John Breuilly, Elie Kedourie, Eric Hobsbawm, Benedict Anderson, and Anthony D. Smith has produced useful hypothetical lenses through which to view the shah's 1953 birthday parade. More importantly, it has generated a series of compelling, nuanced questions to help determine the applicability and utility of their theoretical frameworks and initial leads in our pursuit of suitable research methods to enable us to address these questions. The next step will be to consider the ways in which the work of these theorists has been utilized in existing studies of Iranian nationalism and how these studies might aid our effort to decipher the historical snapshot from 1953.

The Study of Iranian Nationalism: Toward a Dialogic Approach

Despite the fact that modern Iranian history and studies of Iranian politics have flourished in the three and a half decades since the Iranian Revolution, little research has been done on the subject of Iranian nationalism.[80] Embryonic in its development and sparse in quantity, existing historiography on Iranian nationalism has not yet begun to detail the process by which nationalism spread in the twentieth century to the country's many linguistic and religious minorities or its roughly 90 percent Shi'a Muslim majority, of which some 55 percent speak Persian. Throughout the Cold War era, the subject of twentieth-century Iranian national development was approached essentially from two distinct and often ideologically informed points of view in the fields of history and political science. Development was initially written about as part of a general exaltation of a modernizing, secularizing, anti-Soviet, pro-Israel Iran under Shah Muhammad Reza Pahlavi, peaking in the 1960s and 1970s.[81] Analyses of Iranian national institutions and development during the Pahlavi era (1925–79) are distinguished by their dearth of reference to the experiences of anyone but a handful of secular elites.[82] After the Islamic Revolution of 1979, numerous studies emerged to attempt to explain the historical evolution of the movement to overthrow the Pahlavi regime and its leadership.[83] Cold War influences and political turmoil guided much of Western scholarship on Iran from the 1950s through the early 1990s. During this period, however, the specific subject of Iranian nationalism received remarkably little scholarly attention.

As described in this book's preface, Richard Cottam's *Nationalism in Iran*, the single book-length study available on the subject of Iranian nationalism from 1964 to 1993, was shaped by the Cold War and US foreign-policy history in Iran, in which Cottam himself played a role.[84]

Concerned primarily with the prospects for future political stability in Iran, the bulk of Cottam's analysis focuses on the impact of Iranian nationalism on political attitudes and behavior from the 1920s through the mid-1950s and narrates the evolution of the oil nationalization crisis as well as the aftermath of Mohammad Mossadegh's overthrow in August 1953. Although ascribing Iranian nationalism to ancient origins, Cottam viewed it as a modern phenomenon that became politically relevant only after 1890 and that had not yet taken root within the nation's diverse population.[85] Because of the unknown political implications that growing Iranian nationalist sentiment would surely present—whether wielded by the Pahlavi regime or by its manifold opposition—the remainder of Cottam's analysis sought to assess the social base and level of popular receptivity to Iranian nationalism to determine its potential functions in national unification and political stabilization.

As noted in the preface, having completed his field research and relatively short career with the CIA in Iran in the decade following the Azerbaijan Crisis of 1946–47, Cottam was concerned particularly with the issue of Azerbaijani and Kurdish separatism as well as with the potential for a sense of Iranian nationalism as a "terminal loyalty" to be inculcated among Iran's linguistic and religious minorities.[86] Here, alongside Soviet designs and regional irredentism as critical determining factors in the country's territorial cohesion, Cottam plotted the level of allegiance of Iranian minorities and their potential to accept Iranian national identity by way of the proximity of each group's linguistic and religious traditions to that of the Shiʿa Persian majority. Thus, primary loyalty to the Iranian nation would be based on the relative distance or propinquity of a minority group's religious traditions to Shiʿa Islam and of its traditional language to Persian. By this formulation, an Azeri-speaking Shiʿite would more readily accept Iranian national identity than a Kurdish-speaking Sunni, who in turn would be more amenable to Iranian identity and the Iranian nationalist message than would the country's Armenian or Assyrian Christians or Jews.[87] Cottam qualified these logical yet untested assumptions with a series of Cold War what-ifs, such as the impact of Soviet propaganda directed toward Iran's minorities and covert activities in border regions to destabilize the Pahlavi regime.

On October 26, 1953, two months after CIA Operation Ajax succeeded in initiating the coup d'état that overthrew Prime Minister Mossadegh and firmly seated Muhammad Reza Pahlavi back on the Peacock Throne, and two weeks before Mossadegh would face a military tribunal for treason, the shah's thirty-fourth birthday was publicly celebrated at Amjadieh Stadium in Tehran. Drawing insight from Cottam's *Nationalism in Iran* to understand this event and to interpret the photograph of the opening ceremony is particularly apropos considering the concurrence of his research, the book's narrative focus, and its emphasis on the impact of what he saw as the rise of royal dictatorship and movement toward totalitarianism in the wake of Mossadegh's ouster.[88] Seeking to shed the image of vacillation and weakness that was most recently underscored by the shah's escape to Rome at the height of the August coup, the birthday parade is an attempt to demonstrate the shah's power and diverse base of support, the reestablishment of security, and the country's stability. With the purge of the National Front and Tudeh Parties in high gear, the display of Persian nationalist symbols and representation of continuity in the monarchial tradition of the Fourth of Aban parade seek to wrestle back the mantle of Iranian nationalism from the monarchy's competing secular nationalist and Communist opposition. Cottam's detailed account of elite infighting and intrigue in the months following the coup suggests that the show of crowd unity and monarchial loyalty masks infinitely more complex sentiments and likely a sense of unease, fear, and relief in the grandstands. The marching scouts depicted in the photograph of the opening ceremony—probably unaware of the political functions their participation in the event serves or of many applauding onlookers' consternation—are themselves in the process of acquiring a sense of Iranian national identity. Whether these nonelites will ultimately come to accept Iranian nationalism of whatever political orientation as their terminal loyalty in the coming decades will depend primarily on their ancestral language and religion. Per Cottam's predictions, those of a Shi'a Persian background would have a strong chance of developing and sustaining a sense of Iranian nationalism; Sunni Kurds or Azeri Turkish participants would probably do so; and those of Armenian Christian or Jewish ancestry would not.

Five decades since its original publication, *Nationalism in Iran* remains a vital source for understanding the contemporary political context surrounding the 1953 Fourth of Aban parade and offers a logical, if untested, framework for understanding how ethnicity and religion might play a role in shaping the experience of the event's minority participants and their ultimate nationalist allegiances. That Cottam considered Iranian minorities at all is laudable, especially considering that his text has until now remained the only English-language study on the subject of Iranian nationalism that does so. Yet without a lineage of subsequent analyses to test and refine this elementary and inherently cursory work, and in light of the clout he developed as informal adviser to the Carter administration and in testimony before US Congress during the Iranian Revolution and Hostage Crisis, Cottam's conclusions became canonized, even though intervening history would demonstrate his predictions regarding minority allegiances and Iranian nationalism to be far off the mark.[89] Remarkably, it would be almost thirty years before another in-depth study on the subject of Iranian nationalism would emerge to supplement Cottam's influential work.

Mostafa Vaziri's *Iran as Imagined Nation: The Construction of National Identity* (1993) offers the most extensive research into the origins of Iranian national identity to date and (until 1999) remained alongside Cottam's work as one of only two book-length studies in English on the specific subject of Iranian nationalism. In dramatic contrast to Cottam's emphasis on contemporary politics, Cold War lens, and detached position on the phenomenon of nationalism itself, Vaziri's at times polemical contribution centers on the pre-twentieth-century roots of Iranian national identity, viewed through the lens of imperialism and Orientalism. In a radical, constructionist departure inspired and framed via Benedict Anderson's and Edward Said's theories and methods and working primarily through textual analysis of European sources, Vaziri seeks to illustrate his conviction that the very notion of Iran as a geographical designation and Iranian national identity are the inventions of modern European Orientalists and thus imported forgeries.[90]

Vaziri is on solid ground as he details the epistemology of nationalism in eighteenth- and nineteenth-century Europe and describes its effects on the construction of modern Iranian historiography. Tracing the lineage of European philological interpretations and intellectual conceptions of Iran, from Arthur Gobineau's racialist theory of Asiatic–Aryan achievement through the historical narratives of seminal Iranologists such as George Rawlinson, Edward Browne, Vladimir Minorsky, and Richard Frye, Vaziri forcefully and persuasively argues that such outsiders had vast influence in shaping the understanding of what Iran was, where it could be located on a map throughout history, and what linguistic, political, and cultural elements distinguished its people from their Semitic neighbors and carried on through the ages. Ultimately, using the work of Richard Cottam as his central example, Vaziri laments that modern scholars have taken for granted the historicity of Iranian national identity and have unquestioningly adapted the received wisdom regarding Iran's geographical and cultural heritage and national particularism.[91] He asserts that it is contradictory for Cottam to explain Iranian nationalism as a modern phenomenon but then anachronistically assign its historical, racial, linguistic, religious, and cultural basis. "Cottam, like some other scholars, asserts that the greatness of pre-Islamic history gave nationalism (and national consciousness) vitality, but he also admits that 'the uneducated have no idea of Iranian history.'"[92] Hence, Vaziri takes *Nationalism in Iran* to task for its failure to investigate the origins and development of Iranian national identity and to address what he calls the "multilayered identity question" regarding how diverse cultural and linguistic groups "came together to feel Iranian."[93]

Whereas Vaziri's *Iran as Imagined Nation* tackles the origins of Iranian national identity head on, the multilayered identity question Vaziri himself raises is not answered, and the relative success of the effort to create a common Iranian consciousness within a bordered Iranian zone is deemed "an interesting but separate issue."[94] Thus, Vaziri leaves us to speculate about this effort's impact on actual Iranians and their identity in the twentieth century, which is when he claims foreign concepts of Iranian nationalism were successfully imposed. Because his analysis is focused predominantly on what Europeans thought and wrote about Iran, it unfortunately does not detail the actual process by which Orientalist knowledge and historiography affected the construction of Iranian national identity or Iranian sociopolitical developments. Though lacking a base of evidence on which to support such a monologic interpretation of Iran's relationship with the West, *Iran as Imagined Nation* nevertheless places agency in the hands of Orientalists and their indigenous elite tools of the Qajar and Pahlavi eras (such as Ali Akbar Dehkhoda or the Armenian Iranian Muslim Mirza Malkum Khan),[95] who forcibly imposed their "racist" paradigm of Iranian language, identity, and culture within the geographical area now known as Iran. Vaziri explains,

> Iran as a geographical designation was taken by the European Orientalists and transformed into a people endowed with all kinds of national and racial characteristics, in part to serve the ends of the political and racial consciousness being championed by authoritarian European Orientalism. . . . The Orientalists thus forged the name of Iran not only for a people but also for a language family, a civilization, a culture, and a tradition, without fear of contradiction that—in both the ancient and the Islamic periods—there could not have been a homogeneous Iranian world. This conception obviously gained considerable credence in the age of nationalism and overwhelmingly authoritarian Orientalism.[96]

In terms of the process by which "authoritarian" Orientalism shaped the identity of Iranians through the origination of things such as the Aryan Hypothesis and the revival of scholarship focusing on ancient Persian language and civilization, Vaziri offers nothing in the way of supporting evidence, yet he boldly submits that "this anachronistic treatment of Iran by European historiography gave the land's twentieth-century governments and its masses grounds to be content about their forged identity."[97] Vaziri's use of Anderson's theory of imagined community is noteworthy in its interpretation of *imagined* as false, mistaken, or otherwise spurious.[98]

If we accept Vaziri's premise and theoretical reasoning, the shah's 1953 birthday parade can thus be interpreted as an extraordinary example of Orientalist power to fabricate reality and of the Pahlavi regime's complicity in selling a load of Orientalist nonsense to its diverse population. The entire ritual and its trappings reify both the constructed myths of Iran as a nation and legitimately bordered political unit and the lineage of Persian monarchy. They dangerously inculcate bogus concepts of Persian racial superiority and homogeneity. In this view, the participants in this charade, from the field to the grandstands, range from passive victims to insidious indigenous collaborators. The winners are the racists of the dominant linguistic group, and the losers are the participants of all backgrounds, who are being sold a bill of goods at the expense of their true histories, identities, and cultures.

But even if for the sake of argument we agree with Vaziri that European Orientalism was instrumental in the construction of Iranian national identity, why is this bill of goods appealing, and exactly how is it marketed? How do elite and nonelite individuals *use* Iranian nationalism in identity formation and reconstitute it in an annual public event such as the shah's 1953 birthday celebration? Are Iranians merely passive victims of European scholarly fantasy and manipulation? What is in this event for them?

To understand the roots of Vaziri's approach and interpretation, we need to look more deeply into the layers of its theoretical sources, in particular its use of Edward Said's *Orientalism*, now that we have examined Anderson's *Imagined Communities*. To generalize, Said draws from Michel Foucault's analyses of clinics, medicine, prisons, order, and language to develop his theory of the patriarchal Orientalist scholar, who views the East with his panoptic gaze, distinguishing and reifying the Occidental normal from the Oriental abnormal.[99] Antonio Gramsci's theory of cultural hegemony is integrated to describe how Orientalist knowledge, once developed, is monologically imposed on and used to control Eastern societies.[100] Said does not mince words as he characterizes the strength and durability of the Orientalist West, stating that "the relationship between Occident and Orient is a relationship of power, of domination, of varying degrees of a complex hegemony. . . . The Orient was Orientalized not only because it was discovered to be 'Oriental' in all those ways considered commonplace by an average nineteenth-century European, but also because it *could be*—that is submitted into being—*made* Oriental."[101]

This explanation of the relationship between the East and West is problematized by the very theories it draws from. Foucault's variant descriptions of the mechanisms of power relationships do not allow for such a top-down, monologic, juridical, and repressive imposition of power and knowledge. In fact, they point to individuals as the location of power and agency. In response to a question about the historical essences and sources of power that he originally alluded to in *Discipline and Punish* (1975), Foucault states:

> In defining the effects of power as repression, one adopts a purely juridical conception of such power, one identifies power with law which says no, power is taken above all as carrying a force of a prohibition. Now I believe that this is a wholly negative, narrow, skeletal conception of power, one which has been curiously widespread. If power were never anything but repressive, if it never did anything but say no, do you really think one would be brought to obey it? What makes power hold good, what makes it accepted is simply the fact that it doesn't only weigh on us as a force that says no, but that it traverses and produces things, it induces pleasures, forms knowledge, produces discourse. It needs to be consolidated as a productive network which runs throughout the whole social body, much more than as an instance whose function is repression.[102]

Foucault suggests that an *ascending* analysis of power is necessary to understand its mechanisms, which are constituted through "a multiplicity of organisms, forces, energies, materials, desires, thoughts etc."[103] His theories do not dismiss the possibility of cultural hegemony. On the contrary, they support Gramsci's idea (and Said's interpretation of it) that hegemonic activity aside from material force has something to do with the ability of a group (i.e., European imperialists) to seize and maintain power. What they call into question, however, is whether cultural hegemony and the creation of identity can be understood when viewed as monologic, top-down impositions. Foucault instead points to dialogic interactions as the capillary sources of power and to individuals as vehicles of that power. Therefore, if we want to understand how and in what way (or, again, if at all) Orientalism shaped lives and identities in Iran and elsewhere, it is necessary to begin to look at the interactions of individual elites and nonelites in these processes and to find out what significance and meaning—what *uses* and *pleasures*—things such as Orientalist myths and a constructed national identity provided.[104]

Eugene F. Irschick applies this approach in his study of the creation of South Indian identity in the nineteenth century, *Dialog and History, Constructing South India, 1795–1895* (1994). Based primarily on archival and biographical sources, this study examines the creation of knowledge regarding physical space and cultural identity. Irschick explores the process in which a formerly mobile Tamil population became fixed in a resacralized land and demonstrates how this process was useful in various ways to Tamil nationalists, the British colonial administration, and diverse indigenous agriculturalists. Questioning the claim (specifically referring to Said) that knowledge is constructed by willed activity of a stronger over a weaker group, Irschick's research suggests instead that "changed significations are the heteroglot and dialogic production of all members of any historical situation, though not always in equal measure; this is so whether they have a Weberian monopoly on violence or not."[105] In the case of South Indian identity, Irschick's study demonstrates how the process of its development was not only collaborative, but "harmonious" and even "pleasurable," despite the fact that it was in many ways a project of British colonial domination.[106] Active voices from all segments of society—colonizer and colonized, elites wielding juridical power and nonelites often subject to it—came together to create and shape knowledge and identity.[107]

Coincidentally, the third work in the short lineage of studies on Iranian nationalism mirrors Irschick's study of the creation of knowledge regarding physical space and cultural identity in South India and articulates a dialogic understanding of agency in the creative and contested process of identity formation in Iran.[108] In *Frontier Fictions, Shaping the Iranian Nation, 1804–1946* (1999), Firoozeh Kashani-Sabet investigates how territorial defense, delineation of borders, and evolving conceptions of national geography during the Qajar and early Pahlavi eras influenced culture and politics and motivated and shaped Iranian nationalist discourse.[109] While recognizing the utility of Anderson's framework for understanding nationalism and illustrating several of his themes in the case of Iran, Kashani-Sabet asserts that it is the palpable entity of land that enabled Iranians to imagine membership in and develop allegiance to the "deep horizontal comradeship" Anderson describes.[110] An Iranian national community was indeed imagined, she argues, but only after perceptible objects such as land, maps, and historical texts enabled the visualization of Iran as a nation by Iranian intellectuals and political elites and after the subsequent attempt to inculcate a common Iranian national identity, citizenship, and patriotism among Iran's ethnically diverse population by way of mass education and the homogenization of national language and culture. Thus, Kashani-Sabet explains that "the Iranian homeland, though still formally the birthplace of Armenians, Kurds, and Baluchis, as well as Farsis and others, increasingly came to represent the *vatan* of Shi'i Persians through the persistent efforts of the state to extirpate competing cultures. . . . Iran managed to cohere as a territorial unity by emphasizing the shared experiences of its diverse population through a reading of geography and history as well as the suppression of cultural difference."[111]

Although Iranian national unity would prove "spurious" by 1946 despite these cultural projects—evidenced by minorities' discontent with Reza Shah's reign and the Azerbaijan Crisis, which closes Kashani-Sabet's study—the author submits that land and frontier disturbances have remained central to the evolving Iranian nationalist agenda, be it the secular nationalism of Mossadegh and the National Front during the nationalization crisis or the religion-infused Iranian nationalism of the Islamic Republic throughout the Iran-Iraq War.[112]

Although the sophisticated and nuanced theoretical critique of Anderson and other modernists that Kashani-Sabet presents in *Frontier Fictions* is not explicitly associated with existing theorists or theoretical paradigms, her argument, the structure of her work, and its sources are unmistakably ethnosymbolic. Like Smith and the ethnosymbolists, Kashani-Sabet utilizes the scaffolding of the modernist paradigm and the theorists she critiques (Anderson, Hobsbawm, and Gellner) to illustrate "from above as well as from below" how subjective elements such as myths, symbols, memories, and sentiments—in her research regarding land, archaeological reliefs, texts, and maps—evolved over the *longue durée* and to demonstrate their role in sustaining, appropriating, reinterpreting, and reifying conceptions of the Iranian *ethnie* and its historic homeland.[113] Arguing that modern Iranian nationalism was necessarily based on recognizable geographic and historic precedents, which in turn provided modern political elites with viable material for their unification and homogenization projects, Kashani-Sabet's approach, like ethnosymbolism, bridges the gap between perennialist and modernist interpretations.[114] Similarly, in contrast to the instrumentalist reading by Mostafa Vaziri, Kashani-Sabet acknowledges the strong Orientalist influence in the evolution of modern Iranian history and cartography but argues that the appeal and resonance of elite yarns—Orientalist tainted or otherwise—was that they were spun from veritable strands of history and bound via genuine physical and emotional connections to land. Wielding a variety of primary sources that include official documents, maps, journals, newspaper articles, cartoons, travelogues, and personal memoirs, Kashani-Sabet narrates the process by which Iranian patriots, not self-Orientalizing poseurs, revived old myths and created new ones to fortify territorial claims and forge a common Iranian identity.[115] Because *Frontier Fictions* concludes in 1946, its analysis culminates in the death throes of the exclusive ethnic nationalism of Reza Shah's regime, which had the effect of alienating Iran's ethnic minorities and prohibiting the development of national unity. Since 1946, land and frontier disturbances have indeed remained central to evolving Iranian nationalist agendas, but the reorientation of policy to promote an inclusive civic nationalism since 1946, implemented under Muhammad Reza Pahlavi and perpetuated by the Islamic Republic, has arguably succeeded in creating a level of national unity and allegiance among minorities surpassing that of many neighboring countries in the region.[116] What was the nature of these dramatic legal, economic, symbolic, and rhetorical policy changes, and how did they alter the level of nonelite receptivity to nationalist projects in subsequent decades? To illustrate how rapid and significant these changes were, there is perhaps no better moment to consider than the commencement of the 1953 Fourth of Aban parade at Amjadieh Stadium and how it contrasts with Reza Shah's exclusivist policies.

As Kashani-Sabet documents, the Armenians of Iran chafed under Reza Shah's restrictive social and linguistic reforms. In 1927, concurrent with the Motahed ul-Shekl Shodan-e Ahali-ye Iran (Promulgation of Uniformity for the People of Iran) described in this book's introduction, the Interior Ministry demanded that Armenian schools in Azerbaijan remove all symbols that could be perceived to be reminiscent of those used in the short-lived Armenian Republic and immediately convert them to Iranian national symbols. In 1936, the Davudian Elementary School was forced along with other schools to comply with new Ministry of Education regulations demanding that all subjects be taught in Persian, limiting the number of Armenian-language instruction hours to five per week, and requiring an on-site representative/minder from the ministry.[117] From these examples, Kashani-Sabet accurately concludes, "Rival patriotic allegiances, then, could in no way publicly threaten or challenge Persian cultural dominance of Iranian national sovereignty, since the state actively countered such rivalry by imposing its national agenda."[118] By 1938, a majority of Iran's Armenians were alienated by the Persianization effort, as were Iranian Assyrians, Jews, Kurds, Azeris, Turkmen Baluchis, and Arabs. If the story ended here—as indeed *Frontier Fictions* does—Iranian national identity could at that stage accurately be characterized as spurious.

Yet it is well known that after Reza Shah's ouster in 1941, the majority of the regime's restrictive language reforms were either ignored, softened, or eliminated altogether, as were other unpopular reform efforts such as tribal sedentarization and public-dress regulations such as the ban on *hejab* (veiling). The wrenching events of 1946–47 would accelerate this unraveling and under a government split between an increasingly powerful Majles and prime minister, on the one hand, and a weak shah, on the other, would encourage a new approach to national identity, unity, and Iranian minorities. This approach consisted of a rapid, pragmatic shift from exclusive ethnic nationalism to the embrace of elements of civic nationalism.

Bearing the Ararat flag and uniform insignias, which state in Persian "Bashgah-he Varzeshi-ye Ararat" (Ararat Athletic Club) and utilize the red, blue, and orange of the Armenian tricolor, the young scout in the left of the frame in the parade photo keeps perfect cadence as he looks proudly at the shah and his entourage in the grandstands of Amjadieh Stadium on October 26, 1953. What does this overt recognition of Armenian Iranian distinctiveness accomplish for the Iranian political elites looking on? What new national myths are being created and acted out? How does the spectacle and its symbolism shape the sentiments and memories of this Armenian vanguard? This final question is particularly compelling if we remember Richard Cottam's formula for plotting receptivity and allegiance to Iranian nationalism, which places these lead parade participants as the least likely to develop either. Kashani-Sabet's work brilliantly moves the study of Iranian nationalism closer to a dialogic approach and skillfully offers an ethnosymbolic reading of the history of Iranian mapping territorial struggles both physical and intellectual. Yet when we attempt to draw from it to ponder our photograph or, in fact, most developments in Iranian history after the book's conclusion in 1946, it generates as many questions as it answers. In juxtaposition to the examples of abrasive language reforms between 1927 and 1936, what are we to make of the Armenian symbols, colors, and myths on display at Amjadieh in 1953? What changed and why? How did these dramatic policy changes impact the sentiments of the nonelite parade participants? What if any impact did such changes have on the identity and allegiances within the Armenian Iranian community? What about within other Iranian minority communities or within the dominant Shi'a Persian majority?

As we commence this effort to understand the strengths and limitations of enduring theories of nationalism and assess their use in the handful of scholarly works on the subject of Iranian nationalism, it is fortuitous that the most recent book-length study of Iranian nationalism explicitly addresses the evolution, purpose, and features of Pahlavi commemorative activity, such as the celebration of the shah's birthday. In *Nationalizing Iran: Culture, Power, and the State, 1870–1940* (2008), Afshin Marashi explores the social, political, and cultural convergence that enabled a realignment of state–society relations and undergirded the movement from a traditional monarchy under Nasr al-Din Shah Qajar to a modern national state under Reza Shah Pahlavi. By tracing continuities in state institutions, social structures, and cultural forms that transcend the traditional political periodization of modern Iranian history around the change from the Qajar to the Pahlavi dynasty in 1925, Marashi shows how elite state building and cultural production enabled the new framework of Iranian national community to be envisioned and materialized between 1870 and 1940.[119] Tracing European and internal influences that began Qajar experimentation with new ways of self-legitimation during the second half of Naser al-Din Shah's reign, concurrent Orientalist-influenced intellectual crystallization around notions of national culture and history that accelerated through the 1930s, and the resulting educational projects and ceremonial and commemorative activity of the Reza Shah period, Marashi offers an illuminating alternative periodization and narrative to the history of modern Iranian social and political development. Regarding the import of this narrative to subsequent Iranian history, Marashi utilizes the powerful and well-known example of Mohammad Reza Pahlavi's statements at the 1971 Persepolis celebration: "Muhammad Reza Shah Pahlavi's claims of authority, as Shah *of Iran* and Light *of the Aryans* thus were not tied to sources of power above or outside the nation but rather were grounded in the fabric of society itself. This transformation was based on the premise that state and society were tied together by a common culture and that the role of the state was now to be the representative and agent of that common and sharply-delineated culture."[120] Therefore, political actors' ability to claim to speak on behalf of the nation—from Iranian constitutionalists through Iranian president Mahmoud Ahmadinejad (2005–13)—is ultimately reliant on the prerequisite social, political, and cultural changes that took place between 1870 and 1940, which saw the emergence of modern politics around the abstract concept of the nation.[121]

Like Kashani-Sabet's *Frontier Fictions*, which covers analogous chronological terrain (1806–1946), Marashi's study does not subscribe to one or another of the existing theoretical paradigms but rather draws from the work of Anderson, Breuilly, and Kedourie to craft a sophisticated—while still essentially modernist—argument to support his thesis and to define critical operating terms such as *the nation* and *nationalism*. That Marashi views nationalism as a modern political movement and locates the crucible of the nation within the period of political consolidation covered in his book reflects the combined influence of Breuilly and Kedourie's modernist-instrumentalist approaches to nationalism. As described earlier, Breuilly offers a strict definition of nationalism as a political movement relevant in times of political contestation, and Kedourie frames nationalism as an elite political ideology that employs symbols rooted in language, ethnicity, and geography to further political projects as they vie for state power. Yet Marashi finds the definition of nationalism as primarily a political phenomenon relevant only on the field of political contestation insufficient. Drawing from Benedict Anderson's concept of the imagined community, Marashi problematizes Breuilly and Kedourie's definition as too narrow because it neglects to account for the development of the political arena that enables nationalism to come into play in such times of contestation. As Anderson illustrates, imagining membership in a national community requires broad historical transformations within society and culture, which Marashi accordingly identifies and isolates in Iran several decades before the critical moments of political contestation.[122]

Illustrating the nature and function of symbolic commemorative activity and efforts to construct a national memory under Reza Shah, Marashi explains how the invented tradition of the annual celebration of the shah's birthday was but one of many new forms of commemorative practice. Statuary and mausoleums honoring famous Persian poets and writers such as Omar Khayyam, Saadi, and Hafez; state-sponsored Nowruz (New Year) celebrations and ceremonies marking the visit of important literary, cultural, and political figures; and the 1934 Ferdowsi millennial celebration were the creation of political elites and intellectuals intended to produce a uniform national culture with a shared history.[123] In many ways, new rituals such as a parade at the sports stadium for the shah's birthday and the use and appropriation of a pantheon of new secular heroes by the Pahlavi regime dramatically illustrate Hobsbawm's thesis of invented traditions, which, along with the approaches taken by other modernists (Anderson, Breuilly, and Kedourie), informs Marashi's work. Alas, however, a reading of the photograph from the 1953 in light of the attention Marashi draws to Pahlavi commemorations up to the year 1940 still leaves us with essentially the same questions that our review of Hobsbawm's and the other modernists' approaches generated.

Marashi's *Nationalizing Iran* enables us to view the shared salute that commenced the October 26, 1953, birthday rally for Shah Mohammad Reza Pahlavi as a stunning example of the reorientation of the monarchy's claimed legitimacy from divine, cosmic mandate to its relationship with and custodianship of common Iranian people. The large photograph of the young shah in his own scout uniform—that of the all-Persian Pishahangi-ye Iran of the Reza Shah era—is borne by the two Armenian Iranian scouts of Ararat, reifying the notion of an Iranian scouting tradition and its links to the monarchy and symbolizing the new inclusiveness of the institution's orientation. And yet once again, now at the end of our journey through theory and narrative, we come full circle to the questions generated by our coverage of the modernists. Marashi's work provides historical background to enable us to understand the large-scale transformations that enabled such a symbolic event to have meaning as well as the origins and purpose of the specific ritual of the shah's birthday rally itself. Yet it does not explain why the event and its symbolism might be meaningful to the scouts, athletes, and students who participated. What is the role of ethnicity and language in the event's organization, symbolism, and appeal to these nonelite minorities? In what ways does ethnicity relate to their sense of national community and identity? What about the other participants of different backgrounds? Beyond analyzing the event generally as a newly enabled elite commemorative activity, how can we understand how the sublayers of activity—such as the rituals and activities of the scouts themselves—relate to the elites' nation-building efforts, if at all? If the structural relationship between state and society that enabled the comprehension of an abstract, "imagined" national community did indeed emerge in the period 1870–1940 as Marashi argues convincingly, how can we specifically locate and describe the essence and appeal of this abstract community to the birthday event's various participants and the role of language in its evolution now that it has been successfully enabled? To echo the point Smith makes so adeptly, how do we go from imagining the Iranian nation to its nonelites' feeling and loving it? Existing theoretical and historical approaches suggest that answers to these questions will come only through an approach that combines research into elite activities and inventions and study of the activities, perceptions, and memories as well as the "hopes, needs, longings and interests of ordinary people."[124]

Social Biographical Solutions

Social biographical research is concerned primarily with the investigation of the lives of individuals and their social interactions. Most commonly constructed through a combination of relevant documentary evidence from public and private archives, oral interviews with the individual subject and family members and friends, period literature and news articles, as well as secondary sources, a social biography relates the story of an individual's life and contextualizes it through interpretation of the broader events, processes, and structures the individual encountered and through which he or she navigated.[125] Although the idea that research into individual activity and experiences with and expressions of nationalism over time can be conjoined with the many compelling yet speculative theories of nationalism to answer persistent questions about the phenomenon of nationalism is not new, until now such a confluence has been directly called for by only a handful of social historians who have speculated about its potential. The clearest and most direct statement to this effect was first made by Edmund Burke III in the introduction to the first social biographical collection to focus on the lives of ordinary Middle Eastern men and women, *Struggle and Survival in the Modern Middle East* (1993, with a second edition in 2006): "The biographical approach holds out the promise of reinvigorating the relation between theory and empirical research. . . . Social biographies, especially when deployed as part of a broader research strategy, can test and refine social theories, as well as provide an alternative vantage point from which to think about the historical processes by which societies have been continually transformed."[126] Although the volume presents twenty-four social biographies without theoretical structure or analysis, its introduction suggests the potentials of a meeting between social theory and social biography specifically as it relates to nationalism:

> No subject in the modern history of the Middle East has received greater attention from scholars than nationalism. The conventional account stresses the ways in which in response to heroic leaders the masses mobilized to overthrow Western rule. The obvious contradiction between the realities of ethnic diversity and the nationalist assumptions of ethnic unity in Middle Eastern states is simply elided in most accounts. While we know quite a bit about nationalism as an ideology and a political movement, we are much less well informed about how it became the language of politics. The role of nationalism as an ideology in serving the interests of indigenous elites in maintaining their dominance is generally not examined. It is here that the study of ordinary people's lives can contribute a great deal.[127]

Demonstrating how factors such as ecology, culture, ethnicity, class, gender, and personal circumstance influenced the trajectories, options, and strategies of individual Middle Eastern men and women, the social biographies in *Struggle and Survival* are equally effective at illustrating and elucidating the impact of large-scale historical forces (such as the world economy, colonialism, nationalism, revolution, war) on the lives of individuals and how individuals correspondingly have agency and play a role in large-scale forces and events.[128]

Although there has been an abundance of research on the histories of modern Middle Eastern societies, we still know relatively little about the lives of nonelite and minority Middle Eastern individuals.[129] Within the broad field of Middle Eastern history, Iranian history is perhaps the farthest behind in this regard. Slow to move away from traditional document-based research approaches and elite-focused narratives, the field still considers social history a novelty, and oral history is nearly anomalous in it. Of the few established archives that do exist, such as the Harvard Iranian Oral History Project, almost all focus on political elites and take the form of narrative memoirs rather than focused interviews. Although such projects are certainly a start, the area of Iranian oral history is in its infancy, especially as it relates to nonelites of all ethnicities and backgrounds.[130]

In addition to lack of enthusiasm by scholars of Iranian history, political circumstances and events have also played a role in limiting oral history projects on Iran. The dictatorship of the Pahlavi era did not allow for the free expression of ideas at Iranian universities or research centers—especially if they related to anything political—and the government of the Islamic Republic has randomly engaged in the limitation and disruption of scholarship inside the country since the revolution. Fear of both regimes has made many Iranian citizens and expatriates understandably reluctant to discuss their background with a researcher, however apolitical their life or occupation might seem to the outside observer.[131] Furthermore, owing to the ongoing tensions in US–Iran relations, it is exceedingly difficult for scholars from the United States to obtain funding for projects that require research in Iran, which greatly limits the type and scope of projects that can be undertaken.

Despite these obstacles, some of which are common to research in other geographical locations and political regimes (countries in Latin America and many nations of Africa, for example), it is still possible to gather oral evidence to study modern Iranian history. Many Iranian citizens and expatriates are willing to speak openly about their lives and experiences if the researcher is clear about the intent of and possible uses for the research and is willing to be flexible about the necessity to tape record all conversations and about allowing the interviewee/narrator to excise at their discretion material intended for publication.[132] Some narrators request that a pseudonym be used in publication or that recorded conversations not be made public or both. When combined with personal documents, letters, diaries, photographs, and memorabilia, however, detailed interview notes and several recorded conversations can explain much about an individual's life and experiences.[133] All of these materials can then be integrated to create a social biography. Because the written form of social biography does not rely on the direct quotations from the research subject, it is an effective style when developing a biography of an individual who cannot or will not be directly quoted. Combining the methodological strengths of social biographical and oral historical investigation, this stylistic feature of social biography enhances the effectiveness of the format, particularly in the case of Iran and especially in research concerning issues such as personal identity, loyalty, allegiance, and participation in the development of nationalism.

As the methods, uses, and limitations of social biography have been described in past works that have laid the foundation for the present study, I would like instead to address more thoroughly here the relationship between social biography and oral history, both in general and in the chapters to follow.[134] Although existing studies offer proof that insightful and useful social biographies can be based on the interpretation of archival documents, newspaper articles, personal letters, memoirs, photographs, and secondary sources, they also demonstrate that the inclusion of oral testimony by the research subject and optimally by their family, friends, and acquaintances gives such documentary sources deeper meaning and offers the historian insight into personal perceptions, attitudes, and emotions.[135] Probing much more deeply than portraits based solely on documentary evidence, social biographical portraits supported by oral interviews are better suited to answering the questions about receptivity, appeal, and the sublime aspects of nationalism and national identity that emerge from the theoretical discourse and with which my study is concerned.

When relevant oral evidence is possible to acquire and integrate, social biography can be distinguished from oral history (which also draws heavily on nonoral evidence and often focuses on the life of a single subject) primarily through its written form. Whereas works of oral history tend to privilege the subject's voice, interweaving interpretation and detail with quoted words, social biography relies less on direct quotation and is styled around the historian's interpretation of the oral evidence, which is seamlessly integrated with documentary source materials. These divisions are by no means set in stone; past social biographies have been crafted around and based almost entirely on direct quotation with very little input from the historian.[136] However, in my view, the most effective social biographies critically analyze and integrate oral testimony with the other sources at their disposal and are not based on block quotations, as is often the case with works of pure oral history. The social biographical effort, thus, is concerned not only with giving voice to the voiceless, but also with critically analyzing and integrating that voice with other evidence, interpreting it, and creating a portrait of an individual's life and social interactions. To paraphrase Alice Hoffman, it treats oral history as one among several primary sources.[137]

The arguments that call into question the reliability of oral versus documentary evidence and the historian's role in eliciting and interpreting oral testimony are now decades old, and over time they have produced a dialog in which oral historians have vindicated their craft while being prompted to articulate more clearly what oral history's inherent strengths and limitations are.[138] More importantly, this dialog enables a self-conscious assessment and clarification of methods of data gathering and interpretation and a thorough consideration of issues of reliability and validity.[139] Oral historians and social biographers are at this stage well aware of the challenges and responsibilities inherent in gathering and interpreting oral evidence as well as the strength of oral testimony in relation to document-based research.[140]

Whatever the strengths of social biography and oral history, I am not suggesting that they offer a panacea for testing and refining all social theories. What I am arguing, however, is that social biography is the key to providing details that will enable us to respond to the many questions and challenges posed *by theories of nationalism*. What is the impact of mass education and the imposition of a single language on national identity? Why are people responsive to waving flags, anthems, and parades? Where do we locate influences, interests, and agency in the complex process of the development of nationalism and national identity? Why do people kill and die for the nation? Social biographical research into the lives of both elites and nonelites, supported by oral interviews with research subjects, is the most suitable form of historical inquiry to enable us to answer these questions and advance our understanding of nations and nationalism.

PART I

Experiences with Iranian Nationalism

2

Iskandar Khan Setkhanian

A THRONG OF MOURNERS crowded Tehran's Armenian church in April 1953 to pay their respects to the family of retired General Iskandar Khan Setkhanian, who had served in the military under four of Iran's Qajar shahs. Among the mourners were numerous government officials and military officers representing the Pahlavi regime. Following the religious ceremony at Surb Astvatsatsin Church, priests, military officers, and government officials gathered on the stairs outside to publicly extol the virtues of a man who, like his forebears, had long served in the military of Iran. During the eulogy, mourners were reminded that Iskandar Khan had been a respected citizen from a prominent Armenian family that had served the country for more than one hundred years and that he had admirably served three decades in the military. A military spokesman apologized to the family for the small number of officials in attendance, explaining that the current political turmoil made their attendance difficult.[1] The homage paid to the retired general and his family was a reflection of the high esteem in which he was held for a lifetime of service to Iran. During his career, Iskandar Khan had directly participated in significant events that had paved the way for the governing regime. It is also of significance that he had been a close friend to Reza Shah, who had once been his subordinate in the Cossack Brigade.

Iskandar Khan's casket was draped in the Iranian tricolor flag as it left the church and was carried on the shoulders of a military honor guard. At the beginning of Naderi Avenue, a military band stood at attention,

2. Funeral of Iskandar Khan Setkhanian, Tehran, 1953. Unknown photographer. Courtesy of Mara Setkhanian-Martin.

and the streets leading to the Armenian cemetery were lined with hundreds of uniformed soldiers as the procession passed by.

Iskandar Khan's eldest grandson and a nephew carried his military decorations as they walked beside the casket toward Doulab Cemetery and his final resting place.[2] The medals and regalia were but a small part of Iskandar Khan's extensive collection of treasured memorabilia, documents, photographs, and artwork that detailed his military career and life in Iran.[3] To fully understand the life of Iskandar Khan Setkhanian of the Persian Cossack Brigade and his place in Iranian history, it is necessary to consider the family into which he was born in 1865 and the development of the family's relationship and role in the service of the Qajar rulers and Iranian military during the nineteenth century.

The Setkhanian Family in Nineteenth-Century Iran

The Setkhanian family name and many of its family traditions began with Set Astvatsatourian, who was born in Bushire around 1780.[4] Bushire, a port city of the Persian Gulf, was an important center of trade for Armenian merchants of Isfahan, Julfa, and India.[5] Armenian tradesmen had trading houses, distribution centers, and overseers in the seaport. It is believed that the Astvatsatourian family had moved to Iran and become part of the middle class involved in this trade during the reign of Agha Muhammad Shah Qajar (1794–97).[6]

After receiving a rudimentary education and studying the Armenian language with the priest of Bushire's Armenian church, Set Astvatsatourian was sent at the age of thirteen to be educated in English at a school in Bombay.[7] When his education was completed, he worked for an English merchant in India. He returned to Bushire a few years later, by which time his father had died.

Owing to the rarity of educated multilingual individuals in early-nineteenth-century Bushire, Set Astvatsatourian became a translator for the ambassador of Great Britain, who was traveling through Bushire to be received by the court of Fath Ali Shah (r. 1797–1834) in the new Qajar capital, Tehran. From that time, he was given the honorific title *khan* and was thus known as "Set Khan." In Armenian tradition, his sons were later known as "Setkhanian," sons of Set Khan.

Set Khan was employed in the civil service of the Qajar court, and in 1810 he made his first trip to London, most probably as a translator, in the company of the Persian ambassador to Great Britain. After returning to Iran and working for the next decade in the Qajar administration of Tabriz,[8] Set Khan traveled with Ambassador Mirza Saleh Shirazi to London as a military adviser.[9] Continuing in his service to the Qajar administration, Set Khan was selected in 1828 to deliver a letter from Fath Ali Shah to Ottoman sultan Mehmed II, who honored him with a Class One medal, a jewel-studded dagger, and the title *bey*. This successful mission earned Set Khan (or Sedghi Beig) the favor of Fath Ali Shah, who issued two *farmans* (royal edicts) as his reward. The first *farman* allowed him to

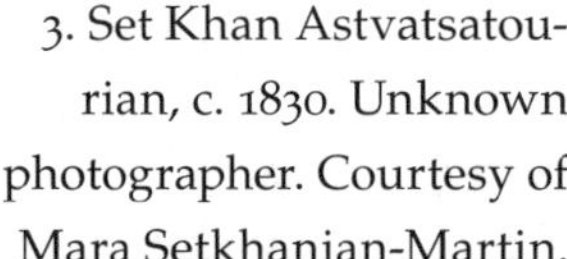

3. Set Khan Astvatsatourian, c. 1830. Unknown photographer. Courtesy of Mara Setkhanian-Martin.

begin precious metals mining in the Minaeh and Gharadagh regions of Azerbaijan and permitted him to go to England for the purpose of contracting experts to work on the excavations. The other gave him permission to import marketable goods from Britain upon his return.[10] Set Khan returned to Tehran with two English mining experts and twenty Greek miners under his employment. He also brought back a quantity of British merchandise, which he sold before heading to the Gharadagh (Kara Dagh) Mountains of Azerbaijan with his mining team.[11]

Around 1830 in Azerbaijan, Set Khan located and mined sites that produced silver, copper, and coal. The modern methods utilized by his mining team had never before been employed in the region and were particularly effective and profitable. Copper was in high demand in Iran because of its uses in cannon making. Set Khan soon concentrated his efforts on cannon smelting, which was considered a breakthrough in Iranian technical and military development. An observer stated, "The honorable Saeed Khan the Christian (*masihi*) last year has cast two 6 lb. cannons, tied them to wheels and has presented them to the Shah as an offering (*pish-kash*). The Shah in return has accorded him an income of 1500 Tumans. He has contracted to manufacture 84 guns to be delivered in six months to the royal court."[12]

At this time, Azerbaijan was the center of Persian military reform under Crown Prince Abbas Mirza, who was attempting to create a modern army with Western-style training, uniforms, and armaments. The new army was called the Nezam-e Jedid, or "New Order," using the same terminology and methods of the contemporary Ottoman reformers Selim III and Mahmud II and of the Egyptian reformer Muhammad Ali. Recent defeats by the Russians early in the nineteenth century had resulted in the 1813 Treaty of Golestan and the 1828 Treaty of Turkmanchai, as a result of which Iran had lost large amounts of territory in the Caucasus and Central Asia as well as rights to use military vessels in the Caspian Sea.[13] The losses compelled the Qajar government, under the leadership of Abbas Mirza and his chief minister, Qa'em Maqam,[14] to try Western-style military training within the country and to encourage the sending abroad of Iranian students to receive an education that included technical and military curricula. In this first era of nineteenth-century reforms, it was thought that the threatening powers of the West—specifically Russia in the North and an increasing British presence in the South—could be held back by the adoption of European military institutions and technical education. The development of a modern army was essential to efforts by the Qajars to retain suzerainty over their territory because of external threats from without as well as challenges from within.[15]

Strong tribes and tribal confederations such as the Qashqai, Lurs, Baluchis, Shahsevan, Kurds, and Bakhtiaris were the true suzerains of their respective regions. The lack of a modern army forced the Qajars to resort to bribes, hostage taking, and divide-and-rule tactics to retain their loose hold on the country from Tehran. Urban corporate groups, such as the ulama (religious jurists), bazaaris, and members of guilds (*asnaf*) and athletic organizations (such as the *zurkhane*, "house of strength"), could pressure the Qajar government to act in their religious and economic interests since the government lacked well-armed security networks and police in major cities to quell protests and riots.[16] In this context, Set Khan's exploitation of the copper mines of Azerbaijan can be seen as an advancement for the Persian military reform effort because previously all large quantities of copper for cannon smelting had to be imported from the Ottoman Empire. Set Khan was able simultaneously to meet the Qajar government's need for domestic weapons production and to enjoy the financial benefits of having secured the demand for his products. His involvement with this initial phase of modernization of the Persian army would initiate a century of his own and his descendants' participation in this process.

The development of domestic artillery production by Set Khan and others helped to further the Azerbaijan-based military reform effort. Its leader, Crown Prince Abbas Mirza, realized the critical importance of the use of foreign techniques and implements in this development because modern gun making and proper use of artillery required an increasingly advanced knowledge of metallurgy, mathematics, chemistry, and military science. Therefore, the long-term success of Abbas Mirza's Nezam-e Jedid depended on the practice of sending students abroad for education concurrent with the attempt to bring foreign instructors and advisers into the country to teach these methods. Abbas Mirza first tried French and then British instructors to train his recruits of the new army. The results of their attempts were not sustained and so produced only more disorganization and confusion.[17] Foreign education was more effective in preparing individuals to fill the ranks of the military than domestic efforts, which were extremely weak throughout the nineteenth century.[18]

Realizing the importance of a formal education for their son, Sattur Setkhanian, and finding no domestic alternative, Set Khan and his wife, Zizi,[19] sent their child from Tabriz to school in England at the beginning of the 1830s. In Tabriz, Set Khan enjoyed a comfortable life and was a prominent leader in the Armenian community. He was a close friend of Abbas Mirza, who was known for his good treatment of religious minorities[20] and who affectionately referred to Set Khan as "Brother Set."[21] The death of the crown prince in 1833 was a personal blow to Set Khan, who lost both a dear friend and a benefactor.[22] He suffered increasingly hard times during the late 1830s and died in Tehran in 1842.[23]

Abbas Mirza's New Order was limited to Azerbaijan during its existence and was disbanded soon after his death. Therefore, unlike contemporary military reforms of other Middle Eastern regions, which progressed slowly but surely throughout the long nineteenth century, similar reforms in Qajar Iran were virtually halted for the next half-century. Firuz Kazemzadeh characterizes the next fifty years of development, or lack thereof, that followed: "Under the inept rule of Mohammed Shah (r. 1834–1848) and his Prime Minister, the grotesque Sufi buffoon Haji Mirza Aqasi, the Persian army lost whatever effectiveness it had possessed in the previous reign."[24] Despite a few attempts to reform aspects of the Iranian military with the use of Western military advisers from a variety of countries,[25] Nasir al-Din Shah (r. 1848–96) did little to remedy this situation for the first thirty years of his reign and therefore would rule during the height of the Persian army's demoralization and ineffectiveness. It would not be until the late 1870s that the Russian-officered Persian Cossack Brigade would be established and developed into a disciplined and effective force.[26]

A young Sattur Setkhanian traveled from Tabriz to England to attend a boarding school. He then obtained a degree in medicine from Cambridge University. After returning to Iran to open up a private practice in the 1850s, Sattur Khan was forced to do surgery on a relative, an experience that forever turned him away from the field of medicine.[27] Because Sattur Khan was highly educated and his father had been a faithful civil servant and close friend of the Qajars, he was appointed as an adviser to Crown Prince Mozaffar al-Din in Tabriz.[28] It was during this time that Sattur Khan was sent on a fateful mission to Georgia. A tale of events has since been handed down through generations of Setkhanians.

> The grand duke of the Caucasus, Mikhail Nikolaevich, had sent a pair of hunting dogs to the crown prince of Iran who, not to be outdone with generosity, decided to reciprocate by sending a delegation headed by Sattur Khan to Tiblisi with a pair of fine Arabian horses for the grand duke. The duke was grateful for the horses and other gifts brought by the entourage, but he was distraught because he feared that his daughter,

> who had fallen down while dancing, had broken her leg. Because of his medical training, Sattur Khan was able to determine that the girl's leg was not broken but had been badly dislocated. He immediately recommended that the duke allow him to send for a *senakhchi* (a type of Persian shaman-chiropractor), who, he was sure, could correct the dislocation. The *senakchi*'s strange bedraggled look upon his arrival worried the duke, yet he permitted the man to perform his procedure. Although the *senakhchi* nearly lost his life to the duke's guards after the young girl screamed and then fainted from the intense pain of the pulls and twists he performed, she awoke later feeling better and was soon able to walk. The duke, who was very grateful for Sattur Khan's assistance and recommendation of the *senakhchi*, inquired about how Sattur had attained his high level of knowledge and refinement, whereby Sattur told him about his British education. The duke proudly stated that this was an insult for Iranians to travel so far for their education when the finest schools in the world (the Russian ones, in his opinion) were so much closer. Sattur Khan responded that it was only because of the fact that his father, Set Khan, had been an adviser to England that he was sent to British schools. Finding this a sufficient excuse, the duke announced that Sattur was forgiven but had to promise him that when his children (who were not yet conceived) reached schooling age, Sattur would send them to Russian schools at the duke's expense. Sattur Khan agreed to this offer, and thus began Sattur Khan's close relationship with Russia and the Russian administration in Tabriz.[29]

While settled in Tabriz and working for the Qajar administration as a military staff officer, Sattur Khan married Ninon Khanom Hovnatanian, the daughter of the famous Armenian Iranian court painter Hagob Hovnatanian.[30] Sattur Khan and his wife, who eventually had three sons and three daughters, chose the Russian general consul in Tabriz, General Stupyn, as the godfather of their son Iskandar (Alexander).[31]

It was at this time that the regular Persian army felt the effects of a serious decline in strength and organization. Corruption and disorganization spread as the reign of Nasir al-Din neared its fourth decade. The army was plagued by the lack of a trained officer corps, a fragmented chain of authority, improper and sometimes nonexistent fund allocations, the lack of matching arms and ammunition, and the practice of giving hereditary ranks.[32]

Debilitated already from these ailments, the army was used nevertheless in the suppression and massacre of the Babis, which resulted in great demoralization within the ranks. Although it did manage to seize the city of Herat in 1857, its losses to nomadic Turkman tribes in Khorasan during the 1860s demonstrated its lack of technical, organizational, and material advancements over its nomadic challengers. Inexcusable losses to British troops in Khuzestan and Fars, where the panicking Persian troops sometimes outnumbered their foes ten to one, left no doubt that Persian forces would be defenseless against other Western aggressions.[33] As a result, the Russian and British Empires would increasingly use Iran as a geostrategic pawn in their nineteenth-century fight for world dominance.[34] The situation for the Persian military was grim in the 1860s and 1870s.

Just as his father had found no local alternative for Sattur's education, and keeping his promise to the grand duke of Russia, Sattur Khan sent his

4. Sattur Khan Setkhanian, staff officer, Tabriz, c. 1860. Unknown photographer. Courtesy of Mara Setkhanian-Martin.

own sons to the military academy in Moscow to receive their primary education and military training.[35] He sent his three daughters to the Gymnasia in Tiblisi.[36] Sattur Khan continued to serve the regular Persian forces as a staff officer and *sartip* (brigadier general).[37] A highly decorated member of the military in Tabriz, he provided his family a comfortable life as he continued with the well-established family tradition of educating his children abroad and serving in the Persian military and diplomatic missions.

Iskandar Khan Setkhanian (1865–1953)

In October 1878, Sattur Khan and Ninon Khanom prepared to send their thirteen-year-old son Iskandar to the military academy in Tiflis, Georgia.[38] To obtain the proper papers and documents for his visas and entrance into the school, they had a certification of birth prepared by the Holy Church of God's Mother in Tabriz.[39] The document prepared by Priest Khosior-ter Gosirorov was transcribed first into Armenian from the "Metric Book" or book of births, deaths, and weddings and stamped with the church's official seal to assert authenticity. On the same document, a translation was made into Russian and authenticated by the Russian general consul in Tabriz, then stamped for a fee of one ruble. Sattur Khan also had to obtain documentation from the Russian consul, which declared that all of Iskandar's papers were in order; the document was also stamped and dated for a fee.[40] By the time of his first journey to Russia, Iskandar Setkhanian had already mastered Armenian and Farsi at the Armenian church school in Tabriz. Over the next nine years, he received a foreign military education and studied the Russian and French languages. His studies and experiences prepared him for his eventual entrance into the ranks of the new Persian Cossack Brigade.

Iskandar Khan's first trip to Russia corresponded with another fateful Russian excursion in the same year. In 1878, as Nasir al-Din Shah made a second trip to Europe and passed through the Caucasus, he was impressed by the uniforms, training, discipline, and weaponry[41] of the Russian Cossack troops. Desiring a similar brigade of his own, Nasir al-Din inquired about how this might be accomplished. Grand Duke Mikhail Nikolaevich, viceroy of the Caucasus, who had been helpful in paving Iskandar Khan's way to school in Moscow, was the intermediary between Nasir al-Din and

5. Ninon Khanom and Sattur Khan Setkhanian with children (Iskandar Khan not present), Tabriz, c. 1890. Unknown photographer. Courtesy of Mara Setkhanian-Martin.

Czar Alexander II, who immediately allowed for a number of instructors to be sent to Iran to assess the military situation and need.[42]

In late November 1878,[43] Lieutenant-Colonel Aleksi Domantovich of the General Staff was advised of his assignment to Tehran for this purpose. With only vague instructions on a course of action, Domantovich arrived in the Iranian capital in January 1879 to begin his assessment of the situation and the creation of the brigade. Despite the challenges posed by the state of the Persian army at this time, he was successful in creating the first detachment of Persian Cossacks by initially enlisting into the brigade four hundred *mohajer*s, descendants of Transcaucasian Muslims who had migrated to Iran early in the nineteenth century to escape Russian rule.[44] After a successful presentation of skills and preparedness for the shah that summer, the brigade was given a budget of 97,000 tumans, to be paid by the Persian government. It was also agreed that the Persian minister of war would have control of the Persian army and the Cossack Brigade would take orders only from the shah and Moscow.[45] The Russians were elated with this arrangement as it essentially gave them military control over northern Iran at the expense of the Qajars. Although the British legation in Tehran complained about this development, it was assured that the single Russian adviser would be the only presence and influence the Russians would have.[46]

Domantovich was replaced by Colonel Charkovskij (first name unknown) in 1881, who oversaw the acquisition of a battery of four horse-drawn cannons.[47] This was the only major development during his five years of leadership, a fact that led the Persian government to cut the brigade's budget by 6,000 tumans. The *mohajer*s had become a liability by this time for leaving their posts and pushing for hereditary rights for their children in the brigade, which necessitated some financial and personnel house cleaning. The next commander of the Persian Cossacks, Colonel Kuz'min-Karavev (first name unknown), entered his position in 1886 facing disorderly troops and with the brigade in deep financial trouble. Despite a lack of improvement of training over the next four years, Kuz'min-Karavev began the elimination of the *mohajer*s and worked diligently on the brigade's finances, leaving his successor, Colonel Nikolai Shneur, with a relatively orderly body of troops and a 4,000-tuman annual surplus over the original budget when the post was assigned to Shneur in 1890.

During this period, Iskandar Khan graduated with honors from the military academy in Tiflis, where he was trained in Cossack cavalry tactics and military sciences, had mastered the Russian and French languages, and studied science and mathematics. From Tiflis, he traveled to Moscow and St. Petersburg to complete his higher education.[48] He was apparently viewed as a model student as well as a model citizen of the Russian Empire, which can be inferred from a document he received in Tabriz in late 1888.[49] Iskandar Khan became a naturalized citizen of the Russian Empire by transfer of *poddantsvo* or "loyalty"[50] from Persia to Russia,[51] after receiving a statement from the police that "he has good behavior and way of life . . . has not been subject to court proceedings or investigations and is reliable in a political sense."[52] Iskandar Khan then immediately entered in the service of the Persian military once back in Azerbaijan (1888) and received a *farman* that placed him in service in Azerbaijan at the rank of *sarhang* (colonel) owing to his level of military and linguistic education.[53]

After four years of service in the regular Persian army as a *sarhang*, Iskandar Khan was given another promotion to the rank of *sarhang* adjutant in 1892[54] through the issuance of a *hokm* (official edict) by the governor of Azerbaijan Crown Prince Mozaffar al-Din.[55] As was not uncommon, the stated reason for the awarding of this rank was not Iskandar Khan's achievements or advancements that year, but rather his father's status as a *sartip*. It was after this promotion in 1892 that Iskandar Khan became dedicated to joining the Russian-officered Persian Cossack Brigade in Tehran, but this plan would be hampered by problems within the brigade that were not unlike those his father and other relatives had been experiencing over the previous decades.

Colonel Shneur, unlike his predecessor Kuz'min-Karavev, was not a master of finances and ran out of money to pay his troops by the middle of 1891. In keeping with traditional Qajar military practice when strapped for funds, he granted indefinite, unpaid leave to his troops, who were demoralized further by the cholera epidemic in Tehran in 1891–92.[56] Shneur was consequently unable to assemble the Cossacks for a review requested by the shah late in 1891. Because he had demonstrated increasingly incompetent behavior as a leader by rendering the brigade useless in the defense of the palace during the Tobacco Revolt in 1892,[57] the brigade's budget was cut by almost one-third, and its active strength reduced to two hundred men. Colonel Shneur had to accept this penalty, which he vigorously fought to keep from being more severe.

Although Iskandar Khan intended to join the brigade, the new order restricting enlistment prevented him. To obtain favor, Iskandar Khan (and most probably his father, Sattur Khan) used some of his family's influence by requesting that a letter to Colonel Shneur be written by the Persian minister and ambassador to Russia 'Ala al-Mulk asking his help on this matter. In an ambiguous response, Colonel Shneur replied to the ambassador on February 25, 1893, that a *farman* had been issued by the shah that limited the Cossack budget and therefore new recruits: "I, this servant, have begged for the writing of this glorious *farman* that forbids completely entrance of new officers into the Brigade." Still, Colonel Shneur agreed that Iskandar Khan seemed suitable for the brigade and stated that it might be possible for him to receive a temporary position and salary until he could become an official member of the brigade.[58]

Shneur was dismissed two months after this response, and the Cossack Brigade was threatened by replacement with German advisers and staff.[59] Although documents confirm that Iskandar Khan was serving in the regular forces during this correspondence,[60] it was not until 1896 that the first award was issued to Iskandar Khan for his services to the brigade. This award places his entry into the brigade around 1894–95.

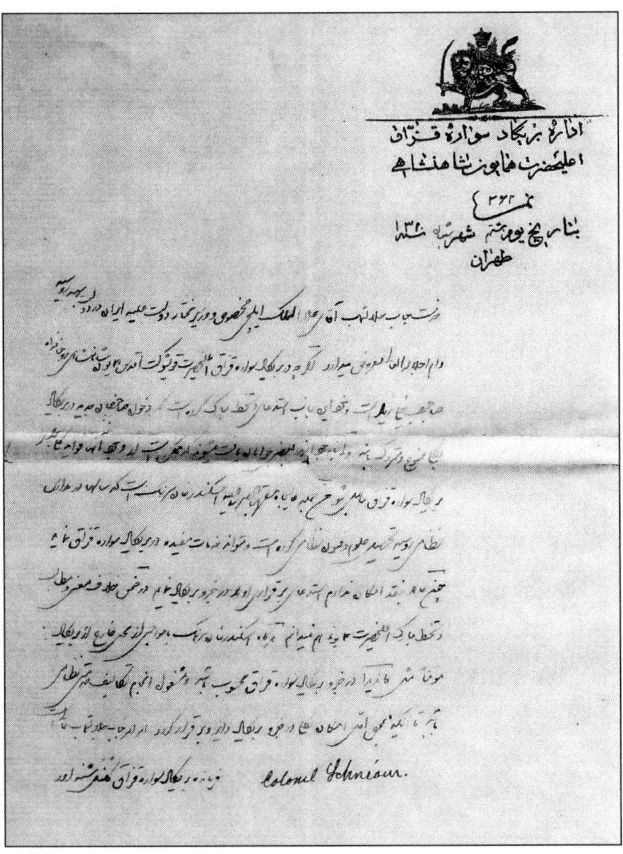

اداره بریگاد سوارهٔ قزاق
اعلیحضرت همایون شاهنشاهی
نمره ۳۶۲
طهران

[illegible]

Colonel Schneiour.

6. Correspondence (in Farsi) from Colonel Shneur to Iranian ambassador in Russia, 1310/1893. Courtesy of Mara Setkhanian-Martin.

Colonel Vladimir Kosogovski of the Persian Cossacks

Finding the German cost for military advisement too high (150 tumans annually for each soldier to be trained), the shah agreed to continue funding the Persian Cossacks. At an all-time low in membership, the brigade was assigned a new commander, Vladimir Kosogovski, late in 1893.[61] Aware that the shah was seeking new advisers, Colonel Kosogovski immediately set out to improve the brigade, and, though in debt and short of horses (as well as trained horsemen), he succeeded in organizing the troops for an outstanding review in September 1894. With the support of the shah again behind the brigade, Kosogovski turned to the task of creating a devoted rank and file and eliminating problem elements in the soldiery.

In his memoirs published in Russian and Farsi, Kosogovski devotes two chapters to the state of the Persian forces upon his entry to his post. The first is a general description of divisions and ranks of the Cossacks and other branches of armed forces—the artillery, infantry, and "irregular" cavalry of tribal forces—and the second is a description of the many problems within the Persian army, titled "Negative Military Discipline."[62] Kosogovski goes into great detail as he recounts stories of theft and property damage by even high-ranking officers that he had witnessed, the poor state of dress and equipment, the laxity in troop training owing to the few number of scheduled days of assembly, and general absenteeism.[63] Kosogovski also details the illicit off-duty and sometimes on-duty activities of many army officers, including a grape-smuggling ring that supplied the underground Tehran winemaking industry with its essential raw materials.[64]

Kosogovski attempted to tighten up discipline, focusing his attention on the subjugation and discipline of the remaining *mohajer*s, who frequently deserted their posts and insisted on continuing the practice of hereditary assignment of positions. Without hereditary appointments, each officer would have to work his way up through the ranks, be worthy of his rank, and remain beholden to his superiors rather than to family members for promotions.[65] As a result of Kosogovski's attempt to reform these practices and punish those who had left their posts, a revolt of the *mohajer*s occurred on May 5, 1895, in which they decided to quit the brigade, taking with them 20,000 tumans of their pay. Subsequent negotiations between Kosogovski and the shah, who was sympathetic to the *mohajers*,[66] yielded an agreement whereby the deserters could return without punishment to the brigade, yet they would be subject to the same duties, rights, and responsibilities as any other brigade member. The Russian commander's power over the brigade would be further increased.

Over the next year, Kosogovski was able to improve the efficiency and discipline in the brigade, making room for non*mohajer* officers such as Iskandar Khan to rise through the ranks on merit and hard work. By the spring review of 1896, the Cossack Brigade had become an increasingly

7. Sartip Iskandar Khan, 1895. Unknown photographer. Courtesy of Mara Setkhanian-Martin.

disciplined and well-trained fighting force. It would soon be tested by an oncoming storm of rebellion and mass political action that in many ways was related to abuses by the Qajar shahs and blatant examples of foreign intervention that emanated from the Cossack Brigade itself.

Nasir al-Din Shah was assassinated on May 1, 1896, by Riza Kermani, a student of Sayyid Jamal-al-Din al-Afghani, who was a staunch opponent of the Qajars and who had been a victim of their political oppression, having suffered years of torture in prison. This event offered the newly reformed Cossack Brigade the opportunity to demonstrate what strength and effectiveness it had outside the parade grounds. Deployed to keep order in the streets of Tehran until the governor of Azerbaijan Crown Prince Mozaffar al-Din and his entourage could arrive from Tabriz in the beginning of June, the Cossacks successfully kept order and were able to deal with the delicate and dangerous issue of succession with the help of Kosogovski's increasing knowledge of the dynamics of court relations.[67] Kosogovski was proud of this achievement, commenting in his memoirs that although ten thousand people had been killed during the accession of the late Nasir al-Din in 1848, not one had died in the transfer of power in 1896.[68]

Shortly after Mozaffar al-Din ascended to the throne, a *farman* was issued with his seals awarding the Shir-o Khorshid (Order of the Lion and Sun) of the Third Rank to Iskandar Khan.[69] The award was given for exemplary service and included a medal or diamond pin (*neshan*, or badge) of the Shir-o Khorshid. Soon after, Iskandar Khan received another *farman* while serving under Colonel Kosogovski that promoted him to *sartip* of the third rank, an award that came with a special sash for his dress uniform. The promotion was once again for outstanding service to the brigade.[70]

Iskandar Khan and the Persian Cossacks continued their service to the shah and the Russians in 1897 as they helped the Russian government extend its intelligence in eastern and southern Iran and hamper British trade between India and Khorasan. Under the pretext of preventing the plague that had broken out in Bombay from reaching Persian and Russian cities, the Russians requested that 150 Persian Cossacks be sent to establish two dozen quarantine posts along the Perso-Afghan border and the highways between Seistan and Khorasan. The quarantine system was a continuous problem for the British, who were unsuccessful for a decade in petitioning for its removal.[71] For his service in this campaign, Iskandar Khan received a *farman* in Farsi and Russian from the emir of Bukhara that awarded him the Order of the Bukhara Star Gold with a gold *neshan*. Indicative of the command structure and interests of the Persian Cossack Brigade, the reason for the award is stated: "In view of the friendship and agreement that unites the Noble Bukhara *with the mighty Russian Imperial Government* . . . [and] so that he may decorate his chest and have feelings of friendliness toward us."[72] Three more years of service to the brigade earned Iskandar Khan a *farman* granting him the rank of *sartip* of the second rank in 1900,[73] a time when dedicated Persian soldiers were few and far between. Iskandar Khan's service to the brigade and thus to Russia was also recognized by the award of the Order of St. Stanislaus of the Second Degree in September 1900.[74]

It was at this time that Iskandar Khan moved from the spartan brigade barracks, the *qazzaq-khane*, to a vast mansion compound near the Tehran city center on Khiaban-e Sepah. When he married into a wealthy family in 1894 following his betrothal to Maryam,[75] daughter of Persian army general Marteros Khan Davidkhanian Amir Tuman,[76] the estate was provided as a dowry.

In addition to the main building, the estate consisted of many separate residences for family members on the grounds as well as ponds, a stable, and workshop. A large *hammam*, or bathhouse, originally built by Marteros Khan also stood on the grounds and was used by members of the Armenian community of Tehran, who called it "Hammam-e Amir," the "Amir's Bathhouse."[77] Considered *najis*, or "unclean," as non-Muslims by many Iranian Muslims and thus unable to use the city's many bathhouses, Armenians were able to bathe at Hammam-e Amir six days of the week, while the seventh was reserved for the Setkhanian family to bathe privately. As Iskandar Khan's father, Sattur Khan, was now in his eightieth year, and the young couple would soon have six sons and a daughter,[78] the estate allowed Iskandar Khan to raise and care for his family away from the orderly but nevertheless unsavory *qazzaq-khane*.

In his biography of Reza Khan, who in 1900 was a *sarbaz* (infantry soldier) in the Cossack Brigade, Donald Wilber describes the features of

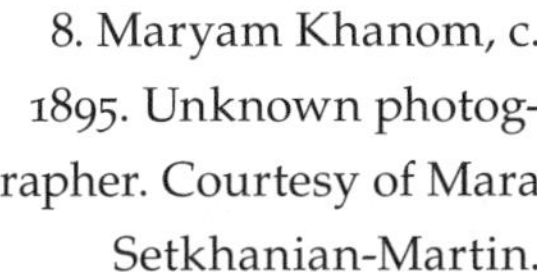

8. Maryam Khanom, c. 1895. Unknown photographer. Courtesy of Mara Setkhanian-Martin.

the *qazzaq-khane* and gives a brief geographical orientation of the area surrounding it:

> Life at the Cossack Barracks was rude and rough, and the pay of the soldiers was very low. The Tehran of that time was quite different from the modern city. It was still encircled by a moat and wall, pierced by a number of faience-clad gates. A few public buildings, some in a modified Russian style, enlivened with whitewash and enamel work, brightened the general mud-brick tone and drab character of the town. The narrow streets and lanes were unpaved, and public transport consisted of horse-drawn trolley lines. Maydan Tup-Khane (Cannon House Square), north of the Gulistan palace, seat of the Qajar dynasty, was the largest open area of the town. Ranged around the parade grounds were the stands of the sellers of tripe—the cheapest of the local foods—of boiled beet root, and of *'araq* (an alcoholic beverage distilled from dates). Off duty the Cossacks would buy food, eat it on the spot, down a bottle of 'araq, and toss the bottle away. Drinking, gambling, whoring, and listening to music and entertainers were the chief means of recreation.[79]

9. Setkhanian family portrait, Tehran, c. 1905. Unknown photographer. Courtesy of Mara Setkhanian-Martin.

To compound problems for the brigade at the turn of the century, there was a general sickness in its horses and donkeys and in the areas adjacent to Golestan Palace. To solve this problem and perhaps to get rid of common subjects on the increasingly valuable land around the Qajar castle, the royal administration put Iskandar Khan in charge of clearing the area of its inhabitants and filth, quarantining the horses of the Qajar palace, and devoting a new area adjacent to the lands of the Qajar castle for a mosque, cemetery, and living quarters.[80] For his efforts in accomplishing this task, Iskandar Khan was promised in a *hokm* issued by Colonel Kosogovski in September 1901 that he would receive hereditary rights to a piece of land on the Qajar palace grounds as well as the materials and assistance to build a house there. A land deed was issued in 1902.[81] He opted to stay at the family estate rather than move to the palace grounds. Through the acquisition of this prime real estate, however, Iskandar Khan was able to prosper economically despite the recurring financial troubles for the brigade.

Iskandar Khan continued to work diligently in the brigade while under the command of Colonel Fyodor Grigoryevich Chernozubov, the Russian commander sent to replace Kosogovski, and thus received another Shir-o Khorshid, this time of the second rank, in March 1903.[82] Owing to a drastic reduction in the brigade's budget in 1904, Chernozubov was forced to reduce the number of active members from the fifteen hundred it had been under Kosogovski to four hundred and to take out a loan from Russian and British banks on his own security to pay the officers he kept.[83] Despite this reduction, Iskandar Khan remained with the brigade and was promoted to the rank of *sartip* of the first rank and received the title *amir panj* (general) by a *farman* issued in 1905 that bore the seal of the minister of war, the *naib ol-sultaneh*.[84] This *farman* was translated into Russian and signed by Captain Zapolski of the brigade.

Although Iskandar Khan's position was secure in these lean times for the Cossack Brigade, the troop reductions made in 1905 had come at a very bad time. They resulted in the brigade's inability to train with live rounds and relegated it to the duties of a palace guard. As a result, it was not able to offer defense against any serious challenge to the rule of the Qajars. Mozaffar al-Din's ninth year of despotic and wasteful rule generated intense opposition, and the Cossack Brigade was increasingly seen as one of the most disturbing elements of his reign. In the growing tide of dissent that had been building since the Tobacco Revolt in 1892, the movement for *mashruteh* (constrained monarchy)[85] emerged in December and

10. Persian Cossack Brigade musters on the *maydan*, 1908 (postcard). Unknown photographer. Courtesy of Mara Setkhanian-Martin.

by June 1906 had grown into the largest demonstration of collective political activity in Iranian history—the Constitutional Revolution.

Iskandar Khan and the Cossack Brigade, 1905–1912

The Constitutional Revolution, which began in late 1905, forced Mozaffar al-Din to sign his acceptance of a constitution and parliament (Majles) in August 1906.[86] Although his successor, Muhammad Ali Shah, swore to uphold and support the Constitution, he immediately came into conflict with the Majles when it tried to begin the complex process of internal reorganization and reform.[87] Members of the first Majles, which met in October 1906, increasingly saw the Cossack Brigade as not only an instrument of Russian influence in Persia, but also as the military bulwark of all foreign interests in Iran.[88] In April 1906, the Cossack Brigade was verbally attacked in the Majles by Sayyid Muhammad Tabatabai, who also protested against its Russian-style uniforms, epaulets, decorations, and practice of showing for review only before the Russian minister in Tehran rather than before the Persian minister of war.[89] He also questioned the brigade's budget and Colonel Chernozubov's effectiveness and honesty.

A committee chosen to investigate the brigade's finances found out that the colonel had been stealing the soldiers' pay, an act confirmed by Russian officers.[90] A month earlier Chernozubov had apparently mishandled pension funds and wills in addition to salaries in overseeing the pension distribution to the ancestors and relatives of the late Marteros Khan Amir Tuman on March 23, 1906. The commission Chernozubov headed had made a decision to give Iskandar Khan Setkhanian (son-in-law of Marteros Khan through his marriage to Maryam Khanom) 32 of the 130 tumans per month allotted in the pension, for the vaguely stated reason that it was "according to the wishes of the Head of the Brigade."[91] This decision was disputed in 1917 by Marteros Khan's own son, who coincidentally was also named "Iskandar Khan." He believed that the colonel had made a serious error in this decision to award Iskandar Khan any portion of his father's pension.[92] Chernozubov was dismissed after the results of the Majles investigation were made known, and on September 15, 1906, a new Russian commander was appointed, the now infamous Colonel Vladimir Platonovich Liakhov. Kazemzadeh summarizes well the effects of Liakhov's appointment:

"Under him discipline was tightened, efficiency improved, and the Brigade was able to play its inglorious role in the suppression of the revolution."[93]

Despite Liakhov's attempts to secure funding for additional officers and arms immediately upon assuming command of the brigade, the Cossacks were in no position to quickly suppress the constitutionalist movement in 1906. Involved in the training of new recruits and reprovisioning the Cossack Brigade during this year, Iskandar Khan (Amir Panj) received the Russian Order of St. Anne of the Second Degree[94] and a gold medal from the Persian Ministry of Education and Occupations.[95] In 1906, he also received one of Austria-Hungary's highest military awards, the Order of the Ritterkreuz.[96] In this time of political turmoil, Iskandar Khan was clearly allied with the Qajars and foreigners rather than with the constitutional movement.

11. Iskandar Khan Amir Panj, Tehran, c. 1908. Unknown photographer. Courtesy of Mara Setkhanian-Martin.

Muhammad Ali Shah, the Cossacks, and the Bombardment of the Majles: 1908–1909

Shortly after taking the throne in January 1907, Muhammad Ali Shah issued a *farman* awarding Iskandar Khan a Neshan-e Khareji, literally "Foreign Medal," for his continued service and dedication to the shah and the brigade and "with hopes that he will rise to the task and apply himself in service and sacrifice."[97] Muhammad Ali Shah worked against the Majles throughout 1907, which—in conjunction with his generally despotic behavior—sparked a failed attempt to assassinate him with a bomb. As 1908 approached, enmity between the Constitutionalists (Nationalists) and the Royalists continued to grow and would soon test Iskandar Khan's devotion to the Qajar regime and the Cossack Brigade.

Although the Anglo-Russian Agreement that was signed on August 31, 1907, declared that under no circumstances would the powers meddle in the internal affairs of the country, both the Russians and the British threatened the Majles with action if the shah's demands were not met.[98] On June 6, 1908, the members of Parliament, fearing imminent foreign intervention, flocked to the Baharistan (House of Parliament), which was promptly surrounded by Nationalist troops who took up strategic positions to protect their representatives. In the well-documented events of the next two weeks, the shah established martial law in Tehran and placed Colonel Liakhov in command of military forces in the city. On June 23, under orders from the shah and most probably directly from the Russian government, Liakhov called out the Cossacks, including a division under the command of Iskandar Khan, to surround the Baharistan and position themselves in strategic places.[99] They were under orders to let Majles members and Nationalists into the building grounds, but to let no one exit. After failed negotiations and the arrest of a delegation of Nationalist representatives, Liakhov, whom historian Firuz Kazemzadeh describes as "a firm believer in the therapeutic value of bloodshed,"[100] increased the number of Cossacks and Royalist troops surrounding the Baharistan to one thousand and gave the order to bombard the building and its inhabitants with heavy artillery.[101]

In the ensuing battle, which lasted more than seven hours, hundreds of soldiers on both sides died or were wounded, but the Nationalists—heavily armed but without cannons—took the most casualties. In concentrated artillery attacks that came from soldiers under the command and instruction of Iskandar Khan and two other high-ranking officers, the Baharistan was bombed into complete destruction.[102] Following the surrender of the Nationalist forces, Majles members were arrested, put in chains, or summarily executed. Majles records were destroyed, the Nationalists' and their sympathizers' homes were sacked and looted, and all of Tehran was placed under martial law under Colonel Liakhov and the Cossack Brigade.[103]

For remaining loyal and following the orders of his superiors[104] and on the recommendation of Colonel Liakhov, Iskandar Khan was promoted one month later to *amir tuman* (which translates literally as "commander of one thousand"), brigadier general, the highest rank in the Cossack Brigade under the Russian commander. An ornate sash that distinguished his new rank accompanied the promotion. The award and promotion were documented by means of a *farman* bearing the seal of Muhammad Ali Shah and the seal of Hussein Pasha Khan Amir Jang, the field marshal who led the combined attack of Cossack and Persian army forces on the Parliament.[105] During this time, news of the events in Tehran spread to Iran's cities and rural areas, causing upheaval and riots in the cities of Tabriz, Isfahan, Rasht, Hamadan, Shiraz, Qazvin, and Mashad.[106] In the absence of any threat from the defunct regular forces of the Persian army, the Nationalist mujahedin (volunteers) seized these cities.[107] As the only trained and equipped modern fighting force in the nation and with a full-scale national revolt on its hands, the Persian Cossack Brigade prepared itself for the inevitable clash with Nationalist forces as the year 1909 approached.

Addressing the Cossack Brigade on October 11, 1908, Liakhov attempted to rally his men for the impending clash with the Nationalist forces. In his speech, which deserves quotation at length, he stressed the threat that the restoration of the Constitution would be to the Cossacks and their families and reassured them that there were larger, more powerful forces at work that would not let them down in their time of sacrifice:

> Brave soldiers and Cossacks! Since the Cossack Brigade was first formed you have on many occasions shewn unparalleled courage, and, in the highest degree, loyalty to the Shah and your superiors. In recognition of this many of you have been honored with decorations, gifts, and all sorts of other favors, *both from the Russian and from the Persian sovereigns*. Your attack on the Tihran agitators assembled in the Parliament buildings and the Sepahsalar Mosque filled the world with amazement. . . . The Shah's throne is [again] in danger. . . . They are striving to compel him again to accept a Constitution. This Constitution will limit and impair the rights and privileges of the Cossack Brigade, and will exercise control over your wages. *The Constitution is your worst enemy*. Against this enemy you must fight till your last drop of blood. . . . You must know that, should you return victorious you will be overwhelmed with money and favors *both on the part of the Russian and the Persian Sovereigns*. . . . [It is] either you or the Constitution! However fierce the foe may be, and however numerous the foe may be, rest assured that you will triumph. The Hidden Hand which has so often aided you will aid you in this campaign also, so that you shall not behold the face of defeat. Do not despair of it, or of God Almighty.[108]

In spring of 1909, Nationalist forces were ready to leave their cities to wage a combined attack on the Cossack Brigade in Tehran to restore the Majles and the Constitution. Fearing traditional retribution (in which they themselves had enthusiastically engaged) and despite Liakhov's words of assurance and praise, officers of both the regular Persian army and the Cossack Brigade began to desert in large numbers. Faced with a dwindling cadre of reliable officers, yet maintaining the extra pay and rations of those who deserted, Liakhov and Amir Jang issued a *hokm* awarding Iskandar Khan a pay raise "because we don't have any more awards exceeding your rank." The *hokm*, which was also stamped by the *moaven-e sultan* (deputy) and Amir Jang, indicated that Iskandar Khan was to receive the increase annually so that he may "receive it with a completely warm heart, and with utmost hope that he will rise to and apply himself to the necessities of service."[109]

Preparing now for the worst, Iskandar Khan and the 750 other remaining loyal Cossacks of the brigade[110] readied their barracks (the *qazzaq-khane* and the central square, Maydan-e Tup-khane) to defend the city and their munitions supplies. They also scrambled to attain documentation of their protection under the Russian embassy should the Nationalists be successful in breaching the minimal Royalist defenses and defeating them. As Nationalist troops began their respective marches in May 1909, Iskandar Khan was able to secure protection for himself from the Russian embassy, which provided him with a document written in Farsi on embassy letterhead declaring this protection.[111]

Resembling a *hokm*, the short statement that was signed and stamped by a Russian official of the delegation certified that "based on the friendship and experience between *Christian* Sir Iskandar Khan *Amir Panj, Translator* of the Cossack Brigade of the Iranian Government, in case of crisis he is under the protection of the embassy and can receive help from the embassy" (my italics). This statement is noteworthy because it is the only document that refers to Iskandar Khan as a Christian (*masihi*), claims that

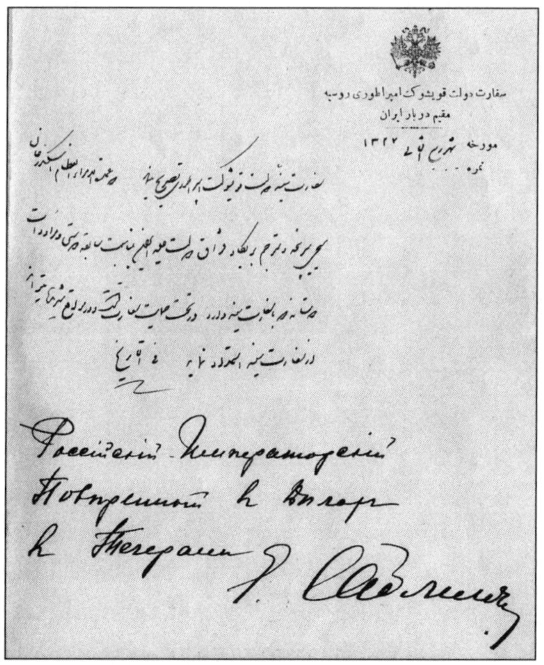

سفارت دولت قوی شوکت امپراطوری روسیه
مقیم دربار ایران

12. Letter from Russian embassy offering Iskandar Khan protection in times of crisis, 1327/1909. Courtesy of Mara Setkhanian-Martin.

he is of a lower rank than he actually was, and implies that his duties were primarily in translation. It can be interpreted from knowledge of his true duties and role during this period that this misinformation and proclamation of protection from the Russian government were generated to assure Iskandar Khan's safety in a possible rout by the Nationalists, who were understandably vengeful after the Cossacks had killed or imprisoned their Majles representatives. It was well known that the brigade had taken violent action against Nationalist soldiers and many prominent members of the ulama, including Sayyid Jamal al-Din al-Isfahani, who was strangled after he fled the bombardment of the Majles in 1908.

It is unlikely that the statement of protection from the Russian consulate gave Iskandar Khan much peace of mind, however, as thousands of Nationalists then converged on Tehran. British newspapers—which followed the events daily owing to commercial interests in the region—ran the headlines "The Persian Crisis: A Dark Outlook" and "Last Stand of the Cossack Brigade." A brigade detachment was sent to guard the approaches to the city, most importantly at Karaj Bridge, which was being approached by thousands of Bakhtiaris from Isfahan. The Cossack Brigade dug in for battle and engaged the Nationalist forces directly at the Karaj Bridge on July 2, 1909.

The force of 360 Persian Cossacks armed with superior artillery under the command of Russian captain Zapolski was initially successful in its defense of the bridge, losing only one Persian officer to the twelve Nationalists killed before forcing a retreat. "Heartened by their successful encounter"[112] and in the rush that followed their victory, the Cossacks literally "tore to pieces" the bodies of the mujahedin they had killed in the first volley.[113] But their celebration was to be short-lived. Although the brigade had stopped the first advance on Tehran by Nationalist troops who were primarily Bakhtiaris, mujahedin forces were approaching the city from all directions and as a result forced the Cossack troops at the bridge to retreat to the outskirts of Tehran to avoid being surrounded outside the city or cut off by a possible Bakhtiari flanking maneuver. Although the commencement of fighting brought a contingent of one thousand Russian troops to Enzeli under the pretext of protecting any Russian subjects and religious minorities, it was clear that the Cossack Brigade and

Muhammad Ali Shah Qajar would be on their own in the days to follow and that the only "Hidden Hand" they could count on to help them would be that of God rather than of the Russian Empire.[114]

By July 13, 1909, after a week of skirmishing back and forth with few casualties on either side, Nationalist forces made their way into the city and forced the five hundred or so remaining members of the Cossack Brigade to retreat with the shah to the Maydan-e Tup-Khane, central square in Tehran, where they barricaded themselves inside. A Russian flag was hoisted over Colonel Liakhov's nearby house, and a regiment of Cossacks was dispatched there to protect Liakhov's wife, who would not seek the protection of the embassy because she wanted to be near her husband.[115] The Royalist and Nationalist forces exchanged gunfire throughout the night at the Maydan and even at the Liakhov residence when the Nationalist troops were fired on by the Cossacks inside the house and decided to return fire despite the presence of the Russian flag.[116]

Fighting continued throughout the next day as Colonel Liakhov dispatched negotiators from the besieged Tup-Khane to the ruins of the Baharistan—where the Nationalist leaders and remaining Majles members had triumphantly returned—to try and secure a temporary cease-fire. Owing to the complete dominance the Nationalists had attained by this point over the three hundred or so remaining Royalist forces, and with casualties and desertion of the remaining Royalist numbers increasing, the negotiators failed in their efforts to strike a deal. Facing imminent defeat at the hands of combined Nationalist mujahedin and Bakhtiari forces, the Persian Cossacks and the shah conceded defeat on the morning of July 16, 1909. Muhammad Ali Shah took refuge in the Russian legation with Iskandar Khan's senior officer, Hussein Pasha Khan Amir Bahadur Jang, and officially abdicated later that evening. Although part of the terms of his abdication to his eleven-year-old son Ahmad Mirza stipulated that there would be a continued cease-fire, the Persian Cossacks under Liakhov were on their own to negotiate a deal with the Nationalists.

After a harrowing incident in which fighting nearly broke out again between the Nationalist mujahedin and Liakhov's Cossack guards,[117] Liakhov was escorted by a troop of victorious Caucasian and Bakhtiari mujahedin to the Baharistan, where remarkably he was able to negotiate a deal that would allow the Cossack Brigade to keep its arms after laying them down for a moment as a token of their submission. They would be employed by the Nationalist government in the policing of now chaotic Tehran and continue to serve under Liakhov's own command. Liakhov would be theoretically subordinate to the new minister of war, the Bakhtiari *sepahdar,* whose troops at the Karaj Bridge had been dismembered.[118] Wanting to demonstrate the amicable conclusion to hostilities, particularly because of the Nationalists' concern about intervention by the imperial "Hidden Hand"—the Russians as well as the British were anti-constitution and anti-Majles—the *sepahdar* emerged from the damaged Baharistan with his new subordinate Liakhov by his side, bringing huge cheers from the throngs of people gathered outside.[119] In the following weeks, there were trials and executions of "those who had most strenuously supported the ex-Shah," including a prominent pro-shah shaykh and "an officer of artillery who took a leading part in the bombardment of the Majlis,"[120] who was executed by hanging in the Maydan-e Tup Khane. However, the Russian legation secured amnesty for Iskandar Khan, who in this way narrowly avoided the tribunals. Thus, once again the conflict between the Nationalists and the Cossack Brigade temporarily ceased, and Iskandar Khan emerged from the most challenging and dangerous year of his life with his family, rank, and property intact.

Iskandar Khan and the Cossack Brigade after the Constitutional Revolution

With two conflicting sources of command—the Nationalist government, which it was supposed to obey, and the Russian government, to which it was truly beholden—the Cossack Brigade was little utilized by either government in 1910. Between 1910 and May 1912, it took a back seat to the Nationalist Gendarme under Yeprem Khan, the popular Armenian mujahedin leader, following the shah's abdication.[121] Iskandar Khan continued in his service as chief translator and general to the brigade, which lost Liakhov in 1911 to Colonel Nikolai Vadbolski[122] and in the year and a half since the Nationalist victory had been relegated to the protection of young Ahmad Shah Qajar and Russian property interests in Tehran.[123] Despite a failed attempt by Muhammad Ali Shah in the fall of 1911 to

13a. Iskandar Khan and the Persian Cossack Brigade with Ahmad Shah Qajar, Tehran, 1909. This widely known photo appeared in American economic adviser Morgan Shuster's book *The Strangling of Persia* with the caption "Russian and Persian Officers of the Notorious 'Cossack Brigade.' This has been one of the chief instruments of Russian influence and oppression in Persia" (p. xxxviii). Unknown photographer. Courtesy of Mara Setkhanian-Martin.

13b. Close-up of Persian Cossacks with Ahmad Shah Qajar. General Liakhoff at left, Ahmad Shah at lower right, Iskandar Khan at right.

regain his throne by rallying Azerbaijani supporters to oppose Nationalist Bakhtiari and Armenian forces under Yeprem Khan, the Cossack Brigade had only limited involvement in these battles, which were finally won by the Nationalists in October.[124] However, that same year the Cossacks were again to be used as an instrument of Russian influence as opposition to the policies of the Second Majles reached a critical point.

The Russians intensely disapproved of Majles-appointed American financial adviser Morgan Shuster, who was working with Nationalist forces to organize Persian finances, create an American-advised tax-collecting gendarme,[125] and arrange the seizure of the estates of Royalists, whose property the Persian Cossacks were guarding. The Cossack Brigade was bolstered by the arrival of Russian Cossacks to add to their numbers and supplies.

14. Postcard featuring Iskandar Khan (*center*) and Russian general, c. 1910. Unknown photographer. Courtesy of Mara Setkhanian-Martin.

The brigade was then used to intimidate Shuster until a full-scale Russian invasion in the North and increasing violence and chaos throughout the country forced the now predominantly Bakhtiari Majles to dismiss Shuster on December 20, 1911.[126] During the next three years leading to World War I, the Persian Cossack Brigade continued to work in the interests of the Qajar family and the Russian Empire, helping to render the Majles ineffective in carrying out its plans for internal reorganization and reform and essentially ending the era of Constitutional Revolution.[127]

For his services to the brigade between 1911 and 1914, and with no higher rank to attain, Iskandar Khan was presented with two *farman*s bearing the seal of Ahmad Shah. The *farman*s praised his services and granted him additional *neshan*s and fine military regalia—silver epaulets and a pendant encompassing a photograph of the late Mozaffar al-Din Shah.[128]

Iskandar Khan again received an increase in his salary and another Order of St. Stanislaus from the Russian government, which was issued

15. Iskandar Khan Amir Tuman, Tehran, 1915. Unknown photographer. Courtesy of Mara Setkhanian-Martin.

16. Iskandar Khan (*seated in rear of carriage*) tours Cossack installations as *amir tuman,* c. 1915. Unknown photographer. Courtesy of Mara Setkhanian-Martin.

on August 10, 1913.[129] On October 3 that year, Vadbolski gave Iskandar Khan two months leave and a two-month visa to travel in Russia, "for the placing of his children in Russian institutions of learning."[130]

Just as his father, grandfather, and great-grandfather had sent their sons away to be educated, Iskandar Khan continued the family tradition. Despite the existence in Iran of a school for children of brigade officers,[131] Iskandar Khan placed his sons in the Lazarev Institute in Moscow with the anticipation that they too would acquire a valuable education and find opportunities such as he had enjoyed while serving the successive Qajar shahs of Iran.

Iskandar Khan became chief of staff of the Tehran headquarters of the brigade in 1915[132] and in this promotion became the commanding officer of a tall, charismatic, popular, and motivated *yavar* (major) named Reza Khan, who would later rise through the brigade to establish the Pahlavi dynasty.[133]

Iskandar Khan and the Rule of the Pahlavi Shahs

World War I brought the armies of four belligerent nations into the country.[134] In the face of foreign military occupation, the Cossack Brigade continued mainly to police Tehran and guard the shah. On a few occasions, they joined Nationalist forces to battle recalcitrant rural tribes. In 1916, the

17. Iskandar Khan (*seated in rear of carriage*) tours Cossack installations as *amir tuman,* c. 1915. Unknown photographer. Courtesy of Mara Setkhanian-Martin.

last year of czarist rule in Russia, the Russian commander of the brigade once again granted Iskandar Khan two months' leave to travel to Moscow.[135] Upon returning from his trip, Iskandar Khan Amir Tuman retired from the Persian Cossack Brigade after more than a quarter century of military service to the Qajar shahs and the Russian Empire.[136]

Immediately after Iskandar Khan's retirement, the Cossack Brigade experienced the most drastic change in influences and commanders in its three decades of existence. Reza Khan, who was merely a *sarhang* (colonel) of the second rank upon Iskandar Khan's retirement, was promoted to *sartip* of the third rank and placed in charge of a regiment in Tehran.[137] The withdrawal of Russian troops from Iran after the end of World War I and the Bolshevik Revolution that followed allowed the British to step in as the primary foreign influence over the brigade. As the new Communist government of Russia left the Cossacks without critical outside support, the British spared no time in recruiting Reza Khan to work in their interests. This was evidently not difficult because the British still had thousands of troops stationed in the South of the country protecting the now vital oil fields, and it soon became clear that the Russians would no longer be providing the support the brigade needed to combat its many enemies in the nation.[138] The Jangali Rebellion of 1920–21 was a serious challenge to the interests of both the Cossack Brigade and the British, and it resulted in their cooperation to thwart the efforts of Kuchek Khan and his supporters in Gilan to establish the Iranian Soviet Socialist Republic (SSR). This cooperation led to British general Edmund Ironside's encouragement of Reza Khan and his partner Sayyid Zia al-Din[139] to launch a coup against the Majles and Sepahdar government in February 1921.

Iskandar Khan was approached by his colleagues to consider opposing Reza Khan, who was now head of the Cossack Brigade himself and had mustered his troops outside Tehran in preparation for seizing control of the government. Iskandar Khan had been fond of Reza Khan while he was a soldier under his command for two years and had developed a personal relationship with him in this time. Having distanced himself from military confrontations, politics, and coups d'état for the first time in a quarter century, and out of great concern for his family, Iskandar Khan chose to stay out of the conflict. When told of an imminent takeover of the city and the nation's military and asked what he was going to do about it, Iskandar Khan is reported to have paused, thought for a moment, and then replied, "I'm very tired. I think I'll go to bed," which he immediately did.[140]

Although Iskandar Khan decided not to take up arms against his former subordinate Reza Khan in the coup of February 1921, neither did he join the procession of people rushing to demonstrate their allegiance and submission to the new minister of war. As April approached and Iskandar Khan had still not yet made his appearance, Reza Khan decided to pay a visit to him at the family estate on Khiaban-e Sepah with an escort of Cossack guards, many of whom had themselves served under Iskandar Khan's command. On Reza Khan's orders, he and Iskandar Khan were left alone to discuss matters, and the two Cossacks walked out into the garden of the estate to circumnavigate the large pond. Halfway around the pond, Iskandar Khan stopped walking, whereby Reza Khan, who was a full head taller, gently put his arm around Iskandar Khan and continued to walk with the older general. Arm in arm and each with a look of resolution on his face, they returned to the main house, whereupon Reza Khan left with his Cossack escorts.[141] Less than five years later Reza Khan

18. Iskandar Khan's son Jahangir poses with horse in front of Setkhanian mansion on Khiaban-e Sepah, Tehran, 1920. Unknown photographer. Courtesy of Mara Setkhanian-Martin.

would crown himself Reza Shah Pahlavi and establish a new dynasty. The fact that Iskandar Khan and his family members survived unscathed the purges that were to come and that he maintained possession of the family's large estate and properties in central Tehran is evidence that the two had struck an agreement.[142]

In 1927, Iskandar Khan, like many other former generals who had taken an oath of loyalty to the Qajars, was required to sit for an official portrait wearing a Kolah-e Pahlavi (Pahlavi Hat)[143] as a show of allegiance to the new regime.

Dressed in military casuals and often sporting his Pahlavi Hat, Iskandar Khan assumed a relatively low profile during the late 1920s and 1930s, enjoying an ideal retired lifestyle, including hunting trips and family gatherings.[144]

19. Iskandar Khan poses wearing the Kolah-e Pahlavi, Tehran, 1927. Unknown photographer. Courtesy of Mara Setkhanian-Martin.

During this period, Iskandar Khan also spent time at the Soviet embassy in Tehran since relations and diplomatic missions had been restored in 1920. Although he was thoroughly anti-Bolshevik, his pro-Russian orientation motivated him to maintain cordial social relations with members of the Soviet diplomatic mission and friendships within the small Russian community.

Iskandar Khan was most fond of rigorous outdoor pastimes such as hunting and fishing in his retirement, but he also engaged in activities that seemed to contrast with his often gruff and strict demeanor.[145] One such pastime was fine woodworking. By mail order, Iskandar Khan developed a dazzling collection of imported specialty tools, with which

20. Setkhanian family portrait, Tehran, 1927. *Standing, left to right*: Hacob, Hovsep, Catharine, Jahangir, Aslan, and Davit. Maryam Khanom is seated at left under the portrait of her father, Marteros Khan Davidkhanian, and Iskandar Khan is seated under a portrait of his father, Sattur Khan Setkhanian (see the top part of the photo). The photos on pedestals are those of son Hovannes Setkhanian and his Russian wife, Yekaterina, who were in Moscow at the time studying law. Unknown photographer. Courtesy of Mara Setkhanian-Martin.

21. Fishing on the Caspian Sea, 1931. Unknown photographer. Courtesy of Mara Setkhanian-Martin.

22. Relaxing after the hunt, March 1930. Unknown photographer. Courtesy of Mara Setkhanian-Martin.

he produced delicately carved picture frames and sculptures that would later be handed down through generations of his descendants. Iskandar Khan was also an avid gardener in his retirement. At one point, he hired laborers to dig out and cart away three meters of topsoil from a large portion of the yard so that loads of highly fertile soil could be brought in to replace it. There, Iskandar Khan planted a large rose garden that became one of his favorite pastimes. In addition to maintaining Hammam-e Amir, the bathhouse, as a service to the Armenian community, in his retirement he also became more involved in the Armenian Church, and made several large donations that the church publicly recognized.[146]

23. Iskandar Khan with members of Soviet legation, 1928. Unknown photographer. Courtesy of Mara Setkhanian-Martin.

Iskandar Khan's death in 1953 was a time for mourning, but as he was laid to rest in the Doulab Cemetery outside Tehran, those at his graveside could take comfort that his life had been long, challenging, exciting, and fulfilling. He had distinguished himself by his steady rise through the ranks of the Persian Cossack Brigade and by his successful navigation through the tumult of the Constitutional Revolution, the invasions and occupation of Iran during World War I, and the changeover to a different political and social order and the quickening growth of Iranian nationalism with the demise of the Qajars and rise of the Pahlavis. Through a combination of grit, determination, and the ability to tactically employ his multiple allegiances and identities to assure his own survival and advancement through to the final moments in Iranian history when such fluidity was advantageous, Iskandar Khan thrived during these troubled years and was able to perpetuate the prosperity of the Setkhanian family in Iran for another generation.

24. Still in uniform at age eighty-seven, Iskandar Khan poses with granddaughters Mara (*left*) and Arlette, Tehran, 1952. Unknown photographer. Courtesy of Mara Setkhanian-Martin.

3

Hagob Hagobian

THE FRIGHTENED ARMENIAN BOY stood in the doorway of his family's home as his mother rushed past him in a vain attempt to protect her husband as he was being attacked by a band of Kurdish men.[1] Following the violent struggle, the Kurds quickly rode away, leaving his parents' bodies in front of the farmhouse. Although Hagob Hagobian was the oldest of three brothers, at the age of seven he was far too young to understand the enormity of what had happened. Seeking help, he sadly led his smaller brothers away from their farming village of Khan-Baba-Khan into the countryside of northwestern Iran. It would be many years before Hagob could begin to understand the political and ethnic ramifications of the violence that orphaned him and his young brothers in 1916.

Intercommunal violence resulting in such scenes was widespread in eastern Anatolia and Azerbaijan before, during, and after World War I.[2] The violence was in many ways related to Young Turk policies concerning Armenians living in the Ottoman Empire, who had been subject to persecution since the reign of Sultan Abdul Hamid began in 1876. Following the occupation of eastern Anatolia and Urmia in 1915 by Turkish and Kurdish forces, the ethnic cleansing and genocidal massacre of the region's Armenian and Assyrian population commenced, vastly exceeding the prior decades of violence in ferocity and scope.[3]

Hagob and his brothers found refuge at the Near East Relief Orphanage in Tabriz, the provincial capital of Azerbaijan. An American-sponsored Presbyterian mission, it was home to them for the duration of their childhood.[4] Orphaned children from areas affected by the massacres, ethnic cleansing, and intercommunal violence arrived at the center almost daily. One such child, Arshalous Harutoonian, a baby girl believed to have been born in Baku, was brought to the orphanage early in 1917 and years later would become Hagob's wife.

The orphanage not only provided a safe haven and the necessities of living but coordinated its efforts with the local Armenian priest to educate the children. With the help of older orphans and adult volunteers from the Armenian community in Tabriz, the priest and orphanage staff instructed the children in the Armenian language and taught them about their rich cultural heritage, rooted in Christianity since the fourth century CE. The boys and girls also attended classes in Persian, English, mathematics, music, and handicrafts such as sewing and carpet weaving, which were

25. The children and staff of the Near East Relief Orphanage in Tabriz, Iran, 1924. The sign to the lower right of the American flag reads in Armenian "Long Live the Armenian Nation." The sign directly under the Iranian Shir-o Khorshid (Lion and Sun) reads "Congratulations and Happy New Year 1924." The sign below that reads "Greetings to the Great American Nation." Hagob Hagobian stands at the far left, top row. Unknown photographer. Courtesy of the author.

taught by local craftsmen. Although Hagob did not have much interest in his academic subjects, he worked for hours on end weaving carpets with other children. This activity produced revenue for the orphanage to reinvest after the items were sold in the bazaar and provided the children with job skills and a way to help pay for their care.

Reza Khan toured Tabriz in 1924 following his rise to power, and the children of the orphanage were gathered to sing for his welcoming parade. In 1925, Reza Khan had the last Qajar shah deposed and proclaimed himself shah and founder of the new Pahlavi dynasty. Soon after this event, Hagob moved into a sparsely furnished room with several boys from the orphanage who at fourteen were considered old enough to support themselves. Each boy occupied a *takht*, or wooden bed frame, and owned his own bedding and some clothing. A woven cotton carpet, or *zelo*, covered the bare floor in the room, which was heated on the coldest nights by a wood-burning stove. Bread, cheese, and sweet tea made up the customary meal, and when work was steady, the boys bought heartier meals of rice, lamb, and vegetables.

At the age of fifteen in 1925, Hagob supported himself by working at small jobs, one of which was unloading goods from carts and the few trucks that made deliveries around Tabriz. Chosen for his capacity to work hard and his great interest in trucks, the following year Hagob became a *shagaird-e shufer*, apprentice driver, in an Armenian and Assyrian transportation guild. This was a prized position for a young man because it provided some income, travel, and the opportunity to work around the rare and powerful vehicles that the master drivers piloted across the mountains to Tehran and then south to the Persian Gulf.

As an apprentice, Hagob was taught the essential skills of load balancing and lashing, which required knowledge of knots, and how different materials would shift and settle over the duration of a trip. Apprentice truck drivers performed maintenance alongside the master drivers and would progressively assume responsibilities as they learned the procedures for truck upkeep and repair. The masters provided the vehicle, the gasoline, licenses (which were required after 1928), maps, and parts, and the apprentices worked for them in two- to three-week shifts that lasted one round trip to the Persian Gulf. Hagob began the driving portion of his training the following year, although it would not be until 1933, after five years of service as an apprentice, that he attained within his guild the status of an *arbab*, master driver. Hagob passed his driver's test[5] and was given a guild pin in the shape of a truck to wear on his lapel.[6]

The travel that Hagob's profession involved inadvertently led to an extremely fortuitous occurrence. While on a layover in Kermanshah, he met a cousin from his home village of Khan-Baba-Khan who joyfully informed him that Hagob's maternal uncle, two of the uncle's five children, as well as a paternal aunt and her three children had also survived the massacre of 1916. Fleeing south toward Baghdad through Azerbaijan and Kurdistan in western Iran, they had found calm and safety in Kermanshah, where, familiar with the language and customs, they began their lives anew. Hagob had fortunately found what remained of his family.

In 1933 at age twenty-five, Hagob made arrangements for his marriage to Arshalous, who was now a young woman of eighteen living with a family in Tabriz, where she sewed to support herself. In a borrowed truck, they drove together from Tabriz to Kermanshah, where she was introduced to Hagob's family. At the American Presbyterian mission in Kermanshah, they were married, with their best man, a fellow Armenian truck driver, and relatives in attendance.

Soon after the ceremony, Hagob and his new wife moved to the growing city of Tehran to be near the hub of the country's trucking and transportation industry. Having no relatives with whom to share a home, as was customary in most Armenian families, Hagob and his wife made temporary arrangements to share rooms with friends from the orphanage in Tabriz who lived in Tehran. Before the birth of a son, Nejde, in 1934, the young couple moved into private rooms located on a narrow *koutche* (alleyway) in an area of the city where some of their neighbors were other Armenian refugees from East Anatolia and Azerbaijan as well Russian-educated Armenian professionals who had immigrated to Iran following the Bolshevik Revolution.

Hagob began driving long-distance hauls between Tehran and the Persian Gulf and soon acquired his own truck through the assistance of his former employer. For an agreed-upon monthly payment made possible

26. Hagob and Arshalous Hagobian, Kermanshah, 1933. Unknown photographer. Courtesy of the author.

27. The Hagobian and Gorjian families, Tehran, 1937. Hagob Hagobian (*front left*), Arshak Gorjian (*front right*), Arshalous Hagobian (*center right*), Jennik Gorjian (*center left*). Unknown photographer. Courtesy of the author.

by their mutual trust, Hagob took possession of the truck immediately with the intention of paying back the debt through the truck's income. Although his life of long-distance truck driving would not enable him to spend much time at home in Tehran with his family, at that time Hagob was most concerned with putting food on the table, trying to save money so he could pay back his debt, and eventually move his wife and son out of the dingy *koutche* and into an electrified residence. The only way to accomplish these goals was to maximize the truck's potential to generate income, which meant spending as many hours away from home as he could bear, shuttling goods across the expanses of the nation.

Shifting Gears in the Desert

While Hagob Hagobian and members of his truck drivers' guild traversed the Iranian deserts and mountain ranges between Tehran and the Persian Gulf during the late 1920s and early 1930s, their minds were not occupied with things such as the historical significance of their activities or the symbolism involved in them because the journey in those years was dangerous and persistently challenging. Pioneering a new mode of transportation in a country that had until the 1920s neglected to develop or maintain its transportation infrastructure, the drivers had to constantly improvise and rely on each other's support and innovation to survive the trip and make trucking a profitable profession.[7] In these early years, drivers needed to caravan in groups of five to ten trucks for safety. Although efforts were being made by the country's new autocrat, Reza Shah (r. 1921–41) to eliminate the threat of banditry by nomadic tribes and create a few well-paved transport routes, it was not until the mid-1930s that brigandage was at least temporarily suppressed.[8] In 1928, the shah's own minister of roads had been killed by nomads opposed to road construction in Lorestan,[9] and thus, fearing a desert breakdown without supplies or attack by mounted hijackers, the drivers drove slowly and stuck close enough together so that they would not lose visual contact through the dust.

In the 1920s, Iran possessed less than two thousand miles of motorable roads,[10] which were for the most part unpaved and ungraded. The result was a ride that punished the occupants, machinery, suspension, and tires of the early-model, six-wheel American trucks that were the industry standard. It was not uncommon to go through two full sets of tires in one round trip between Tehran and the gulf, and the drivers, with no formal training, had to perform all truck maintenance as well as carry or fabricate any needed spare parts. The precipitous passes of the Zagros and Alborz Mountains contained hundreds of hairpin turns and switchbacks, each of which required precise maneuvering in turns and backups. Many truck drivers of this generation perished as their crudely serviced and unbalanced trucks (usually overloaded to three or four times their capacity) cartwheeled down the mountainside—with other guild members often looking on helplessly.[11]

In his retirement, Hagob Hagobian would refer to this endeavor and the four decades he labored in it as "shifting gears in the desert." A corresponding hand gesture mimicking first-through-third was obligatory and signified the repetitive and mundane nature of it all. The time required away from his family in Tehran and years of monotonous rides over bumps and ruts so familiar they were given names left him with few romantic memories of truck driving during this era. Although he never intended this phrase to be a trope, in the context of the economic and political history of modern Iran it turns out to be a fitting metaphor to figuratively link the national and economic transformation that occurred during the 1920s and 1930s to his tedious but much-needed profession. As perhaps the "latest" of the developing nations of the Middle East, Iran was heavily dependent on the trucking industry in the initial phases of modernization and industrialization. Without a rail system and constrained by the absence of navigable waterways, trucking was the primary mode of transportation by which economic and cultural links between the distant ports and urban centers of the newly consolidated nation were created.

The caravans of motorized trucks that appeared on the Iranian landscape in the late 1920s were both physically and symbolically indicative of the radical changes the country was undergoing during this decade. Once again replacing the camel as the primary means of long-distance transport for the first time since the fifth century CE, wheeled vehicles—now motorized rather than drawn—retook the roads and caravansaries.[12] The increasing presence of truck caravans, as they linked the distant ports and urban centers secured by Reza Shah's military efforts, was a loud, rolling testament to the industrialization and consolidation of the nation and the recent but progressive development of the country's transportation infrastructure. The caravansaries and *chai-khaneh*s (roadside rest stops, literally "teahouses") along the way, generally owned and operated by Muslims, were soon converted to "truck stops" and provided the predominantly Armenian and Assyrian[13] truck drivers (of Christian religious heritage) such as Hagob Hagobian and Arshak Gorjian some comforts and relief from the harsh road environment. The cultural and economic interactions and spirit of cooperation experienced within this multiethnic transportation network of Iranian citizens was, in an ideal sense, the stuff of Iranian nationalism.

Concurrent with this profound physical transformation was a structural change in Iranian urban economic institutions. The process of Iran's incorporation into the world economy, which had been slowly progressing since the beginning of the nineteenth century, was accelerated by trucks during the 1920s and 1930s.[14] The impact of this structural change was felt in centers of Persian handcraft production throughout the boundaries of

28. Arshak Gorjian (*second from left*) with fellow truck drivers. Photo by Hagob Hagobian, c. 1936. Courtesy of the author.

the new nation. Although trucks provided a means of export for items from the cities of Iran, they also brought inexpensive imports—most notably, textiles—which undermined local craft industries and, through this, the craft guilds in Iran. This issue, upon close examination, reveals an interesting paradox.

Pressed by the unique demands of the Pahlavi regime and the challenging nature of the profession in the 1920s and 1930s, Iranian truck drivers found support and organization in their craft guild, an institution that had helped sustain urban Iranian workers of all trades since the fourteenth century.[15] Guild organization provided the drivers with an exclusive network of protection, access to truck parts, information, and credit as well as a collective means of voicing concerns about matters such as governmental pricing, road safety, and licensing issues. But although it was the guild that enabled Hagobian and his fellow truck drivers to persist and prosper in their trade, it is evident that their trade was destructive to Iranian guilds in general. To fully understand this paradox, it is necessary to briefly describe the development of the truck transportation industry in Iran as well as the structural shifts in Iranian economic and productive institutions during the 1920s and 1930s.

The Development of the Iranian Truck Transportation Industry

Iran's transportation infrastructure in the first quarter of the twentieth century was, even by the standards of other developing Middle Eastern countries, extremely poor in quality and extent. At the onset of World War I, pack animals were still the basic mode of transportation because automobiles had yet to be introduced to Iran. As previously mentioned, Iran did not have a rail system[16] or navigable rivers. A British source on Iranian trade and foreign competition attested to this condition and some of the problems of pack-animal transport at the turn of the century:

> The only method of transporting goods in Persia is by pack animals. Camels, mules, ponies and donkeys are all used in different parts of the country and under different circumstances. The ordinary load for a camel is about 400 lbs. . . . 200 to 250 is a fair load for a mule or pony, and a donkey load may be reckoned at 130 lbs. Both loads and prices depend

> much on the nature of the country and the season of the year. The cheapness or scarcity of forage also naturally affects prices. In summer drivers feed their animals by allowing them to graze for many hours daily by the road and this habit makes the time occupied on a journey longer in the summer than in winter.[17]

Charles Issawi's analysis of these observations and statistical data about transportation costs between major ports and cities in 1903 reveals seasonal price fluctuations, which often related to fodder availability, road security, and road conditions.[18] The Qajar shahs, who from Tehran ruled Iran from 1789 to 1925, never achieved more than a weak suzerainty over the various regions of the country and, as discussed in detail later in this chapter, did not actively seek to reform their military, economic, and industrial infrastructure in the nineteenth century. As a result, tribal nomads were able to continue the practice of caravan raiding, which was compounded by the problems faced by the transport industry. The country's increasingly anarchic political conditions following the unsuccessful 1905–11 Constitutional Revolution exacerbated the problems of what was already a very unpredictable transportation system, causing a sharp price rise in the years 1911 and 1912.[19]

During this period, road surfaces were often in such bad repair that pack-animal transportation—slow under the best conditions—was made even slower. At times, impassable roadways stopped movement altogether. Various Russian and British plans for graded carriage roads were developed in the North and South of Iran (respectively—reflecting the "spheres of influence" these two countries had over Iran from 1907 until 1921).[20] The eruption of World War I prevented their implementation. A manager of the (British) Persian Transport Company described the decrepit road conditions:

> The state of the Bakhtiary road is unsatisfactory in the extreme. In many places it is little better than a goat track. It was bad enough when I went over the road in 1910 and it has since deteriorated to an alarming degree. Since that year the number of camels plying between Ahwaz and Isfahan has been reduced by 50 per cent, largely due to the fact that they

> are of little use on a road which abounds with stretches of rough, rocky track, and before long we shall be compelled to abandon camel transport altogether.[21]

Issawi cites British sources from the period 1913–14 who mention "robberies", "insecurity", "the exorbitant price of fodder," and "menaces to traffic."[22] The abysmal conditions for transportation obstructed trade, and under Qajar rule attempts to develop this critical infrastructure remained sporadic and largely unsuccessful. With the advent of the automobile and its introduction to Iran in limited numbers after World War I, it became even clearer to the era's three contending powers that Iran's transportation infrastructure was in vital need of improvement and further development.

The Qajars, the British, and the Russians all had military and economic interests in a more extensive and efficient Iranian transportation infrastructure. From each of their perspectives (grossly simplified), its development would yield better control of the Qajars and British for the Russians, better control of the Russians and Qajars for the British, and better control of regional tribal and ethnic challenges for the Qajars, who were too weak to have influence over the imperial powers. The three governments recognized that expanded transportation furthered their interests in increased trade and the efficient collection of tax revenues. Before World War I, 80 percent of Iran's trade was with Russia and Britain, and more than 60 percent of that was with Russia.[23] An increase in trade was seen as desirable by all three governments despite their individual differences and agendas. The question of how to modernize the infrastructure began to be pursued.

Moustafa Fateh, an Iranian economics student studying abroad at Cambridge in the 1920s, was concerned with these issues as he wrote his doctoral thesis on the state of the Iranian economy and industrial infrastructure. *The Economic Position of Persia*, published in 1926, analyzes data from 1919–23 to describe the situation and makes recommendations for future economic and industrial development. The study included an assessment of Iran's roads and transportation completed during the transition from pack-animal to motor-powered transportation. Fateh explained,

> Persia possesses at present about 1500 miles of roads which can be used for motor transport, and there are many natural roads connecting the large cities which could easily be reconstructed and used for this purpose. The bulk of commercial goods is transported on pack animals, and the high cost of such a primitive system of transport is responsible for the undeveloped resources as well as the meager trade of the country. . . . There is a project before the Government for the construction of roads throughout Persia and the repair of the existing ones, which would involve a total expenditure of over £5,000,000. It is hoped that this project will be approved and the necessary sums provided for this very important and vital question. In the case of a railess [*sic*] country like Persia it is most vital to have good roads for developing the motor transport service, which is becoming very popular in the country.[24]

Writing during the transitional period from Qajar to Pahlavi rule (1921–25), Fateh was keenly aware of the national debate over future infrastructural investment and development because this period of conflict and change at the national political level found its parallel in the transportation industry. The Fourth and Fifth Majlis (parliamentary assemblies of 1923–25), featured debates over whether to invest the country's limited financial resources in railroads or in roads and trucks as a means of increasing the extent and capacity of the transportation infrastructure. Although a rail network was most desirable for its capacity to transport heavier loads at greater average speeds, time and money ultimately decided the order of investment. A functional system of rail was at best years away, while trucks could be used effectively after the relatively simple grading, graveling, or paving of existing roads. Fateh explained, "There are some people who favor an extensive system of motor transport for the present, as less costly and more adaptable to present needs [than rail]. . . . The Persian Government is bent on building and maintaining good roads, which, in the absence of railways, are essential for the development of vehicle and especially motor transport."[25] It was soon realized that trucks would be an essential part of the effort to build a national railroad anyway, and so this debate did not progress past 1925. The Pahlavi regime, established officially in 1925 after Reza Shah's self-coronation, would work to develop both; they would begin with trucks and roads and use them to quicken the rail effort.

At this historical juncture, men began to make their living shifting gears in the deserts of Iran. In doing so, they encountered the same problems with this new method of transportation as those before them had in pack-animal transportation—as well as a host of new ones. Fuel supplies were distantly spaced, parts were in short supply, and mechanical knowledge was generated by trial and error. Nevertheless, with a payload of thousands rather than hundreds of pounds, and in a country with a newly developing oil and fuel industry, trucks began to proliferate, although truck driving was still considered a novelty rather than a profession in the years between 1920 and 1925.

Arthur Chester Millspaugh provides statistics from his 1926 economic survey of Iran that set the number of vehicles in 1925 at 3,000, with 529 of them imported in 1925–26, an increase of 35 percent over the 1923–24 total of 392.[26] The Fourth Majlis appropriated almost ten million rials for road construction in 1925, which funded the grading and graveling of existing roads.[27] The Majlis organized an economic committee, which took up the freeing of the roads from the payment of the *rahdari*, a toll previously paid for maintenance and protection; the abolition of dues payable at city gates (in 1924 Tehran was still surrounded by walls); and the removal of customs duties on materiel destined for projects such as road maintenance, construction, and transportation services.[28] The Government Alimentation Service purchased at once a fleet of 198 trucks and 60 trailers to carry foodstuffs from surplus to areas hit by the famine of 1925,[29] which simultaneously increased governmental reliance on this new technological advancement and the number of trucks in the country. As the number of vehicles and miles of motorable road grew, so did the ranks of laborers in a newly created profession. Peter Avery describes the truck drivers of this era,

> whose fatalism seems to preclude the thought that their particular vehicle will ever go over the precipice or be the one to be carried off by a torrent, or so loaded that sooner or later it will roll over. Lorry drivers undertake repairs on the road, miles away from anything remotely resembling a garage or workshop, which would daunt automobile engineers who are

> far better equipped and more experienced. Often a lorry is taken down and overhauled, on a mountain road, in an operation that takes several days before the truck is again grinding its way over the steep passes. Ignorance may be bliss, but also the ingenuity and aptitude of the Iranian workmen are manifest in the skill of these patient and courageous mechanics, who manage so well on such slender means.[30]

Managing on slender means was made easier through membership in a guild.[31] Members of Hagob Hagobian's truck drivers' guild, which included Hagob's brother Aram and his best friend, Arshak Gorjian, shared with each other vital knowledge of the trade, such as the best routes between destinations and techniques to keep the trucks running. Road conditions fluctuated, depending on the weather, construction, and the political climate. Without road maps, the guild members relied on oral transmission of directions or scribbled notes detailing natural features (such as trees or large boulders) that would alert them to perils such as truck- and cargo-smashing potholes. Iran's highly variant physical terrain, which ranges from endless expanses of desert to snowy mountain passes, posed additional problems that compounded the lack of paved surfaces. Landslides and washouts, the result of rain and snow, were of concern in the winter months, and summer posed the challenge of sandstorms and up to 118-degree heat.

Guild members kept each other informed about the political situation in various regions, which often had a direct and immediate effect on road security. The hijacking of vehicles by bandits and associated violence were commonplace in the Iranian countryside in the 1920s. This continued to be of concern to Hagob and his fellow truck drivers even after Reza Shah largely suppressed such activities in the mid-1930s. Because of the many unpredictable dangers, truck drivers in Iran caravanned in groups, finding strength and security in their numbers. Driving in shifts, the truck crews of two, ordinarily the *arbab* and his *shagaird-e-shufer*, alternated sleeping and driving eight to ten hours, with the driver at the wheel keeping the other trucks in sight.

Trucks and their components were imported from abroad, and there was an acute shortage of all parts. US-manufactured single-cab, six-wheel trucks such as Hagob's 1932 International were the industry standard in Iran. The early trucks were especially vulnerable to the frigid air and ice of the mountains as well as to the desert environment, where heat and sand were brutal on the machinery. Up to two full sets of spare tires might be needed during one round-trip due to the ravages of the unpaved roads. In the absence of a truck-service industry, when trucks broke down on the road, the men had to improvise ways to repair them, although they had had no formal training.[32] Guild organization provided a network that helped Iran's first generation of truck drivers contend with these challenges.

In addition to these trucking-specific functions, the guild performed other functions that were common to Iranian and Middle Eastern guilds of other occupations. These functions included cultivating a quality-control consciousness, lending cash resources, participating in an information network,[33] and attempting to keep the ranks exclusive. Another characteristic of the guild was its ability to influence rates and price setting; only the truckers knew how much a roadside overhaul cost in time and parts, and they could collectively assert operating costs to influence pricing in the transportation industry. The truck drivers' guild in Iran was thus created by the adaptation of traditional guild functions to new technology.

Another adaptation of traditional Iranian institutions facilitated the development of the truck transportation industry while making life a bit easier for the drivers. A haven to which Hagob Hagobian and his driving colleagues could go for rest and some restocking of supplies in the 1920s and 1930s was the rural teahouse, or *chai-khaneh*. The teahouses, in effect truck stops, were the former caravansaries, which for centuries had been way stations for travelers and traders in camel caravans. Hagob and his fellow truck drivers paused at the shelters to eat a hot meal, buy supplies, and spend a night before beginning another grueling twenty-four-hour shift. If time permitted, the drivers would enjoy the common pastime of playing cards and *nardi* (backgammon) while drinking tea. Owing to the unpredictable hygienic conditions of the *chai-khaneh*s and a general fear of disease and parasites, truckers rarely accepted the rooms and beds that were offered. They instead slept in or on top of the trucks, using their

29. Galoast Bagdasarian (*far left*) and Hagob Barsamian (*far right*) observe overhaul of truck engines, Chaparkhane District, Hamadan, mid-1930s. Unknown photographer. Courtesy of the author.

personal sleeping gear. This practice also served the function of providing security for the valuable trucks and cargo, which were vulnerable to thieves if the drivers slept elsewhere.

Iranian truck drivers, predominantly Christian Armenians and Assyrians, enjoyed a unique status in the nation as the operators of novel and complex machines. The *chai-khaneh* owners were Muslims who, in Islamic tradition, provided a hospitable environment to every guest. Thus, although the *chai-khaneh* owners and the truck drivers came from different religious backgrounds, they formed a trusting and enduring relationship that became an integral part of the transportation industry of Iran.

These pioneers of Iran's transportation revolution demonstrated remarkable ingenuity and patience in their labor, but they were also part of a process that was not always beneficial to all Iranians. Interest in roads and trucking was generated by elites in the Iranian government, foreign powers, and large-scale traders. On most societal levels other than the elite milieu, however, the development of the country's transportation had mixed, though generally disruptive effects. In fact, this transportation revolution was to be one of the greatest dislocating forces to enter Iran since the advent of gunpowder weapons.

Military use of a road network would, for perhaps the first time in history, seriously challenge regional and tribal political power in Iran.[34] Expanded transportation meant the proliferation of Western goods and ideas, which would threaten and anger traditional urban groups such as the bazaaris and the ulama. As previously mentioned, most sectors of traditional handcraft production—the primary producer of goods in Iran—would suffer from exclusion in the expanding world economy. The weakening of handcraft production as a result of imports and the government's investment in industrialization would work to undermine the craft guilds, which were simultaneously the targets of governmental regulation to limit some of their traditional responsibilities.

In 1926, the year that Hagob Hagobian entered his guild apprenticeship, the Sixth Majlis approved two unrelated pieces of legislation: a law that provided funding for roads and a law that took away the power of guilds to collect taxes. The latter was a function the guilds had served for more than four hundred years and that had provided them with influence and importance. The Pahlavi regime's sharp break from past centuries of Iranian governmental policy on the guilds and the progressive assault of imports brought by the newly developed truck transportation industry in the 1920s altered guild functions and threatened their existence. A look at the position of the guilds in Iran in the nineteenth century and through the rise of Reza Shah in 1925 reveals their strength and pervasiveness and helps explain why the agenda pursued by the Pahlavi government would be only partially successful.

Guilds on the Eve of Pahlavi Rule

From the height of Safavid rule in the mid–sixteenth century until the beginning of the nineteenth century, the *asnaf* (guild) had remained relatively unchanged as the primary labor-organizing and tax-collecting institution in urban and much of rural Iran.[35] Although the gradual integration of Iran into the world economy had already begun to change the nature of Iranian craft industry by the mid–nineteenth century,[36] the guild structure endured, as did the guilds' productive and administrative responsibilities. Descriptions of industry and trade in Hamadan, Mashad, Tabriz, Kerman, Kashan, Tehran, Isfahan, and Shiraz supply us with data from which a general picture of the Iranian guilds during this time can be drawn.[37]

All artisans working in the bazaar, including Europeans and other foreigners, were required to be members in a guild that represented their craft. Each different occupation had its own guild, and bazaars were often set up by and for the use of single guilds. Bakers, water sellers, cobblers, stonecutters, blacksmiths, druggists, butchers, carpenters, barbers, and caravan leaders were organized into guilds, as were more obscure occupations such as washers of the dead, executioners, acrobats, passion-play actors, professional mourners, and even thieves.[38] Each guild was constructed hierarchically in a vertical pattern based on skill, responsibility, and power. An informal but mandatory apprenticeship period preceded full entry into the guild.

An individual, often in his[39] early teens, would begin his work as *shagaird*, or apprentice, using the shop, tools, raw materials, and guidance of his superior, the *ustad*, or master craftsman. After a few years of training, the exact amount of time depending on the trade, the *shagaird* would be promoted to the rank of *ustad*.[40] The mainstay of craft production in Iran, the majority of craftsmen consisted of the masters.[41] Above the masters were the guild elders.

The guild's head, called a *naqib* or *ustabashi* (literally "head master"), was an elected or hereditarily assigned position, which performed several important functions for the guild, most importantly serving as the sole intermediary between the guild and the central government.[42] It was the *naqib* who collected and paid the taxes to the central government, arbitrated disputes within and outside of the guild, organized corvées, and negotiated with the government to fix minimum prices. Tax collection was the most important duty of the guild elders, who engaged in negotiations with the government about the amount of tax, or corvée, for the entire guild before allotting shares and organizing payment for members—often on an installment plan.[43] The *naqib* was also the legal intermediary between individual guild members and between guild members and the central government, who dealt with the representatives of corporate groups rather than with individuals.[44] He was paid a fixed salary by the guild for his work.[45]

The Qajar shahs competed with a diversity of strong corporate groups that challenged and limited their power: tribal confederacies, the ulama and the *bazaar* classes, with the various *bazaar* strata composed mostly of guild members. The urban portion of the challenges to Qajar rule, the ulama and the bazaaris (a term that does not reflect the diversity of groupings and interests in the bazaar) had demonstrated brief but important success in their collective efforts to establish a constitution and parliament. Many of the guild members and especially the guild heads and larger merchants (*tujjar*) were influenced by the ulama, to whom they were tied to by religious practice, education, and often marriage.

Of equal importance to the elite strata were the lower ranks of the guilds, including *ustad*s and *shagaird*s. They fell under the category of *pishivaran*, generally middle- and lower-class bazaar artisans, excluding the *tujjar* and the *ustabashi*s.[46] The *pishivaran* became closely related to many of the Iranian secret political societies, *anjuman*s, which sprang up at the turn of the century in various corporate and hybrid milieus.[47] They were also linked to the *futuwwat*, spiritual-athletic organizations (specifically the *zurkhane*, "house of strength") in Iran, which literally provided extra muscle for street demonstrations. These groups played an increasingly assertive role in Iranian politics during the Qajar era, beginning with the well-documented Tobacco Revolt of 1891 and peaking during the Constitutional Revolution of 1905–11, in which they were the central agitators of the movement.[48]

In the latter revolt, the *pishivaran*, motivated by the ulama and guild elders to protest, were demonstrating their concern about the selling out of the country's resources to foreigners and the devastating economic and social results of this betrayal. As noted earlier in the story of the Constitutional Revolution, the interests of those we are concerned with here were to limit the powers of the Qajar shahs, the Russians, and the British by the adoption of the institutions of the constitution and parliament. It was hoped that political representation would alleviate the problems posed by weak shahs and their economic concessions to foreign interests.[49]

The First Majlis, meeting in 1907, had sixty Tehrani delegates, thirty-two of which were representatives from the local guilds, in compliance with the First Electoral Law of 1906. This was a large percentage—70 percent of the Tehrani delegates, and 22 percent of the national delegates—because the guilds constituted only 12.5 percent of Tehran's population of roughly 280,000.[50] The rest of the seats from Tehran went to the ulama, who held four seats, and to the *tujjar*, who held ten.[51] Therefore, guild representation and involvement in the Constitutional Revolution were considerable. The Iranian guilds were organized, pervasive, and influential at the end of the long nineteenth century.[52]

Although the guilds became weaker in the decade between the revolution and the accession of Reza Khan's government in 1921, they maintained substantial political and economic influence and continued to collectively voice political opinions in the form of letters, strikes, and demonstrations through 1922.[53] What was unique about the Iranian guilds during this period was not their ubiquity, political activity, or central role in the economy, but rather their strength vis-à-vis the government as a result of its inchoate bureaucracy. A look at some of the similarities and differences between contemporary guilds of other Middle Eastern nations and those of Iran provides a broader context for the analysis of development and the trucking industry during the reign of Reza Shah and for understanding the place of the Armenian–Assyrian truck drivers' guild in the history of Middle Eastern guilds during the nineteenth and twentieth centuries.

Nineteenth-Century Craft Guilds in the Middle East

There are remarkable similarities in the structure and range of trades and occupations that were organized into guilds in Iran and other Middle Eastern territories such as Egypt, the Ottoman Empire, and Arabia throughout most of the nineteenth century.[54] However, the Iranian guilds for the most part experienced this period differently from their counterparts in other regions of the Middle East. Whereas there were only subtle variations in guild organization and functions in this period, the pace and scope of nineteenth-century developmental efforts in each of these countries produced remarkably different results for guilds in the twentieth century.

To generalize a bit, the reforming sultans of the Ottoman Empire and the khedives and British in Egypt provided their countries with one hundred years of slow but progressive modernization and bureaucratic reform by the dawn of the twentieth century. As mentioned, Iran experienced little of either under Qajar rule. Whereas the Ottoman and Egyptian governments were able to suppress or co-opt many of the important and influential corporate groups in their societies as they attempted to take control of their economies and develop extractive bureaucracies (the ulama; military, tribal and regional forces; as well as the guilds), these groups gained strength in Iran during the nineteenth century. An intermittent but progressive movement toward these economic developments in nineteenth-century Egypt and the Ottoman Empire led to the decline of their guilds by the twentieth century.

Economic reformers of nineteenth-century Egypt and the Ottoman Empire used the guilds as transitional fiscal administrators until the machinery of their respective national bureaucracies were set up. Gabriel Baer explains that although Muhammad Ali and his descendants would have liked to have done away with the corporative structures of the ubiquitous Egyptian guilds, this would have required the previous establishment of a state taxation bureaucracy and employees who would assume the responsibilities of the guilds and guild shaykhs.[55] The guilds, by necessity, served the government in a transitional role, while the government worked simultaneously to create a bureaucracy for taxation and to undermine the guilds.

During the 1880s and 1890s, the Egyptian government issued decrees that led to a loss of guild functions and power. Guild shaykhs were no longer allowed to issue professional permits and were denied influence in wage fixing. In 1881, they were relieved of their tax-collecting duties and other fiscal functions and were further weakened by Egypt's continued integration into the world economy as a periphery area.[56] Baer attributes this weakening to the decline of the crafts and artisanal guilds with the coming of industrialization.[57] Therefore, the Egyptian guilds, already impaired because of exposure to the world economy, lost cohesion and influence. In 1880, the guild was still the basic form of Egyptian labor organization and fulfilled a number of important economic functions. By the end of that decade, however, they lost many of their responsibilities and progressively dissolved.

Baer charts the demise of most Egyptian guilds by 1910 except for, notably, the transport industry.[58] He does not offer any explanation as to why this guild was able to persist, but I will venture to say that the nature of inclusion of a core or periphery area into the world economic system necessitates a functional transportation network. The transportation trade endured, but to the detriment of crafts and the local economy in general as local products were replaced by imports and raw materials were extracted. Survival in this context meant the ability to adapt to new technologies and market realities.[59]

Baer qualifies his work on the Ottoman guilds by explaining that a detailed study had not yet been done. However, there is ample evidence to attest to the strength and large numbers of Ottoman guildsmen during the eighteenth century and the beginning of the nineteenth century and to conclude that the Ottoman guilds were similar to Iranian and Egyptian guilds in their functions and organization.[60] Although Baer's assessment of the Ottoman guilds at the turn of the century is not sufficient in supporting evidence or references, it reveals a chain of events concomitant with Egyptian developments: government policy led to the dissolution of the Ottoman/Turkish guilds. Although Baer stresses that we do not have enough evidence to chart the various stages of the guilds' decline, it is known that in 1910 the Ottoman government abolished the guilds of Istanbul by law and successfully enforced this legislation within the remaining domains of the empire (including Syria, but not the Hijaz) over the following two years.[61] Ottoman and Turkish government policy toward the guilds in the early twentieth century was distinguished by its direct legal movement to eradicate them.

Abraham Marcus's study of Aleppo in the eighteenth century, *The Middle East on the Eve of Modernity*, yields some relevant details about the guilds in Aleppo and Damascus. The Syrian guilds were organized and served functions that were almost identical to those of the Iranian guilds.[62] In the eighteenth century and beginning of the nineteenth, Allepine guilds regulated professional licenses, production, price, wages, and quality control. They also mediated between the government and guild members in legal issues.[63]

By the second half of the nineteenth century, the Syrian guilds showed various signs of decline. World economic penetration, facilitated by the relatively flat geography of the Levant, weakened Syrian handcraft producers. During this time, the Ottoman government worked to assert its power over the guilds. Guild shaykhs and *naqib*s were no longer hereditarily appointed or elected by guild members after the government began requiring its approval of positions. Government licenses to own shops were required, which took away one of the guild's basic functions as labor organizer and its ability to ensure quality control. In 1912, a law providing for the establishment of trade chambers or syndicates was created by the Young Turks as a means of ending once and for all the presence of the Syrian guilds. The outbreak of World War I two years later ended almost eight hundred years of Ottoman/Turkish rule over the Levant, including recent Young Turk legal decree.[64] This pause in the efforts against the guilds allowed the Syrian guilds to persist until the 1920s, where under the British Mandate they were finally superseded by chambers of commerce and labor unions.[65]

Although what eventually became Saudi Arabia after the Uqair Conference of 1922 was technically part of the Ottoman Empire until 1916,[66] the political structure and infrastructure of the region (aside from the Hijaz Railway, completed in the 1890s) was not affected by the nineteenth-century Tanzimat reforms. Like Iran, efforts at economic and industrial reform did not begin in Arabia until the 1920s and were effective only in the 1930s. The similar chronology of development that Arabia shared with Iran in the nineteenth and twentieth centuries make it a particularly important case to examine.

At the turn of the century and during the final dismemberment of the Ottoman Empire after World War I, various tribal elites competed for influence in the Arabian Peninsula, where power was distributed regionally rather than centralized. The Nejdi faction, which had been in control of Riyadh since 1902, eventually won out and formed a pact with their biggest rivals, the urban Hijazi faction, who were prominent in the Holy Cities of Mecca and Medina. Throughout this period, roads and transportation remained in as undeveloped a state as in Iran, and trade was similarly hampered by tribal interference and political instability. Ibn Saud was proclaimed sultan of Najd and its dependencies in 1921, solidifying his military rule of Arabia, just as the coup d'état in Iran elevated Reza Khan's status to *sardar-i sepah*, the Iranian commander in chief. In 1926, the same year Reza Khan crowned himself shah of Iran, Ibn Saud was declared king of the Hijaz.[67] Ibn Saud had to contend with organized urban corporate groups as he established his dynasty, perhaps most importantly the influential craft guilds of the Hijaz, which, like their Iranian counterparts to the north, continued to organize trade, collect taxes, and mediate in legal issues.[68]

The Saudi regime faced monumental extractive and administrative tasks following military unification.[69] In the absence of their own fiscal-administrative apparatus, the Saudis used the guilds of the Hijaz, which were highly organized and powerful after centuries of economic influence, as they created a national market and bureaucracy.[70] Rather than being displaced from traditional economic activities and subject to restrictive laws, the highly organized craft, service, and trade guilds continued to act as the units of fiscal administration and extraction, in essence becoming "labor savers"[71] to the Saudi regime as it developed its national economic infrastructure. Although the agricultural populations of Asir, Nejd, and Hassa were subject to the government's direct extractive and coercive efforts, the urban population of the Hijaz for the most part retained economic and legal independence throughout this period. In addition, the transport and other guilds continued to administer justice within their own ranks and provided an informal insurance system between importers and retailers, which linked retailers and importers in ports and cities.[72] This structure persisted in Saudi Arabia throughout the 1930s until the new bureaucracy was slowly able to take over the guilds' fiscal-administrative responsibilities in the 1940s.[73]

Structural shifts in the Arabian economy were also responsible for the eventual weakening of the Hijazi guilds. The creation of a national market eliminated the restrictive market-sharing agreements that had formerly sheltered the guilds, and the introduction of new technologies created disputes that increasingly necessitated governmental mediation and, thus, control. The introduction of automobiles disrupted long-established relationships and agreements between insurance and transport guilds as everything from profit-sharing arrangements to the schedule of transfer payments became points of contention.[74] The demands of integrating economic practice in the various domains of the nation led to an expanding state role in all economic affairs, which was finally complete in the 1950s.[75]

The history of national economic development in Saudi Arabia demonstrates a progressive transition to a national market through a process of gradual and inclusive reform implementation, without shock and dislocation caused by the immediate dissolution of corporate groups. The experience of the Arabian guilds as well as the variant treatment of the Egyptian, Ottoman, and Syrian guilds outlined earlier provide relevant cases to compare with the Iranian guilds' experiences during Reza Shah's reign[76] and enable an assessment of the complex relationship between the guilds and the emerging truck transportation industry in the period 1925–41.

30. Heavily laden trucks and buses at a former caravansary, Shahrud, 1937. Axel Von Graefe, *Iran Das Neue Persien* (Berlin: Atlantis-Verlag, 1937), 96. Courtesy of the Von Graefe family.

Trucks and Guilds in Pahlavi Iran, 1925–1941

When Reza Khan deposed Ahmad Shah—the last of the Qajars—and assumed full control of the government in 1925, he moved swiftly to implement his economic reform agenda. Over the next fifteen years, his regime engaged in a textbook "big push" economic reform and industrialization effort to make up for Iran's lack of development.[77] Industry accounted for less than 10 percent of Iran's gross domestic product at the turn of the nineteenth century, and this statistic did not change over the next quarter-decade. It was hoped that a firm government hand in economic affairs and the promotion of import substitution would invigorate the economy by allowing industry to develop in a sheltered economic environment. Interested in creating national self-sufficiency based on a diversified industrial economy, Reza Shah used the puppet Majlis to initiate a national economic reform effort based on import substitution.[78] Peasants, guilds (especially the artisans and small traders of the bazaar), and the new industrial labor force were to pay the high price of Iran's late industrialization.[79]

The Fifth Majlis of 1925 met without even symbolic representation from the guilds or *pishivaran*. When in December 1926 the Sixth Majlis passed the Law on the Abolition of the Guild Taxes, which eliminated the taxes on 230 specified guilds and abolished forty-six other taxes related to bazaar artisans and traders,[80] the Iranian craft guilds were relieved of all fiscal-administrative duties. Reza Shah's goal was to establish a government-run bureaucracy that could levy taxes on individuals; therefore, eliminating the guilds as the corporate agents of tax collection was one of the necessary steps in doing so. The new autocrat's rush to impose governmental control on the economy caused him to rid the guilds of their fiscal-administrative tasks almost immediately rather than attempting to use them in a transitional role as the Egyptians, Ottomans, and Saudis had. The Egyptian, Ottoman, and Saudi cases suggest that this process could be completed only after the development of a functioning government bureaucracy for taxation and that there was a sequence necessary for completion. Reza Shah did not follow the same sequence because in 1926 the Iranian government had not yet developed a bureaucracy for taxation.

The effort to immediately remove the guilds from their position as fiscal administrators in Iran was made more difficult by the cohesiveness and ubiquity of the guilds at the time of the restricting legislation. The government relied on the guilds' ongoing productivity while it was carrying out its modernization reforms, so all other guild functions except taxation remained legal. A kind of Darwinian economic expectation among idealistic members of the government and economists such as Millspaugh and Moustafa Khan Fateh predicted the rapid decline of traditional modes of production, which would be supplanted by more efficient industrial production.

The continued existence and popularity of the guilds during this period of industrial expansion form one factor that distinguishes the Iranian case from the others analyzed and raises another question. If Reza Shah wanted to eliminate the guilds and replace them with modern industrial production and organization, why did he allow them to exist at all? Willem Floor's work in *Labour Unions, Law, and Conditions in Iran, 1900–1941* and articles on guilds provides data that can be interpreted to provide a few possible reasons.

Aside from the unnatural developmental atmosphere created by import substitution, problems with industrialization in Iran during this period also related to the abuse and disenchantment of the industrial labor force. Mistreatment by industrial management and the wide-scale employment of women and children in the new factories led to resentment by many Iranian workers, who were used to the paternalistic family and ethnic organization of the traditional guild system.[81] Industrial management was seen as lacking the moral responsibility demonstrated by guild *ustad*s and *naqib*s. A British observer of Iranian economic development in 1935 wrote, "For an additional rial or two per day the factory worker has lost the personal association with his employer. There is not, as yet, adequate provision for injury or for unemployment to replace the moral responsibility of the old-type employer."[82] This situation produced essentially two reactions among malcontent Iranian urban workers: a return to the weakened but functioning craft guilds and brief involvement in socialist trade unions.

Although the Soviet-influenced trade unions, which emerged concurrently with the rise of Reza Khan, were active only in the northern Iranian cities of Tehran, Tabriz, and Enzeli and had at their height only a few thousand active members, they were seen as a threat to the Pahlavi economic development effort. They were also perceived to be a threat to national security, especially following the suppressed Jangali Rebellion of 1920 in Gilan, which received Bolshevik encouragement.[83] The unions were organized with the help from the Profintern (the Moscow-based International Trade Union Movement) between 1921 and 1923 and then by the Communist Party of Iran (CPI) until 1925.[84] In the years between 1921 and 1925, they organized several isolated but successful strikes, rallying weavers, bakers, printers, and dock workers to protest working conditions and wages. When Reza Khan took full control of the country in 1925 as shah of Iran, he immediately declared the CPI an illegal organization and had all of the trade union leaders arrested or killed.[85]

As opposed to the trade unions, which, combined with the availability of Marxist ideology and aggressive Soviet activity in the Caucasus and Central Asia, were a constant worry to two generations of Pahlavi dictators, the traditional craft guilds were not seen as a direct physical threat. Even though the selection of various positions of authority within the guild was electoral or hereditary, Floor contends that Iranian guilds (and other guilds of the world) were created from the top down; government sponsorship of corporate bodies of craftsmen for productive, administrative, and fiscal purposes had brought guilds into being. Government elites had relied on qualified nonelites to perform various duties for centuries, including important fiscal-administrative functions. Governments had benefited from the expertise and production of each corporate group and saved resources by treating them legally as one entity.[86]

Despite origins that were generated by and served the interests of the government, the Iranian guilds were not characterized by strict hierarchy or class conflict within their ranks. On the contrary, their political activities in the nineteenth and early twentieth centuries seem to demonstrate solidarity between their various strata against the government. The effective protests of the 1905–11 Constitutional Revolution were led and constituted predominantly by guild members and included joint demonstrations by apprentices, journeymen, and masters.[87] Social bonds forged in the close working environment of the bazaar, *chai-khaneh*s that were specific to guild but not to rank, and the solidarity felt by guild members of similar ethnic backgrounds prevented interclass strife within the guild hierarchy. Crafts and trades were often particular to an extended family, which precluded the possibility of labor disputes. There was not a rigid structure to the apprenticeship system, and there was not a rigid distinction between apprentices and assistants. Also, most guild members were masters (*ustad*), who in most cases shared the same economic benefits as their colleagues and were sometimes no better off than their apprentices. Floor offers these details to explain why the Iranian guilds did not grow directly into modern trade unions and remarks that this common platitude connecting the two has no basis in fact.[88]

In 1925, after the annihilation of the trade union movement, the Pahlavi regime attempted to further bury the option of union organization by verbally demonstrating support for the guilds and inducing workers to join them.[89] Thus, although the guilds were not used as transitional fiscal administrators, it seems as though they were viewed as "labor savers" to the government in another capacity. The guilds' efficient and well-developed organizational abilities gave some security, insurance, and morale to Iranian workers, saved the Pahlavi regime the effort required to provide state-organized and controlled industrial employment, and helped eliminate the troubles (real or imagined) that Soviet-influenced socialist trade unions would cause.

It appears that the 1926 Law on the Abolition of the Guild Taxes was the only direct step the Pahlavi regime took to weaken Iranian craft guild organization, which otherwise remained intact. The previous analysis might explain why Reza Shah did not disband the guilds immediately by employing the same strong-arm strategies he so successfully used on the leaders of the CPI and the trade unions. Guild meetings were monitored by government police for the duration of Reza Shah's reign,[90] but there is no evidence of a crackdown even remotely comparable to the one he exacted on trade unions. Although it is not clear how taxes were collected between 1926 and 1931, it is known that the Pahlavi regime had not yet developed a bureaucracy that could levy taxes on individuals, and there was a four-year gap between the law abolishing guild taxes and further legislation on taxation.[91]

When the Majlis met in 1931, a new tax law was passed alongside the Foreign Trade Monopoly Law to tax individual guild members. The new law divided guild members and merchants into three and four categories, respectively. The breakdown of guild members was based on income, where those making more than 40,000 tumans paid 100 tumans annually; those who made between 20,000 and 40,000 tumans in a year paid 48 tumans; and the third category, those making between 5,000 and 20,000, paid 18 tumans per year.[92] Floor suggests that the process of categorization of guild members for individual taxation must have been problematic because no receipts or records detailing annual sales or profits were required through 1941.[93] Nonetheless, evidence of the existence and continuity of guild organizational structures and production during the 1930s can be demonstrated by this legislation as well as by the history of the truck drivers' guild.[94]

It was 1926 when Hagob Hagobian entered the guild of Armenian and Assyrian truck drivers and became a *shagaird-e shufer,* apprentice driver. Hagob's involvement with the truck drivers' guild during the 1920s and 1930s demonstrates the persistence of all traditional guild functions, excluding the fiscal-administrative ones. Despite legal restrictions, the persistence of guild credit networks in the next decade is demonstrated by the fact that in 1933, after completion of a traditional apprenticeship, Hagob Hagobian was able to acquire his own truck through the assistance of his former *ustad* rather than being assigned one by the central government.

Although it was the guild structure that initially facilitated Hagobian's entry into the profession and made trucking at all safe and profitable, trucking ironically did as much to damage the guilds as the legal decrees by Reza Shah and his Majlis. The advent of motorized trucks caused a revolution in Iranian transportation, the main indicators of this upheaval being the cost of moving goods to and from the Persian Gulf and Tehran. In 1920, it took two months and cost $200 a ton to move goods from the Persian Gulf to Tehran. A decade later, the same trip took a little more than a week and cost only $50 a ton.[95] The number of vehicles rose from the roughly 3,000 that Millspaugh calculated in 1925[96] to almost 20,000 in the late 1930s. In 1935, nearly 2,000 trucks and more than 1,000 motorcars were being imported each year. By 1938, 14,000 miles of new roads, including 3,000 miles of "first class highways" had been constructed.[97] The expansion of the trucking industry during the 1920s and 1930s had these important economic implications as well as significant military ones. Trucks allowed for the rapid movement of troops along the newly constructed roads, which increasingly became the conduits of central governmental control. By 1934, the *amnieh*, or road guards, were disbursed over 12,000 miles of Iranian roads to stop the robbery and violence caused by bandits.[98] In essence, regional power and the strength of urban corporate groups such as the guilds had been preserved by Iran's underdeveloped transportation infrastructure in the nineteenth and early twentieth centuries.

The impact of Reza Shah's total reform package rendered the decade between 1931 and 1941 arguably the worst in the five-century history of the Iranian guilds. Although they were able to maintain cohesion and importance after their fiscal-administrative duties were taken away, the new economic policies substantially challenged them. The policy of

31. Sadi Street, Shiraz, c. 1947. Photo by Mirza Hassan Akkasbashi. From Mansour Sane, comp., *Remembering Shiraz (Be Yad-e Shiraz)* (Tehran, 2009); not copyrighted in the United States per US Copyright Office Circular 38a, see 17 U.S.C. § 104(b).

import substitution vigorously pursued over the decade of the 1930s protected the many new factories that were established with government subsidies, which further displaced the Iranian craft guilds by increasing local competition. Government monopolies removed the traditional Iranian producers and their methods from certain important areas of production completely, such as textiles and carpets.

Therefore, the governmental attack on the traditional modes and centers of production was a multifaceted endeavor, which intended to replace them completely with modern factories and government-controlled workers' organizations. Hagob Hagobian and his fellow Iranian truck drivers, whose labor in the 1920s and 1930s pioneered a new profession, straddled a central position in the history of twentieth-century Iranian development while they "shifted gears in the desert" to make a living. The roads in Iran became the first injection points of new goods, influences, and power relationships vis-à-vis the new government, and the truckers, whether they knew it or not, were the pilots of this mechanized economic assault.[99]

The damage done to the guilds by the transportation revolution cannot really be quantified in numerical or monetary terms because of the multiple challenges to guilds that emerged in the 1920s and 1930s. However, we can safely infer that there is a link between the health of handcraft production and craft guild size and strength and thus conclude that trucking helped to weaken the uniquely strong and organized guilds in Iran, while simultaneously emerging as a new and important trade through which the centuries-old institution of the guild flourished and found new relevance. The paradox remains that while the guild structure allowed the trucking industry to be as productive as it was, the trucking industry had perhaps the most detrimental effect on the guilds. The Law on the Abolition of the Guild Taxes was a legal blow to the guilds' power, but the true basis of their livelihood—craft production—was threatened primarily by the trucking industry.

Conclusion

A turning point in Iranian history occurred in 1941, bringing an end to the phase of industrial, economic, and legal change initiated by Reza Shah. Reza Shah's exile by the occupying Allies in 1941 and the lack of a strong central government caused the temporary unraveling of many of his regime's previous successes. Sedentarized tribes resumed their nomadism and brigandage, the ulama and other corporate groups again became involved in the political process, and the guilds were persistent and organized enough to resume their fiscal-administrative functions.[100] The Allied invasion also led to an instantaneous and dramatic change in the trucking industry as all available trucks and spare parts were directed in a coordinated effort to keep Allied supply lines moving to the southern Soviet border.

At a time when multiple systems of support were becoming efficient and trucking had become profitable, the Allied occupation during World War II created troubles for Hagob Hagobian and some members of the Iranian truck-driving industry.[101] As the transportation needs of the occupying force took precedence over private ownership and private transportation, many large vehicles were impounded for war use. At the onset of the Allied occupation of Iran in 1941, Hagob's truck was being loaded by his assistant in Tabriz while Hagob was visiting his family in Tehran. Aware that trucks were being commandeered by Russian troops, some drivers and their assistants removed the tires and other crucial operating parts in time to avoid their loss. In Hagob's absence, however, his truck and its car were confiscated. His repeated appeals to the Soviet embassy in Tehran were futile, and he thus lost his only means of livelihood; he never received compensation.[102]

Further complicating his existing problems, Hagob became ill with malaria in 1942. By mortgaging the family's Persian carpets to the state bank, a common practice in Iran, and with support from his relatives in Kermanshah, his family, which grew in 1943 to include a daughter, survived unexpectedly trying times. Hagob returned to his trucking activities in 1945 with the help of a loan from relatives that enabled him to purchase a dump truck. For the next several years, Hagob transported construction materials to job sites in and around the growing city of Tehran in partnership with fellow guild members. By the early 1950s, he had purchased a ten-wheel truck and again began more profitable long-distance hauling to the Persian Gulf. This journey was becoming quicker and safer with the continued construction of modern roadways.

Again earning a stable income, Hagob repaid his debts and over the next few years began planning and saving for his son's higher education. He took advantage of a program offered by the Iranian government that paid half of the educational expenses for students who passed a qualifying examination and received an acceptance from an accredited university abroad. In 1956, Hagob sent his son to the United States to earn a university degree. In 1964, while still engaged in long-distance hauling from the Persian Gulf to Tehran, Hagob sent his daughter, accompanied by her mother, to the United States to begin her university education. A serious trucking accident near Kermanshah in 1966 necessitated his wife's return from abroad to care for him and forced his retirement. During the next decade, Hagob Hagobian and his wife were visited frequently by their adult children, who had established careers in the United States, but the continual separations were insufferable for a couple who had spent their youth as orphans. In 1975, Hagob and Arshalous Hagobian moved to the United States to be with their children's families and resettled in a California community in which Armenians in the diaspora had again established their churches, schools, and cultural centers.

4

Sevak Saginian

AT AGE FIFTEEN IN 1937, Sevak Saginian made the unfortunate observation that the Armenian and Assyrian kids in his Tehran neighborhood seemed to be on the receiving end of increasing verbal and physical punishment from their Persian Muslim counterparts, some of whom they had played with as small children. Although decades later Sevak would attribute this change to the effects of the extreme Iranian nationalist rhetoric and policies that typified Reza Shah's reign after 1934, all he knew at the time was that things were getting rough and that something needed to be done about it.[1] With the closure that year of his Armenian school due to an explicit decree by Reza Shah that only the national language, Persian, be taught and the resulting transfer of most students to the integrated Alborz American College—a high school with only a Persian and English curriculum—the situation got worse. Now, on the way home from school, lone Christian teens were routinely getting clobbered, and Sevak shared their growing fears. It was not often that blood would be shed, but a great amount of pride was lost in these engagements.

One day after encountering yet another after-school brawl, Sevak made the observation that the reason the Persian kids seemed to always get the better of their Armenian or Assyrian classmates was that most of the Persians possessed at least rudimentary wrestling skills. The fight would begin evenly, then, inevitably, the Persian contender would drag the Christian down, incapacitate him, and then proceed to issue standard wrestling torment.[2] Sevak reasoned that the key to winning, or at least to fending off such an encounter, was to stop it before it got to the wrestling portion of the match. So he took up boxing, and his brother, Artashes, quickly followed suit. Emboldened by their rudimentary boxing skills, over the next year the two developed the effective, if not chivalrous, strategy of "hit and run."

Sevak's boxing exploits in school eventually led to his development of a small gang of predominantly Armenian students who took up boxing as well as any other martial arts skills they could obtain.[3] Soon Sevak, always a leader in his youth, and his gang of friends became an unofficial after-school escort service for Armenian students, often using their bicycles to quickly race to the scene of an altercation. As Sevak continued to hone his boxing skills on the street, he also engaged in amateur boxing tournaments in Tehran.

As well as in athletics, Sevak Saginian excelled in academics. Although his schoolwork and social life were disrupted in eleventh grade after Reza Shah's language curriculum decree was extended to American and European schools, and Sevak had to transfer to a public high school from the private Alborz American College, his grades held fast. With his high exam scores when he was a senior, Sevak Saginian won the award for top valedictorian in the nation. His combined athletic and academic abilities as well as his excellence in Persian brought him to the notice of members of

32. Sevak Saginian at the Danashkadeh-ye Afsari, military-technical college, 1946. Unknown photographer. Courtesy of Sevak and Nella Saginian.

the Armenian clergy, who began to call on him to translate at gatherings and, in short order, in exchanges and meetings with various Iranian government officials.[4]

Sevak spent 1941–44 working as an interpreter, writing occasional news stories for *Alik* (Wave) newspaper, boxing, and developing an extended peer group of young Armenian athletes and intellectuals, with whom he spent much time engaged in sport and entertainment. Although Sevak was interested in pursuing a law degree, his family's long history of military service to Iran motivated him to enroll at the Danashkadeh-ye Afsari (Officers College), the military-technical college that taught tactics of traditional and mechanized cavalry. An exceedingly confident young man, Sevak was sure he would quickly rise through the ranks as his great-great-grandfather, great-grandfather, and grandfather had before him.

The Saginians in Qajar Iran

Part of a splinter group of Armenians who escaped south during Russo-Persian war of 1804–13, Sevak Saginian's great-great-grandfather David Saginian and his younger brother, Zal, immigrated to Tabriz with their family in 1811.[5] Having studied Russian military sciences at an academy in Tiblisi as teens, both David and Zal joined the military of Fath Ali Shah Qajar (r. 1797–1834) and quickly distinguished themselves owing to their advanced knowledge of field tactics. Following the disastrous war with the Russians in 1826, "David Khan" was put in command of a regiment created to subdue recalcitrant nomadic tribes throughout Qajar Azerbaijan, especially in the region of Orumieh.[6] Because of David Khan's success in suppressing tribal revolts in the country's northwestern region, the heir to the Qajar throne, Crown Prince Abbas Mirza—known widely for his pro-Christian policies and connections within the Christian community in Tabriz—promoted him to the position of *sartip* (brigadier general).[7] David Khan Saginian was then sent south with a regiment of Nezam-e Jedid (New Order) artillery troops to put down tribal rebellions around Isfahan, Shiraz, and Bushire.[8] Again successful in carrying out his orders, Sartip David Khan was awarded two additional titles by Fath Ali Shah: *farmandeh* (supreme military commander) of the provinces of Shiraz and Isfahan and *sarperast-e Aramane* (guardian of the Armenians). Thereafter, aside from his military responsibilities, David Khan was given the task of overseeing the administration of the Armenian populations of Isfahan and Shiraz, which included assuring their physical protection in their urban quarters and mediation in legal disputes.[9]

With the deaths of Crown Prince Abbas Mirza in 1833 and his father, Fath Ali Shah, the following year, the titles *farmandeh* and *sarperast-e Aramane* were confirmed by Fath Ali Shah's successor, Mohammad Shah Qajar. Throughout Mohammad Shah's reign—which ended with his death in 1848—and into the beginning of the reign of Nasir al-Din Shah (r. 1848–96), David Khan retained these titles until he retired from the military in the 1850s.[10] Goorgen Khan Saginian, David Khan's oldest son and Sevak Saginian's great-grandfather, also joined the Qajar military and attained the rank of *sarhang* (colonel), but he died in his forties while his father David Khan was in retirement. Around the time of David Khan's death in 1867, Goorgen Khan's son Solayman, Sevak Saginian's grandfather, entered the Persian army and rose through the ranks to become *sarhang*. He was also bestowed the title *sarperast-e Aramane* for the region of Tabriz, although it is not known what regional responsibilities and powers were specifically granted through the title. In 1875, Sarhang Solayman Khan Saginian, who had become fluent in French, was placed in charge of the telegraph system in Iranian Azerbaijan (later conjoined under the title PTT: Post, Telegraf va Telefon), which he oversaw until his death in 1913.[11]

Zohrab Saginian and the Iranian Majles

Solayman Khan's oldest son, Zohrab Saginian, was born in Tabriz in 1883. Unlike his male ancestors, Zohrab was not fond of the idea of military service, and as a teen he sought instead to distinguish himself in academics. Solayman Khan supported his son's academic pursuits and funded Zohrab's study of political science in Geneva, Switzerland.[12] Returning to Iran in early 1910 as a budding political activist, Zohrab took up residence in Tehran and quickly fell in with members of the Armenian Revolutionary Federation—known widely as the Dashnaksutiun (Dashnak) Party—who were active participants in the Constitutional Revolution. A prolific writer of poems, editorials, and news stories, Zohrab became a frequent contributor to the Dashnak newspaper *Aravot* (Morning), dedicated primarily to Dashnak perspectives on contemporary politics. His editorial articles in *Aravot*, often written under the pseudonym "Rostampour" for anonymity, most often revolved around three related topics: political tenets of the Dashnaksutiun; the adoption of European political institutions to strengthen Iran; and the importance of the development of a literacy corps to prepare the citizenry of both Iran and the Caucasus for participation in the political process.[13]

Dashnaks had been active in Iran since the 1890s with cells and small military training centers in cities with substantial Armenian populations such as Tabriz, Salmas, and Khoy.[14] Although the organization's activities were initially focused solely on the issue of Armenian liberation and the protection of Armenian populations from Kurdish and Turkish aggression, it became directly involved in the Iranian constitutional movement after the Fourth General Congress of 1907 in Vienna, where the party's loose socialist ideals and goal of Armenian liberation were deemed compatible with the Iranian movement's progressive, antiautocratic aims.[15] The Dashnaksutiun had developed a particular antipathy for czarist Russia, which had closed Armenian schools and confiscated Armenian

33. Zohrab Saginian, Dashnaksutiun *fedayi*, Tehran, 1910. Unknown photographer. Courtesy of Sevak and Nella Saginian.

church properties in an attempt to homogenize the Christian populations of the Caucasus, and which was viewed as the primary threat to both Armenian and Iranian sovereignty.[16] Unlike the Hnchak Party, which remained ambivalent toward physical involvement in the movement, the Dashnak Party entered into an alliance with the Iranian Social Democrats and joined directly in the constitutionalist struggle to counter what they deemed "reactionary feudalism."[17]

Becoming better connected in the Dashnak hierarchy in Tehran and known for his linguistic skills in Armenian, Persian, French, and Russian, Zohrab acquired a combined position as secretary, interpreter, and "public-relations" mediator for *fedayi* (literally "devotee," referring to the Nationalist forces) leader Yeprem Khan (Yeprem Davidian, 1868–1912), who spoke little Persian. Yeprem Khan was a Dashnak activist and fighter who became a leader in the military struggle for Tabriz, Gilan, and Tehran during the Constitutional Revolution and was selected by the Majles to serve as chief of police of Tehran in 1910.[18] Zohrab Khan was present in September 1911 when Yeprem Khan's forces defeated those of Muhammad Ali Shah Qajar and again in the battle of May 5, 1912, against Muhammad Ali Shah's brother Salar al-Dowleh, in which Yeprem Khan was killed.[19] With the death of Yeprem Khan and the withdrawal of the Dashnaks from Iranian politics in late 1912, Zohrab returned to Tabriz. Here, his family connections and his diverse language skills paid off again as he first began working for the PTT, which soon led to his acquiring a job as translator in the Iranian administration in Azerbaijan under Mokhber al-Saltaneh. In this job, Zohrab's experience stands in dramatic contrast to many of the immigrant Armenian and Azeri Transcaucasian mujahedin who fought under Yeprem Khan and were left without support upon his death in 1912. Lacking knowledge of Persian, yet unable to return to their homes owing to fear of the Ottoman or Russian governments, some turned to a life of begging or crime.[20] In contrast, Zohrab obtained steady employment and remained loosely connected with the government.

In 1915, Zohrab Saginian was married to Sandokht Badmagurian, daughter of the Qajar military commander Ardashir Khan Badmagurian. The following year the couple moved from Tabriz to Tehran so that Zohrab could attend the Daneshkadeh-ye Hoquq (College of Law)—an

34. Sandokht Saginian, c. 1920. Unknown photographer. Courtesy of Sevak and Nella Saginian.

extension of the Dar al-Fonun (military/technical school)—to obtain an advanced degree in law. It was also in 1916 that Zohrab's brother, Alex Saginian, opened up the first movie house in Iran. Located in a hall of the French Mission in Tabriz, it was named "Cinema Soleil" and showed primarily Russian and European films.[21] While studying at the Danesh-kadeh-ye Hoquq in 1917 and 1918, Zohrab again became involved in the Tehran branch of the Dashnak Party and in closely following the politics of the Iranian Majles, which had been disbanded in 1915 and was now being slowly reconstituted through a fresh election process.[22]

It could be said that in May 1918 Zohrab Saginian reached a crossroad in his life, for on that day the Dashnak-dominated Armenian National Council proclaimed an independent Armenian republic in the Caucasus.[23] Dashnak activists from Iran were leaving for the new republic to assist in its administration and defense, and Zohrab—with his linguistic skills and advanced education in political science and law, as well as his record of service with Yeprem Khan during the Constitutional Revolution—would have been a prime candidate to enter the Dashnak-run republican government. Yet, despite the fact that he was an ardent Armenian nationalist with a social democratic bent, the Saginians had lived in Iran for more than a century, and Zohrab considered it his country. The disruption of the Iranian Majles, politics, and the economy as well as the abusive regime of Ahmad Shah strengthened Zohrab's resolve to work for political change in Iran and, like his ancestors, to work to safeguard the interests of Armenian Iranians. Furthermore, there was much he could do in Iran in the way of continuing to support the Dashnak movement, which was habitually short of arms and funds and desperately needed articulate and sympathetic representation in surrounding nations.[24]

After the failure of the Dashnaksutiun-led Republic of Armenia and the establishment of the Armenian SSR on April 21, 1921, many Armenian Iranian Dashnaks who had moved to Armenia as well as Dashnaks from Russia and the Caucasus were forced to flee to Iran to avoid arrest and execution by Soviet secret police. The refugees from Yerevan were generally welcome in Iran, especially after a contingent cooperated with Iranian troops under General Amanallah Jehanbani in the suppression of a Kurdish insurgency.[25] With this dramatic turn of events, the ranks of the Tehran cells of the Dashnak Party reformed rapidly, and the Soviet Union edged out Turkey as enemy number one of the Dashnaks. The effect of these events on Zohrab was to solidify his interest in reforming the Iranian government and working to improve life in Iranian Azerbaijan after a decade of war and revolution had shattered its communities and economy.

During the 1920s, the Dashnak and Hnchak Armenian revolutionary organizations competed with each other and a variety of political parties and unions to gain the sympathies and support of Iran's roughly 150,000 Armenians, whose participation spanned the political spectrum. Armenians were prominent in the Tabriz Social-Democratic Group and the Tabriz-based social democratic party Ferqeh-i Edalat (Justice Party). The Justice Party was sympathetic to the Bolshevik movement, attempted to organize the Iranian laborers in the oil fields of Baku, and sent delegates to the Bolshevik Congress as well as to its own Caucasus-wide congress in 1920.[26] Armenians were also members of the Rasht militia that supported the 1915–21 Jangali Rebellion led by Kuchek Khan, and hundreds fought for the establishment of the SSR in Gilan.[27] In addition, Armenians were highly active in the Communist Showra-ye Mutahedeh-ye Ittehadieh Kargaran (Central Council of Federated Trade Unions, CCFTU), which was founded in 1921 and composed of an urban Armenian and Azeri rank and file from northern Iranian cities and rural Armenian cells.[28] After growing up in rural Iranian Azerbaijan and Rasht, Ardashir Ovanissian participated in the Jangali Rebellion, was an early CCFTU organizer, and later became head of the CCFTU's youth organizations. Ovanissian would ultimately become leader and primary spokesman of the Communist Tudeh Party in Iran during the 1940s and 1950s.[29]

In the 1920s and 1930s, Armenians were used to form and support networks of Soviet secret police in Iran, also known as the Cheka. Because the Dashnaks advocated armed opposition to Soviet rule and were considered by Moscow to be Menshevik subversives, the primary responsibilities of the Soviet secret police in Iran were surveillance of Dashnaks and efforts to thwart their organization and membership while working covertly to promote communism and the Soviet Union.[30] Armenian agents posing as Dashnak defectors from the Armenian SSR as well as sympathetic local Armenian Iranians were ideal for the purposes of infiltration and spying. As a result, Cheka agents and spies in Iran were overwhelmingly of Armenian descent.[31]

Within this politically charged milieu, Zohrab Saginian decided to seek candidacy for the Iranian Majles. The elections for the Fifth Majles were genuine: independent candidates such as Zohrab campaigned in major cities and drew on their bases of support to acquire votes (money, family connections, or, in Zohrab's case, a combination of family connections and Dashnak support) rather than being hand-picked by the ruling regime.[32] After campaigning throughout Iranian Azerbaijan and Gilan in 1923, a region where his family had been involved in the military and culture for a century, Zohrab was elected in 1924 to the Fifth Majles as representative for the Christians of northern Iran and Iranian Azerbaijan. At the time of the Fifth Majles, 4 of the 130 total seats were designated for religious minorities. Christians received two representatives, one based in Tehran to cover the northern portion of the country and one based in Isfahan to cover the south. Because the Armenian population of Iran exceeded that of the Assyrians, Armenians always won both parliamentary seats and became de facto representatives for the Assyrians. In addition, Jews and Zoroastrians received one seat each. For the duration of the twentieth century, Majles representative was the highest position in the Iranian government an Armenian civilian could acquire.

In 1924–25, Zohrab was a supporter of Reza Khan, whom he saw as a reform-minded, secular republican leader. In the only period of his twenty-year tenure as Majles member when he was free to vote his conscience, Zohrab voted in 1925 for Reza Khan's appointment as prime minister, for Reza Khan's universal military conscription bill, and for Reza Khan's bill requiring family names and abolishing honorary titles.[33] However, Reza Shah quickly assumed dictatorial powers over every aspect of national governance, and the Majles was reduced to a rubber stamp. Between 1925 and 1941, which encompassed the Sixth through the Thirteenth Majles, all Majles members were either hand-picked or individually reconfirmed by Reza Shah, and elections were thoroughly rigged.[34] Although Zohrab's attitude soured as Reza Khan abandoned the idea of an Iranian Republic, crowned himself "Reza Shah Pahlavi," and moved toward dictatorship and extreme Iranian nationalism, his support for the shah in the Fifth Majles would ensure him a long career as Majles member and relatively good relations with the monarchy.

Despite the fact that Reza Shah quickly became a repressive dictator, the reforms initiated by the Pahlavi regime to promote national development, unity, and cohesion were not altogether unappealing to Zohrab Saginian. In fact, most of Reza Shah's reforms were in line with Zohrab's own secular, Western-oriented sensibilities, Iranian patriotism, and anti-Communist sentiment. As a secular-minded lawyer trained in French and Swiss law, Zohrab supported Reza Shah's Western-oriented legal reforms and moves to limit the powers of the Iranian ulama. He was also supportive of Reza Shah's policies concerning the status of women and the issue of *hejab* (veiling). With the banning of the chador, Armenian women would blend with rather than stand out in a crowd. Armenian Iranian women had, furthermore, always played a more prominent role in public life than Persian Iranian women, and Zohrab was supportive of the elevation of all Iranian women's status. Because Armenian Iranians did not tend to wear any particular ethnic clothing, the banning of tribal wear and headgear in 1928 did not offend any of their cultural traditions or sensibilities. Furthermore, many Armenians in Iran were tailors and importers of Western fashions, so Zohrab's constituents would benefit from this reform economically as well as socially.

Zohrab, a staunch modernizer, saw Reza Shah's subjugation of Iran's nomadic tribes as well as his agenda for nationwide industrial and infrastructural development as a necessity for Iran's cohesion, security, and economic growth. He also saw a larger defense budget and universal military conscription as beneficial both to Iran as well as to Armenian Iranians. A strong military would be able to defend Iran's borders, in particular Iranian Azerbaijan, from attack by Turkey or the Soviet Union—two bordering countries that Zohrab despised. Moreover, Armenian Iranians such as his own Saginian ancestors David Khan, Goorgen Khan, and Solayman Khan as well as his relative through marriage, Iskandar Khan Setkhanian, had attained high ranks and leadership roles in both the Persian army and the Cossack Brigade, and there was no reason in the late 1920s and early 1930s to think Armenian Iranians would not continue to excel in the Iranian military.[35]

Also a staunch Iranian nationalist, Zohrab was supportive of Reza Shah's efforts to combat foreign influence, in particular his attempt, albeit unsuccessful, to end the unfavorable Anglo-Iranian oil concession in 1932.[36] Reza Shah's policy concerning Communists was also supported by Zohrab, who as a Dashnak loathed communism and the Soviet Union and was happy to see CCFTU and CPI members driven underground or arrested.[37] Although many urban and rural Armenians were organizers and members of these organizations, Armenian Iranian Communists, in Zohrab's view, undermined not only Iran's national integrity, but perhaps more significantly the effort to discredit the Soviet Union and the work for the liberation of Armenia from antireligious Communist imperialism.[38] From the viewpoint of Armenian Iranian Dashnaks, the arrest and persecution of Communist activists and spies were thus beneficial for Iran and Armenia.[39] Zohrab was a strong proponent of increasing literacy and access to education, so he initially perceived Reza Shah's educational reforms, which drastically increased the budget for education and expanded enrollment and schools at all levels, as ideal.

Throughout most of the 1930s, Majles members worked only three days a week, and their positions became ceremonial. Although Zohrab had been loyal to the regime and thus far had never publicly criticized Reza Shah, in 1931 he was put under full-time surveillance along with many of his fellow Majles members. Not altogether a negative experience, the surveillance was, however, a daily reminder of Reza Shah's ubiquitous power and authority.[40] In this period, being a Majles member could be dangerous, and the minority deputies were not immune to the hazards of their public positions. The Jewish representative to the Majles, Samuel Haim, was accused of plotting against Reza Shah, tortured, and executed in 1931.[41] Saharoukh Keykhowsrow, the Zoroastrian deputy who had supported Reza Shah since 1921, was killed by Iranian police in 1940 after it was learned that his son had broadcast pro-Nazi speeches in Germany.[42] Knowing full well that his Dashnak activities could get him into trouble with the regime, Zohrab did his best to keep his ongoing participation and support of the organization at a low profile. The covert battle between the Dashnaks and Armenian Chekists was heating up, and Zohrab did not want to serve as Reza Shah's scapegoat should he become aware of its extent.

The conflict between Iranian Dashnaks and Soviet Armenian agents became public knowledge in March 1931 with the execution of an Armenian named Garnik, who ran a coffee shop in Tehran on Khiabane Istanbul apparently as a cover for his covert political activities. A newcomer to Tehran, Garnik had immediately joined the Dashnaks and earnestly attended several meetings before background checks revealed that Garnik's brother was working for the Cheka in Baku, and it became obvious that the coffee shop's income was being heavily subsidized. After Garnik was found stabbed in the doorway to his home, there was a roundup of nearly fifty Armenians despite a total lack of evidence that any were involved in Garnik's murder or affiliated with the Dashnaksutiun. After a few days had passed and no killer had been found, the police chief was fired, presumably because of the failure to obtain solid evidence as well as the failure to detect Communist activity in the nation's capital.[43]

However Zohrab might have attempted to downplay or hide his extracurricular Dashnak activities, we know that his connections with the Dashnak Party were not lost on the informants to American diplomat Charles C. Hart, who had filed a report on the murder of Garnik in 1931. In the 1932 "Report to the Honorable Secretary of State," Hart offers summaries of the basic tenets of Hnchak (social democratic), Dashnak (Armenian revolutionary/nationalist), and Ramgavar (liberal democratic) Parties in Iran, stating,

> Of the Persian Armenians, it is generally estimated that 85 per cent are Gregorians and ten per cent Uniates. The remaining five per cent are Protestants, members of the Armenian Evangelical Church, the result largely of American missionary endeavor during the last century in the Ottoman Empire and northwestern Persia. In the latter group are included about 500 Seventh Day Adventists. As to the political affiliations of these groups, it may be said, first, that practically all Persian Gregorians are either active Dashnakists or Dashnak sympathizers and that practically all Persian Dashnakists are Gregorians. I am reliably informed that the doctrines of the party are held by the two Armenian deputies to the Persian Majles (Sohrab Khan Sakinian, representing the Armenians of Azerbaijan, and J. Z. Mirzayantz, Deputy for the South Persia Armenians) and are taught by both priests and teachers, in the churches, schools and social clubs maintained by the Gregorian communities. Some 85 per cent of the Persian Armenians are, therefore, either actively or potentially anti-Soviet.[44]

If Zohrab's connection to Dashnak was so obvious a fact as to be brought to the attention of an American diplomat, why wasn't he called to answer for the death of Garnik or even arrested himself for membership in an illegal political organization? As part of an anti-Communist force that had originally supported Reza Shah's ascension to power, Iranian Dashnaks were not actively pursued by the Pahlavi regime in the early 1930s, which instead focused its repression on the CPI and trade union movements. With the suspicion and fear that large numbers of Armenian Iranians were Communist sympathizers, the Dashnaks of Iran would be one of the last Armenian political organizations Reza Shah would want to suppress or alienate at the time. This point was clear to Charles Hart, who, in concluding his 1932 report's overview of the Dashnaks of Iran, stated, "I may add that I have gained the clear impression that, of all the Persian Armenians, they [Dashnaks] stand highest in official esteem, because of their present anti-Soviet and traditionally anti-Turkish policies."[45] Thus, owing to Zohrab's support of Reza Shah's positions and Reza Shah's tacit approval of the Dashnak Party, for the time being he remained safe from arrest or persecution.

The year 1934 marked a watershed in the relationship between Reza Shah and the Armenians of Iran, however, in that the shah's widely publicized visit to Turkey in June of that year was considered to be the catalyst for his progressively anti-Armenian and nationalist policies of 1935–41. Whether it is historical fact or not, the perception that Mustafa Kemal Atatürk had persuaded Reza Shah to crack down on the Dashnaksutiun and make life hard for Armenian Iranians was universal in Iran's Armenian communities. After several Dashnaks who had been known to the regime for years were arrested and interrogated, the organization went deep underground.

Although the Dashnak Party was indeed targeted by the Pahlavi regime after 1934, the historical record suggests that the Armenians of Iran were not singled out by Reza Shah as a special case for repression. Rather, all linguistic and religious minorities as well as many traditional-minded Muslims suffered from the shah's policies to promote national unity and modernization through linguistic and educational reforms emulating those of Atatürk.[46] Reza Shah's minister of education, Ali-Asghar Hekmat, explained that the shah's policy was that "all Iranians must have one language, one writing, one culture and even one attire. They must all be equal before the law and no difference should separate the Muslims from the non-Muslims," and that "the unity of discourse [*vahdat-e kalameh*] must be fully observed everywhere in the country."[47]

For the Armenian Iranians, the revoking of their school licenses in 1938 was an outrage. Like the Baha'is, Azeris, Kurds, Arabs, and Assyrians—other Iranian religious and linguistic minorities whose schools were also shut down in the attempt to impose Persian as the standard national language—Armenian Iranians saw this act as an attack on their ethnicity and an attempt to eradicate their culture.[48] Arrest and interrogation of Armenians in Tabriz, Tehran, and New Julfa—most often for suspected Communist activity—continued in 1938, further alienating the Armenian population. To make matters worse, as Ervand Abrahamian observes, in 1938 "*Itila'at* (Information), the semiofficial government daily, waged a front-page campaign against the Christian minority by running a series of articles on 'dangerous criminals,' all with obviously Armenian and Assyrian names."[49]

Despite Zohrab's status as parliamentarian, speaking out in Majles directly against these developments was out of the question, and, like his fellow minority Majles deputies, Zohrab was forced to remain silent about these issues. Thus, he was resigned to the fruitless task of letter writing to other representatives and the protective measure of assessing Armenian properties in case of confiscation by the government. The latter was always a possibility because several of the schools continued to illegally teach private Armenian-language classes.[50]

It was paradoxical that Zohrab was himself an Iranian nationalist. He considered himself an Armenian Iranian and was beholden and loyal to the Iranian nation.[51] He was supportive of most of Reza Shah's secularizing reforms as well as of his policies to modernize and strengthen Iran. Yet Reza Shah's closure of the Armenian schools and effort to homogenize Iran's language were indicative of a fundamental difference between how the two Iranian nationalists perceived ethnic minorities. For Reza Shah, the nation would be cohesive only when the Armenian Iranians had become "Iranian Christians."[52] For Zohrab, the nation would be cohesive only when the state recognized and celebrated the contributions and loyalty of its diverse population.[53]

With the Allied invasion of Iran in August 1941 and Reza Shah's exile, newspapers and political parties again flourished. After winning his seat in the Thirteenth Majles (November 1941–November 1943), Zohrab knew he was finally free to publicly pursue the issue of Armenian-language schools.[54] Heir to the Pahlavi throne, Muhammad Reza Shah was not feared by the Armenian community as his father was, and the open political atmosphere finally allowed criticism of the Pahlavi regime. In January 1942, Zohrab wrote an open letter to Majles members and to *Alik* (a

Tehran-based Dashnak weekly newspaper) declaring that Reza Shah had closed the Armenian schools illegally.

It is not clear who beat whom to the punch, but in 1942 the Tudeh Party, led by the Armenian Ardashir Ovanissian, also called for the opening of Armenian- and Azeri-language schools throughout Iran.[55] Irrespective of who made the first public statement, beginning in 1942, when it became clear that Reza Shah would not return, the Armenian schools were slowly reopened on an ad hoc basis. Across the nation, groups of Armenian teachers and administrators simply returned to their schools and reopened them without permits from the Ministry of Education. By 1944, almost all of the Armenian schools that had been closed after 1936 were reopened, albeit with unaccredited status because they had not been officially recognized and certified by the Iranian Ministry of Education.

Between 1941 and 1944, the Soviet secret police had free reign in northern Iran. The Cheka ruthlessly pursued and arrested suspected members of the Dashnak Party and were able to obtain British cooperation in their attack on the supposed "fifth columnists." As Major Edward S. Kennedy noted in an American military intelligence report of 1944, "The Allied invasion of Iran in 1941 ended the power of Reza Shah, but the Soviets have become an even greater scourge than he. If any former Dashnak goes to a Russian official and confesses the error of his ways, the reformed one is invariably made to act as an agent, spying on the activities of his former associates. The Soviets are not willing that he live a quiet, nonpolitical life."[56] Kennedy's report offered descriptions of six Armenians in custody, and he concluded that some, such as Dr. Artashes Babalian, were genuinely innocent, whereas others, such as Manuk Martin and Khachik Melconian, were most likely real fifth columnists.[57]

In 1944, with the Red Army firmly entrenched in his representative district of northern Iran, and as a known Dashnak supporter and loyal deputy under Reza Shah, Zohrab Saginian had little chance of winning the election for the Fourteenth Majles (January 1944–January 1946). More important perhaps was the conjunction of a sentiment to clean house and, with the reemergence of political parties, a growing array of new alliances and voices for change.[58] In the electoral campaign for the Majles in 1944, pro-Soviet Armenians in Tabriz supported a member of the Tudeh Party,

Qazar Simonian, for their representative against the Dashnak-supported candidate, Zohrab Saginian's colleague and former representative for the southern district Dr. Alex Aghayan. The leftist newspaper *Azhir* (Alarm) published by Iranian Communist organizer Javad Pishevari endorsed Simonian while criticizing Aghayan's connections to the Pahlavi regime and his silence when the Armenian schools were closed in 1938.[59] When the votes—however externally influenced—were tallied, eight Majles seats went to pro-Communist deputies, including the northern Armenian post, which was assumed by Simonian.[60] After serving twenty years in the Iranian Majles, Zohrab retired from politics in 1944 and returned to the PTT and part-time university teaching.[61] Shortly after his retirement, his oldest son, Sevak, entered the Danashkadeh-ye Afsari.

Sevak Saginian, Ararat, and the Iranian Majles

In addition to carrying on his family's tradition of military and political involvement in Iran, Sevak Saginian was motivated to join the military specifically because of the brewing Azerbaijan conflict. Beyond the liberation of Tabriz and Iranian Azerbaijan, which had been the home of the Saginian family for four generations and their burial place, Sevak was interested in fighting Communist Soviets. His father's Dashnak orientation, Iranian nationalism, and activities in the effort to help both Caucasus Armenians and Armenian Iranians, combined with Sevak's education in Armenian and Iranian schools, had inculcated in Sevak a deep-seated contempt for Communists. He loathed the Soviet Union in particular, which he viewed as both a threat to Iran and the oppressors of Armenia. In 1945, he was promoted to lieutenant in a mechanized division in the Iranian army and became excited when it seemed that the army would most probably be going to Azerbaijan to face the Soviets. But Sevak also began to notice that strange things were happening within the ranks. Armenian officers who should have been promoted to high leadership positions were not receiving promotions, and rumors circulated that it was owing to the perception that they might have Communist leanings. Paranoia about Communists in the Iranian military was high, and in 1945 leaders of the gendarme, such as Colonel Zanganeh, openly considered Armenians and Assyrians potential subversives.[62]

These rumors were confirmed one day shortly after Sevak had been transferred from the cavalry division to artillery. He was standing in the barracks and overheard two Persian officers talking about a Soviet spy who had been caught on a nearby base. As Sevak looked over toward them, one of the officers dropped his eyes, nudged the other, and said, "Shhh, a *brother* is among us." In that moment, Sevak's hopes for a career in the military were dashed. If his fellow Iranian soldiers and officers wouldn't trust him and share their secrets, he was sure the military would be a dead end.[63]

Although any suspicions about Sevak's stance on communism and questions of his loyalty to Iran were unfounded, the Iranian government and military had ample reason to think that many Armenians were either Communists or Communist sympathizers.[64] As Abrahamian's in-depth analysis of the pro-Soviet Tudeh Party in *Iran between Two Revolutions* demonstrates, the party appealed in particular to Iranian Christians (almost all being of Armenian or Assyrian descent) but failed to motivate Iranian Sunnis, Baha'is, Jews, and Zoroastrians for a variety of reasons.[65] Attributing Iranian Christians' involvement in and support of the Tudeh Party to factors of class and geography, Abrahamian demonstrates statistically how urban Armenian and Assyrian workers such as shoemakers, carpenters, tailors, truck drivers, and mechanics as well as middle-class professionals and clerks were involved at all levels of the Tudeh in numbers disproportionate to their percentages within the Iranian population as a whole.[66]

Armenian and Assyrian support for Communist parties came from rural peasants and the commercial middle class as well as from intellectuals and the urban working class. Abrahamian notes that the Armenian merchants and retailers of the Hnchak Party were closely affiliated with the Tudeh and the Soviets, and the predominantly Christian guilds of pharmacists and food sellers joined the CCFTU. Outside of urban areas, in regions with a high concentration of Christians such as Urmia, rural Assyrian and Armenian peasants embraced the Soviets and the Tudeh, expelling Iranian landlords, officials, and gendarmes shortly after the occupation and setting up independent village councils.[67] In 1945, Armenian and Assyrian peasants were active volunteers in the revolt against the Iranian government, comprising in one engagement near Urmiah forty-one of fifty-five rebels killed.[68] Abrahamian speculates that in addition to these factors of class and geography, the Tudeh appealed to Iranian Christians because it was the only political party to champion their causes, such as the reopening of Armenian schools, the establishment of Assyrian schools, and the addition of a seat for an Assyrian deputy in the Majles.[69] In contrast to the now underground Dashnaksutiun, whose reputation was damaged after Reza Shah turned against linguistic minorities and closed their schools after 1938, the Tudeh was not connected with the Pahlavi regime.[70] Furthermore, the Tudeh was the one movement offering full citizenship and true equality between Christians and Muslims.[71]

In August 1945, the Tudeh Party seized Iranian government buildings in Tabriz and issued a statement calling for the cultural and administrative autonomy of Azerbaijan as well as the right of Iranian Azerbaijanis to speak their native Azeri language. Soviet troops countered any defensive efforts by the small number of Iranian soldiers stationed in the region, blocked a contingent sent from Tehran, and cut telegraph communications between Tabriz and the capital.[72] Although the Iranian government was able to regain control of the buildings seized in September, by October new Red Army contingents were entering Iran. The dispute between Iran and the Soviet Union over Iranian Azerbaijan would initiate the first Cold War political crisis in 1946–47 and in April 1947 would fall under the scope of the Truman Doctrine. Military aid followed in 1948, and thereafter the United States increasingly became a major player in Iranian politics and foreign policy.[73]

Whatever the reasons for some Armenians' gravitation to the Tudeh Party and the global implications of the Azerbaijan Crisis, Sevak Saginian's experience in the Iranian army was disconcerting and offensive because his loyalty had been questioned simply because he was of Armenian descent.[74] Nevertheless, Sevak had options outside the military. Having been a successful student, athlete, translator, and social organizer before he entered the army, he decided that instead of pursuing a career as an officer, he would go to law school and begin a legal practice in Tehran.

While in law school at Tehran University in 1946, Sevak quickly reconnected with his athletic and intellectually oriented friends, including some who were original members of the teen bicycle vigilantes and boxing club and others who became friends and acquaintances following high school. Soon the group, heretofore unnamed and unorganized, was so large that a permit was required for its gatherings.[75] Sevak Saginian successfully applied to the Ministry of Education for a permit, which was put in his name. He also became a permanent member of the board of directors, which initially consisted of one woman and eight men.[76] The official name chosen for the group, which was required for the permit, was Anjoman-e Parvaresh-e Afkar-e Javanan-e Aramane in Persian, which translates as Organization for Fostering the Thoughts of Armenian Youth. Members soon began informally calling the group "Ararat" after the sacred mountain central to Armenian mythology, lore, religion, and nationalism.[77] The abbreviated name reflected the Armenian culture on which the club was intended to be focused; it was short, catchy, and easily recognizable. As an unintended bonus, the name was visually pleasing and easily identifiable when spelled in Persian.[78] The organization's first permanent meeting hall, rented between 1946 and 1950, was located on Khiabane Ghavam al-Saltaneh above a Persian-owned bakery producing *sangak* (flatbread).

In the early period of Ararat between 1946 and 1950, membership rose sharply as activities became better organized, and the loose-knit

35. Founding members of Ararat, 1946. Sevak Saginian at lower right. Unknown photographer. Courtesy of Sevak and Nella Saginian.

groupings of Armenian youth ranging in age from roughly ten to thirty years congealed around the activities of sports, theater, music, and literature. Intellectuals in the early days of Ararat were oriented primarily toward the political left, but at that time there was no semblance of unity on political ideologies or positions. Reading groups would meet and discuss various texts on politics, philosophy, art, history, and Armenian culture. An orchestra was created for the musically inclined, and classic plays such as Shakespeare's *Othello* were translated into Armenian and performed for parents and the community. Theater also included groups performing traditional Armenian dances and incorporated the skills of those interested in visual arts such as painting and set design. Sports-minded Ararat members practiced and competed with each other at soccer, boxing, weightlifting, and track and would compete in national Iranian competitions under the Ararat banner. In addition to these more standard forms of athletics, mountaineering and rock climbing became popular with many intrepid Ararat members, who found the Alborz Mountains, in particular Mount Damavand, to be a beautiful and challenging place to practice and develop their skills.

As permit holder for the Ararat organization, Sevak Saginian was responsible for obtaining gathering permits for all large group activities such as plays or large sports outings and competitions. He also acted as the primary intermediary between Ararat and the government, most commonly interacting with the Ministry of Physical Education.[79] In mediating between the Pahlavi government and Ararat, Sevak was increasingly required to utilize his knowledge of both entities as well as his linguistic skills and *ta'arof* (traditional Persian manners and etiquette) to smooth interactions and create a trusting relationship. For example, when it was decided to officially change the name of the organization to "Ararat" at the end of 1949, Sevak was asked in a meeting with officials of the Ministry of Physical Education to explain what the name meant.[80] Quick to understand the implications of this question, Sevak instantly replied that it was a mountain of religious importance to Christians because of the perception that it was the location of Noah's Ark. This was apparently an acceptable answer, for the ministry issued Anjoman-e Javanan-e Ararat its new permit in 1950.

36. Ararat board of directors and founding members, Tehran, 1950. Sevak Saginian at the front right, wearing army reserve uniform. Unknown photographer. Courtesy of Sevak and Nella Saginian.

Mountaineering proved to be a complex issue that also necessitated Sevak's quick thinking and personal judgment. Despite having quit the army in large part owing to his awareness of the Iranian government and military's paranoia regarding Armenians and communism, it was nevertheless a surprise to him when he was called to the Ministry of Physical Education to explain what groups of well-equipped Armenian Iranians were doing setting up encampments in the mountains and engaging in activities such as rappelling and rope-bridge building. The Ararat climbers' outings had apparently not gone unnoticed by the military, which had suggested that perhaps the Armenian youth were storing arms or training for a Communist insurrection of some kind or both. Sevak explained that they were simply hiking, rock climbing, and practicing outdoor skills—much like Pishahangi-ye Iran (Scouting of Iran), which had been founded under Reza Shah. Told that the Pishahangi-ye Iran had been declared illegal after Reza Shah's exile because its members were "against Islam," Sevak asserted that for Christians scouting was not against their religion and mentioned the fact that some Persian scouts were still organizing outings, only without uniforms. Despite this explanation, the Ministry of Physical Education revoked Sevak's request. Undeterred, Sevak tried another route; after rephrasing the discussion with the ministry and request for a permit in a personal letter to Mohammad Reza Shah, the ministry's decision was overridden, and Ararat was issued a permit for both mountaineering and scouting.

This interaction had the combined effect of allaying the government's fears about Ararat's camping and mountaineering activities and of paving the way for the development of Ararat boy and girl scouts, who would take their first oath in 1952. It was also a lesson for Sevak in how to effectively deal with the government. He learned to try the standard routes to get things accomplished, but then, if unsuccessful, to appeal directly to the shah.

In 1950, Ararat's meeting site moved to Khiabane Yusefabad across from the Park Hotel. By 1954, membership swelled again and required an even bigger facility. Thus, Sevak applied for and received a permit allowing Ararat to move to a two-story building with an adjacent auditorium on Khiabane Noh Bahar. In this period, Ararat chapters were also founded in Isfahan and Tabriz.

Sevak became increasingly busy with his activities in Ararat while attending law school at Tehran University between 1946 and 1953. In this tumultuous period in Iranian history, the political system was free and vibrant, with the secular nationalist National Front and Communist Tudeh reaching their height of power and influence in Iran. The ascension of Mohammad Mossadegh to the position of prime minister and the oil nationalization crisis intensified the already strained relationship between royalist, secular-nationalist, Islamicist, and Communist political parties. Armenian Iranians were by no means a politically cohesive minority, with members in almost all Iranian political parties.

It was during this period that the politicization of Ararat occurred. Although in the 1940s Ararat members leaned to both the left and the right politically, the popularity of the Tudeh Party and the overt courting of the organization by the Tudeh and the Soviet embassy in 1948 and 1949 (both of which had sent the organization gifts and invitations to functions) alarmed Dashnak activists of Tehran, many of whom were either members of or parents of members of Ararat, such as Zohrab Saginian. As much a product of the loss of members to the popular Tudeh as pressure exerted on Ararat by the Dashnaks, by 1950 Ararat had become a bastion of Dashnak political ideology and anticommunism and had correspondingly developed a well-known although publicly denied reputation as such. Yet Ararat and the Dashnak Party were not synonymous. Aside from the unofficial Dashnak newspaper, *Alik,* to which many intellectually inclined Ararat members contributed, Dashnak Party literature and propaganda were never to be found on the premises of the clubhouse or utilized in any public Ararat function.[81] Ararat members who were also Dashnaks, such as Marzbet Marzbetuny, would privately engage in a number of activities ranging from discussion and analysis of contemporary political events vis-à-vis the Dashnak Party to fund-raising and gun running for the organization.[82] Although Iranian Dashnaks' gun-running activities peaked in the late nineteenth and early twentieth centuries when they were devoted to supporting Armenian defense brigades and volunteer militias in the Ottoman Empire as well as the Nationalist, anti-Royalist causes of the Constitutional Revolution, it became evident during the chaotic years of 1951–53 that these activities had continued underground throughout the 1940s.

Over the course of Prime Minister Mossadegh's tenure in office and the oil nationalization effort between 1951 and 1953, increasingly large and often violent street brawls were breaking out between pro- and antishah supporters. Seated squarely on the side of the shah and anticommunism, male Ararat members such as amateur boxer Sevak Saginian and some of the larger Ararat boy scouts, such as Nejde Hagobian and Artash Yerganian, were becoming regularly involved against the Tudeh.[83] In their view, it was already bad enough that Armenia was under a Communist system and Soviet rule. Thus, the potential bruises and puncture wounds associated with the street fights of the day were a small price to pay to protect their own country from being ruled by Communists and falling under the sway of the Soviet Union.[84] Although physical altercations with pro-Tudeh Iranians (who often included other Armenians) were not considered to be a threat to Ararat's standing with the government, Ararat's well-known Dashnak orientation made its members and property an obvious target for pro-Communists in Tehran and especially in Tabriz. There Ararat was almost as low profile as the underground Dashnak Party itself owing to threats made by pro-Tudeh and pro-Soviet agitators. Therefore, caches of Dashnak guns were opened and weapons distributed to trusted members in Tabriz and Tehran in anticipation of riots in which Armenian churches or the property of Dashnaks or Ararat members might be threatened.

On one particularly chaotic night of protests, street fights, and riots in July 1953, a rumor spread that pro-Communists were planning on ransacking and burning the Ararat club. When Sevak called the Tehran police to ask them to come to protect the club, he was told that the police had hundreds of similar calls from fearful property owners, and unless the club was actually attacked, Ararat would be a low priority. Seeing that the club's protection was in the hands of its members, Sevak contacted Marzbet Marzbetuny, who quickly showed up at the Ararat facility on Khiabane Yusefabad with an assortment of previously loaded rifles and handguns to distribute to Sevak, Nejde Hagobian, Artash Yerganian, and several other Ararat members. After spending the night in defensive positions taken up in small windows on the basement floor facing the street, awaiting an attack that never materialized, Saginian and Marzbetuny collected the guns and secreted them back to their hiding place.[85]

Although historical hindsight allows us to view the coup d'état of August 19, 1953, and the return of Mohammad Reza Pahlavi to dictatorial powers as events funded and to a large extent orchestrated by the US CIA,[86] at the time it was clear only that there were many conflicting rumors and conspiracy theories about what had transpired and that the shah was back in power. Almost immediately the restored Pahlavi regime initiated a purge that would eventually eliminate or drive underground those who had opposed the shah between 1951 and 1953, especially members of the Tudeh Party and the National Front.[87] Simultaneously, those who had openly supported the regime in protests and street fights were recognized and rewarded.

In mid-September 1953, Sevak Saginian and thirty other Iranian citizens known for their anti-Communist and anti-Mossadegh activities in the previous two years were invited to the Golestan Palace for a reception with the shah, where each was awarded a medal, the Neshan-e Rastakhiz-e Darje-ye Yek (Order of the Resurgence of the First Degree). During the reception, the shah, flanked by one of his top generals and a secretary, circulated around the room to speak individually to his guests. Many of them repeatedly kissed his hands or fell to kiss his feet or both, which Sevak noticed elicited a neutral reaction from the shah. Mohammad Reza Pahlavi would then thank each guest for their support and find out if they needed compensation for losses or injuries sustained in their encounters or the rioting. Sevak observed that all of the invitees seemed to have a story about property burned or a terrible beating they had sustained in a fight that made it impossible to work for weeks or months. The shah would respond that the guest would be duly compensated, the guest would thank him and kiss his hands or feet again, and the shah would move on to the next person.

By the time the shah reached Sevak, who was one of the final medal recipients he greeted, the routine had perhaps gotten old. As Sevak bowed his head in respect as the secretary introduced him, the shah said, "I suppose the Tudeh must have beaten you up pretty badly too." Sevak looked up and replied, "No, Your Majesty, they didn't beat us, we beat them."[88] The shah seemed amused with this unique response, mildly chuckled, and asked if Sevak would nevertheless like monetary compensation like the others. Sevak replied honestly, "I'd rather have a gun." This response again seemed to please and pique the interest of the shah, who told Sevak that it would be arranged and shook his hand before moving on to the last few guests.

A few days later a government courier delivered to Sevak a stunning polished and etched revolver in a wooden box with a permit signed by the shah allowing Sevak to possess and wear the gun in public, an almost unheard of liberty at the time in Iran for anyone not associated with the police or the military.[89] Like the other recipients of the Neshan-e Rastakhiz, Sevak also was provided with a small *hokm* (written edict) declaring the reasons for the awarding of the medal and containing Sevak's own photograph attached with an official seal. More than just an award, this document was copied and carried around as a sort of "secondary" identification to show officials and to lubricate the wheels of justice and bureaucracy in the years following Bist-o Hasht-e Mordad (Twenty-Eighth of Mordad [Coup]), as the events of August 19, 1953, became known in the collective Iranian memory.[90]

Although Sevak had recently finished his law degree and successfully passed the bar exam, in late 1953 he did not have enough money to open his own law firm as he had planned. He therefore applied for a position in the Point Four program in Tehran and was hired to work in the legal department. Sevak divided his time between work, Ararat, and his future wife, Nella. He also wrote articles for *Alik* newspaper and continued working as a translator between Armenian Church officials and the various Iranian government ministries.[91] Sevak continued his activities and oversight of Ararat, and on the Fourth of Aban (October 26, 1953) he proudly stood in the stands as the Ararat boy scouts and girl scouts led the annual parade for the shah's birthday (see chapter 1).

In November 1953, Sevak received a message requesting that he come to the office of General Abbas Izadpanah, who was at the time the head of the Ministry of Physical Education. Because Sevak was the permit holder and Ararat's chairman of the board, he correctly assumed the meeting had something to do with the organization's sports activities. First, Izadpanah inquired generally about the status of Ararat in Tehran and Tabriz, and Sevak explained to him that Ararat was well organized, yet much less public and bold in Tabriz owing to the overwhelming number of pro-Communist Tabrizis. After a few more questions about Ararat's activities and size, Izadpanah asked if Sevak would be willing to accompany himself and the shah to Tabriz as a representative from Ararat and the Tehrani recipients of the Rastakhiz medal. Izadpanah explained that the shah would be attending a concert, a sports exhibition, and a reception for Tabriz sports and youth organizations and asked if the Tabriz branch of Ararat was well enough organized to meet personally with the shah for a review and reception. Sevak replied that the group would be both honored and ready, and so immediately after the meeting with Izadpanah he contacted members of the Ararat branch in Tabriz to prepare the athletes to meet with the shah.[92]

The following week Sevak traveled with General Izadpanah, the shah, and his entourage to Tabriz; owing to the shah's other scheduled meetings and banquets, Sevak was given an extra day to further organize for the sports exhibition and reception. With solid preparation, Ararat's participation in the exhibition was impressive. At the reception following the sporting events, the shah asked Sevak to introduce him to the Ararat athletes and paid close attention as Sevak presented each of them.

Sevak answered the shah's numerous questions about the organization and its activities and continually demonstrated the utmost respect and deference toward the young king who was only three years his senior. The experience of personally traveling with the shah, being awarded the Neshan-e Rastakhiz, and receiving the trust that the gun permit implied significantly boosted Sevak's confidence, and he quickly became comfortable and relaxed in their interactions. To Sevak, this relaxation seemed to have a reciprocal effect in that the shah was increasingly kind and affectionate and soon came to treat him like a friend.[93]

Back in Tehran, Sevak was again contacted by Izadpanah, who told him that the shah had been very impressed by Ararat's showing at the exhibition as well as by Sevak's leadership skills. In their conversation, Izadpanah also asked Sevak if he had any connections or sway within the Assyrian community in Tabriz—which Sevak took to imply some sort of government position. Although he had none, Sevak emphasized his family's long history in Tabriz and vaguely said that he would see what

37. Sevak Saginian introduces Mohammad Reza Shah to Ararat athletes, Tabriz, 1953. Unknown photographer. Courtesy of Sevak and Nella Saginian.

he could arrange. Considering his growing leadership skills, legal education, family history, and now the establishment of a relationship with the Pahlavi regime, Sevak Saginian decided that, like his father Zohrab, he would run for office as Majles representative of the Armenians of northern Iran.

Having missed the elections for the Eighteenth Majles in 1953, Sevak had two full years to campaign throughout the northern part of the nation. The only problem was that he had more time on his hands than money. When the underground Dashnak body in Tehran learned that Sevak was planning to run for the Majles, they gave him their blessing, with the caveat that because he didn't have any money, he would probably lose the election. Still, they reasoned, he was relatively young, so should he lose the next election in 1956, he could always run in the following one or switch to try to represent the Armenians of the South, who—as it was

38. Sevak Saginian (*right*) marches with Ararat scouts to the Fourth of Aban parade, 1955. Unknown photographer. Courtesy of Sevak and Nella Saginian.

explained to him—were generally worse off than the Armenian Iranians in the North and needed a representative well connected in the capital and to the regime.

Sevak was determined to win the 1956 election for the North. This would be an important election because for the first time Majles appointments were being extended to four years from two. In the summer of 1955, after marrying Nella in a huge wedding attended by hundreds of Ararat members at Tehran's Armenian Surb Astvatsatsin Church, Sevak set off on a three-month tour of the cities of Iranian Azerbaijan to campaign for the Majles.

Sevak met with Armenians and Assyrians in Tabriz, Salmas, Shapour, Marageh, and Rezayeh to hear about their problems and tell them what he thought could be accomplished in Parliament. Here Sevak's family history was important. Many Armenians and Assyrians remembered his father and other ancestors who had assisted Christian minorities in the region, so they pledged their support. Sevak did not, however, win over everyone. The Assyrian community was itself divided in opinion, and in several meetings his potential Assyrian constituents began energetically arguing between one another in Azeri or Assyrian, two languages Sevak did not speak, and so leaving him out of the dialog entirely. Moreover, the mayor

39. Sevak and Nella Saginian pass Ararat girl scouts at their wedding. Tehran, 1955. Unknown photographer. Courtesy of Sevak and Nella Saginian.

of Rezayeh explicitly told Sevak not to run, but without expressing why, and the governor of Azerbaijan suggested that Sevak's young age and lack of money would surely doom his campaign and that he should renounce his candidacy and go back to Tehran.[94]

Although Sevak's low-budget campaign could not compare to the high-priced entertainment and gifts his wealthier opponent was offering, the Christians of Azerbaijan appeared to be supportive. Perhaps most importantly, the shah of Iran liked and trusted him. It is certainly possible that Sevak Saginian could have won his Majles seat based on the votes cast by individual Iranian Christians in the North, but the facts of the regime's strict control of the election in 1956 indicate that their votes were irrelevant. Most probably the representative for the Nineteenth Majles could be said to have won his seat in November 1953 following the shah's trip to Tabriz and introduction to Ararat members by Sevak Saginian. Whatever the results of the voting, Sevak Saginian was elected to the Nineteenth Majles in 1956.[95]

In 1956, Sevak Saginian began what would be a twenty-two-year career as a member of the Iranian Majles, representing the Armenians of the North for his first four-year term in the Nineteenth Majles (1956–60) and the Armenians of the South for the other five terms.[96] After the shah's opening speech to the Nineteenth Majles in which he outlined what he would like to see the assembly accomplish in its term, Sevak began a weekly schedule that would fluctuate little in his long tenure. He and his fellow Majles members worked six days a week. For the most part, three of those days were focused around meetings of the entire assembly that lasted from 9:00 a.m. to 1:00 p.m., while the other three days of the week would be dedicated to smaller committee meetings and hearings. No work was performed on Fridays. Because Majles members were not granted offices, work and meetings would often take place at home. Although each of the Majles members was provided with a cabinet to store their personal documents and effects—and were told that each possessed the only key—the deputies would routinely keep their files at home for convenience and privacy.[97]

One of the youngest Majles deputies at age thirty-four, Sevak quickly learned how to interact in the assembly and conduct himself around his older and more experienced fellow deputies. Moreover, Sevak soon made several general observations about how the Majles functioned and, after confirming them with his father Zohrab, formulated pragmatic strategies to approach working in the interests of his Armenian Iranian constituents.

Sevak understood from past Iranian history and his father's experiences that there was an inverse relationship between the shah's power and that of the Majles. Basically, the Majles had been created to limit the power of the shahs. Yet when the shah was strong, such as between 1925 and 1941, the Majles was weak and became his ceremonial rubber stamp. Thus, when in a position of strength, the shah had the elections rigged as he saw fit, and Majles members had no option but to cast their votes for proposed legislation according to the shah's wishes. When the shah was weak, such as during the period between 1941 and 1953, Sevak observed that the Majles and the prime minister were the country's primary political leaders and could exert their will over that of the shah. Individual Majles members were then free to vote their conscience and speak their mind in the assembly. A case in point was that his father, Zohrab, was able in 1942 to complain vocally and in writing that the Armenian schools had been closed down illegally by Reza Shah but was forced to remain silent about the same issue in the three-year period in between the time the schools were closed and Reza Shah was forced to abdicate the throne (1938–41). In 1942, the young successor Mohammad Reza Shah was much too weak to do anything about the dramatic upsurge in political freedoms and demands and had to choose his battles wisely if he chose to engage at all. However, after the coup of August 1953 the shah's power rose quickly, and by 1955 it was clear that Mohammad Reza Pahlavi was becoming the nation's sole power and a true dictator like his father. Supported by the CIA and Mossad-trained Iranian secret police, the Sazeman-e Ettela'at va Amniyat-e Keshvar (SAVAK, Organization of Intelligence and National Security) and bolstered by increasingly large offers of financial aid and arms from the United States to strengthen his military, the shah was arguably at his peak of power over Iranian politics, economy, and society during Sevak's entire tenure as Parliament member. Although he could not have predicted such a long streak of power by the shah when he was becoming acclimated to the Majles in 1956, Sevak realized that, at least for the time being, he would have to make the system work for his constituents in whatever way he could.

In assembly legislation or in votes about national issues such as the economy, education, foreign policy, and the selection of the prime minister, there was basically no choice in how the Majles would vote, and this was an unspoken but unanimously recognized fact. Unofficial go-betweens referred to as "representatives of the court" or even "friends of the Shah" (*rofagha-ye Shah*) would circulate among the Majles members and would make "recommendations" that would inform everyone what the shah's wishes were. Although there was some leeway in assembly speeches in terms of Majles members' ability to engage in light criticism or concerns about a particular piece of legislation, there were never any surprises when the votes were finally tallied: the shah's will would inevitably prevail.[98]

In regards to proposed legislation, a Majles member had two routes. One was to try to individually motivate other Majles members to vote for a bill by delivering speeches outlining the plan(s) and meeting with other deputies to try to gain their support. If the member's bill or expenditure proposal gained enough votes, a general vote would be advanced to the Majles, and it would become active as law. This was a time-consuming

40. Sevak Saginian with Empress Farah and Mohammad Reza Pahlavi, 1968. Unknown photographer. Courtesy of Sevak and Nella Saginian.

and risky process, however, both owing to the fact that the shah pulled the strings. First, it was time-consuming because beyond selling the other Majles members on a proposal, one would also have to somehow assure them that this proposal would please or at least be in line with the shah's wishes. It was possible, but not easy. Second, it was risky because should the shah disapprove of a proposal, it might harm an established personal relationship with him, which was one sure way to be ignored in the assembly and "voted" out of office.

The second route Sevak saw as a path to getting things accomplished in the Majles for his constituents was through his personal relationship with the shah, which was predicated on trust and loyalty. Since their first encounter in 1953, Sevak had felt comfortable around the shah and as a Majles member had never had difficulty obtaining appointments to see him to talk about Sevak's own proposals or problems administering the northern Armenian Iranian community.[99] Although Sevak chose his issues and meetings wisely and sparingly, he was never denied access to or rebuked by the shah, who was responsive to his requests and supportive of his suggested legislation regarding the Armenian Iranian community.[100] Sevak quickly realized that this direct route to the fundamental source of power in Iran was by far the safer and most effective of the two. Thus, although he cultivated close relationships and alliances within the Majles that would be beneficial in his proposals for education, committee work, and disputes between different regions and constituencies, his primary concern was to remain a loyal supporter and friend of the shah so that any challenges he or his constituents might face in the Majles or one of the ministries would be manageable.

Two issues predominated in Sevak's first four years while serving as northern Armenian Majles representative: solidifying the position of Armenian education in the country, which had flourished since the ouster of Reza Shah but still lacked official sanction and support, and keeping Armenian Iranian organizations and culture strong and distinctive.[101] Although Armenian schools had been reopened in 1942, since their closure in 1938 they had not received full certification from the Ministry of Education, and the status of some school properties was still unsure. Working with the Ministry of Education, Sevak was able to negotiate an agreement in 1957 whereby Armenian schools were fully accredited and Armenian language and history could be taught, provided that they be offered as "electives" that did not count toward a student's grade point average and that the school taught other subjects such as math, science, and Iranian history in Persian to prepare the students for the national exams. To solidify the position of Armenian school properties, Sevak mediated between the Armenian and Iranian property owners and the Armenian Church diocese in Tabriz and Tehran to have the properties deeded to the church in perpetuity.[102]

Between 1956 and 1960, Sevak Saginian also worked to maintain the independence of the Ararat boy scouts and girl scouts against a concerted effort by the Ministry of Sports to integrate them fully into Pishahangi-ye Iran. As well as continuing to act as permit holder and board chairperson of the then seven-hundred-member Ararat, Sevak was also the honorary scoutmaster of the Ararat scouts. In their fourth year in 1956, the scouts had grown to well more than two hundred in number, with branches in Tehran and Tabriz, and had been a model for Mohammad Reza's reinstitution of Pishahangi-ye Iran in 1954[103] after a thirteen-year interregnum

41. Sevak Saginian (*second row, second from right*) with Armenian community leaders and bishops of Isfahan, 1966. Unknown photographer. Courtesy of Sevak and Nella Saginian.

following protests by the ulama and conservative members of the Majles after the exile of Reza Shah in 1941. By 1956, the Ministry of Physical Education under Dr. Hossein Banai was pressing for the full integration of the Hay Ari (Armenian Scouts) into Pishahangi-ye Iran, which was being reconstituted across the nation. Banai sought to subsume Ararat under the banner "Yek Mellat Yek Pishahangi" (One Nation, One Scouting Organization). Determined to keep the Ararat scouts independent of the national organization, Sevak adopted the countermotto "Yek Mellat Doh Pishahangi" (One Nation, Two Scouting Organizations), and he did everything in his power to thwart Dr. Banai's efforts.

When Dr. Banai suggested in 1958 that the Ararat scouts become a numbered division of Pishahangi and adopt Persian script in lieu of Armenian on uniforms and badges, Sevak argued effectively that Ararat and its scouts were funded entirely by member dues and should be under its own name. Furthermore, Sevak argued that Ararat would not abandon its girl scout program and mixed functions, which made it incompatible with the all-male Pishahangi-ye Iran. On these issues, compromises were reached whereby Ararat scouts would be considered a troop of Pishahangi-ye Iran but would keep its distinctive name. Banai was adamant about the removal of the Armenian uniform script, so it was thereafter changed to Persian, but many of the awards and badges continued to contain Armenian characters: the name "Pishahangi-ye Iran" appeared along with "Hay Ari" (Armenian Scouts) in Persian. The position of the Ararat girl scouting program was also assured.[104]

For the shah's Fourth of Aban birthday celebration parade in October 1960, Ararat scouts and athletes marched once again at the head of the parade as they had since 1952 and were initially announced under the organization's name, "Ararat." In all previous exhibitions of their skills at the Fourth of Aban event, such as marching and erecting rope and wood bridges or assorted fortifications, the scouts had always been introduced as "Pishahangan-e Ararat" or "Pishahangan-e Aramane" (Armenian Scouts). However, during the scouting skills exhibition in 1960, in which Ararat boy scouts competed against other troops of Iranian scouts in a bridge-building contest,[105] Banai described the Armenian scouts over the public-address system only as Pishahangan-e Iran. Sevak Saginian was furious and decided he would demand in any future events that Banai introduce the Ararat scouts as such.

At the end of October 1960, the shah's first son, Crown Prince Reza Pahlavi, was born, and the Ministry of Sports soon held another sports and scouting exhibition at Amjadieh Stadium to honor him. Because Sevak knew the Ararat scouts would be engaging in a similar competition with Pishahangan-e Iran at this event, he approached Banai and insisted that he use the name "Ararat" when introducing the Armenian scouts in the competition, for that was what they had agreed on in their past negotiations. Because Banai responded neutrally to his demand, Sevak took steps to assure that the Ararat scouts would be introduced by name at the event: he told the scouts that in the competition they were to remain in line at attention and not to begin building their bridge until they heard the name "Ararat" over the loudspeaker.

Sevak was in the stands a few rows away from Banai and the shah when Banai began announcing the event. As expected, Banai announced that "Pishahangan-e Iran" was now going to conduct a skills exhibition, waited for the scouts to take their places behind the starting line, and then stated, "Amadeh! Pish!" (Ready! Begin!). Immediately, the two other troops competing ran to their piles of materials to begin assembling their structures, but the Ararat scouts remained in their places. Banai immediately bellowed again, "Amadeh! Pish!" The Ararat scouts stood still. After an uncomfortable eternity, or what in reality was perhaps only ten to fifteen seconds, Banai yelled in the same tone, "Pishahangan-e Ararat, amadeh! pish!" and with that the Ararat scouts immediately ran to their pile and began their construction. To add insult to Banai's injury, the Ararat scouts won the competition despite their fifteen-second disadvantage. This would be the last time the name would be contested. Thereafter, Banai used the name "Ararat" consistently when addressing the Armenian scouts.

In the Twentieth Majles elections of 1960, Sevak Saginian won the position of Armenian deputy from the South, a position he held for the next eighteen years.[106] In this position, he concentrated his efforts on further expanding Armenian education on both a local level and a national level, obtaining state funding for the rebuilding of Armenian churches in

42. Ararat scouts in construction competition, Amjadieh Stadium, Tehran, c. 1958. Unknown photographer. Courtesy of Sevak and Nella Saginian.

cities and rural areas throughout the South, and working to develop the infrastructure of rural Armenian villages in the region of Isfahan.

The expansion of Armenian education in Iranian universities was Sevak's toughest challenge, and after the solidification of the legal status of Armenian schools between 1956 and 1960, it was the most important for Armenian education at all levels. To provide the schools with top-notch instructors of Armenian history and language as well as qualified administrators and principals, it was necessary to develop degree programs in Armenian studies at Iranian universities. Sevak set his sights high, proposing at the beginning of the Twenty-First Majles (1964–68) to establish an Armenian studies chair at the University of Tehran and a program offering masters degrees and PhDs in the subject. To accomplish this goal, he utilized Majles procedures as well as his personal relationship with the shah.

After receiving the full support of the northern Armenian representative, Felix Aghayan, Sevak drafted a letter outlining for the Majles's Education Committee the plans for the Armenian studies program and a proposed budget. Before attending the committee meeting in which it was to be voted on whether the initial proposal was worthy to pursue in full assembly, Sevak visited each of the committee members privately to try to obtain their support, explaining the proposal in detail and attempting to respond to any criticism of its feasibility, intent, or budget. Once he obtained a passing vote in the committee, the next step was a vote on the Majles floor, which was scheduled a few months in advance. In between the committee meeting and the time the Majles voted on the proposal, Sevak Saginian and Felix Aghayan made an appointment to visit the shah and explain the proposal to him. In their meeting, Sevak emphasized the fact that Iranian universities taught several foreign languages and that this request should be considered in that context. The shah told the two deputies that he did not see anything wrong with the request to extend Armenian studies to the university level and said he would have the *vazir-e darbar* (minister of the court) inform the *nakhost vaziri* (prime minister) of his support for the proposal. Accordingly, when the vote came up in the Majles assembly a few weeks later, it was approved almost unanimously.[107]

Although the decision had thus been made to establish and fund the Armenian studies program in 1965, by late 1966 the University of Tehran had not done anything in the way of establishing it. When Sevak inquired as to why the university was apparently stalling in initiating the program, he was told budget issues were prohibiting the initiation of the chair and degree programs. He indirectly learned that the underlying issue was the fact that members of the Ministry of Education were concerned about national security and were opposed to anything that might feed student radicalism at the University of Tehran, the site of numerous demonstrations in the early 1960s. Because many in the government perceived Armenians as activist in nature or as on the left in the political spectrum or both, the ministry feared that the Armenian studies program would be a magnet for student protestors.

Whether this logic was accurate or not, Sevak's inquiry led to the Ministry of Education declaring that there was no space at the University of Tehran for the Armenian studies program and that a master's degree program would be established at the University of Isfahan. Although Felix Aghayan, deputy from the North, and the Armenian Church bishop of the Tehran diocese were vocal in their complaints about the ministry's unilateral decision to change the proposal, Sevak was less adamant, figuring that an excellent program in Isfahan (his own district) could be used as a model for a future PhD program at the University of Tehran. The only problem remaining, he thought, was to find properly certified instructors. Although there were many Armenian Iranian scholars worthy of teaching the courses, none had graduate degrees in Armenian studies, which would have required study abroad. An instructor without proper credentials would be allowed to teach, but the Ministry of Education would pay only a salary far too low to obtain an excellent instructor. Although local Armenian benefactors had made significant donations to support the new chair, enabling the instructors to receive supplemental pay, Sevak's interest was in establishing it officially and in perpetuity as a government-sponsored program; he thus wanted the first instructors to receive full compensation from the start.

To obtain the first qualified instructors for the program, Sevak finally turned to the Armenian community of Lebanon for assistance. He flew to Beirut to meet with the Armenian Catholicos (the chief bishop and head of the Armenian Church), who referred him to two younger members of the Beirut clergy who were more than qualified for the positions and willing to move to Isfahan to teach. Yet Sevak discovered that they too lacked higher degrees in Armenian studies and thus would also be denied a proper salary by the Iranian Ministry of Education.[108] He had come too far and worked too long to let this issue slow the establishment of the program any longer and soon realized the answer to the problem. Before returning to Iran, he purchased spurious diplomas in Armenian studies and teaching credentials for each of the two clergy members. When they showed up in Isfahan to teach, the Lebanese clergymen received the full teaching salary accorded to other new instructors, which was supplemented further by the previous donations made by the Armenian Iranian community.

The final, unforeseen hurdle Sevak Saginian and the Isfahan Armenian studies program faced was the lack of students interested in the program in its first year. Most Armenian Iranian college students at the time were pursuing degrees in subjects such as medicine, engineering, business, and law. Armenian studies was a subject that did not seem to offer a well-paying, prestigious future. As such, in the first year of instruction there were only a few students in the program. Through announcements and flyers at Ararat gatherings and other Armenian Iranian public functions, Sevak stressed the applicability of the master's degree to practical careers such as the teaching of history and language, school administration, translation, and PhDs in linguistics. Through these efforts and word of mouth, the program became better attended the following year, and by 1968 it was full. Finally, after four years of instruction at the University of Isfahan, in 1971 a PhD program was established at the University of Tehran with qualified Armenian Iranian instructors, requiring only that potential PhD students first obtain their master's degree from the University of Isfahan. Through his efforts with Felix Aghayan in the Majles, relationship with the shah, networking of Armenian Iranian community leaders, and successful navigation through every imaginable channel, Sevak Saginian was able to firmly establish Armenian studies at two of Iran's finest secular institutions of higher learning. It was an achievement that gave him great satisfaction and pride.

In 1970, Sevak was successful in obtaining funding through the Majles to restore rural Armenian churches throughout the nation, many of which, along with their small classrooms, had fallen into a state of decay. As a result of his observations and interactions with local villagers, during the Twenty-Second and Twenty-Third Majles he focused his attention on bettering the lives of Armenian Iranian agriculturalists in the rural regions surrounding Isfahan. Helping small farmers obtain more land to cultivate while obtaining funding to expand irrigation in their districts, Sevak encouraged them to put their land to maximal use and diversify their crops beyond the standard wheat and barley. Two villages in particular were in dismal shape, Namagerd and Khoygan, neither of which had piped water or electricity. In the Majles, Sevak received funding to bring water mains and electricity to both villages as well as funding to expand farm irrigation in the region. Construction began in 1973.[109]

As southern Majles representative for the Armenians, Sevak usually focused on large-scale issues such as the community's education, infrastructure, and economy. The Armenian Church diocese in Isfahan generally had jurisdiction over domestic matters such as divorce, disputes, and the administration of estates.[110] The church's decisions in these matters were considered binding, even where the decision differed from Iranian laws.[111] The Armenian Community Council was in charge of church upkeep, community welfare, and health issues.[112] Occasionally, however, circumstances emerged that required Sevak's mediation and sway at higher levels of government.

One such circumstance occurred in Abadan, when an Arab-speaking Iranian taxicab driver picked up an Armenian Iranian nurse who was returning home from a house call.[113] Her body was found the next day, and the evidence suggested attempted rape, yet the local police seemingly did nothing to try to apprehend the cab driver and question him. Upon hearing the details from the woman's family and questioning the Abadan police, who were within Sevak's geographical sphere of responsibility as Majles representative for the South, Sevak determined that little was being done to solve the crime and that he needed to take the issue to Majles. In Tehran, he subpoenaed the minister of justice to answer questions about the conduct of the case by the Abadan police and was rebuked for three reasons. He was told, first, that Majles members did not have the individual right to subpoena anyone; second, that he was out of his jurisdiction; and, third, that he was a religious minority! Sevak immediately issued a complaint outlining the issues to the Speaker of the House, who concurred with him and asked that the matter be discussed before a larger, special committee of deputies.

As Sevak was busy preparing his questions for the upcoming session regarding the Abadan investigation, the minister of justice stopped him in the hall of the Majles building. After a bit of small talk, the minister casually informed Sevak that the previous day an Armenian Iranian man had killed a popular Isfahani *pahlavan* (athlete) in a street fight and was claiming self-defense. The minister of justice was somber as he explained that the *pahlavan*'s family wanted the death penalty and that it would be hard for the judges to rule otherwise. Then he immediately changed subject and brought up the case of the Armenian nurse, reasoning that unfortunately there was nothing that could be done for her, but that perhaps there was a way to save the life of the young Armenian man. Sevak instantly knew what the minister was suggesting. The fact was that neither of them wanted to go before the Majles special session to get into these issues, and Sevak knew that the minister of justice basically held the Armenian youth's fate in his hands—whether he was guilty of the alleged crime or not. If Sevak persisted in having the minister appear before the special committee, the Armenian suspect was going to suffer for it. Together the two went to the House Speaker and privately told him that the issue was to be dropped. Instantly inferring that some sort of deal had been negotiated rather than asking the deputy and the minister to explain their reasoning, the Speaker chuckled and said, "You see? You can get more accomplished in the outside halls of this place than inside!" Sevak did not disagree with this accurate observation but dwelled on what he perceived to be the real justice denied the Armenian nurse, the Armenian street fighter, as well as the Isfahani *pahlavan* when a few days later the Abadan police dropped whatever case they had developed on the Arab Iranian cab driver, and the Armenian Iranian was speedily acquitted. Sevak later requested the report and read that the matter of the *pahlavan*'s death was dropped in the preliminary hearing as a clear-cut issue of "defense of honor."[114]

Outside of his work as Majles representative during the 1960s and 1970s, Sevak Saginian continued to act as chairperson and permit holder for Ararat and worked to expand the organization in Iran's southern cities. Although membership had dropped to around 300 in 1960–61, by 1968 Ararat membership had grown to 1,700 nationwide, with the largest branches in Tehran, Tabriz, and Isfahan. The scouting and athletic programs continued to flourish, and Ararat music and theater groups put on increasingly complex and large-scale plays and concerts. Outside of his family, which by 1972 had grown to include four children, Ararat was one of the primary joys in Sevak's life. It was also the center of his social world, and he did whatever he could to promote it.

In Sevak's view, his activities as Iranian Majles representative and as Ararat leader were compatible because he viewed Ararat as a vehicle for sustaining Armenian national and cultural identity as well as Iranian nationalism.[115] By supporting its activities and regional expansion and showcasing the organization in national events, the government enabled Sevak Saginian and many Ararat members to develop a feeling of inclusion in Iranian society and a love of and patriotism for Iran that was not in conflict with their Armenian identity. The state's recognition of their Armenian heritage and language and of their legal status as equal

43. Sevak Saginian leading Ararat members in the Fourth of Aban parade, Amjadieh Stadium, Tehran, 1968. Unknown photographer. Courtesy of Sevak and Nella Saginian.

members of society facilitated rather than hindered their acquisition of a compound national identity.[116]

In 1972, Sevak was invited to a ceremonial *dast-busi* (hand kissing), a reception in which the shah would usually distribute gifts and favors to the invited elites, who at this particular event included other Majles deputies, various ministers, and members of the shah's family. At that event, Sevak informed the shah of Ararat's attempts to obtain funding to build a complex on Armenian Church–owned land in the Tehran suburb of Vanak.[117] Although Ararat members and Armenian Iranian elites had donated money to build the complex, the donations were not nearly enough to cover the building costs for what was planned. Sevak, not imagining that the shah's contribution to the project would be as vast as it turned out to be, was overjoyed to learn that the shah decided to build Ararat its own state-of-the-art sports arena to seat ten thousand, with adjacent facilities that included an auditorium, meeting halls, and several smaller classrooms. The site was blessed by an Armenian priest, and ground was broken in May 1973. The Tehran branch of Ararat moved from its home on Khiabane Noh Bahar to the complex when it was completed in 1974.[118]

In 1976, Sevak Saginian was elected to the Twenty-Fourth Majles, which was scheduled to last until 1980. However, his plans for that session, which included more village electrification projects in the South, were cut short. In 1978, popular uprisings against the repressive Pahlavi regime took center stage as the events of the Iranian Revolution unfolded. Although some intellectuals and socialist-minded Armenians took part in the movement, Armenian Iranians were for the most part ambivalent about participating in it.[119] In spite of the political repression they had suffered along with their fellow Iranians, many were conflicted about whether to speak out against a regime that had treated them relatively well. As an easily recognizable religious minority, and with no way to predict the future, they feared retribution by both the Pahlavi regime and the powerful forces for Islamic revolution should they become involved on either side. As a result of their trepidation, the vast majority of Armenian Iranians sat on the fence in 1978 and nervously watched as events seemed to spin out of control.

In early December 1978, Bishop Ardak Manoukian called Sevak and requested that he come to the Surb Astvatsatsin Church to speak to members of Tehran's Armenian community about the growing unrest.[120] Sevak gave a speech in which he expressed his confidence that Armenians in Iran would be left alone no matter what the outcome of the political struggle and urged the group not to worry. Sevak knew, however, that in the event that the movement to establish an Islamic republic was successful, his own ties to the Pahlavi regime were too strong to allow him to stay and feel that he and his family would be safe from arrest or retribution.

Sevak's perception of the situation was confirmed when he immediately began receiving telephone death threats after the Majles verified the shah's nomination of Shapour Bakhtiar as prime minister on December 30, 1978. The callers stated that the Majles had not been elected under Islamic law and that Sevak and his fellow deputies had forty-eight hours to resign or face eventual execution.[121] In spite of these credible threats,

Sevak stayed on for the single month of Bakhtiar's provisional government, in which Bakhtiar gave several speeches to the Majles explaining that there would be no power-sharing agreement with Ayatollah Ruhollah Khomeini, who had appointed Mehdi Bazargan as the prime minister of the Islamic Republic. Although in his thirty-seven days in power as prime minister Bakhtiar ordered the freeing of thousands of political prisoners, the reopening of the Iranian press, and the disbanding of SAVAK, it was much too little, much too late. On February 11, 1979, the same day Bakhtiar fled Iran, Sevak also boarded a jet with his family, leaving his career, Ararat, his possessions, and his country behind.[122]

5

Lucik Moradiance

THE LOCOMOTIVE strained to gather momentum and began to pull out of Tehran's central train station as the group of recent college graduates bid good-bye to family and friends, waving to them from the station platform. Three young women and their fifteen male colleagues, all selected for on-site internships at the Abadan refinery in the summer of 1954, settled in for their twenty-four-hour journey. For Lucik Moradiance, a twenty-three-year-old chemical engineering graduate, it was the first time she had traversed the length of the country along the route of the Trans-Iranian Railway, and she was amazed to see the major infrastructural construction that enabled transportation of people and goods from north to south.[1] Completed in 1938 with primarily German technical assistance, the railroad was a remarkable engineering feat and quickly supplanted buses and trucks as the primary means by which people and goods were shuttled between the Persian Gulf and the nation's capital. Marveling at the bridges, tunnels, and complex passages while traveling to her internship at a petroleum facility, Lucik could hardly have imagined that she would soon be applying her scientific knowledge at the core of the nation's infrastructural development projects, engaging in technical work and research that only a decade earlier had been predominantly the domain of foreigners and the exclusive domain of men.

While comfortably relaxing in their sleeping cars and taking in the view as the train rolled southwest through the Zagros Mountains, passengers became aware of their entrance into Khuzestan Province as the terrain flattened, date palms proliferated, and the air thickened with humidity. In Khorramshahr, the interns and other Abadan-bound passengers left the

44. Lucik Moradiance (*far left*) and fellow engineering students Hirair Maroukian, Genoush Hovanessian, and Nazik Sarkissian depart from Tehran, 1954. Unknown photographer. Courtesy of Lucik Moradiance-Melikian.

train and boarded a bus, and soon the unmistakable sight of giant, aboveground storage tanks and smokestacks as well as the now-enveloping sulfurous smell signaled that they had reached their destination.

At first sight, the enormity of Abadan was stunning. In 1954, the Abadan oil complex was still the largest in the world and occupied a roughly ten-square-mile island mudflat along the Arvand Rud (Shatt al-Arab in Arabic), where the Tigris and Euphrates Rivers join together before exiting at the head of the Persian Gulf. Established as the Anglo-Persian Oil Company in 1909 when the local population numbered in the hundreds, by the mid-1930s the complex had become the world's largest crude-oil-refining facility, employing laborers from throughout the nation, who were managed by British expatriates and technical staff.[2] The name was changed to the Anglo-Iranian Oil Company (AIOC) in 1935 to conform with Reza Shah's decree that the country be referred to as "Iran," not "Persia," and then was changed again to the National Iranian Oil Company (NIOC) after the nationalization of the Iranian oil industry and AIOC facilities in May 1951. Manucher Farmanfarmaian—a young petroleum engineering graduate who would later become the head of NIOC and play a major role in the establishment of the Organization of Petroleum Exporting Countries—provides a vivid description of his own first visit to Abadan in 1941:

> The refinery was awe inspiring. It was the biggest in the world and was shipping 300,000 barrels a day. Laid out in a huge set of interlocking grids along the coast, it sprang from the earth in a plethora of smokestacks and piping. Gas burned off in towering flames like torches to Zoroaster. I breathed in the heavy smell of sulfur and kerosene and felt transported. The great holding tanks looked like bastion towers plucked from the walls of citadels and placed into perfect rows along the quay. The heat from their metallic sides shivered in the air, turning the whole vast, smoking, spitting complex into a wavering mirage.[3]

Farmanfarmaian also describes Abadan in 1941 as "a slice of Britain. It was on Iranian soil, but it was English to the core." He lamented, "Even in my own country, Abadan would make me second class."[4] Although all British AIOC employees had been ejected from the facility during the oil nationalization effort and subsequent global boycott of Iranian oil (1951–53), Lucik's internship in 1954 coincided with the return of some British personnel and increasing numbers of American technicians, contractors, and consultants.[5]

For anyone but the local Khuzestani population, who are primarily Arabic-speaking Shi'ites, summer in Abadan is an unforgettably hot and muggy ordeal, and the majority of workers at the refinery—including Lucik and her fellow interns—were not locals. In July and August, the temperature averaged higher than 110 degrees Fahrenheit and often exceeded 120, making work in the late morning through late afternoon torturous. The facility's machinery and piping further stoked the cauldron.[6]

By 1954, most laboratories and offices as well as housing for management, technical staff, and interns had become generally more tolerable, primarily owing to upgrades completed by the AIOC before nationalization. Laboratories and offices featured stand-alone air-conditioning units, and housing units in the former AIOC "company town" of Braim—which had been off limits to Iranians before 1951 but was now inhabited by mixed Iranian and foreign personnel—were supplied with air conditioning, electric coolers, fans, or a combination of the three. Management and staff could also retreat to the "Annex" cafeteria and lounge, another formerly exclusive AIOC facility that was perhaps frequented more for its powerful centralized air-conditioning system than for its cuisine.

Lucik and each of her two fellow female interns were assigned to a spacious one-room apartment in Braim, each with a kitchenette; the three apartments were located side by side in a bungalow designated for single women. The fifteen male interns were given similar accommodations in a separate building, but each shared an apartment with another male intern. Although strictly segregated in living quarters, male and female interns had identical responsibilities and roles and worked alongside each other during their average eight- to ten-hour workdays. Serving on one of three consecutive eight-hour shifts that kept the facility running day and night, those interns and staff who were off in the slightly cooler morning hours ran the necessary errands for themselves and their roommates. Yet owing to the high humidity, even the early-morning heat outside was stifling, and one would perspire profusely to the point that eyeglasses would fog up from the inside. As Lucik walked in the door to her apartment from a dawn walk to buy groceries one morning soon after they had arrived, she startled and concerned her roommate, who took one look at her and demanded to know who had doused her with water. Despite relatively comfortable accommodations in Braim compared to those of the unelectrified Abadan workers' slum known as Kaghazabad (Paper City), the summer of 1954 would be the hottest Lucik would ever experience.

Although the Abadan refinery had been at the epicenter of the nationalization effort during the three years prior to Lucik Moradiance's arrival, as an intern she heard no discussion of those events or of the new American, British, and French consortium among workers, staff, or other interns.[7] Although unable to gauge the political climate in Abadan at that time, Lucik rather enjoyed this break from political turmoil—especially after the disturbing events she had witnessed in Tehran the previous winter—and she now vividly remembers her excitement at being exposed to so many new things on a daily basis as interns were kept to a rigid schedule as they worked throughout the site.

45. Interns, including Lucik Moradiance (*seventh from left*), set out on the Arvand Rud (also known as the Shatt al-Arab waterway) to tour offshore portions of the Abadan oil complex, 1954. Unknown photographer. Courtesy of Lucik Moradiance-Melikian.

Interns rotated to different stations around the refinery every two weeks as they learned about the various chemical processes undertaken in each distinct section of the facility and studied the workings of the mechanical components and hardware necessary to complete these processes. Receiving hands-on training during the day and poring over relevant technical manuals at night, Lucik learned the rudiments of crude-oil refining, catalytic cracking, bituminous material processing, and the function of specialized on-site laboratories. With virtually no nightlife or entertainment to distract or occupy one's off hours, and considering the forbidding summer heat outside, the three-month Abadan program offered interns the opportunity not only to focus on their training, but simultaneously to ponder whether they could handle a career in Abadan's stark industrial environment or similar petroleum facilities in the South.

Upon completion of their arduous training, the interns were invited to the home of the refinery's general manager, Dr. Reza Fallah, and over tea they were informally encouraged to apply for positions in the refinery. It was understood that interns would first be taking a break to visit their families, so their decisions were not expected immediately. On the return trip to Tehran, Lucik once again marveled at how the nation's topography was finally being tamed through engineering and science; meanwhile she pondered the pros and cons of a job at the Abadan refinery.

When Lucik spoke with her parents about her internship experience and Dr. Fallah's suggestion that the interns apply for a position at the refinery, her father was particularly concerned about what it would mean for a single woman to be working in a hot, remote, industrial, and almost exclusively male setting.[8] Gevork Moradiance was not explicit about his deeper concerns, but with the long Moradiance family history of wavering fortunes owing to changing political circumstances, the idea of his daughter living and working at the heart of what had the year before been the vortex of an international political and economic crisis weighed heavily on his mind.

As far back as Lucik Moradiance can trace her parents' ancestors, they lived for generations in and around Haftvan village in the Salmas region of western Iranian Azerbaijan.[9] For more than two thousand years, Armenians lived in the cities of Urmia, Salmas, Khoy, and Maku to the west and north of Lake Urmia. Scores of surrounding villages such as Haftvan had remained predominantly Armenian up to the early nineteenth century, despite repeated war and conquest over the centuries; a "recent" shortlist of invaders from only the previous twelve hundred years would include Arabs, Persians, Mongols, Turks, and Russians. Neighboring towns of integrated Armenians and Christian Assyrians, such as Khosrava, and of Sunni and Shi'a Muslim Azeri Turks and Sunni Kurds were interspersed, and some mixed villages of Christians and Muslims existed.[10] Located near the crossroads of the Russian, Persian, and Ottoman Empires, and coveted by several competing nationalisms (and their prospective European patrons), the region's mixed population would experience long nineteenth and twentieth centuries marked by hunger, violence, and uncertainty, punctuated with periods of relative abundance, stability, and hope.

In the wake of the Iranian loss in the Russo-Persian War of 1826–28, Russia extended its territory south to the Aras River, seizing the provinces of Yerevan (eastern Armenia) and Nakhichevan. Of the many punitive outcomes for Iran, the Treaty of Turkmanchai, signed by Fath Ali Shah in 1828,[11] set the border between Qajar Iran and the Russian Empire at the Aras River and enabled thousands of Armenians to immigrate to the city of Yerevan and villages of eastern Armenia and Nakhichevan.[12] Among these Armenian immigrants were hundreds of families from the region of Salmas, but even before this the majority of these families had already left villages where Turks or Kurds were a majority. Demographic consolidation in the remaining Christian villages and Armenian villages such as Haftvan, Mahlam, and Payajouk received additional (Armenian) immigrants. Although economic motivations in the late nineteenth century and political events of the early twentieth century would motivate Lucik's ancestors to temporarily move north to Russia, in the aftermath of the 1826–28 Russo-Persian War both her mother's and father's ancestors decided to remain on their land in Salmas rather than immigrate to Yerevan or Nakhichevan.

As natives of Salmas and like most other rural Armenians in the region, Lucik's ancestors were in one way or another involved in agriculture. In the late 1880s, her father's grandparents grew bulk vegetables (primarily tomatoes), while her mother's grandparents maintained fruit orchards. Lucik's maternal great-uncles established a fruit-distribution business in Russia that was based in Astrakhan and opened branches as distant as Tashkent and Simbirsk. Although Lucik's maternal grandfather eschewed agriculture and worked at first as a schoolteacher in Haftvan, after he and Lucik's grandmother were married, they decided to move to Simbirsk, where he took a job with his brothers-in-law in the fruit business.

Lucik's mother, Vardanoush Kazarian, was born in 1908 in Simbirsk, and her mother's brother, Smbat, her only sibling, was born in Astrakhan in 1911. She graduated high school in Astrakhan in 1925, and Smbat completed high school in 1928. Smbat went on to obtain a college degree in Russia and became a teacher in Leningrad before he was arrested in 1939 by the Main Directorate for State Security and was never heard from again. The family assumed that he was executed or died in a prison work camp in the East, but his fate remains a mystery.[13]

Lucik's father, Gevork Moradiance, was born in 1900 in Haftvan, where he attended primary school. In 1912, owing to the decrease in security in the region, his parents moved to Astrakhan with their three sons, Garekin, Gevork, and Mourad, the youngest. Gevork's father started a new business growing tomatoes and manufacturing tomato paste for bulk sale. The business began to turn a profit the following year, but the family's decision to move north for safety did not have the intended results. With the outbreak of World War I, security and transportation conditions in Astrakhan declined, as elsewhere throughout Russia and the Caucasus, and at the height of the war food became scarce. On a winter evening in 1917, leaving a hungry and worried family behind, Gevork's father and eldest brother, Garekin, harnessed their horse to a carriage and set out for surrounding villages hoping to exchange a bit of gold or some valuables they had collected for flour to bake bread. They were never seen again. Gevork's grieving mother surmised that her husband and son had probably been robbed and killed for their horse and carriage as well as their valuables, but no witnesses emerged, and their bodies were never found. Gevork, then seventeen years old, was put in the position of having to care for his mother and his ten-year-old brother, Mourad. Compounding the tragedy, shortly after this terrible incident the boys' mother became bedridden with an undiagnosed illness that took her life two years later.

Despite these immense challenges and the October Revolution of 1917 that brought the Bolsheviks to power, Gevork Moradiance continued his father's small tomato paste business in Astrakhan for more than ten years. The business survived both the period of "war communism" in which agricultural goods were requisitioned for support of the Red Army and the battle for Astrakhan in October 1919, in which White Army forces and the Astrakhan Cossacks were defeated (by the Reds). Because private enterprise in agriculture was allowed under the first Soviet New Economic Policy (NEP) of 1921–28,[14] the business flourished. As a result of his regained stability and success, in 1924 Gevork married and had a daughter, Marianna. Within four years, however, large-scale political events would once again lead to hard times. With the death of Lenin and the end of the NEP, the Soviet leader Joseph Stalin instituted the First Five-Year Plan, which initiated forced collectivization of Soviet agriculture. At the same time, Gevork's wife fell ill, and her health rapidly deteriorated, leaving Gevork a widower with a child.

Gevork's late wife and Vardanoush Kazarian were second cousins who had endured similar hardships, and after establishing a relationship of their own, Vardanoush and Gevork were married in 1929. However, the comfort of their union was mitigated by the dim realities of the situation they were facing. With the demise of the NEP and nationalization of private enterprise, the beginnings of forced collectivization of agriculture, and a general increase in political repression under Stalin, the Moradiance family made plans to leave Russia and return to Iran. Because Gevork's business had employed only family members rather than peasant laborers and profited only enough to sustain the small family and perpetuate the business, the Moradiances were not necessarily considered *kulaks* (rich farmers to be liquidated by the Five-Year Plan) but nevertheless faced certain forced collectivization. Now under its fourth year of Pahlavi rule, following the ouster of Ahmad Shah Qajar by Reza Khan and his subsequent self-coronation in 1926, their ancestral homeland again looked appealing because it was relatively stable economically and appeared increasingly secure. Shortly after the birth of daughter Lucik in Astrakhan in 1930, Gevork traveled alone by train to Tabriz to find a home to rent and look into business possibilities. When he was successful on both fronts, Vardanoush brought the two girls and the family's remaining possessions to Tabriz in July 1931.

Collaborating with his brother, Mourad, who also decided to make the move from Astrakhan to Tabriz, Gevork established a small winery near Azarshahr thirty miles southwest of Tabriz. By the mid-1930s, the Moradiance brothers were able to expand the business to include a food-canning factory, which was one of the first of its kind in the region. Vardanoush contributed to the family income as well, working long hours after the three children had gone to bed (a son, Garekin, was born in 1932). Sewing colorful fabric flowers for women's hats at night, she unwittingly was poised to dominate a local market niche that would be opened by the Pahlavi regime. Owing to Reza Shah's decree in January 1936 that women must remove their chadors in public, Western-style women's hats began flying off the shelves. As such, Vardanoush could not keep up with the demand for her flowers, which had formerly been worn only by Armenian and Assyrian women but were increasingly becoming in demand in Tabriz. Although the Moradiance family did not become wealthy overnight, by the late 1930s they had established what would be considered a stable, comfortable, middle-class living and maintained high hopes that the days of political turmoil and insecurity that marked their earlier years were past.

Lucik's first memories are of this tranquil period—playing in and around her family home during the time she was attending kindergarten at the age of four. In 1934, the Moradiance residence was located in Karashenk (Armenian for "stone buildings") between Leilabad and Aramian, which were two major Armenian communities in Tabriz. Situated on a quiet cul-de-sac, the house had a small yard that was shared by another Armenian family living in a single-story house and was adjacent to a larger two-story building with two residences and a large yard. In the wintertime, children would play in the small yard, where snow piles could last for months. The snow could be piled high enough to allow the children to slide on a piece of wood from the top to the bottom. Although the ride was only several feet, it was exhilarating to five-year-old Lucik. When the weather got warmer, she and the neighborhood kids would play in the big yard and enjoy eating the berries from the large mulberry trees, much to their mothers' consternation.

In 1934 and 1935, Lucik attended an independent Armenian kindergarten that was managed by an Armenian woman, Astghik Hacobian. It was located in the small park adjacent to the residence of Archbishop Nerses Melik-Tangians and operated under supervision and financial assistance from the Armenian Relief Society.[15] Having acquired Armenian as her primary language in the home and at kindergarten, and having played almost exclusively with other Armenian children in Karashenk, Lucik was a bit confused when she found out that the following year in elementary school her teachers would be speaking a different language. It was called Farsi.

In 1936, Lucik entered into the newly renamed Farrokhi Girls' School, which had opened on the grounds of the Armenian elementary school known as the Gymnasia. The Gymnasia and other "foreign-language" and missionary schools—including those with primary instruction in Azeri-Turkish, Kurdish, and European languages—were nationalized by decree of Reza Shah as a component of his program to bolster Iranian national identity, in this case through linguistic and curricular uniformity.[16]

Persian headmasters were assigned to assure compliance with new directives, which included Persian as the primary language of instruction. Several Armenian teachers remained after these changes were imposed, but language instruction in Armenian or religious instruction was prohibited, and teachers who were known to be members of the Dashnaksutuin were not rehired.[17] Conformance with government policy was required not only of foreign-language and missionary schools. In 1936, the Ministry of Education fired a girls' school principal in Sabzavar for public pronouncements against mandatory unveiling and rehired her only after she recanted.[18] Although the process was still incomplete by 1940, the Pahlavi regime actively worked toward the standardization of school curriculum and imposing oversight of the Ministry of Education.[19]

Between 1923 and 1941, the Iranian government invested more in the reform and growth of secondary and postsecondary schools than in other areas of education,[20] which considerably increased the number of male and female students attending them. Although the percentage of female students would continue to lag far behind that of male students, the improvements in gender equalization in this period are noteworthy nevertheless. Between 1924 and 1944, the total number of female students enrolled in Iranian schools grew from nearly 17 percent to 28 percent, and the number of female high school graduates increased from none in 1921 to 356 by 1936. The number of male students completing high school grew nearly ten times between 1921 and 1938, and the number of both male and female students to enroll would continue to increase until the period of Allied occupation (1941–45).[21]

The classes taught at Farrokhi Girls' School while Lucik was in attendance from 1936 to 1942 included Persian, reading, writing, natural sciences, mathematics, history, geography, drawing, and singing. Lucik's favorite classes were math, natural sciences, and singing, while drawing was her least favorite. Her years at Farrokhi were formative: she excelled in school, and her consistently high scores reflected a genuine passion for learning and study that would last throughout her life. It was here, in Farrokhi's ethnically and religiously diverse classrooms—where Persian and Azeri Muslims sang and read and drew along with Armenian and Assyrian Christians—that Lucik first became aware of other languages and religions.[22] It was here, too, as she learned to sing the national anthem in Persian with her schoolmates in classrooms uniformly outfitted with the Iranian tricolor and a requisite portrait of Reza Shah Pahlavi, that she first became aware that she was considered Iranian.

In primary and secondary school, Lucik recalls that she was not treated differently (either positively or negatively) because she was an Armenian, nor did she see any other Armenians treated differently. As a child, she was unaware that equal treatment of minorities had been mandated from above by Reza Shah as part of his broader program of inculcating Iranian national identity. It was true that under his rigid, exclusive formulation of Iranian nationalism (which would contrast significantly with that of his heir in subsequent decades) religious and ethnic minorities chafed at the blanket label of "Iranians" bestowed on them all—as opposed to being permitted a hyphenated, layered national identity. Yet under Reza Shah's configuration, although an Armenian Iranian or Assyrian Iranian was now to be considered (and ostensibly to consider himself or herself) an "Iranian Christian," the removal of ethnic distinctions also brought relative equality in public education and in the growing Iranian civil service.[23]

During these years of Lucik's primary education, important foundations were being laid for her eventual rise through the Iranian public education system and into a professional career. In addition to a leveling of the playing field for religious and ethnic minorities, Reza Shah's modernizing, westernizing, and secularizing agenda also called for the integration of women into the workforce and civil service. Described by historians alternatively as a bold, transformational "state feminism" project that marked a watershed in the making of the modern Iranian woman and society[24] or as window dressing enabling the appropriation of a genuine women's movement to confirm the regime's power and to maintain "patriarchal consensus," the Nahzat-e Banovan (Women's Awakening) of 1936–41 was undoubtedly essential to Lucik's future options and trajectory.[25]

Certainly, the imposition of unveiling laws in 1936 was by far the most overt, dramatic, and controversial aspect of the Women's Awakening.[26] But arguably the most important and long-lasting element of the project came the year before its official inauguration, when after lively debates in the Majles and the press throughout 1934, in which voices both for and against women's higher education focused almost entirely on implications for home life and motherhood, the Iranian government endorsed women's higher education in 1935.[27] Eighty women were admitted to Tehran University the following year, and by the academic year 1937–38 female students were majoring in foreign languages, Persian literature, history, archaeology, natural sciences, philosophy and rhetoric, mathematics, physics, and chemistry. In addition, in 1937 the first women entered programs in pharmacology and dentistry, and by 1941 more than eighty women were studying medicine at the university.[28] Soon integrated into the various student institutions of Tehran University, by 1937 women held offices and acquired executive board status in campus clubs and organizations such as Yearbook, Forensics, Theater, Sports, and Foreign Relations.[29]

Although the regime's program for women's education and the gains made by women at Tehran University would persist beyond 1941, Reza Shah's tenure as shah would not. The Soviet entry into World War II, British concerns over AIOC facilities in the South, Reza Shah's pro-German orientation, and the presence of hundreds of German technical advisers and expatriates in Iran combined to motivate an Allied invasion of Iran in August 1941.[30] Reza Shah's subsequent abdication and exile signaled the end of the Women's Awakening project, which, like most of Reza Shah's programs and laws, was either shelved for several years or scrapped entirely. Nomadic tribes previously forced to sedentarize again took to the hills with their flocks, Muslim women were free again to wear the chador in public if they chose, and "foreign-language" schools reopened and began teaching their nonstandardized curriculum.[31] The number of women attending Tehran University dropped dramatically during the war years but began to rebound by academic year 1947–48, two years before Lucik Moradiance would herself enroll there.[32] Failing to persist as government policy, the Women's Awakening of 1936–41 had nevertheless successfully established a tradition of women's higher education in Iran that would persist through war, revolution, and radical social and political reorientation.[33]

During the summer of 1941, Lucik's family took what had become an annual vacation in Azarshahr, staying in a residence adjacent to her father's factory, which was surrounded by orchards. Late that August, hearing the news that the Soviet Union had invaded Iranian Azerbaijan and that Reza Shah had abdicated the throne, Lucik's father wondered what the impact would be in Tabriz and Azarshahr and vexed over what this might mean for his business and the family's general welfare. Aware of little beyond playing in the orchards with her siblings on long summer days, eleven-year-old Lucik was likely to have been more surprised than her parents when a small group of Iranian soldiers wearing only long underwear emerged from an orchard and approached the factory. After a short conversation with her father out of the family's earshot, the group of apparent deserters was given some old clothing and invited inside for a meal. As agreed with her father, after eating they left the property the way they came, resembling a group of local agricultural workers.[34]

Such was the scene across northern Iran as Iranian soldiers for the most part fled their barracks in the face of a Russian attack.[35] Although Gevork Moradiance had little choice but to assist the group of soldiers, he was in fact genuinely sympathetic to their situation because he was essentially neutral regarding the entire conflict. Neither strong Iranian nationalists nor Communist-loathing Dashnaks like some of their relatives, Lucik's parents were not pro-Soviet owing to their experiences there and the fact that the family believed that Stalin was responsible for the execution of Lucik's uncle Smbat, but they were not against Russia or disdainful of Russian people like the Dashnaks were. Nevertheless, Iran was their ancestral homeland and had again become a stable and safe place to live and do business. The anticipation of what the Soviet occupation would mean put a damper on the family's remaining days in Azarshahr. Little could they have imagined that it would be the end of Soviet occupation rather than its imposition that would bring about the destruction of their factory and the return of hard times.

Despite the concerns of the adults around her, Lucik began sixth grade at Farrokhi two weeks after the Soviet invasion in September 1941 and was glad to see her friends once again and to get back to classes and learning, which she enjoyed more and more each passing year. The adults also soon relaxed; rather than seeing his business seized, collectivized, or otherwise restricted, by winter 1942 Lucik's father was attempting to increase the output of canned food, which was, somewhat remarkably, purchased for a relatively fair, negotiated price by the Soviet military to feed troops garrisoned in the region.

By spring of 1942, the future was again looking bright for the Moradiances, and the family was looking forward to a summer vacation in Azarshahr. It was a particularly memorable academic year for Lucik as she received the highest score possible on the national exam.

Lucik entered Dabirestan-e Parvin (Parvin High School) for girls in 1943. The school building was originally constructed to house the American Missionary Memorial School for boys, which Presbyterian missionaries had established in 1891. Well known as the first institution of its type in Tabriz, the Memorial School had been the workplace of an American *shahid* (martyr) of the Iranian Constitutional Revolution, Howard Baskerville.[36] Like the Gymnasia, however, the Memorial School, as a "foreign-language" institution, had been switched to an Iranian administration, staff, and curriculum in 1936, which were maintained, albeit temporarily, under Soviet occupation.

Girls entered Parvin High School in the seventh grade and took introductory classes in major fields taught by predominantly male teachers. Persian, English, Arabic, natural sciences, chemistry, physics, math, drawing, sports were required in the basic curriculum. Beginning in tenth grade, students were divided into two tracks, and the curriculum varied accordingly. Those who did not want to continue their higher education beyond the twelfth grade (a decision almost always made by parents) took courses in *khane dari* (the domestic sciences), which included continuing study in the three language courses, some classes in basic natural sciences, and an added emphasis on childcare, hygiene, cooking, and home economics. For those who planned on continuing their education beyond high school, study continued in all of the areas taught in the previous years, with the addition of advanced math, geometry, and algebra. In the twelfth grade, students were again branched into different tracks or majors. One track was a social sciences group for those who wanted to pursue literature, history, or geography. A second in natural sciences was designed for those who wanted to apply for medical college, pharmacology, or dentistry. A third was a mathematical sciences track for those who wanted to major in engineering, physics, or mathematics. The latter track

46. Lucik Moradiance (*fourth from left*) with classmates at Dabiristan-e Parvin (Parvin High School), Tabriz, 1946. Unknown photographer. Courtesy of Lucik Moradiance-Melikian.

was most appealing to Lucik, whose interest in mastering these subjects and her hard work studying routinely generated top exam scores.

In 1945, in Lucik's ninth grade year at Parvin, Iranian Azerbaijan was again thrown into a state of political turmoil. In a new variation of the same geopolitical power struggle that had distinguished the long nineteenth century, the region became the epicenter of a new type of global conflict—the Cold War—and served as its first point of crisis when the short-lived Soviet puppet Azerbaijan People's Government (APG, November 1945–November 1946) was declared and to the south the independent Kurdish Republic of Mahabad (1945–46) was established. Breaking the wartime agreement that occupying powers (i.e., the United States, Soviet Union, and the United Kingdom) would withdraw their forces within six months after the cessation of hostilities, the Soviets intended to support and protect these fledgling socialist states and to cultivate proxies. Putting the newly founded international organization called the United Nations to an immediate test, the United States and Britain exerted sufficient pressure on the Soviets to force the withdrawal of Red Army forces, which spelled certain doom for the APG and the Mahabad Republic.

When the Red Army pulled out of Azerbaijan in November 1946, the APG lost its critical military support, and as Iranian military forces neared Tabriz, APG leaders fled north to the Soviet Union or went underground.

Until Iranian forces were able to assert authority and impose security throughout Tabriz and in surrounding regions, mayhem, looting, and widespread settling of scores commenced. Because the Moradiance family's factory had canned and sold food to Soviet soldiers and also made and distributed wine, a local *mujtahid* (Muslim jurist) publicly declared the factory to be *najis* (unclean). Lucik's father and uncle were in Tabriz, so they were not injured when the factory was attacked and put to the torch by a mob. Although the workers tried to save the business after the mob dispersed, there was little they could do to douse the flames, and the structures and machinery were totally destroyed. Thus, instantaneously and unexpectedly, large-scale, global events over which the family had no control had once again turned their fortunes. The Soviet withdrawal and subsequent fall of the APG left the Moradiances with a destroyed factory, heavy debt, and consternation about the future.

Seeking employment in the wake of this family disaster, Gevork's younger brother, Mourad, moved with his wife and son to Tehran to seek work and try to establish a business, but Lucik's parents, now with four children (daughter Anahid was born in 1944), remained in Tabriz. At first, they tried a home canning business, but it was neither profitable nor sustainable. Branching out from their traditional business skills, they started a small beverage-distribution business to supplement canning, and it quickly became the mainstay of family income. Gevork eventually opened a wholesale distribution shop for alcoholic beverages in 1949. Employing mostly Turkish men, he sold wine and arrack that were made locally on a small scale, cognac imported from Rezayeh, and larger supplies of vodka, arrack, bulk wine, as well as an occasional liqueur imported from Tehran. The operation was licensed by the state, which required that each bottle sold have a stamped seal indicating that the required tax had been paid to the finance office. Around this time, Gevork fell ill with diabetes. Despite access to insulin, Gevork's combination of poor diet and stress owing to his repeated financial losses took an enormous toll on his health.[37]

In its short period of existence, the APG had established the University of Tabriz (originally the University of Azerbaijan) in June 1946, offering advanced degrees in medicine, education, and agriculture. Because Lucik's older sister Marianna and two other young women, Hasmik

Haroutunian and Jemma Mouradkhanian, did not have the required twelfth year of science and mathematics necessary for entrance, they had to get private tutoring to gain admission to the Medical School that fall. In November 1946, however, when the women had taken three months of coursework, the APG fell, and the university was immediately closed by the Iranian government. When it was announced that the university would be reopened in the fall of 1947, Marianna and her friends were told by the new staff that they would not be able to return to the university (i.e., they were expelled) because they hadn't been "legally admitted." No amount of pleading changed this decision, which was determined to be final. When Muhammad Reza Pahlavi visited Tabriz for the first time since Iranian governmental authority had been restored, Hasmik Haroutunian, undeterred, attempted to present a letter directly to the shah, crafted and signed by all three women, explaining their plight and requesting readmission to the university. Between the shah's tight security and the throngs of supporters who came out to demonstrate their allegiances or to present damage and loss claims, the closest she got was to one of his assistants. Nevertheless, Hasmik was promised that the letter would be given to the shah. Apparently this promise was not just *ta'arof* (Persian ritual courtesy): the shah received the letter and ordered that the Ministry of Education allow the three Armenian Iranian women to continue with their studies. They were therefore the first women ever to attend the University of Tabriz Medical School.[38] After Marianna graduated, she was hired as assistant professor at the Medical School and ran a private practice in the evenings.

Like Marianna, who set a good example by excelling at school, the greatest influence in Lucik's path to higher education and a professional career was that of her parents, who instilled the idea in their children's elementary school years that a high school education was an important step, but that it should not constitute the end of a man or a woman's education. Drilling home the motto that "the only thing that will stay with you throughout your life is education," Vardanoush was Lucik's primary mentor. She made sure that Lucik received the proper private tutor for Armenian, English, and Russian and set a positive example by always reading something if she had free time and encouraging the children to join her with their own reading. When Lucik returned home from school on exam days, her mother waited at the window to gauge whether her expression was happy or sad, and she always seemed to have the right words of support on challenging days.

Although it was back in her first years at Farrokhi elementary school that Lucik discovered that she enjoyed science more than any other subjects, it was an influential tenth-grade teacher who solidified her interest in science and made chemistry particularly appealing. After the fall of the APG in 1946, groups of recent college graduates were sent from Tehran to Iranian Azerbaijan to replace faculty who had been fired after having been accused of involvement with or support of the Pishavari government and to bolster the Pahlavi regime's image in the region. Lucik was fortunate to have one of these young, energetic teachers for tenth-grade chemistry. Mr. Mansour was highly organized and would always challenge the class to grapple with difficult and at times potentially volatile chemical combination problems, while remaining relatively empathetic of students and enthusiastic about the subject. With this infusion of new teachers, Lucik's other classes became more enjoyable as well, but chemistry remained her favorite subject. In eleventh grade, she received the highest score for her school on the national exam, which was a thrilling experience and achievement for a young female student.[39]

With this kind of positive support for her education from immediate family members and dedicated teachers at the fine schools she attended, Lucik was free to select the path she most liked. But her parents' own experiences and memories certainly shaped their advice and guidance. Although Lucik's initial interest in high school was to become a chemistry teacher, Vardanoush often reminisced of her father's and brother's negative experiences with teaching (however common or unique they might have been) and was thus cool to the idea. It was clear that both of her parents would have been happy for Lucik to follow in Marianna's footsteps and attend medical school in Tabriz, but Lucik abhorred the type of rote memorization that medical school demanded of her sister, so this was out of the question. Though the family was financially strapped at the time owing to the loss of the canning factory, and despite the fact that arrangements would have to be made for Lucik to move to Tehran for her studies, when she arrived at the decision to major in engineering, both of her parents supported the idea enthusiastically.

Aside from her mother's aversions and perhaps superstitions about teaching as a profession, Lucik was never pressured by anyone—parents, teachers, clergy, friends, or neighbors—to pursue a different educational or career path such as nursing, teaching, or something more traditionally "feminine." Yet this is not to say that the entire idea and utility of women's education was not questioned or even dismissed. When Lucik graduated, she refused a marriage proposal because she preferred to continue her education, which led family members and friends to assert that she was making a mistake, arguing emphatically that a woman couldn't do much with education and that only marriage made her complete.

Because there was no twelfth-grade mathematical science branch for girls in Tabriz, and girls could not attend boys' schools, Lucik had to move to Tehran to pursue an engineering major. Because it was out of the question for a young woman to live alone in the nation's burgeoning capital, arrangements were made for Lucik to stay with relatives in Tehran so that she could attend Nurbakhsh Girls' High School (formerly the American Bethel School for Girls) in academic year 1949–50, which offered the twelfth-grade curriculum in math and science required for university entry.[40] The moment Lucik stepped onto the Nurbakhsh school grounds, she was impressed. From its large, spacious classrooms to its well-dressed student body and its highly professional teaching staff, the campus exuded a serious and prestigious air. She was even more impressed to discover that her math teacher, Professor Fatemi, the chemistry teacher, Mr. Pezeshkpoor, and the physics instructor, Dr. Sedighi, were authorities in their respective fields and had authored some of the textbooks used in schools nationwide. Acclimating easily to her new school, Lucik was excited about the move to Tehran and was not often homesick because she was able to return Tabriz during summer and Nowruz (New Year) vacations,[41] and her mother and father made trips to Tehran to visit her when they could.

Having completed the required coursework at Nurbakhsh, Lucik was finally ready to apply for college. The Tehran University College of Engineering campus was located near the center of the city on Shah Reza

Avenue with another entrance off Takht-e Jamshid. In the late 1940s and early 1950s, owing to limited facilities and faculty, each first-year class was admitting a maximum of one hundred students. The entrance procedure for the college required applicants to take a general entrance exam—a written test that took a full day, covering math, physics, chemistry, and the English language. In the year Lucik applied (1950–51), there were roughly eight hundred applicants, but only eighty qualified. Because the government heavily subsidized the tuition—rendering the annual fee at the Engineering School a manageable eight hundred rials (twelve dollars), including workshop and laboratory costs—admission rather than expense was the biggest hurdle for the majority of applicants. The aspiring college students were well aware that they were essentially competing against each other and that at best only one in eight of them was going to make the cut, so the tension was palpable in the examination rooms.

Four female and seventy-six male students were admitted to the College of Engineering at Tehran University in 1950. Of the four female students, three were Armenians: Lucik Moradiance, Nazik Sarkissian, and Genoush Hovanessian. Pouran Shahandeh, a civil engineering student, was the single female Persian Iranian student. Out of the one hundred students admitted, twenty-four were Armenians. Thus, approximately one-fourth of the entering student body at that time, this proportion of Armenians was high considering the fact that Armenians constituted less than one percent of Iran's population.[42]

Several years ahead of Lucik's class with four female students were two women who were considered pioneers because they were the first women admitted to the engineering program in 1947. Arshalous "Milik" Voskian majored in chemical engineering, and Touran Khodabandeh majored in mechanical and electrical engineering. Lucik remembers well the other female students on campus during her first year—after all, they totaled only eight. In addition to her three fellow classmen and the two female senior pioneers, there were three female students who entered in 1948, including Nina Oganian in civil engineering; Nadia Kharchenko, a Russian Iranian student; and Malihe Khatibi, a Persian Muslim. No women had been admitted to the program in 1949, and four (including Lucik) were admitted in 1950.

The first-year coursework covered a general engineering curriculum, including the basics of civil, mechanical, electrical, and chemical engineering. The second- and third-year curricula covered some general courses, such as mineralogy, hydraulics, thermodynamics, and industrial electricity. The fourth year was devoted almost entirely to a student's selected area of specialization, which in Lucik's case meant intensive study in chemical technologies and petroleum engineering.

The College of Engineering had a high attrition rate, which Lucik attributes to a stringent minimum grade-point average requirement and very demanding professors. In her second year, Lucik was one of five chemical engineering students, but three failed during the next three years, so in 1954 only two chemical engineering students graduated from the college: Lucik Moradiance and a male Armenian Iranian, Goorgen Zargarian.

Because the Iranian education system had not yet developed the capacity to produce its own university professors, the majority of Lucik's professors were educated in Europe, and almost all of them treated both male and female students politely relative to rigid Iranian primary- and secondary-school traditions.[43] However, one engineering professor clearly disliked the presence of women at the university and would routinely tease them or go out of his way to try to embarrass them in his classes.

Although in terms of statistics and in historical hindsight Lucik's university education was a new and relatively rare thing (she was part of a small handful of female students attending university at the time), Lucik experienced neither positive nor negative reactions to the fact that she was a female college student other than from the aforementioned matchmakers and the one infamous professor.

In general, Armenian and Persian students did not socialize outside of school, and female Armenian students maintained closer relationships to each other, as did their female Persian (i.e., Muslim) counterparts, although relations were always cordial. During breaks between classes, Armenian female students socialized with Persian female students (initially only one, Pouran Shahandeh), although this necessitated a shift to the Persian language, sometimes in midsentence, to be respectful to someone joining a conversation in progress. Lucik remembers walking out of class one day during her freshman year chatting in Armenian, when

Pouran reminded them in mock exasperation, "Again, Armenian. I don't understand a single word!"

Owing to the small number of female students on campus, Lucik was able to cultivate a bond with all of them, but she had relatively little contact with male students. Some of Lucik's fellow female students later married male classmates who were attending concurrently, so acquaintances were being made, and there was certainly flirting going on, although not obvious or in the open. Male Armenian students treated the female Armenians differently than the male Persian students did, maintaining friendly rather than formal relationships with them. Persian underclassmen would occasionally joke or act up, but Lucik's recollections of such circumstances suggest that they were very tame by today's standards.[44]

Lucik usually socialized with her fellow first-year students on campus and would join Nazik and Genoush to study with other Armenian students at the university library. Armenian students socialized outside of the university as well. Aside from personal friendships and small gatherings attended by fellow Armenian students, there was also the Hay Hamalsaranakanneri Miutyun (Society of Armenian Graduates), which organized lectures and parties. Some Armenian students also socialized at the right-leaning Ararat club, which had been established in 1946 by Armenian intellectuals and athletes as a social and cultural organization. Ararat sponsored and organized public events such as plays and concerts, which were well attended by a cross section of Tehran's Armenian Iranian population, and many local youth participated in Ararat's sporting and scouting activities. Yet Ararat's clear but unstated orientation toward the Dashnak Party as well as the obvious but unstated membership of most of its founders in that party meant that some Armenians would attend only its public events, and others—in particular those who supported the Communist Tudeh Party—at best wanted nothing to do with the organization and at worst wanted it liquidated.[45] Armenians constituted more than half of Tudeh Party leadership and a large part of its constituency in the late 1940s, so the Dashnak's vociferous anticommunism kept many Tudeh supporters at a distance from Ararat.

Lucik was basically apolitical in her young adulthood and was not drawn to the sports and theater-oriented activities of Ararat or other social clubs as much as she enjoyed her own academic pursuits and spending time with her family and her close group of friends. Nevertheless, as a Tehran University student during this period of relative freedom of speech and press, she was well aware of important contemporary issues facing the country and, having witnessed some of the positive changes brought to Tabriz by the APG, was not completely closed to the ideals of socialism or the potential for better government in Iran. Thus, although not a member of Ararat, she was a member of the Society of Armenian Graduates and volunteered to tutor Armenian high school students in preparing for their university entrance examinations in chemistry.

Lucik attended concerts and theater presentations and had many friends who were Ararat members, but she was always short on extra time owing to her studies (and later to her professional life). If she had more time, she would have taken English classes rather than pursue more Armenian-related activities. Lucik's attitude about Soviet Armenia was not the same hard line the Dashnaks took. In her view, although the regime was not desirable, she appreciated the scope of progress in education, health care, art, and military protection the Soviet Union provided. Because there were no direct channels of communication between Armenia and Iran, radio broadcasts from Armenia had to suffice for news and information, and although she was aware that much of the news was infused with state propaganda, she nevertheless enjoyed hearing Armenian folk music and was proud that Armenian musicians, writers, and artists were making progress. She thought that nothing should be done for the goals of nationalism or independence that might hinder the advances of Armenians in Armenia or stunt their progress in art, science, and industry in the Soviet Union. As Lucik reasoned at the time, had Armenia become independent, the next day Turkey would have invaded, so what would have been the point? In considering the choice between being under Soviet control (and thus its protection) and fighting the Soviet Union for Armenian independence, Lucik preferred the former, even if it was not optimal.

Like millions of fellow Iranians and most of her fellow students at Tehran University, Lucik initially supported Prime Minister Mohammad Mossadegh's effort in 1950 to renegotiate the AIOC concession to obtain a fifty–fifty split akin to that struck by Saudi Arabia and Aramco that same year and the subsequent nationalization of all AIOC fields and assets in Iran when those negotiations failed in March 1951. Yet as the AIOC global boycott of Iranian oil began to severely weaken the economy, and street violence between pro-shah, pro-Mossadegh, and pro-Tudeh Iranians grew over the next two years, Lucik became more ambivalent about Mossadegh. Also like many fellow Iranians, Lucik was unaware that the United States had gone through its own process of disillusionment, and under the new leadership of the Eisenhower administration had directed the CIA to work with British MI6 to overthrow the Mossadegh government and restore Pahlavi dictatorship through a series of covert activities, culminating in the August 19, 1953, coup d'état that eliminated Mossadegh from his elected post.[46] Although American and British activities at that time were purposefully murky, the anger over American involvement in Iran and the shah's return became shockingly clear to Lucik in December 1953.

Less than four months after the successful coup d'état, on December 7, 1953 (Azar 16, 1332), US vice president Richard Nixon visited Iran in a demonstration of support for the shah, who had not yet crushed pro-Tudeh and pro-Mossadegh opposition and whose legitimacy had suffered when he fled the country while the coup was carried out.[47] Although the morning began uneventfully for Lucik, who was prepared for her regular schedule of classes and lab work, she was surprised to find outraged students at Tehran University, primarily pro-Tudeh but also supporters of the National Front and Pan-Iranists, gathering to protest and express their anger over US interference in Iran. They were milling about outside the main building as she entered to attend morning classes, trying to explain the reasons for their anger to fellow students and a few faculty onlookers. Lucik had mixed feelings about politics and sympathized to an extent with the student protesters, but skipping class to attend the rally was for her simply out of the question. Her primary concerns at the time were her education and her family, whatever the nature or merits of her fellow students' grievances.

Suddenly, in the middle of her morning class, the bell rang, and the dean's assistant entered the room to tersely announce that all students, staff, and faculty were to leave the premises immediately. Although he left to inform the neighboring class without further explanation, the noise of the protestors outside chanting antishah and anti–United States slogans made it obvious to everyone why the university was being closed. What was unknown to those inside the College of Engineering was that the Iranian military, specifically the shah's elite Javidan (Immortal) Guard had entered the university compound to confront the protesters, and the situation outside was deteriorating quickly. Lucik and her classmates joined in with the scores of students leaving other classes and moving through the hall and down the stairs. She had just reached the ground floor when the deafening sound of gunfire erupted inside the main hall, sending everyone instinctively diving for cover. Petrified with fear, Lucik thought for a moment she had been shot or injured when she felt warm liquid on her back, only to realize that it was water escaping from the radiator along the wall that had been punctured by a stray bullet. After a few moments of quiet, someone opened the door, and students began to spill out of the building once again. What Lucik saw as they filed out of the main hall shocked her and would forever leave a searing image in her mind: three young students, soaked in blood, were lying dead on the marble floor.[48] She became physically ill, and the trauma of the event left her bedridden for several days.

As witness to what would thereafter be annually remembered on Azar 16 as "Student Day," and with family history that had mixed experiences under monarchial, socialist, Communist, and secular democratic political systems, Lucik internally maintained strong convictions regarding social justice in Iran and complex thoughts about its political future. By the time she reached early adulthood, however, the culmination of her experiences and family history taught her to choose her words carefully and to confide only in trusted relatives and friends. As such, with her penchant for study and technology, and with a warm but reserved nature, Lucik developed a reputation on campus and later in professional life and social circles as a no-nonsense person, at ease with both highly technical and light conversation, but ever elusive on the subject of politics.

During spring term 1954, as a sense of normalcy returned to campus, Lucik immersed herself in her studies and Engineering College field trips, trying to look forward to her upcoming graduation and investigating internship and job options to pursue after she obtained her degree in chemical engineering.

47. Tehran University engineering students, including Lucik Moradiance (*second from left*), inspect a Gilan facility that chemically treated wood for railroad ties, spring, 1954. Unknown photographer. Courtesy of Lucik Moradiance-Melikian.

At that time, two internship programs were accepting new applicants; one was in Abadan, the other at an oil hydrogenation plant in Tehran. Although the Tehran internship would be closer to her parents and thus preferable to them, Lucik opted for the Abadan program, where she would be able to learn about the inner workings of a large-scale petrochemical plant. She applied and was accepted, entering a three-month summer training course at the Abadan refinery, which began in June.

Lucik's parents were standing in virtually the same spot where they had bid her good-bye three months earlier, excitedly waving hello as the dusty train slowed to a stop at Tehran Railway station. Pondering whether she should apply for a job at Abadan for most of the overnight return trip, she realized the pros (relatively high pay, fascinating work, an important national concern and duty) and cons (the heat, the harsh industrial environment, the distance from her family, the humidity, the almost total lack of other women, and, again, the heat) were about equal, so she was essentially neutral about the idea. After she discussed her experiences and the potential position with her parents, her father was not adamant that she turn down the offer, but his expressed concerns as well as Lucik's concern

48. Interns at the Abadan oil complex return from a tour of offshore facilities, summer 1954. The three female interns are (*front to back*) Hydeh Mehri, Nazik Sarkissian, and Lucik Moradiance. Unknown photographer. Courtesy of Lucik Moradiance-Melikian.

for his declining health led her to reject the potential job at Abadan, and she began looking for a position in Tehran.

Because Dr. Fallah had been so quick to suggest that Lucik apply for a job in Abadan, she had hoped that job leads would be as easy to come by in Tehran, but unfortunately this would not be the case. Whereas Abadan was continually expanding and in the wake of the nationalization turmoil would slowly be restaffed with a higher proportion of Iranian (rather than foreign expatriate) technicians, the oil boycott imposed by the British had severely weakened the Iranian economy, and technical and engineering jobs in Tehran were sparse in late 1954.[49] Unable to obtain work in her field immediately, Lucik temporarily took a position with Pfizer Pharmaceuticals as a sales and distribution representative, continuing to keep an eye out for new openings in chemical engineering throughout 1955. Although nothing explicitly suggested that her gender was a primary factor in her difficulty in finding another position, Lucik had the sense that it was certainly not a benefit. All she could do was to continue applying for relevant openings while using her University of Tehran affiliation to access the library and remain updated on the latest developments in the field so she could be sharp in interviews.

While checking out books at the College of Engineering, the librarian mentioned to Lucik that a new Soils Laboratory had been established at the university. Out of curiosity, Lucik walked directly over to the laboratory and met Mr. P. Robinson, who was the British manager of the John Mowlem Soils Laboratory in Tehran. After a long, spontaneous conversation in English in which she had the opportunity to describe her educational background and training at Abadan, Robinson asked Lucik if she would be willing to return the next day to the Mowlem Lab to meet their employment officer, even suggesting that she might be able to start work the following week. After a similarly fast-moving interview in Mowlem's employment office, Lucik was hired as a laboratory assistant.

Established in 1822, Mowlem was one of Britain's largest construction and engineering companies. Originally engaged in road construction in Iran, Mowlem then moved into consulting for soil physics, chemistry, and mechanical engineering.[50] As the only soils engineering laboratory in Iran until the late 1950s, Mowlem received almost all contracts for material analysis. In 1960, the American firm Ammann and Whitney temporarily took over the Mowlem Soils Lab facilities, before the entire operation was taken over by the Iranian government and put under the control of the Plan Organization in 1962. By directing Lucik to the Mowlem employment office before she had a chance to establish a relationship with the university's new Soils Lab, Robinson had precluded the potential opportunity for Lucik to be offered a position by the university and brought her to what would become her daily workplace for the next eleven years.[51]

In 1957, Lucik married Artavast "Levon" Melikian, a jovial and quick-witted Armenian Iranian lawyer and writer whose grandparents, like

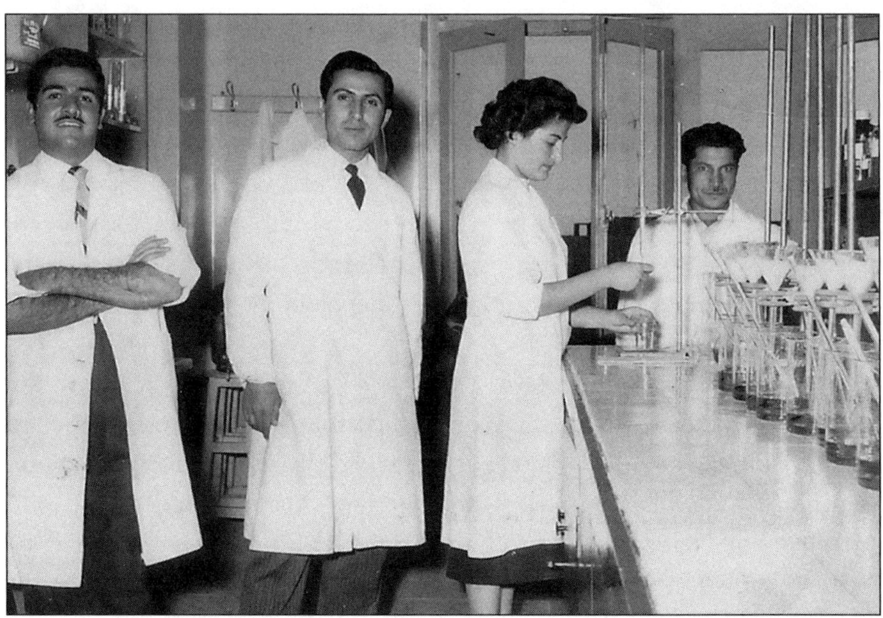

49. Lucik Moradiance and Iranian coworkers at the John Mowlem Soils Laboratory, Tehran, 1957. Unknown photographer. Courtesy of Lucik Moradiance-Melikian.

Lucik's, were born in Salmas.[52] The two had met at Tehran University, where Levon attended law school from 1949 to 1952. As a progressive thinker with complex but generally left-leaning political views, Levon was completely supportive and proud of Lucik's professional career. This, of course, was key to their compatibility because Lucik never entertained the thought of not working in some professional capacity.

In her first year at Mowlem (1956–57), Lucik Moradiance was the only female engineer at the lab, although there were female employees in the secretarial staff. As soils engineering was a new direction for Lucik, and as it required its own specialized training, she took advantage of a scholarship opportunity to advance her knowledge of soils chemistry and engineering. The British Council in Tehran announced that it was offering five one-year full scholarships to study at British universities in various fields, which ranged from education and English-as-a-second-language teaching to economics and engineering. Because tuition, room, and board were covered by the scholarship, it was highly competitive, with fifty to sixty

50. Lucik and her supervisor Mr. Robinson respond to the questions of Plan Organization director Abolhassan Ebtehaj, John Mowlem Soils Laboratory, Tehran, 1957. Unknown photographer. Courtesy of Lucik Moradiance-Melikian.

applicants. In addition to bringing the competition to Lucik's attention, Mr. Robinson wrote a letter of recommendation in support of her application, attesting to her character and explaining the responsibilities she had taken on thus far at the lab, which was no doubt key in making her one of the two female and three male applicants eventually selected. Having won a scholarship, Lucik applied and was accepted to attend Aberdeen University in the United Kingdom to obtain a diploma in soils sciences in the academic year 1958–59. Traveling to England by air, she spent the first seven of nine months there alone, renting a room near the university from a British family. As they had planned in advance, Levon joined her in Aberdeen for the final two months of her stay, before the two traveled a purposefully circuitous route back to Iran overland via combination of car, train, and ship that enabled them to see as many different countries as possible. Lucik and Levon's six-week-long journey together through western Europe in the summer of 1959 was unforgettable and a needed break before Lucik would need to return to the lab in the fall of 1959 to assume most tasks related to chemical testing of construction materials, water, and soils.[53]

With the Iranian government's takeover of laboratory facilities in 1962, the Mowlem site became known as the Plan Organization Technical and Soils Laboratory. Lucik became manager and director in charge of the chemical engineering laboratory, which incorporated the physical testing sector of the lab in 1963. The lab's primary mission was to conduct precise and accurate materials testing in accordance with international standards. As manager, Lucik was responsible for day-to-day activities of the chemical physical sections, including supervision of the chemical and physical analysis of soils and of building materials such as cement, asphalt, concrete, limestone, water, steel, and paints. She was also responsible for the creation of technical reports, preparation of new technical manuals and

51. Lucik and Levon Melikian and Lucik's sister Anahid Moradiance at Abali ski resort in the Alborz Mountains, Iran, 1965. Unknown photographer. Courtesy of Lucik Moradiance-Melikian.

instructions for utilizing various instruments in the lab, and interviews of applicants. Under her management during the 1960s, with the large volume of materials testing for infrastructural construction (dams, bridges, roads, airports, railways, ports, petroleum facilities), the laboratory became recognized as the national center for quality control of cement products in accordance with British and American Society for Testing Materials Standards. As such, the laboratory's standards certifications and reputation led to the proliferation of private contracts (for reliable test reports) so that, aside from Iranian governmental institutions, most private companies operating in Iran were using the laboratory's services.

The most common types of materials that the laboratory would analyze to verify that they met requirements for specific use or international standards or both were bituminous materials, which included the

52. Lucik Moradiance gives a tour of the former Mowlem Laboratory facilities to Dr. Asfiya and Dr. Behnia of the Plan Organization after nationalization of the facilities, Tehran, 1961. Both served as Lucik's professors at Tehran University. Unknown photographer. Courtesy of Lucik Moradiance-Melikian.

materials for domestically produced asphalt as well as soil and limestone for the manufacture of cement and bricks. Through a variety of tests on equipment that ranged from flame photometers and spectrophotometers to large hydraulic presses that gauged maximum loads and compressibility of materials' flexibility and consistency, samples were checked to see if they met international standards and contract specifications. The tests would be requested by the owners or managers of a project, who usually submitted initial samples, but also sometimes submitted "problem" samples that contractors felt warranted analysis. Because most of the major projects consultants were foreigners (with an increasing number of Americans in the 1960s) and standards were in English, most of the reports produced by the lab were written in English.

Through her acquired expertise in international standards, Lucik was appointed by the Ministry of Development as an active member of the Standardization Institute of Iran Building Materials Committee in 1969–70. The purpose of her appointment to the institute was to bring her years of hands-on experience with building materials to the new organization, which sought to compile a set of new Iranian standards based on combined international standards. Whether owing to her specialization in international standards and quality control or her businesslike, no-nonsense personality at work or a combination of both, Lucik was never approached or asked to falsify findings of reports while she was working for the Plan Organization. Whether contractors followed prescribed recommendations and maintained standards throughout the process of construction was the responsibility of inspectors, and this is where corruption flourished. The only real evidence of "corruption" noticed at the lab concerned materials samples that were rejected because they were taken improperly or the location of the sample core extraction was in doubt.

Although by the mid-1960s many Iranian women held equivalent and higher positions both in governmental and educational institutions, Lucik had no female peers at the Plan Organization. The accounting section eventually hired a female university graduate, and in later years one female engineer and several female chemists were reporting to her, but the only female employees she worked with initially were secretaries and one administrator; all of the engineers were male.[54]

53. Lucik Moradiance (*seventh from right*) with female assistant and Plan Organization colleagues at the Abadan refinery, 1968. Unknown photographer. Courtesy of Lucik Moradiance-Melikian.

In 1970, Lucik transferred from the Soils Lab to work for the Plan Organization Industrial and Mines Division. Her primary task in this position, which she maintained until 1975, was to evaluate feasibility studies prepared by various engineering firms and governmental agencies for allocation within the national budget. Studies included cost–benefit analyses of such variables as product demand, manpower and energy availability, natural-resource requirements, and overall project value for the gross domestic product. One of her most memorable challenges during these years was the preparation of a voluminous report detailing Iran's existing chemical industries, their production capacities, and the availability of indigenous raw materials to plan for future expansion in view of projected domestic demand and the objectives of Iran's Fifth Development Plan (1973–78).

In 1975, Lucik changed positions once again, this time taking a job at the National Iranian Petroleum Company (NIPC). Distinct from the NIOC, which was responsible for the exploration and extraction of crude oil and the refining and distribution of petroleum products, the NIPC and its subsidiaries focused on fertilizer, feed, and petrochemicals. Here, Lucik's tasks shifted to studying projects conducted at the NIPC, including the production of catalysts consumed in refineries and manufacture of protein from hydrocarbons for animal feed. This job would bring her full-circle back to her Abadan experience in 1954. Although she never had to stay for more than a few days, she visited Abadan and nearby Kharg Island and Bandar Shapour several times over the next two years, but now by plane instead of by the overnight train. Abadan was much the same physically, but it was now staffed predominantly by Iranian technicians and managers. Yet despite the fact that the makeup of technical and managerial staff had changed to become predominantly Iranian by the late 1970s, and the conditions, wages, and job security had "turned the oil industry's labor force into something of a labor aristocracy," it would soon become dramatically clear that the relative affluence and security attained by Abadan workers had not resulted in loyalty to the Pahlavi regime.[55]

There was no single incident during Lucik's professional career in which she felt discriminated against because of her gender or ethnicity. Her supervisors, Dr. Ahmad Nowban and his assistant Mr. Taraji, as well as her male coworkers at the Plan Organization were uniformly polite and respectful, and she felt that she always had their cooperation. On the contrary, she believes that she received more respect as a woman in Iran. The Iranian government's policies had by the 1970s integrated women into the highest areas of the workforce and sought to make this fact well known.[56] In 1975, Lucik was sent as one of five NIPC representatives to the International Petrochemical Conference in Baghdad, an international symposium to discuss current petrochemical projects in the Middle East and areas of future expansion and potential cooperation.

The other four representatives sent to the conference were male engineers, and the NIPC representatives who joined them were also male. Lucik believes she was chosen to participate specifically because she was a woman and a Christian and it was thought this would demonstrate the progressiveness of the regime and the NIPC.[57] Yet when she had traveled to Japan two years earlier as part of a Plan Organization delegation for a conference on protein manufacture from hydrocarbons for animal feed, consisting of three women and six men representing the NIOC, NIPC,

54. As an NIPC delegate to the International Petrochemical Conference, Lucik Moradiance is introduced to the oil minister of Iraq, Baghdad, 1975. Unknown photographer. Courtesy of Lucik Moradiance-Melikian.

Plan Organization, and Agriculture Ministry, she had learned that she could not expect the same kind of consideration in other countries. When the representatives were met by their Japanese counterparts at the airport, their male hosts promptly greeted the three Iranian men and hastened to take their luggage and lead them out of the terminal, leaving Lucik and her female colleague standing there, somewhat bemused. A bit of awkwardness ensued as their male colleagues realized what had happened and turned around to take the women's luggage, smiling and bemused as well.[58] The female delegates and delegates' wives were also not invited out with the men for dinner or the requisite after-dinner socializing, which Lucik also found markedly different from her experiences in Iran.

As Levon was doing very well in his law practice and had developed a stable range of clientele, and Lucik had now been working for twenty-two years in various technical jobs, the two decided that it was time to expand the family. In April 1978, Lucik retired from the NIPC so she could stay home and care for their son, George. After decades of study and technical work to better herself and the Iranian nation, Lucik Moradiance had attained a stable upper-middle-class existence and now looked forward

55. Conference delegates, including Lucik Moradiance (*standing fourth from left*) from the NIPC tour a Japanese chemical plant, Osaka, 1973. Unknown photographer. Courtesy of Lucik Moradiance-Melikian.

to having the opportunity to relax and enjoy family life. Yet how many of Lucik's forebears had achieved stability and looked forward to the same, only to have their hopes dashed by large-scale political events completely out of their control?

Protests against the Pahlavi regime had been gathering steam over the course of 1978, but a series of bloody events quickly elevated the intensity and scope of dissent. On August 20, 1978, a fire tore through the Cinema Rex movie theater in Abadan, killing more than four hundred people, predominantly workers at the refinery and their family members. Blamed alternately on SAVAK and Islamic revolutionaries, and later becoming fertile ground for conspiracy theories, at the time it was widely believed that the shah's forces were responsible for setting the blaze and ordering local police to ensure that none of the audience could escape or be rescued. The origin of the Rex theater fire remains murky, but there is no question who was responsible for the massacre of antigovernment demonstrators in Tehran's Jaleh Square on Friday, September 8, 1978, when the Iranian

56. Garni Society of Armenian Engineers and Architects annual gathering (Lucik Moradiance, *center*, number 39), Tehran, 1976. Unknown photographer. Courtesy of Lucik Moradiance-Melikian.

army itself demonstrated its might via machine guns and tanks. There is also no question regarding the impact Black Friday had in hastening the fall of the Pahlavi regime.[59]

Within a month of Black Friday, the oil workers at Abadan joined other industrial workers across the country and went on strike. Almost instantaneously the nation's industrial production came to a grinding halt. Although relatively small, Iran's industrial working class occupied a strategic position in the nation's economy, and thus their mass strikes, which included the shutting down of oil pipelines and a halt to exports in October 1978, were critical to the revolution's success.[60] Three months later the shah of Iran and his family would be in exile, and Ayatollah Ruhollah Khomeini would be greeted by millions of ecstatic Iranians as he returned from his own.

What would the future bring, Lucik wondered as she, Levon, and close friends waited for news reports with mixed fascination and apprehension. Certainly many of the initial, idealistic rallying cries of the revolution had merit: freedom of speech, press, and assembly; a more equitable distribution of wealth; and the end of the regime of fear inculcated by SAVAK. But Lucik was not naive and from the beginning remained skeptical that the promises of a new dispensation of love, justice, and equality would be met or that the rights and status that Iranian women and religious minorities had attained under the Pahlavis would be maintained under a theocratic political system, which seemed a likely outcome in February 1979. Would political change once again bring a radical shift in family fortune, stability, and location? Were these natives of Salmas unfortunate heirs to a lineage of instability and challenge? Lucik had far too rational and technical a mind to believe in curses. Had such disruption and tumult become an unfortunate Moradiance family legacy? Perhaps, yet so too had perseverance.

6

Nejde Hagobian

AS HE SLOWLY SHOOK HIS HEAD, Dr. Hossein Banai looked both amused and slightly perturbed.[1] The previous evening he had warned the Persian scoutmasters to be on alert during the night to defend against the classic ritual attack that occurred at boy scout jamborees, but they had obviously disregarded his warning. As a result, their outer clothing had been purloined in the early morning hours of August 26, 1954, and hoisted to the top of the flagpole. Thus, when Dr. Banai sounded the morning reveille, almost all of the Persian scoutmasters were stuck in their tents while the Armenian Iranian scouts of Ararat who had perpetrated the requisite deed quickly and quietly lined up in front of the flagpole pretending not to notice the garments gently swaying in the breeze over their heads. Putting on the best poker face he could under the circumstances, the twenty-year-old scoutmaster of the Ararat group, Nejde Hagobian, ordered one of his Armenian scouts, in Armenian, to untie the line and lower the load to the ground. Banai, the head of the Iranian scouting organization under the Iranian Ministry of Physical Education, then ordered one of the few Persian scoutmasters to emerge from his tent fully clothed to quickly distribute the items to their rightful owners. All joking aside, the shah was due to arrive in two hours to review this first Iranian boy scout jamboree since 1940, and everyone—especially Banai and Hagobian—wanted to make a good impression.

Dr. Banai wanted to demonstrate to Shah Mohammad Reza Pahlavi his effectiveness in reviving the Pishahangi-ye Iran (Scouting of Iran, alternatively known as Sazman-e Pishahangi, the Organization of Scouting), which had been disbanded because of pressure from the ulama and conservative Majles members following the exile of Reza Shah in 1941 and had not been reorganized until spring of 1954.[2] Nejde Hagobian, in contrast, was seeking to show the shah—honorary president of all Iranian scouting groups—that the Armenian Iranian scouts were the nation's best-organized and disciplined scouting troops and to imply that the scoutmasters of the Pishahangi-ye Iran were being schooled by Ararat in scouting activities and rituals. Certainly the salaried Persian scoutmasters learned something about the nasty side of scout rituals that morning, but the prank did not mar the overwhelmingly positive spirit of cooperation and healthy competition that otherwise marked the scouting event. Hagobian was relieved that Banai took the "underwear ritual" in stride and glad that he had had the foresight to issue specific instructions that Banai's tent be left alone in the roundup.

When the shah, dressed in full military regalia, arrived with his entourage of military officers, ministers, and a group of reporters and photographers, Banai and Hagobian greeted him with smart salutes before showing him around the encampment.[3] To Dr. Banai, walking

57. The shah arrives at the joint scouting jamboree encampment at Manzarieh, August 26, 1954. *Left to right*: George Patgorney, Shah Mohammad Reza Pahlavi, Dr. Banai, Nejde Hagobian. Unknown photographer. Courtesy of Nejde Hagobian.

beside the shah and answering his questions were routine, for he was a member of the government who regularly interacted with the shah. For Hagobian, who was quite a bit younger than Banai, an ordinary citizen, and a religious minority as well, it was exhilarating to walk beside the country's leader and describe to him aspects of the Ararat scouts' organization, activities, and skills. Although he had briefly met the shah once before at a reception for scouts and had marched before him several times at parades, Hagobian had never before had the opportunity to interact with anyone from the government, let alone the nation's king, for such an extensive period of time. So he was proud to be able to show off the well-organized Ararat scouting encampment and the various wilderness survival projects the scouts had been working on during the event and glad that he could explain everything in excellent Persian. Although at age twenty Nejde Hagobian was still in the process of learning what it meant to be a member of a minority group in Iran, he was acutely aware that it was important for the Ararat scouts to look their best, for they represented not just a neighborhood or city, but Iran's Armenian community.

Born on August 8, 1934, in a midwife's residence in the Armenian quarters of Tehran to Arshalous and Hagob Hagobian, Nejde Hagobian was named after Dashnak general Garegin Nejde, whom his parents admired. Because the couple had met in an American Presbyterian-sponsored orphanage in Tabriz for Armenian children after having lost their own parents to the Armenian massacres and intercommunal violence that wracked the Caucasus between 1914 and 1918, it was fitting that they decided to name their son after an Armenian who had fought for the liberation of Armenia.

When Nejde reached the age of five, the family moved out of the sparse accommodations they had rented in the Armenian *koutche* (alley) off Khiabane Sepah Salar to a more spacious and electrified house off Khiabane Estakhr in central Tehran. The new residence was located several blocks away from the royal palace complex of Marmar in what was then a mixed light-industrial and residential neighborhood. One of thirteen buildings on a cul-de-sac owned by a wealthy Muslim bazaar merchant named Abdoulahian and rented to predominantly Armenian families, the Hagobians' two-story brick unit consisted of four rooms, a water closet,

58. Nejde Hagobian in front of Hagob Hagobian's and Arshak Goorjian's six-wheel trucks, Vanak, 1937. Unknown photographer. Courtesy of Nejde Hagobian.

and a shower room on the top floor and two rooms, a water closet, and a kitchen on the first floor. The unit also included a small yard that had a large pine tree, fruit trees, and a shallow goldfish pond in the center. Like most of the other tenants renting from Abdoulahian, the Hagobians sublet the rooms on the bottom floor to other Christian families to lower the overall price of their rent. Thus, although nine of the buildings were officially rented to Armenian families, two to Assyrian families, and one to a Jewish family, and the other, newest unit was inhabited by the Abdoulahian family, at any given time as many as twenty families were living in the Abdoulahian compound. This meant that there were usually at least fifteen to twenty children of all ages for Nejde to play with in the narrow paved street that connected the houses. As turnover of tenants was quite low, the families and children got to know each other well, and the small neighborhood took on a life and rhythm of its own.

Although the cul-de-sac consisted of thirteen buildings, only ten of them were inside the walled compound protected by the old, heavy wooden gate that remained open most of the time. The large Abdoulahian family inhabited one of the houses inside the compound, seven were rented to Armenians, and two to Assyrians. Although the Hagobians' unit was considered to be inside the compound, its main entry door was outside of the wooden gate, and a side door opened into the compound behind the gate. Of the three buildings on the cul-de-sac situated outside the gate, one was rented by a Jewish family that had recently fled from Poland to Iran, another by an Armenian family, and the third by one of the founding members and leader of the Tudeh Party, Dr. Fereydoun Keshavarz, who had converted the house into a bustling pediatric clinic.[4] It was in this controlled neighborhood environment that Nejde Hagobian spent his childhood and learned about Armenian and Iranian culture.

Because Nejde's father, Hagob Hagobian, was a long-distance truck driver who was often away from home for extended periods, the Hagobian family benefited by having a family live downstairs, and the close-knit neighborhood was ideal. It offered security and companionship to Arshalous, who socialized with the other women living in the compound while at work or rest, shared babysitting duties, and often made trips with them to the bazaar. Nejdik (Little Nejde) safely played with the other neighborhood children in the narrow paved street that connected the houses without fear of traffic or the approach of strangers.[5]

As the son of a truck driver, Nejde had easy access to what was then a particularly precious childhood commodity: wheel bearings. Because

59. Nejde Hagobian (*center*) poses with friends north of Tehran in Vanak, 1938. The boy on the right is an original Iranian *pishahang* (scout). After Reza Shah's exile, the Pishahangi-ye Iran was disbanded until 1954. Unknown photographer. Courtesy of Nejde Hagobian.

of the harsh, sandy conditions his father drove in to make his round trips between Tehran and the Persian Gulf, wheel bearings had to be changed often and could not be remachined or rebuilt because of their precise tolerances. Although they were unserviceable for further use on trucks, a pair of used wheel bearings was a coveted item among Tehrani children, who could combine them with two pieces of wood and large bolts to create a two-wheeled *rowrowak* (scooter). Despite the fact that the steel rolling surface of the wheel bearing offered at best a bone-jarring ride on pavement and a noise that tested the parents' patience, *rowrowak*s were the ultimate form of transportation, and soon all of the neighborhood children were racing around on them.

Because both Hagob and Arshalous had been orphaned and had little formal education, they were lacking role models that demonstrated how to interact in a parent–child relationship. Thus, although Nejde's well-being and health were of primary concern to his parents, his inquisitive mind was nurtured by neither his mother nor his father. Hagob was away on long-distance trucking hauls most of the time. When he was at home, he would seldom, if ever, take the time to explain to Nejde what was going on around him or how things worked. Hagob was rarely available or willing to answer a child's most common question: Why? Arshalous, who often played the role of both parents while Hagob was gone, was herself busy doing everything necessary to maintain the household and had little time or patience for Nejde's persistent questioning. He was dearly loved, and his healthy cheeks were often pinched in delight by his proud parents with a traditional Armenian Iranian exclamation of parental love, "Bouyeet mernem! Ghorbaneternem!" (I die for your stature! I sacrifice myself for you!), but Nejde had to look elsewhere to satiate his desire to learn about and understand the world around him.

Luckily for Nejde, on any given day from early morning to late afternoon the street became the scene of intense hustle and bustle as Persian vendors of all kinds would turn into the neighborhood while making their rounds and announce their presence with a distinctive chant. At that time, Nejde was unaware that the vendors were different than himself and his neighbors except for the fact that they spoke a different

60. Hagob, Arshalous, and Nejde Hagobian, Tehran, 1938. Unknown photographer. Courtesy of Nejde Hagobian.

language, Persian, which he spoke and understood perfectly. While most of the other neighborhood children would be zigzagging around on their *rowrowaks* among the vendors and the women of the compound who would flock out to examine the wares and make their purchases, Nejde was fascinated by the vendors and the skills they demonstrated; he never tired of observing them and asking questions. Almost all of the Persian vendors were extremely kind and willing to explain, often in great detail, what it was that they were selling or doing.

On a typical summer weekday, the vending began with the arrival of a horse-drawn tanker carrying fresh drinking water and the chant "Abi!" Neighbors would line up with their large clay chalices, and Abi (as the water man was known) would fill each vessel individually using a section of a bicycle inner tube as an extension from the large brass faucet. As Abi was busy filling the neighborhood's water vessels with Ab-e Shah (King's Water, as the clean drinking water was known), other produce and goods vendors would begin turning onto the cul-de-sac, chanting their individual slogans, and lining up behind Abi's tanker.

There was Yakhi, "Ice Man," whose donkey bore two large burlap rice sacks containing big, irregular chunks of ice. On hot days, Yakhi was a favorite vendor of the children, who would laugh and squeal with delight as he would break the ice into smaller pieces with swings of his pick, producing a hail of fine ice chips that would land on their heads and faces. The numerous fruit and vegetable vendors were less intriguing, but Nejde never tired of watching the morbid activity going on around Morghi, "Chicken Man." Morghi would stop his donkey in the center of the street and remove strips of burlap that shaded large cages made of woven twigs hanging on either side of the donkey and containing scores of live hens. Women of the neighborhood would gather around Morghi and specify the approximate size of the hen they wanted for that evening's meal. With this information, Morghi would then blindly reach into the cage and pull out a random hen that would be frantically squawking and trying to escape. The customer would examine the hen, and if it was not acceptable—as the first one to emerge rarely was—Morghi would throw that hen back in the cage and reach for another one. Sometimes Morghi would pull out the same hen and exclaim, "Now *this* is a truly superb hen!" although he rarely fooled his customers or Nejde, who watched the haggling in rapt fascination. After continuing that process until an acceptable chicken was found, Morghi would then nonchalantly sever the head of the chicken with a large knife hanging from the side of his donkey and then hand the still-kicking chicken to the satisfied customer. During this slaughter, the cry "Zoghaly!" announced the arrival of the charcoal man, who was followed closely behind by Nafty, who sold kerosene. Sheeshe Khoordei bought broken glass and bottles, and Kot-Shalvari bought and sold used clothing. The procession continued for most of the morning.

Specifically for children, there was Shahrefarangi and Jegh-jeghe-i.[6] Shahrefarangi would set up a table with an indigenously made stereoscopic photo viewer and charge a half-rial to transport the children to far-away lands by showing them technological wonders old and new: Jerusalem, Taj Mahal, L'arc de Triomphe, the pyramids of Giza, a white paddle wheel steamboat on a river in America, the Great Wall. Shahrefarangi also showed paintings of European artists such as Raphael, DaVinci, and Michelangelo. While turning the crank to change the photos for the children, whose faces were excitedly glued to the viewing lens, Shahrefarangi would look through a separate viewport and describe in deep, animated tones what it was they were seeing, which incited the other children to beg their parents for a coin so that they too could see the show. Sometimes Shahrefarangi's pitch was so compelling that the adults would be motivated to shell out a whole rial and see the photos for themselves. With Shahrefarangi's descriptions in the background, Jegh-jeghe-i would appear and lower the large basket of toys and candy he bore on his head down to the ground. Jegh-jeghe-i specialized in toys such as pinwheels, fans, and noisemakers that were like kazoos and were called *jirjirak* or *ghargharak* depending on their tone. He also purveyed hard candy and sweets such as shaped rock sugar candy filled with rose water. His appearance initiated another round of skirt tugging as children asked their mothers for another half-rial. Before long, the kazoolike sounds of the *ghargharak* joined the cacophony.

Although most of the neighborhood children would lose interest in the vending activity after Shahrefarangi and Jegh-jeghe-i packed up and left, afternoon was most entertaining and informative for Nejde because it was then that the Persian service vendors would appear to mend household items or custom fabricate new ones. Unlike the food and goods vendors, whose loads, often borne on beasts of burden, were configured for quick and easy removal, the service vendors would usually appear with only their unique tools and a large canvas cloth. Selecting a choice spot on the side of the street in the shade, the service vendors would spread out the cloth and neatly arrange their tools while neighbors would bring out items such as broken pots and dishes, dull kitchen knives, and used bedding for mending, restoration, or recycling. The service vendors would remain at the compound for hours—or as long as there was work—and seemed happy to allow Nejde to scrutinize their activity and to patiently answer his flood of questions about everything they were doing. To Nejde, the most intriguing of the service vendors were the *shekast-e band* (repairer of broken items, also known as *chin-i band*) and the *la-haf dooz* (quilt maker). They worked methodically, used many different tools and techniques to accomplish their tasks, and produced dramatic results in a relatively short amount of time.

Chinaware and porcelain were expensive in Iran, especially for working-class Iranians. Therefore, when a china plate, platter, or teapot broke, it would be fixed rather than discarded. All of the pieces, no matter how small, would be carefully saved, and when a family had accumulated several items that needed mending, they would take them to the *shekast-e band* to fix. First, the craftsman would sit cross-legged on his cloth and carefully examine, clean, and separate into piles all of the pieces given to him. Then, while holding the broken sections of ceramic between his bare feet, he would use a rudimentary drill, staple-gauge wire, a small hammer, and dry grout to bind the pieces together and waterproof the crack. The resulting pattern, which resembled a zipper or stitches running the length of each crack, was not aesthetically pleasing, yet it was highly effective and practical at a time when throwing such an item away was not an option. Oftentimes, months or even years later, a platter or pot that had been fixed before with this method would be brought back a second or third time, yet the new break would inevitably be in a different spot: a testament to quality workmanship that the *shekast-e band* never failed to modestly point out.

Another Persian service vendor who served an important practical necessity while entertaining and providing Nejde with information about his craft was the *la-haf dooz* (quilt maker). Most Iranians, irrespective of religion or ethnicity, generally slept on bedding consisting of thin quilted wool-and-cotton mattresses that were placed directly on the floor, with lighter wool or cotton comforters on top when needed for warmth. These items would routinely become worn out, compressed, and soiled, necessitating the services of the *la-haf dooz*. In the Hagobians' neighborhood, the women would bring mattresses and comforters outside, remove the stitching, and separate the stuffing from the covering cloth. After washing the raw wool and cotton stuffing, they would lay them out in the sun to dry and await *la-haf dooz*. Like the *shekast-e band*, *la-haf dooz* would spread out his cloth, remove his shoes and socks, and carefully arrange his tools before surveying the amount, type, and condition of the wool and cotton stuffing and pieces provided by the customer. After brief negotiations about the size and thickness of the items he was to recycle, he would begin his work. After spreading out the stuffing on his cloth and lightly wetting it with a sprinkle of water, he would use sticks of various thickness and lengths to whip at the pile and fluff the material until it was gathered in a separate pile that was two or three times its previous bulk. After all of the material was fluffed, the craftsman would stuff it back into the large washed sacks and sew the opening closed. He would then squat and proceed to quickly stitch beautiful patterns through the material to shape and even out the thickness of the item. By the end of the day, *la-haf dooz* would have several mattresses and comforters neatly folded and stacked for the owner to pick up. By that time, he would also have detailed the entire procedure several times for Nejde, who was fascinated by the process and the various looms and implements the quilt maker used and so always had another question.

By far the most exciting days of vending and observing in the neighborhood for Nejde would culminate with the appearance late in the afternoon of Ab-i Hozi, "Pond Water Man." Ab-i Hozi specialized in the cleaning of water ponds and cisterns, which were an integral part of the neighborhood's water system. Unlike Abi, who brought Ab-e Shah early in the morning, Ab-i Hozi carried only his tools (a bucket, various brushes, shovels, and scrapers), which were used to drain the reservoirs and remove the accumulated dirt and sludge. His presence meant that all of the children would get to stay up until at least two o'clock in the morning and play in the dark that night, for Ab-i Hozi visited the neighborhood only prior to water nights.

Every other week, on predetermined and fixed dates, the neighborhood would have its scheduled water night. On these designated nights, Tehran water officials would release water through a system of open channels that would be diverted to flow through the irrigation system of a particular section of town. Gravity would cause the water to flow through the concrete-lined square gutters (*joubs*) that ran the length of both sides of each street. Because the system was open to the air, the officials distributed the water in the middle of the night to cut down on the amount of dust and contamination.

Tehran's *joub* system, which most foreigners assumed was an open system to carry sewage, was constructed for two specific functions: to serve as storm drains to keep streets from flooding when it rained and as the primary residential system for nonpotable water, which was to be used for washing, bathing, and watering gardens. From the main *joub* running down the side of Khiabane Estakhr, there was a diversion gutter leading past the wooden gate and into the cul-de-sac, running the length of the small street.[7] From that smaller *joub*, each of the thirteen houses in the neighborhood had its own, smaller diversionary channel that would divert the water into that home's yard, where it would first fill up the central pond (now sparkling after Ab-i Hozi's visit) and then overflow to fill up an underground, concrete-lined water reservoir.[8]

Because it was not known at what hour the water would arrive, the neighbors would gather after ten o'clock at night outside to socialize and make final preparations. While the young children ran in circles and chased each other on their *rowrowak*s, the women would bring out tea, sit on the steps, and chat with each other, and the men would smoke and prepare their gutters. Finally the sound of water flowing past the main *joub* on Estakhr would signal the water's arrival, and the action would begin. One of the men would walk out to the main *joub* and divert it with a large piece of wood into the compound's smaller gutter. Although the water would soon be overflowing this dam and continuing on down the *joub* on Estakhr to other residents of that section of Tehran, the diversion would send water cascading through the compound's gutter and into the neighborhood's water reservoirs. Despite the fact that the water was quickly and efficiently flowing through the channel system, the entire process of topping off the neighborhood's water supply took a few hours, and the children took full advantage of the activity to continue frolicking in the dark.

One particular water night in 1940 that Nejde distinctly remembers, everything was flowing along as usual when suddenly the adults began using hushed tones and motioned for the children to be quiet. Curious about what was going on, Nejde looked out toward Khiabane Estakhr and saw an exceptionally tall man dressed in a black cape and black riding boots talking to an Armenian neighbor who had been manning the wooden dam. The hulking man was gesturing with a cane at the *joub*, and Nejde's neighbor was bowing, nodding his head, and answering the man's questions. As quickly as the lone giant had arrived, he walked briskly away down the street, and Nejde's neighbor ran over to tell everyone what had happened. The man was none other than the country's king, Reza Shah Pahlavi, who had walked down the street from the palace to personally observe the distribution of water and ask about the punctuality of water service. The neighbor had humbly explained to Reza Shah that the service was quite regular and thanked him profusely for the city's efforts to provide the citizens with water. After listening to this news with quiet fascination, the adults uniformly told the children to hurry inside and then dispersed to their own houses. As usual, Hagob and Arshalous did not take the time to explain to Nejde what this visit meant or why families had to go in early, but he assumed it had something to do with the king, whose visit seemed to fill the adults with both excitement and fear.

The only other occasion Nejde could remember the adults of the neighborhood acting in such a way was the time the old wooden gate had to be closed, which also had something to do with Reza Shah. It was in the month of Shahrivar in 1941, immediately following Reza Shah's exile, when Hagob Hagobian returned home in a panic, having heard a rumor that there were likely going to be marches and riots near the palace and that looting and mayhem might spill over into the surrounding neighborhoods. Other neighbors had also heard this rumor, including the Muslim landlord, Agha-ye Abdoulahian, who decided that it would be best to close the gate. Although there was no explicit rumor that religious minorities were to be singled out by the anticipated mobs, the anti-Armenian, nationalist tone of the late 1930s combined with the strongly Islamic tone of the voices to emerge after Reza Shah's exile led to wild rumors of lawlessness in the community and perhaps a bit of paranoia, so that the event would hence be remembered as the "Shahrivarian Incident."

While the Hagobians and their downstairs tenants were bolting the front door to their residence, which was not protected behind the wooden gate, their Jewish neighbor Pauline knocked on the door and asked to speak with Arshalous, who was her best friend in the neighborhood. Afraid that their home would be targeted by the anticipated mobs because they were European Jews, Pauline asked Arshalous if she would be willing to hide their family jewels and silverware in her home, apparently reasoning that as Armenians the Hagobians would be less of a target. Without hesitating or conferring with her husband, Arshalous told Pauline that she would help and waited by the door for Pauline's son, Albert, to bring over a small wooden trunk, which she took upstairs to hide under some linens. Upon finding out about the agreement between the two women, Hagob became concerned, feeling that somehow the presence of the hidden jewels would attract the angry mob that was growing by the minute in the neighbors' minds.

Looking down from his upstairs window at the closed gate, Hagob seriously assessed the security of the house and gated neighborhood for the first time. He realized that there was one fatal flaw. The Hagobians' house was the only house on the cul-de-sac that had its main door outside of the wooden gate, and a side door that opened into the compound behind the gate. This meant that in order to gain entry into the compound an attacking mob would likely attempt to break down the front door of the Hagobians' house first so that they could circumvent the thick wooden gate that was essentially impenetrable. After sharing his fears with Arshalous and the tenants downstairs, a plan was devised to protect the house and compound. In the downstairs kitchen, large pots of cooking oil and water were set to boil on the stove, and a path was cleared to enable easy access from the kitchen to the stairs. In the event that a crazed mob tried to breach the Abdoulahian compound either though the front gate or through the Hagobians' residence, the pots of boiling liquid would be hauled upstairs and dumped out of the upstairs window onto the heads of the attackers. Hagob stoked the medieval defensive weapon all night, but the angry, chanting mob never materialized. For the rest of that week, the main gate was left closed, but quiet prevailed on Khiabane Estakhr, and the neighborhood soon returned to its normal pace.

In the fall of 1941, Arshalous enrolled seven-year-old Nejde in a coeducational private grammar school called Mehr (Kindness) that was run by Iranian Presbyterians. Although the Hagobians were Gregorian Christians, Hagob and Arshalous had been raised in a Presbyterian-run orphanage in Tabriz, where they had met. They were later wed by an American Presbyterian minister in Kermanshah. Thus, they always held a special affinity for Americans as well as Presbyterians. In addition to this positive affiliation with the Presbyterian Church in Iran, Arshalous chose Mehr for her son because it was one of the few Christian schools still open after Reza Shah's closure of all foreign-language schools in 1938—including those run by Armenians and Assyrians. Because Mehr was attended by children of prominent generals, ministers, newspaper publishers, and government functionaries, its student body was a mixture of Persian Muslims, Persian Christians, Persian Jews, Armenians, Assyrians, Zoroastrians, and some Baha'is. Although Nejde had been speaking Persian and interacting with Iranian Muslim vendors on the neighborhood cul-de-sac since he was a toddler, it was at Mehr that he first became aware of differences between Armenians and Iranians of other religions and ethnic backgrounds.

The language of instruction at Mehr was Persian, and before classes every day the students, regardless of their religion, would congregate in the adjacent church hall to sing songs from Christian hymnbooks translated into Persian and to listen to their female principal read selections from the Ketab-e Muqadas (Holy Book/Bible). At play, all the students would speak, yell, and scream in Persian, so no linguistic differences separated students or outwardly suggested different religions or ways of life. The first major difference that Nejde noticed between himself and his Persian Muslim classmates was something very basic: lunch.

When it was time for the children to eat, Nejde and other Armenian and Assyrian children would reach into their sacks and produce a rolled sandwich made of flat bread and cold meat that sometimes included pork. The students would usually run around in the schoolyard during lunch and play while holding the tubular sandwich in one hand, stopping every so often to take another bite. In contrast, the Persian Muslim children would gather in the room that served as a cafeteria and open up covered bowls that usually contained rice with an aromatic stew such as *ghorma sabzi* or strips of *kubideh* (ground, spiced kebab). The children of the military generals would often receive their food hot, delivered by soldiers serving under their fathers, who would return later to pick up the empty pots.

One day it started raining before lunch, and all of the students were directed to the cafeteria to eat. As Nejde sat down on the floor and unwrapped his sandwich, his Persian Muslim friend Ali sat next to him and opened up his pot of hot rice and kebab that had just been dropped off by his father's servant. The smell of the warm kebab overcame Nejde, who forgot himself and stared longingly into his friend's pot. Noticing Nejde's obvious interest in his food, Ali suggested that they exchange lunches. Nejde nodded his head in agreement and proceeded to dig into the rice and kebab while Ali devoured his cold-cut sandwich. After they were done eating, Ali told Nejde that he loved eating the Armenians' sandwiches but that he wasn't allowed to. Perplexed and in true form, Nejde asked why this was the case. Without mentioning the Islamic ban on pork, Ali explained that it was because he was a Muslim. Nejde didn't really understand but was happy when Ali then suggested that they exchange lunches more often, and the two made a pact to keep their activity a secret. The day before, Ali would specify what type of sandwich he wanted, often knowing the names of the cold cuts better than Nejde, and Nejde would ask his mother to make that kind for school the next day. Whatever type of Persian food Ali was delivered was fine with Nejde, and he couldn't wait for exchange days. Arshalous may have become suspicious when Nejde began coming home smelling spicy and asking her for strange cold-cut combination sandwiches for lunch, but as far as Nejde knew, exchange days with Ali forever remained a secret.

The first day of September 1943 was a memorable day for nine-year-old Nejde because it was the first day of Ramadan and the day on which his sister Rima was born. The night before, Hagob had taken Arshalous to stay at the residence of an Armenian midwife after the midwife had determined that Arshalous would soon give birth. While Nejde and Hagob were sleeping upstairs at home, Nejde was suddenly jolted awake by the thunderous sound of cannons going off. Scared out of his wits, he ran into his parents' room, dived into his father's bed, and frantically tried to hide under the covers. For the first time in his life that Nejde could remember, and what he would later recall to be a rare occasion in his youth, his father, instead of becoming perturbed and telling him to be quiet or go back to sleep, took a moment to explain to Nejde what was going on and why: it was the Muslim holy month of Ramadan, in which all Muslims in Iran and around the world did not smoke, eat food, or drink from dawn until dusk. The cannons were set off just before the break of dawn to signal to Muslims that the fast had begun. With that lengthy explanation, Nejde was kindly told to be quiet and go back to sleep. But he could not. Nejde lay in bed thinking about this month of Ramadan, the cannons, what it would be like to go all day without food or water, and why Armenians did not act in the same way. Shortly thereafter the sun rose, and father and son walked to the midwife's house to check on Arshalous. As they approached the residence, the midwife emerged to tell Hagob and Nejde the good news that Arshalous had just delivered a healthy baby girl.

As Nejde entered his preteens, he began to notice other differences that distinguished Persian Muslims from Armenians. The Jewish family that had lived next door moved and were replaced by a large Persian family that included boys and girls who were Nejde's age and older. Because their mother and Arshalous became close friends and would often go out shopping together, Nejde noticed that their mother would don a black chador (the traditional Iranian form of *hejab*) before leaving the house. Nejde also observed that that the older girls, whom he found very attractive, would do the same. However, most striking to Nejde were the relationship and interactions he witnessed between the young males and the females of the family, which differed drastically from his own relationships with female friends and relatives and those he observed within the other Christian families in the neighborhood. Unlike in his own family, where his mother was the primary disciplinarian even when Hagob was at home and the person whom Nejde was never to talk back to or question, the Persian boys next door were encouraged by their father to act in an authoritative manner from an early age such that their older sisters and even their mother had to accept their commands and treat them with deference. This, thought Nejde, was an ideal way to live.

Another observation Nejde made around this time was that all his Persian friends at school and in the neighborhood seemed to be able to escape music lessons, while almost all of the Armenian children were forced by their parents to endure dreaded private music instruction. Boys were usually given the choice between violin and accordion, and girls were given the sole option of piano. Nejde hated the violin and wished he could play piano, but his parents were determined that he learn to master the stringed instrument and forced him to practice daily. Every time the family would have guests in their home, Nejde would be required to play several Armenian songs, which he would have to improvise because his teacher taught only European classical music. The scales were wrong, the songs would be painfully off key, and Nejde and his captive audience would wince as his proud parents smiled and offered encouraging words. Guests would always applaud politely and call for another song, but Nejde hated the whole affair, wondering why Persian kids never had to take music lessons unless they wanted to. Why couldn't Armenians be like the Persians? he often thought.

In 1946, Arshalous walked Nejde down the street from Mehr after school to a building on Khiabane Ghavam al-Saltaneh to register him for after-school activities. There above a Persian bread bakery was the clubhouse for the Anjoman-e Parvaresh-e Afkar-e Javanan-e Aramane (Organization for Fostering the Thoughts of Armenian Youth), which would later become known as Ararat. This newly established Armenian youth organization, which had members ranging from age seven to mid-forties, offered group music classes and the opportunity for Nejde to play in a small orchestra. Ararat also offered classes on Armenian literature and culture and an environment in which Armenian was routinely spoken and Armenia was often a topic of discussion. The organization made an agreement with Mehr whereby the school's soccer field could be used by the Ararat soccer team after hours, so Ararat activities were initially like an Armenian cultural supplement to Nejde's schoolday at Mehr.

Although Nejde still continued to loathe the violin, perhaps even more in a group setting, he was very impressed with Ararat and its older members and leaders, and he thrived in an environment where interaction and questions were encouraged. The setting seemed familiar, for, as at home, Armenian was the only language spoken at Ararat. The organization's athletes, who participated in track, soccer, weightlifting, and mountaineering, greatly inspired Nejde, who would over the coming years in Ararat be motivated to try all of these activities, eventually focusing on soccer and weightlifting. Aside from the fun and glory promised by sporting activities, many of Ararat's early members were intellectuals, and they would become involved in intense political discussions which

Nejde intently listen to and tried his best to understand. Often the discussion centered on the subject of the Soviet Union, communism, and Armenia, and Nejde noticed that opinions within Ararat at that time differed sharply on these issues, even if he could not fully understand why.

In 1948, when Nejde was fourteen, the Hagobian family moved out of the Abdoulahian compound and up the street to a new four-story apartment building on Khiabane Estakhr that housed predominantly Armenian tenants. The Hagobians' next-door neighbor, Megardich Megardichian, was the publisher of the unofficial Dashnak daily Armenian cultural and community newspaper *Alik*, of which Hagob and Arshalous were avid readers. In summer of that year, Nejde graduated from Mehr and was registered at Dabirestan-e Firuz Bahram, a Zoroastrian-sponsored boys high school of five hundred students that was well known in academics.[9] Most of Nejde's Armenian friends from Mehr and many of them from Ararat were instead enrolled in the newly opened Armenian high school Hayots Dprots, which taught half of its classes in Armenian.[10] Because Hayots Dprots had only recently added its upper-division high school classes, Hagob and Arshalous made the decision to send him instead to Firuz Bahram. The extra Armenian-language skills Nejde would acquire at Hayots Dprots were not worth the risk that he might do poorly on the national exams, which were offered only in Persian.

In his high school history and geography classes at Firuz Bahram, and through his interactions and conversations at Ararat, Nejde began to learn more about the relationship between the Soviet Union, communism, and Armenia. Events that had happened in his short past suddenly began to make much more sense as Nejde began to recall his random experiences with the Soviet Union up until that point. There was the time in August 1941 when the annual family vacation to the Armenian village suburb of Vanak was cut short after the Soviets bombed Tehran,[11] and days later when his father and mother were devastated with the news via telegram that Hagob's truck had been seized by the Red Army as it invaded Tabriz. Nejde remembered the arguments between his parents and his aunt and uncle, Hripsik (or Morkur, "Aunt") and Hovannes Mouradian, both of whom spoke fluent Russian and were strongly pro-Soviet, and the stories they would repeatedly tell about their die-hard support for Russia.[12]

He would detect his father's disgust during the war when Hovannes and Morkur would listen to the shortwave radio and gleefully move little red flags westward across a map of eastern Europe they had up on the wall, tracing the Soviet advance to Berlin. Nejde remembered their heated conversations about Armenia and the words *socialism* and *communism* recited often. Nejde recalled the time when during the occupation of Iran in 1944 the family vacationed in Ghazvin and a Red Army soldier gave him a small medal with a red star and hammer-and-sickle insignia. When he showed it to his father, Hagob promptly smashed the item and offered no explanation to his distraught son. By high school, Nejde began to make sense of these arguments and attitudes: his father hated the Soviet Union because of its hold on Armenia and because of its invasion of Iran, during which the family lost its livelihood and Iran was occupied. Nejde would later learn that the Dashnaks with whom Hagob sympathized and often donated to, were hunted down, arrested, and often executed by the Soviet occupiers during the war. Until his adulthood, Nejde perceived the land of Armenia as the Armenians' original motherland that now, unfortunately, was a Soviet republic with a population of mostly Communists.

Although his understanding of events, ideology, and details was extremely basic, Nejde nevertheless quickly learned to despise the Soviet Union and communism and was never short of an ally at Ararat when he began to engage in his own discussions on these topics with Ararat club members. In these engagements, he learned the terminology and buzzwords of the debate. Pro-Communist or sympathetic Ararat members would harp about the "masses" and "workers" and "Marx" and the "bourgeoisie," while trying to explain an ideology Nejde couldn't seem to understand and didn't really care to learn about. They would call Nejde and his anti-Communist friends "imperialists" and "servants of the shah." As modeled by older and at the time better-educated Ararat leaders such as Sevak Saginian, Nejde would retort that communism was antireligious and anti-Armenian and that Communist sympathizers were traitors to Iran and the shah. He couldn't argue with the point that his anti-Communist, pro-shah arguments were intellectually unsophisticated because they were. That would hurt, so Nejde would retort that communism was the bane of the free world and that pro-Communist Iranians were Soviet lackeys.

While finally finding an academic subject, mathematics, that he enjoyed and excelled at, Nejde continued to learn about Persians, Armenians, Communists, and Iranian politics at Firuz Bahram. He learned about Islam and Zoroastrianism in required classes on religion. History classes covered Persian history only from the time of the Achaemenids through the Qajars, and political science focused on the Iranian Constitution, so Nejde's education in Iranian and international politics occurred outside the school compound rather than inside. At Firuz Bahram, with its large, mixed student body, student cliques and gangs were often formed around the predominant political parties that were active between 1948 and 1953. Fistfights would often occur between pro-Tudeh students and those sympathetic to the Pan-Iranists or the Somka (National Socialist Workers Party of Iran), which was an extreme nationalist group whose supporters at the school wore distinctive black T-shirts.[13] In these engagements, punches were exchanged rather than party ideology and rhetoric. Yet however impelled by teen angst and bravado, it was clear that the underlying divisions were political.

The Soviet Cultural Library faced the intersection where the high school was located, and the students would pass by it on their way to

61. Nejde Hagobian (*third from right along wall*) in the hall at Dabirestan-e Firuz Bahram, Tehran, 1952. Unknown photographer. Courtesy of Nejde Hagobian.

and from school. Taped to the windows from inside were large posters of Russian women happily engaged in agricultural work on collective farms. Nejde would always notice how the stout women smiled and showed their gold-capped teeth, and through conversations with friends about the photos he added another word to his rapidly growing lexicon of political terms: *prupagand* (propaganda). The street on which the high school was located came to a dead end in the next block at the gate of the Soviet embassy. The latter large walled and wooded property, several blocks in length and width, was never open to the public and became an object of curiosity and constant speculation about its contents and purpose.[14] Two blocks up the street in the other direction was a new multistory building built by the US State Department to function as an office extension and information center. Downstairs was a beautiful library stocked with books and periodicals in English, a language that Nejde was now studying at Firuz Bahram. Rows of polished American cherry-wood bookshelves and tables were interspersed with comfortable couches, and the library featured paintings of American presidents on the wall.[15] Nejde and his friend Henry Gabrielian would visit the American library every week. They usually would sit in the periodicals section and leaf through American magazines such as the *Saturday Evening Post*, *Life*, and *Look*. Nejde found the photographs of campus life in the United States most interesting and often admired the detail in the cover work by Norman Rockwell. Also of interest to him was the large collection of technical and engineering reference books the American library offered, although they were not to be checked out, and most of the words were indecipherable to him with his limited English.

Between 1950 and 1952, membership in Ararat fluctuated, and the clubhouse moved twice, eventually ending up in a two-story building on Khiabane Noh Bahar. Many of the older college students of the original group, especially those interested in the political left, quit the organization to focus their attention and efforts on Iranian national politics and parties. At the same time, Ararat's athletic activities, especially mountaineering, gained in popularity. Involved in several athletic activities and having made good friends, Nejde spent most of his waking hours at Ararat when he was not at school. During summer breaks, Nejde and his Armenian friends would be at Ararat or on the playing field from early morning to late evening, When school was in session, Nejde's social life was divided between his Persian and Assyrian friends at Firuz Bahram and then his Armenian friends and teammates at Ararat.

Membership and activities at Ararat could be highly structured and organized, such as the track and field and gymnastics groups that competed in national competitions under the Ararat banner, yet many activities were loosely organized, and participation fluctuated. Depending on individual interest and motivation, Ararat members could participate in several activities concurrently or none at all. Although a substantial number of Armenian Iranian teenagers seemed to show up at Ararat only to socialize and flirt, no one seemed to mind, even their parents, who were happy that the youth were passing time in Ararat's safe, Armenian-oriented environment and avoiding trouble out on the streets.

In 1951, Leonidas Ohanian, a twenty-two-year-old member of Ararat who had been active in Armenian literature classes and theater, proposed to the permit holder and chair of Ararat, Sevak Saginian, that a scouting group be developed to give the preteens and teenagers something else to do with their time that was constructive. Not all of the youth were musically inclined or interested in theater; organized sports weren't for everyone; and mountaineering, although popular, involved training, detailed planning, and proper equipment. Scouting, Leonidas thought, would offer Ararat teens an organized outdoor, social, and physical activity that taught practical skills and upheld Armenian culture and the values of the Armenian community. Sevak agreed with him and informed Lolo (as Leonidas was called by his friends) that he had in fact already been granted a permit for scouting that had been issued when the shah intervened the previous year to allow the organization to have mountaineering as an activity.[16] Thus, all that was left for Lolo to do was to find a group of teens interested in scouting activity and to learn about scouting himself, for, aside from the fact that they wore uniforms and practiced marching regularly, Lolo admittedly knew very little about scouting activities and traditions.[17]

When Lolo approached Nejde, then seventeen, and some of the older teens to find out about their general level of interest in scouting, he got mixed reactions. Although some, such as Nejde's good friend Artashes

"Adzi" Yerganian, were enthusiastic after hearing only the initial concept, Nejde was more skeptical and wanted to find out more about what scouting entailed before signing up for yet another Ararat activity. To him, scouting implied only "uniforms," which at first did not seem particularly appealing.

Lolo was undeterred and within a short period of time had signed up about twenty-five *hay ari* (Armenian boy scouts) and twenty *hay arenush* (Armenian girl scouts). Ararat leaders agreed upon a style of uniforms, which looked like a hybrid between those of the American Boy and Girl Scouts and the Soviet Pioneers.[18] Equally important as the style was the consistency of the color of the cloth, which was a contested issue before a standard light khaki was agreed upon. Orders for labels and badges were placed at a local trophy shop, and these items were fashioned after those of military and other scouting organizations. Scouts had to have a parent take them to the tailor for measurement for their custom uniforms, which would have the name "Ararat" embroidered in Armenian script above the breast pocket and on the arm. Soon decked out in their khaki uniforms and neck scarves, the boy scouts and girl scouts were organized to learn the skill of precision marching for parades and flag bearing, which they practiced for weeks on end in the large yard behind Ararat. Occasionally watching with some of the other Ararat teens, Nejde noticed that the practice was paying off, but he would repeatedly tell Lolo that there had to be more to scouting if he were to consider joining the group.

Two months after the establishment of the Ararat scouts, Ararat was making plans to host a dinner and reception for a visiting Armenian American dignitary from the United Nations Food Program, George Mardikian. Lolo seized the opportunity to have the scouts' first dedication ceremony and oath coincide with what would be a large community event. On the night of the dedication, Nejde looked on as a spectator while his friends marched by him in uniforms carrying the flags of Iran and Ararat to music of the Ararat marching band. The parade went without a hitch, with the exception of the clarinet player, who emitted a high-pitched squeal every time he stepped in one of the many holes that pocked the yard. The oath ceremony was solemn as the scouts pledged in Armenian before the crowd that they would be faithful to "Astsus, azgis yev hayrenikis" (My god, my nation, and my homeland).[19] As Lolo had hoped, in the weeks following the impressive awards ceremony the ranks of the scouts doubled. But almost as soon as the new recruits were outfitted in uniforms, the novelty of the awards ceremony and marching before the crowd wore off on the original inductees, and the scouts started verbally complaining and dropping out.

One day while Lolo was discussing the situation with some of the other Ararat members, Nejde Hagobian suggested that Lolo contact his Iranian American friend George Patgorney, whom Nejde knew to be somehow affiliated with the Boy Scouts of America. Lolo asked Nejde once more why he wouldn't join the scouts, this time boosting his ego by saying he knew Nejde was a leader and challenging him to put his mind to work to develop some activities to keep the scouts interested. Having already been intrigued by the induction ceremony, Nejde agreed on the spot to join the scouts and help out—with the condition that he begin at the level of assistant scoutmaster.

Before the next scout meeting, Nejde and Arshalous went to the neighborhood tailor, bringing a bolt of khaki cloth the color of the other Ararat scout uniforms and the correct patches and badges purchased from the trophy shop. Two days later the uniform was ready, and when Nejde appeared at the next Ararat scout meeting, he was greeted by the cheers and hugs of his good friends who were already scouts. But Nejde still knew next to nothing about scouting. So, acting on his own suggestion to Lolo, he contacted George Patgorney, who attended the American school next to Nejde's former primary school Mehr. Patgorney lent Nejde a used copy of the *Boy Scouts of America Field Book*, which contained hundreds of pages of instructions and photos depicting activities, including signaling, stalking, knot tying, first aid, wilderness survival, cookery, camp crafts, and the building of rope structures. Patgorney explained that because there was no Iranian scouting, he and a loose-knit group of half a dozen sons of American expatriates would go camping together in the hills north of Tehran and practice wilderness skills. All of them, including Patgorney, wore the uniforms of the Boy Scouts of America. Although they engaged in scouting activities without a proper permit, they were a small group, so no one from the government seemed to mind.

Nejde rushed home with the boy scouts manual and studied it intently, using the many descriptive drawings to aid in his understanding of the English text, which he still had difficulty fully understanding. He practiced the knots for hours and then advanced to assembling wood and rope structures in an empty lot. He also learned about the concept of merit badges for community service and projects. Over the next six months into the summer of 1952, Nejde shared the knowledge he acquired from the field manual at Ararat scout meetings. The scouts were rearranged and structured into patrols like the Boy Scouts of America,[20] a program of merit badges was initiated, and outdoor hikes and camping trips were planned that included activities in wilderness survival and the construction of rope structures. As an added symbolic touch, badges were ordered to emulate the American motto "Be Prepared!" The closest approximation in Armenian was "Misht Patrast": Always Prepared. As before, the scouts marched and marched, but their morale had been raised considerably with the injection of new ideas and scheduled outings.

The first Ararat camping event took place in the spring of 1952 in the mountains north of Tehran at the Manzarieh campgrounds. Sevak Saginian obtained a permit for a large group to camp at the spacious, woodsy park, which featured a swimming pool, campgrounds with fire pits, and abundant trails for hiking. Best of all, it offered use of camping equipment stored on the site, such as canvas tents and cookware for large groups. Although the equipment had been left unused for more than a decade after the disbanding of the Pishahangi-ye Iran following Reza Shah's exile in 1941, it was in fairly good shape and enabled the generally unequipped Armenian scouts, all from the city, to enjoy a true outdoor camping experience. The first camping trip was attended by a group of about thirty-five boy scouts and was scheduled to last for a week.

Mornings at camp began with the sound of reveille blown by an Ararat trumpet player. Within five minutes, the scouts were expected to be in uniform at the flagpole, where the Ararat flag would be hoisted under the Iranian national flag. Scouts who didn't hear the bugle or who pretended not to would be dragged out of their tents by the other scouts and forced to stand in their underwear or pajamas for the flag raising. All would then state the Ararat oath to uphold allegiance to God, the nation, and the

62. Scouts gather for a portrait at the first campout at Manzarieh, 1952. Unknown photographer. Courtesy of Nejde Hagobian.

homeland. Breakfast, cleanup, and wilderness activities followed. After lunch, a one-hour rest would be taken in tents before the group would reconvene for more activities and training until dinner. Each day would culminate with a big bonfire.

One day during the middle of the trip was designated for a visit by parents and Ararat girl scouts. This was a special event because the boy scouts, most of whom had never spent a night away from home, hadn't seen their parents for days, and several of them had girlfriends in the girl scouts and were by then lovesick. The night before, the scouts carefully laid their uniforms under their sleeping pads so the following day they would look as if they had been pressed, and everyone did their best to clean themselves and the campgrounds in anticipation of their guests. The parents and girl scouts arrived at ten o'clock in the morning, carrying home-cooked food and changes of clothing. After lunch, parents relaxed outdoors and spent time with their sons while other scouts went on a group hike. Some of the scouts who had visiting girlfriends showed off the couple's initials secretly carved on a remote tree because the practice was contrary to scout rules.

The final day of the first Ararat camping trip was full of mixed emotions for the scouts, who had developed a tremendous amount of camaraderie in their week of camping and activities together. Although many were content to be going home after a week of outdoor life, some had tears in their eyes as they took down the tents and dismantled the structures they had built together over the week. From the moment they left Manzarieh, the scouts became nostalgic about the trip, and for the next several months they would proudly display the badges they had earned and share often exaggerated stories of incidents that had occurred while at camp. The first Ararat scout campout had been a huge success and would thereafter become a regular biannual event for the organization.

In September 1952, Lolo Ohanian informed Ararat leader Sevak Saginian that the scouts were ready to march with the Ararat athletes in the annual parade at Amjadieh Stadium for the shah's birthday on the Fourth of Aban, a state holiday that fell on October 25 that year. Sevak told Lolo to take the preparation for the event very seriously and that the scouts had better be prepared and look their best. Sevak knew that Ararat athletes

63. Nejde Hagobian holds the Iranian tricolor at Manzarieh, 1952. Unknown photographer. Courtesy of Nejde Hagobian.

traditionally led the Fourth of Aban parade owing to the parade's alphabetical organization and that the shah would again be standing and saluting while observing the parade.[21] Furthermore, he was aware that there would be scores of photographers covering the event, so it was important that the Ararat scouts march in perfect formation. Heeding Saginian's stern advice, Lolo made sure they prepared for a full month for the Fourth of Aban parade in 1952.

At Amjadieh Stadium, with thousands of spectators looking on, the state marching band finished playing the patriotic anthem "Shahanshah," and the drummers broke into marching cadence. Bearing the Ararat flag, which states in Persian "Bashgah-he Varzeshi-ye Ararat" (Ararat Athletic Club) and utilizes the red, blue, and orange of the Armenian tricolor, and flanked by his close friends David Davidian and Rubik Voskanian, Nejde Hagobian was the lead flag bearer in the parade of Iranian sports and athletic organizations. As the scouts passed the shah's observation box in the stands, Nejde lowered the Ararat flag parallel to the ground as instructed. The shah, dressed in his military regalia, stood at attention and saluted while the parade passed by.

Through the experience of leading the 1952 Fourth of Aban parade, Nejde's sense of loyalty to the shah grew. It was exciting to lead the procession, and it was an honor to be recognized and saluted by the nation's ruler. Furthermore, the shah's recognition of Ararat itself—an Armenian

64. Ararat scouts, including Nejde Hagobian (*center with flag*), lead the Fourth of Aban parade, 1952. Unknown photographer. Courtesy of Nejde Hagobian.

social and cultural organization—gave Nejde a feeling of belonging and inclusion because it seemed as though there was no difference in the shah's treatment of and respect for all Iranians participating in the event, whatever their religion or ethnic origins. The experience also boosted Nejde's interest in scouting further, and because of his dedication and involvement he was promoted by the scouting council to the position of scoutmaster.

In the spring of 1953, the Ararat boy scouts and girl scouts from Tehran took a trip by bus to Isfahan under Nejde's leadership. In Isfahan, the scouts were treated to receptions by members of the city's Ararat branch, introduced to important members of the local Armenian community, and given tours of the city's historic sights. During the three-day trip, the scouts were taught about the commercial and artistic contributions of the Armenians of New Julfa under the glorious reign of Shah Abbas, which simultaneously deepened Nejde's sense of Iranian patriotism and Armenian pride and elevated his awareness of the long history of Armenians in Iran.

Nejde was aware of rumors that the Dashnak Party, which sponsored the daily newspaper *Alik,* which his parents avidly read, had a grip on Ararat and that the group's members were affiliated with the party. It was true that many of its leaders were either rank-and-file members of the party or Dashnak sympathizers—or even Dashnak pretenders because it was trendy in those years to hint at one's activity in the covert, underground organization. Yet Nejde never detected a hint of party ideology in Ararat meetings or activities and never received or heard of any directives or indoctrination sessions to advance the party's nationalist, socialist philosophy. As far as he was aware, Ararat's purpose was purely athletic, cultural, and social—dedicated to sustaining the Armenian language and strengthening the bonds within the Armenian Iranian community.

Despite the organization's outwardly apolitical appearance, Ararat members found it difficult to avoid becoming drawn into the politically motivated street demonstrations and altercations that typified the year 1952–53. Members who were strongly pro-shah and anti-Tudeh, such as permit holder Sevak Saginian (who also happened to be an excellent boxer) basically sought out physical confrontations with Communists at street rallies and demonstrations. Motivations were different for younger members such as Nejde Hagobian, Artash Yerganian, and David Davidian, who were drawn in at demonstrations and fistfights more as a result of their age, the allure of being a part of a powerful mob, and the excitement of the moment rather than any strong political convictions regarding issues such as the leadership of Prime Minister Mossadegh or concerns about the Iranian economy. Throughout the winter and spring of 1953, street fights between pro-Tudeh gangs—which would at times include some Armenians—and supporters of the shah were commonplace, and Ararat members and scouts were increasingly becoming involved.[22] Entering his nineteenth year and having been weightlifting for five years at Ararat, Nejde had become one of the largest of the Ararat scouts. After a few engagements with pro-Tudeh youth, Nejde discovered that he could hold his own in a fight when he had to and so quickly shed his apprehension about getting involved in street mayhem on the side of the shah.

On Noh-e Esfand (February 28), 1953, Nejde and several other Ararat members attended a demonstration outside the royal palace in support of the shah when it was rumored that Prime Minister Mossadegh had persuaded the shah to leave the country.[23] Nejde was amazed by the huge crowd of people gathered, many of whom were flagellating themselves with their bare hands or stooping to rub grass or dirt in their hair to express their consternation over the thought that the shah might leave. A clash was inevitable when a previously planned pro-Tudeh march against the shah and a large pro-Mossadegh rally converged on the palace from opposite directions. The Ararat members joined in with their fellow pro-shah Iranians as they vented their anger with a hail of pro-shah chants, sticks, bottles, rocks, and fists. The shah remained in the country, and Nejde was proud that he had participated in what seemed to be a critical demonstration of support.[24]

During another pro-shah demonstration in the summer of 1953 that got out of control, a large crowd had formed outside of a compound near the royal palace where Prime Minister Mossadegh and his foreign minister, Husayn Fatemi, were meeting. Although Nejde wasn't sure what the crowd's intentions were once they gained access to the compound, he joined in with scores of Iranians and a few of his friends from Ararat

65. Nejde Hagobian in "counterdemonstration" attire, Tehran rooftop, July 1953. Unknown photographer. Courtesy of Nejde Hagobian.

in pushing collectively on the front gate to break it down. After someone in the crowd yelled that the security guards were fleeing out a side door and over a neighboring wall, the crowd heaved mightily, and the gate flew open. In a mad dash, the mob rushed the compound's main building, with Ararat member Chalo Amirkhanian leading the charge through the front door. When Chalo emerged from the building, which was being ransacked and looted by the crowd, he was holding a leather briefcase and looking simultaneously excited and scared: it was Foreign Minister Fatemi's notes and documents. As Chalo and the other Ararat members ran off with the bag, Nejde hurriedly walked home, thinking that matters were getting serious.

On yet another occasion in 1953 that demonstrated how political turmoil was escalating, Nejde, Lolo, and three other Ararat members were walking down Khiabane Yusefabad when they were suddenly surrounded by a large group of pro-Tudeh youths and young adults, who began verbally accosting them and provoking them to fight. As one of the Tudehists squared off with Lolo, Nejde assessed the situation and realized it was hopeless: they were totally outnumbered and were surely going to suffer a severe beating. The crowd closed in on the Ararat members, and fists and sticks started flying. Then, just as suddenly as the gang of Tudeh supporters had appeared, there was a screeching of tires on the street and pounding of feet on the pavement, and Nejde heard someone yelling, "Bachaha-ye Ararat!" ("Ararat kids!"). He looked up to see the towering local *pahlavan* (athlete) of the *zurkhane*, ardent pro-shah agitator, and mob organizer Shaban Jafari (widely known as "Shaban Bimokh," Shaban the Brainless) tearing into the crowd of Tudehists, followed by a large gang of other stout pro-shah *pahlavan*s, who had arrived in Jeeps.[25] Within moments, the Tudeh gang was beaten back and sent running down Yusefabad with a number of *pahlavan*s in pursuit. Lolo and Nejde approached Shaban Bimokh afterward and thanked him profusely for saving them from what would have no doubt been a brutal thrashing. As Shaban shook their hands, he smiled crazily and explained that it was his pleasure to beat up Tudehists. With that, he hopped back in his Jeep and led the caravan of *pahlavan*s away. Nejde and Lolo were thoroughly impressed.

Thus far such fistfights and demonstrations had seemed relatively harmless and were extremely exciting, but fear set in late one day in July 1953 when a well-substantiated rumor circulated that Tudehists planned on burning down or otherwise attacking the Ararat building on Khiabane Yusefabad. It was surmised that Ararat was viewed as a pro-shah organization. Ararat leader Sevak Saginian called Nejde and a number of other scouts and Ararat members to the club, where they took up positions in the lower windows of the building with an odd assortment of loaded guns that Marzbet Marzbetuny had miraculously produced. Nejde had always guessed that Marzbet had a direct connection to the Dashnaks, but now he was certain. When a patrol of the Tehran police finally showed up that evening—hours after Sevak Saginian had placed a frantic call to them with the rumor—the patrol chief walked around the building, looked into the basement, and returned outside to report to Sevak that there shouldn't be a problem, joking that the club was already being defended by more firepower than the gendarme had at its disposal.[26] Furthermore, he explained, the police were too busy trying to deal with rampant protests and rioting around the city to assign guards to Ararat based on only a rumor. After waiting anxiously until dawn at the windows without detecting a single Communist agitator or saboteur, the scouts returned their weapons to

Marzbet and Sevak. They were sent home yawning, with instructions not to tell their parents what had happened, for Ararat was supposed to be a place that kept Armenian kids off the streets and out of trouble.

On the days leading up to Bist-o Hasht-e Mordad (Mordad 28, 1332; August 19, 1953), Hagob Hagobian made Nejde stay at home, not even allowing him to make the walk across town to attend Ararat functions. Demonstrations and riots were becoming even more violent, and Hagob was afraid Nejde would get seriously hurt in the street clashes between the pro-shah, National Front, and Tudeh forces. When it was announced that Prime Minister Mossadegh had been arrested and the shah was firmly back in power, Nejde could never have dreamed these events had been shaped by a CIA/MI6-inspired and funded coup d'état; in his understanding they were simply the result of a popular outpouring of loyalty and support for the shah and a rejection of the leadership of the Tudeh and Mossadegh.[27]

In early September, barely two weeks after the coup d'état, Nejde received an unexpected award for his participation in the demonstrations in support of the shah during that period. He was declared the recipient of the Neshan-e Rastakhiz-e Bist-o Hasht-e Mordad Darje-ye Seh (Order of the Resurgence of Bist-o Hasht-e Mordad of the Third Degree). In addition to a medal, he was given a document, affixed with his own photograph, that declared him a recipient of the award.

Upon receiving the award through Ararat leader Sevak Saginian, Nejde found out that he was not the only Ararat member to receive a medal for Bist-o Hasht-e Mordad. Scout leader Lolo Ohanian and Nejde's friend Artash Yerganian had also been given the award of the third rank, while Sevak Saginian and Chalo Amirkhanian (the "liberator" of Fatemi's briefcase) were awarded the Neshan-e Rastakhiz-e Darje-ye Yek, which was the same award but of the highest rank. Nejde was proud of his award, wearing his Rastakhiz medal on his Ararat scout uniform, showing off the certificate to all of his friends and relatives and describing in detail the street engagements that, he surmised, were the reasons he received the award.[28] Soon Nejde found out that beyond impressing friends and relatives, the certificate could play a very practical purpose in lubricating the wheels of Iranian bureaucracy.[29]

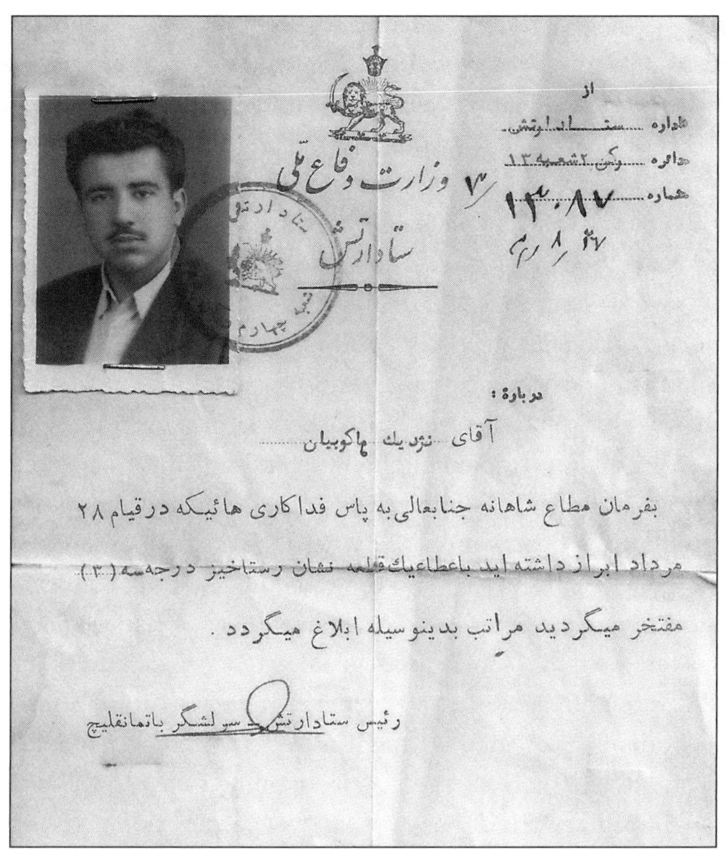

وزارت دفاع ملی
ستاد ارتش

از
اداره ستاد ارتش
دایره رکن ۲ شعبه ۱۳
شماره ۱۳۰۸۷
۲۷ / ۸ / ۳۲

درباره :

آقای نژدیک هاکوبیان

بفرمان مطاع شاهانه جنابعالی به پاس فداکاری هائیکه درقیام ۲۸ مرداد ابراز داشته اید باعطاءیک قطعه نشان رستاخیز درجه سه (۳) مفتخر میگردید مراتب بدینوسیله ابلاغ میگردد .

رئیس ستاد ارتش سرلشگر باتمانقلیچ

66. *Hokm* certifying the Neshan-e Rastakhiz-e Bist-o Hasht-e Mordad Darje-ye Seh awarded to Nejde Hagobian. "Ministry of Defense—Armed Forces Agha-ye Nejdek Hakobian, By order of the king, because of the heroism/sacrifices you have demonstrated during the uprising of Bist-o Hasht-e Mordad, you are being honored with the Order of the Resurgence of the Third Rank. The proceedings are related to you by this means. General Batmangholitch, Head of Armed Forces." Courtesy of Nejde Hagobian.

Just two months after Mohammad Reza Shah's throne had been restored by the coup d'état of August 1953, the Ararat scouts again led the Fourth of Aban (October 26, 1953) parade at Amjadieh Stadium for the shah's birthday.[30] This was perhaps one of the most exciting events of Nejde Hagobian's youth, for he was selected to march alone at the very front of the parade and by his salute provide the cue for the shah to rise for his review of the procession. Thousands of spectators filled the stands, flashbulbs were popping, and cameras filming the nation's movie theater news shorts (known as *akbar*) were rolling as Nejde led the Ararat scouts and Iranian athletic organizations around the track at Amjadieh to honor the shah. Marching directly behind Nejde were two younger Armenian scouts bearing a large, framed photograph of the shah as a teenager wearing the uniform of the Pishahangi-ye Iran. As instructed, when Nejde was in front of the observation box where the shah stood amidst Majles members, generals, ministers, and other members of the political elite, he turned to the shah, saluted, and then dropped his hand smartly. With this honorific cue, the shah stood up at attention, saluted back at the honored scout, and remained standing in review as the Iranian scouts, athletes, students, and an assortment of representatives from social and cultural organizations from Iran's cities marched past to the cadence of the national military band. For Nejde, it was an exhilarating experience that he relived for months afterward as clips appeared in movie theaters in Tehran and around the nation.

After the parade but preceding the main event, which was a soccer game between the two best soccer clubs in the nation, the Ararat scouts exhibited their newly acquired skills erecting flag posts, observation towers, and suspension bridges for river crossing out of wood and rope. Engaging in a timed competition between troops and observed by the shah with binoculars and the crowd in the stadium, the competing troops lined up at opposite ends of the track field with organized piles of precut timber and ropes on the ground in front of them. On Nejde's signal, which was a sharp blast of a whistle,[31] the troops would scramble to pick up the ropes and timber and run to their preplanned positions to begin erecting the structures. After the constructions were completed and the crowd applauded for the winning troop, Nejde signaled again, and the scouts competed to dismantle their constructions, organize their materials, and move back into formation. After another round of applause and another signal from Hagobian, the scouts marched off the field in a synchronized fashion, carrying their building materials.

Less than two weeks after the highly successful Fourth of Aban parade, the Ararat scouts were invited to a special reception held at the new palace complex in Tehran by the shah and his second wife, Queen Soraya.[32] There the scouts were photographed meeting the shah and treated to an elaborate buffet. Afterward, the shah circulated around the room to talk to some of the scoutmasters. In a relaxed conversation in which Nejde felt oddly comfortable considering the circumstances, the shah asked him about the activities of the Ararat scouts and seemed interested in hearing the details. He seemed particularly pleased when he asked what manual the Ararat scouts were using, and Nejde replied, "*Boy Scouts of America.*" Nejde was proud when the shah told him to keep up the good work with the scouts.

Shah Mohammad Reza Pahlavi had a sincere interest in scouting in 1953 and 1954, for he was planning to revive the Pishahangi-ye Iran under

67. Hagobian and Ararat scouts at reception with Mohammad Reza Shah and his second wife, Soraya, November 10, 1953. Unknown photographer. Courtesy of Nejde Hagobian.

the Sazman-e Pishahangi (Organization of Scouting), which had been disbanded in 1941 when his father, Reza Shah, had been deposed and he had been installed as successor. From the perspective of the Pahlavi regime, scouting was a vehicle for the inculcation of secular nationalism and patriotism that instilled in youth a sense of community and taught practical skills that were paramilitary in essence. Mohammad Reza Shah hoped that he could quickly establish groups of boy scouts and "girl guides" in every sizeable city and village in Iran.[33] To achieve this goal, the shah employed the skills of Dr. Banai, recipient of a doctorate in physical education from the University of Tehran, to head the Sazman-e Pishahangi under the Ministry of Physical Education. In 1953, Dr. Banai attended an international scouting jamboree in Britain to obtain literature and information about scouting and by 1954 had put together a staff of paid adult scoutmasters to lead the new *pishahangan*—of which the shah would serve as honorary president.[34]

To move the project forward in the summer of 1954, Dr. Banai contacted Sevak Saginian, who was permit holder of Ararat and its honorary scout headmaster, and proposed a joint scouting jamboree to be held at Manzarieh. It would include the Ararat boy scouts, which by now had grown to well more than two hundred members ranging in age from seven to twenty, Banai's group of paid scoutmasters, all of whom were in their thirties and numbered about twenty-five, and the small band of American scouting enthusiasts associated with George Patgorney. Sevak was particularly pleased when Banai added that the shah would be visiting and reviewing the encampment, and he told Banai that the jamboree sounded like an excellent idea.[35]

Held during the last week of August 1954, the first joint Iranian scouting jamboree was a huge success. On Banai's insistence, all the scouts pitched their tents together rather than in the separate Armenian Iranian and Persian Iranian groups that were taking shape before he intervened. Despite a highly successful covert attack by the Armenian scouts to pillage the outer clothing of the Persian scoutmasters the night before the shah's visit on August 26, the overall group otherwise interacted in a strong spirit of cooperation. Because Nejde Hagobian had previously met the shah and marched before him at the Fourth of Aban parades,

68. Nejde Hagobian (*center left*), George Patgorney (*center right,* wearing Boy Scouts of America sash) with a group of Armenian and American boy scouts at the scout jamboree, Manzarieh, August 26, 1954. Unknown photographer. Courtesy of Nejde Hagobian.

and because of the strict discipline of the Ararat scouts under his direction, he was able to remain calm in his interactions with the shah and relished the opportunity to walk beside him and answer his questions about the various wilderness survival projects on which the scouts were working, the organizational structure of the Ararat scouts, and their various activities outside of camping while photographers took pictures and generals and reporters followed behind. At one point, the shah asked Nejde what one of the Ararat scout badges said because it was written in Armenian script. Nejde instantly replied that the patch said "Bardzratsir Bardzratsur" (Elevate Yourself and Lift Up Others). Instantly realizing by the shah's expression that the Armenian phrase was unclear, Nejde instantly tried the closest approximation in Persian he could think of at the moment, which was "Boland sho Boland kon." With that, the shah and Banai looked at each other and chuckled. Then Banai softly explained to Nejde that although the Persian approximation that he came up with didn't have the wholesome connotations he intended, they nevertheless got the gist of what "Bardzratsir Bardzratsur" meant.[36]

The excitement about the shah's review dissipated shortly after he and his entourage left when news arrived at the camp that one of the head scout leaders, Felix Menatsakanian, had died in a mountain climbing accident. The news put a damper on the end of the jamboree, and the next several months were a very sad period for Nejde and Felix's friends in Ararat.[37]

In the fall of 1954, the Ararat scouts had grown to more than three hundred in number and were divided into subsections of cub scouts, girl scouts, and boy scouts. At this time of increasing popularity in scouting, a number of Ararat members older than twenty wanted to join the scouting ranks or stay in the organization but were considered too old for the boy scouts. Although Nejde was content as a scoutmaster of the boy scouts, he was interested in trying something new and in consultation with the potential new members decided to create a division of *yerets*: senior scouts like the American Explorers.[38] After he was unanimously voted to be the leader of the new division, Nejde selected a uniform color of dark green with white belts and dusters. He also set up a small room at the Ararat club to serve as the *yerets'* headquarters, which was decorated with the flags of Iran and Ararat as well as a painting of the shah. Ararat leader Sevak Saginian was invited to pose for photographs with Nejde and the *yerets* scouts to mark the occasion.

Nejde's next challenge was going to be how to keep this older group of somewhat unruly scouts—a few of whom were wrestlers and martial arts athletes—in line, busy, and entertained. He soon realized that it would be necessary to eliminate much of the synchronized marching and instead subject the *yerets* to rigorous, out-of-the-ordinary outdoor activities. During the Fourth of Aban celebration of 1954, in which the Ararat boy scouts and girl scouts again led the parade at Amjadieh Stadium, the ten senior scouts under Hagobian's leadership were away on a remote backpacking trip in the high elevations of the Alborz Mountains in which they had to carry in all of their equipment for miles and put many of their wilderness survival skills to use. In January 1955, Nejde led the *yerets* on a trip to the outlying hills around Rasht (near the Caspian Sea) with the goal of catching a live bear and returning with it to Tehran in the back of one of Hagob Hagobian's dump trucks,[39] where it would be donated to the

69. Hagobian and Ararat Yerets (senior scouts) pose with Sevak Saginian under flags of Iran and Ararat and a photo of the shah in the new Ararat headquarters, Tehran, 1954. Unknown photographer. Courtesy of Nejde Hagobian.

city zoo. Although they were well equipped with thick ropes and nets, Nejde realized that his planning had been too hasty when bemused locals explained to the scouts while they were setting up camp that there were very few bears in Rasht and that the ones that did inhabit the region were hibernating at that time of year.

Later that year Sevak Saginian was informed that the Tabriz branch of Ararat had a growing group of boy and girl scouts who were afraid to wear their uniforms in public owing to harassment by pro-Communist youths who were still quite active in that city and resented Ararat's Dashnak, anti-Communist, pro-shah orientation. When Sevak informed Nejde about the situation, Nejde saw another challenge for his *yerets* and immediately planned a trip to Tabriz. He coordinated with the local Ararat chapter in Tabriz to organize a reception and oath ceremony much like the one he had watched his friends take in 1952 and then sought to invite guests to further distinguish the affair. With Sevak Saginian's guidance, Nejde wrote letters to Governor Golshayan of Azerbaijan, the mayor of Tabriz, and the Armenian prelates.

Two days before the reception, Nejde Hagobian, Ashod Safarian, Amour Mouradian, and several other Ararat *yerets* arrived in Tabriz to tour the city and prepare for the reception at the Ararat club. They were surprised to be welcomed by the local Ararat members as though they were heroes, even though they had done nothing to deserve such admiration. When they went to visit Governor Golshayan, who had accepted the invitation to attend the oath ceremony, the scouts were given the red-carpet treatment. When a clerk of the governor protested that the scouts should first remove their large, sheathed hunting knives before entering the governor's office, Golshayan rebuked him and invited the scouts into his office, where he listened intently as they described their organization and its activities.

Yet not everyone in Tabriz welcomed the Ararat *yerets*. While walking around the city and taking in its sights following their meeting with the

70. Ararat scouts, including Nejde Hagobian (*third from right*), visit the office of Governor Golshayan, Tabriz, 1955. Unknown photographer. Courtesy of Nejde Hagobian.

governor, Nejde and four other scouts were on a small side street when one noticed that they were being followed by a group of eight to ten youths that looked menacing. As the scouts quickened their pace and turned to assess their pursuers, they observed that they were outnumbered two to one and that the pursuers had also quickened their pace. Despite the fact that two of the scouts were Ararat martial arts competitors, Nejde was a capable street fighter, and all of them had knives, they were in an unfamiliar town being chased by a gang of young men they didn't know. As Nejde quickly went over their options and ruled out another miraculous appearance by Shaban the Brainless, he decided that the best course of action would be to run as fast as they could rather than making a stand. The *yerets* raced down the street without looking back. Although they had no way to confirm it, they unanimously concluded that their pursuers were pro-Communists who had singled them out as Dashnakists because of their Ararat uniforms.

That night at the Ararat reception, which was attended by army general Governor Golshayan, the local Armenian patriarch, and a number of other high-ranking generals and officials, Nejde made a speech in which he explained the principles of Ararat scouting and announced that this oath ceremony would mark the official opening of the Tabriz branch of the Ararat scouts. After Nejde's introduction, Governor Golshayan spoke, pledging the government's support of Ararat and praising the organization. Following the solemn oath ceremony, the newly christened branch of the Ararat boy scouts and girl scouts posed for photographs with their honored guests and enjoyed a roaring bonfire.

Soon after the trip to Tabriz in 1955, the chief Ararat scout leader who had taken over after Felix Menatsakanian's death left for Italy to go to college, and Nejde Hagobian was named chief scout leader of Ararat. For the duration of that year, Nejde devoted his time to benefiting all ranks of the Ararat scouts—passing the leadership position of the *yerets* on to another scout. Yet with Nejde's own high school education finished and a year of advanced mathematics courses under his belt, he too would be leaving for college soon.

In May 1956, Nejde said farewell to his parents and a large group of friends and scouts who were gathered at Tehran's Mehrabad airport to

71. Iranian generals and government officials with the Tabriz branch of Ararat boy and girl scouts, who had just taken their first oath of allegiance, 1955. Unknown photographer. Courtesy of Nejde Hagobian.

wish him and his fellow Ararat member Andre Minassian a safe journey to the United States.

Both of them had gained acceptance to Pepperdine University in Los Angeles to study mathematics and take pre-engineering courses. Both Nejde and Andre were able to afford tuition owing to a new Iranian student aid program that would equally match their parents' financial contribution if they submitted a written promise that they would return home and work in Iran after their education abroad was completed. Nejde knew of many Iranians who went to college in the United States and Europe and never returned, elongating their stay through graduate school or marriage or both so that they could acquire foreign citizenship and stay abroad.[40] As they flew over Tehran and banked to the west, Nejde already missed his family, his friends, and his country and vowed to work as hard as he could while in the United States so that he could finish his education and return to work in Iran as he had promised.[41]

Nejde found the United States exciting and appealing and quickly developed an interest in American popular culture as his English-language skills increased and as he made new American friends. His awareness heightened by the classes he was taking and a growing interest in

72. Armenian Iranian boy scouts, including Victor Martin (*center with flag*) and Nejde Hagobian (*far right*), of the Ararat organization march down Tehran's Istanbul Avenue to Sepah Palace on Nowruz (New Year), where they were greeted by Shah Mohammad Reza Pahlavi and presented with gold medals as an *eidi* (Nowruz gift), 1955. Unknown photographer. Courtesy of Nejde Hagobian.

73. Nejde, Rima, Hagob, and Arshalous on the front porch the day Nejde left for the United States, May 26, 1956. Unknown photographer. Courtesy of Nejde Hagobian.

74. Nejde Hagobian and Andre Minassian turn to bid their friends and families good-bye, Mehrabad Airport, Tehran, May 26, 1956. Photograph by Hagob Hagobian. Courtesy of Nejde Hagobian.

civil engineering, Nejde was amazed at the vast physical infrastructure of the United States and its engineering marvels, such as the Hoover Dam and the Golden Gate Bridge. He had read about and seen these sites in photographs and textbooks but was nevertheless impressed when he visited them in person during class outings.

Nejde was also amazed by how little Americans seemed to know about Iran and Iranians compared to how much he and his Iranian peers knew about the United States. Fortunately, he encountered very little, if any, discrimination, and although misunderstandings occurred often, they could be quite amusing. At the YMCA where Nejde and Andre attended dinners hosted for foreign students, he was asked by an elderly gentleman how it felt when he came to the United States and wore his first pair of shoes. When another asked if his family lived in a tent, he was very surprised to hear that they did not and remained skeptical. In the fall of 1957, while inspecting a potential rental unit in Champaign-Urbana after transferring to the University of Illinois from Pepperdine with his roommate and best friend Andre Minassian to pursue his new-found passion of civil engineering, Nejde was in the bathroom looking at its fixtures and storage. When he opened the cupboard above the toilet to see the space inside, a towel fell out and landed squarely in the toilet bowl. As he was wringing the water out of the towel, the female landlord who owned the duplex walked in, took one look at Nejde, and sweetly but firmly exclaimed, "Oh NO, sweetheart! We wash our faces in the *sink*, over here!" Before he could explain what had actually happened in his still-broken English, Nejde and the landlord were greeted by the mad howl of her Siamese cat, which Andre had assumed was feral or a stray based on his experience with cats in Iran. As the potential landlady and Nejde emerged from the bathroom, they observed Andre hurling the writhing cat out the front door before he slammed it shut. Grinning broadly, Andre thought he was doing the horrified landlady a favor. Needless to say, the Armenian Iranians weren't offered the unit to rent.

After earning his bachelor's of science degree in civil engineering at the University of Illinois, where he had become a die-hard "Illini" football fan, dated American women, and loved the close-knit midwestern college lifestyle, Nejde Hagobian returned home to Iran in 1961 to see his friends

75. Iranian college students in America, Nejde Hagobian at left, Los Angeles, December 1956. Unknown photographer. Courtesy of Nejde Hagobian.

and family for the first time in nearly five years and to serve his country as he had intended. Although it was extremely difficult to leave behind close friends and a culture and society he was beginning to greatly admire, Nejde had never questioned the fact that he was going to return to Iran upon completion of his studies. He felt indebted to his loyal family and was determined to work as an engineer to develop Iran's infrastructure.

Although many positions were available in the engineering field working on rural road and bridge projects, Nejde's goal of finding work in Tehran as an entry-level civil engineer was challenging. After unsuccessfully applying for positions with a number of local building contractors, Nejde was interviewed at the John Mowlem Soils Laboratory. The largest of its kind in the Middle East at that time, it employed almost four hundred engineers and technicians. The British construction and engineering firm John Mowlem had established the laboratory in the early 1950s as a component of its infrastructural projects, and the lab had become critical to the Seven-Year Plan Organization for the implementation of the country's infrastructural development.[42] Nejde was interviewed by the British director of the firm that had originally established and managed the lab, Mr. P. Robinson, and his soon-to-be successor, a Dutchman by the name of Simon Van der Wal working for the Plan Organization. After hearing Nejde describe (in his now very good English) his major in structural engineering and soil mechanics, the two seemed impressed and offered him a job as lab engineer on the spot. When Nejde inquired about the salary for someone like himself with a diploma from an American university, Van der Wal explained to him matter-of-factly that if he had been an American expatriate with the same educational background, he would receive a salary of $1,200 to $3,000 a month, a housing allowance, a car with a driver, and a thirty-day paid vacation in Europe or the United States.[43] However, because he was an Iranian, his salary would begin at $100 per month with no benefits. Nejde was both astounded at how much the foreigners made and offended by Van der Wal's overall tone, but he desperately wanted the job at the lab and therefore accepted the offer.

From the very first day he started working at the lab as a geotechnical engineer, Nejde could tell things were amiss. Many of the highly paid foreign employees would work only a few hours a day, and when they were in the lab, they openly demonstrated their ignorance of the testing equipment and procedures. Most of the work was carried out by the Iranian employees, all of whom shared a dank basement office. Resentment was high among the Iranian employees, who gossiped about their foreign bosses without proper credentials such as the former butcher from Italy who was incompetently working for $2,000 per month plus benefits as an expert on concrete and a former Manila taxi driver making a comparable salary and benefits as manager of project quality control. Stories of waste and corruption were commonplace. Nejde found it hard to believe that the foreign employees could be as bad as the Iranian employees were describing until a slew of incidents proved to him that the situation was at least as bad and perhaps even worse.

After only ten days on the job, he began noticing egregious errors in record keeping and calculations. In one instance, Nejde was working nearby on a project when he overheard an Italian cement "specialist" directing some of the Iranian employees in mixing a test batch of cement for a road project[44] give a major miscalculation in the water-to-cement ratio, telling them to add water by a ratio of 5, when 0.5 was the correct proportion. Nejde watched in fascination, not saying anything, as the specialist complained to the Iranian employees that the cement was not solidifying because they were not stirring the mix fast enough and began to castigate them for their supposed lack of proper mixing technique. Nejde's sense of right and wrong, his sense of Iranian nationalism, and his professional sensibilities suddenly combined and manifested themselves in the form of the very undiplomatic statement, "You really are incompetent, aren't you?" The specialist and the Iranian workers who spoke English looked shocked. When the specialist gruffly asked Nejde what he was talking about, Nejde persisted with his observation. "It's true, you are completely incompetent!" In a huff, the specialist turned and walked up the stairs to Van Der Wal's office to inform him of Hagobian's rudeness and insubordination after only a little more than a week on the job. The Iranian workers, including future friend Shahen Askari, looked nervous and as though they believed Nejde had lost his mind.[45] Almost immediately, Mr. Van der Wal and the specialist returned, and Van der Wal asked Nejde to explain what was going on. Nejde pointed out the basic error in the water–cement ratio and the soupy mess the specialist was having the workers stir. Then Nejde turned the question to his boss, asking rhetorically of Van der Wal if this was how precision testing and analysis were achieved in the Plan Organization lab. Before Van der Wal could answer, Nejde added, melodramatically, that if this was the way things were conducted around the lab, it was a huge waste of Iranian resources and put people's lives at risk through improper construction. Van der Wal looked genuinely concerned and said he was going to investigate cement consistency at current projects. Two days later the Italian cement specialist was fired—to the glee of the Iranian workers in the basement.

In another incident that stretched the bounds of Nejde's imagination for how corrupt and unsafe the Plan Organization lab could be, several foreign Plan Organization technicians were sent on a one-week trip to collect core samples for a bridge project in the South. When they returned and submitted to Nejde their samples for processing, Nejde was incredulous. The core cylinders were packed with a color and grade of rock and gravel that he knew well from his camping trips in the mountains *north* of Tehran, not the type of fine clay he was sure the tests in the South should have produced. Again taking up the issue with Van der Wal, who agreed with Nejde's initial instincts, Nejde was pleased to hear that another investigation was going to be launched. After a few weeks, the investigation revealed that the samples had indeed been taken from some region in the foothills of the Alborz and that the employees, who were fired for their dishonesty, had more than likely gone to the Caspian on illicit vacation for the week and taken the core samples on their inbound or outbound journey.

It was not only a matter of nationalistic pride, ego, and offense over bogus expenses squandering Iranian resources that motivated Nejde to expose such incompetence. Especially in a seismically active country such as Iran, improper construction of large-scale engineering projects such as bridges or refineries owing to poor-quality materials or faulty determinations of the consistency of the underlying earth could cause structural failures that could conceivably hurt or kill many people. Nejde thought such behavior was not only dishonest but criminal, and he was astounded at the number of such incidents he witnessed at the Plan Organization lab in 1961. Having been promoted several times by Van der Wal so that he was soon in charge of technical testing for all major engineering projects around the country, Hagobian was pleased to see other Iranians being hired to replace the outgoing Americans and Europeans, although there was still no corresponding pay increase for any of them.

In 1962, the contract with Ammann and Whitney for management of the Plan Organization lab expired, and the Iranian government nationalized the facility. Van der Wal, who was leaving Iran to return to the Netherlands, recommended that Nejde Hagobian be his replacement for overall supervision of the laboratory. Furthermore, owing to the insistence of the current prime minister, Ali Amini, the Plan Organization was instructed to replace any foreign workers where there was a competent Iranian replacement, and thus qualified Iranians soon staffed the entire office. The morale at the technical lab was considerably raised, and quality increased considerably by 1963.[46]

For the next eighteen years, working as a consultant for the Plan Organization and the Iranian Oil Operating Consortium and eventually as a partner in the American engineering firm Dames and Moore, Nejde Hagobian would continue to apply his engineering and leadership skills to develop Iran's physical infrastructure, eventually moving into seismic, geotechnical, and environmental engineering and tackling increasingly large-scale projects such as dams, petrochemical complexes, airports, and seaports.[47] By the late 1960s, Nejde estimated that he had saved the Iranian government tens of millions of dollars in fees that would have been spent on unnecessary or redundant structural foundations based on improper assessment of Iranian geology and seismic activity.[48]

Former connections served Nejde well in these heady days of vast national engineering projects and hectic international business travel. In 1965, shortly after opening the Tehran branch of the engineering firm Dames and Moore, Nejde gave an important task to one of his new employees, Amour Mouradian. It was critical that by the next morning fifty copies of a report totaling more than two hundred pages be ready for a meeting with the Iranian Oil Operating Consortium. Thumbing through the master copy, Amour said he wasn't sure how this was going to be accomplished so fast because the copy machines they had access to did not collate, but that he would somehow find a way to get the job done in time. The next morning, as Nejde arrived at the office, he was stunned to find it staffed with a dozen or so Ararat scouts, who were putting the finishing touches on the reports, which they had sorted and collated by hand. From across the room, Amour, who had been one of Nejde's Ararat *yerets*, smiled proudly.

PART II

Experience and Theory

7

Learning from Theory and Social Biography

HAVING EXPLORED CONTEMPORARY QUESTIONS and problems posed by theoretical accounts of the development of nationalism in chapter 1 and investigated the activities and experiences of a group of Armenian Iranian individuals through social biography in part I, this final chapter demonstrates how social biography and theory can be utilized to respond to persistent recurring questions and refine our understanding of nationalism. It explores the insight that the theories offer to help us better understand the experiences of the individual subjects with Iranian nationalism and their participation in its development as well as ways in which social biographical research can be used to ground and refine theoretical speculation on the evolution and mechanisms of nationalism.

Social biographical research into the lives of Sevak Saginian and Nejde Hagobian enables us to respond to many of the questions generated in chapter 1 surrounding the photograph of the 1953 Fourth of Aban parade. Here, as in chapter 1, the photograph serves as a means of illustration as the theoretical discourse on nationalism is brought together with the social biographical sources that inform us of the event's details and personal meaning. We now know that the citizens leading the parade and bearing the photograph of Mohammad Reza Shah as a young scout in Pishahangi-ye Iran were Armenian Iranian scouts of the Ararat organization. Wearing locally tailored copies of contemporary foreign scouting uniforms with patches, badges, and uniform script reproduced in Armenian characters, these religious minorities were selected to lead the parade ahead of the other Iranian organizations simply because the name of their troop, "Ararat," when transliterated into Iran's official language, Persian, begins with an *alef*—the first character in the Persian alphabet—thus placing them at the front of the alphabetically organized procession. Having been established in 1952 before the umbrella organization Pishahangi-ye Iran was reconstituted in 1955–56, the Armenian Iranian boy and girl scouts were also the only Iranian scouting organization participating in the parade.

Nejde Hagobian, the *sayar* (explorer) in the photograph whose salute cues the shah to rise to his feet and begin his review of the parade, was excited beyond telling as he rounded the corner of the track and approached the grandstands. Confident that his fellow Ararat scouts were rhythmically in step behind him, Nejde concentrated on his own cadence and posture and basked in the glory of the moment. As he saluted the nation's leader and marched past the political elites in the stands, he was feeling a sublime sense of Iranian nationalism. However paradoxical, the Pahlavi regime's willingness to allow Nejde and his fellow Armenian scouts to express and sustain their Armenian cultural heritage enabled him to develop a strong sense of Iranian national identity and patriotism that would last throughout his lifetime.[1]

From his perspective in the grandstands as Nejde Hagobian saluted the shah and the Ararat scouts marched past, Sevak Saginian felt a complex blend of Armenian and Iranian pride. Foremost, he was extremely proud of his Ararat scouts and athletes and of the Armenian social and cultural organization he had helped to establish and grow. In his view, on that day Ararat scouts and athletes publicly represented the Armenians of Iran, and they performed flawlessly. The organization's placement in the parade alphabetically and the allowed use of Armenian uniform scripts were to Sevak a public indication of the regime's recognition of the Armenian Iranian community as a distinct yet integral component of the nation that shared equal status with other Iranian ethnic communities and corporate groups. At the Fourth of Aban parade in 1953, Sevak Saginian's feelings of Iranian nationalism were supreme. He was simultaneously proud to be an Armenian, proud to be an Iranian, and relieved that the shah had weathered the political storm of the previous few years. It was truly a momentous occasion.[2]

Beyond the parade's overt purpose as an annual public gathering of citizens to honor the king's birthday and the sublime feelings of nationalism inspired in individual participants, the broader historical context provided by the biographies of Sevak Saginian and Nejde Hagobian can shed light on other functions and purposes this event served the Pahlavi elites. As well as an annual occasion to demonstrate the country's modern, dynastic secular nationalism, in 1953 the Fourth of Aban event supplemented the propaganda effort to restore the image and legitimacy of Mohammad Reza Shah and the Pahlavi regime, which just two months earlier had narrowly survived the challenge posed by the various forces rallying around Prime Minister Mossadegh and the Tudeh. One of the first public opportunities after Bist-o Hasht-e Mordad to attempt to display the shah's power and his subjects' loyalty and admiration, the event was also broadcast live on national radio and then repeated nationwide in theater *akbar*, news shorts, for months. It is a fact that the coup d'état of Bist-o Hasht-e Mordad was funded and orchestrated by the CIA, but it is also true that the CIA was able to accomplish the covert effort to undermine Mossadegh and the Tudeh with such little effort, planning, and funding owing to a sharply divided Iranian populace and some genuine outpouring of support for the shah.[3] Because Armenian Iranians had participated on all sides in the political struggles of 1951–53 and during the street riots prior to and on Bist-o Hasht-e Mordad—including Ararat members such as Hagobian and Saginian, who had received medals for their participation in support of the regime—the official recognition and support of Ararat implied by the organization's participation in the Fourth of Aban parade in 1953 was congruous with the regime's attempt to reward its supporters, demonstrate its legitimacy, and reestablish its relationship of authority over its diverse and politically polarized citizenry. Thus, in addition to the pleasures of self-exaltation and glorification the event provided to the shah himself, we can speculate that the event was meaningful to Pahlavi political elites because of the functions it served in the effort to project the shah's legitimacy and omnipotence at this critical stage in his reign as well as the simultaneous opportunity it afforded the regime to publicly demonstrate its Western orientation and dynastic secular nationalist character.

But to specifically address the questions raised about the event in the theoretical discussion in chapter 1, why was the event meaningful to its variety of participants, and where was agency in this process located between Iranian elites and nonelites? How and why did such an event resonate with its various participants and inspire a sublime sense of nationalism? What was the role of culture of origin, ethnicity, and language in the event, and how did it relate to a sense of national community and identity? How was nationalism reconstituted by nonelites, and was their sublime sense of national community and identity congruent with that of the political elites? Finally, was the event or Iranian nationalism itself imitative or pirated or European inspired or all of these things?

Social biographical research reveals that Iranians in attendance were receptive to the event's symbolism for a variety of intermingling reasons, which depended on multiple factors such as ethnicity, education, family values, and personal experiences. The event was meaningful and appealing to Sevak Saginian because of the positive implications of the participation and performance of Ararat scouts and athletes for the organization and for the Armenian Iranian community. The event's symbolism and rituals appealed to Sevak's already well-developed sense of Iranian nationalism and secular leanings, and its explicit purpose appealed to him as a staunch supporter of the shah, whose birthday was being celebrated. Nejde Hagobian was receptive to the event and its symbolism on one level purely because marching at the head of a national parade and being filmed while saluting the king were exciting, but on another because his scouting activities and ethnicity were being recognized and honored by the state. Occurring within weeks of his receiving by surprise a medal and *hokm* for his activities in support of the regime during Bist-o Hasht-e Mordad, the parade solidified Nejde's evolving sense of Iranian national identity and feelings of loyalty to Mohammad Reza Pahlavi.

The issue of agency, or "who rides whom and how,"[4] is demonstrated as reciprocal in the case of the birthday rally—there was a dialogic power relationship between the regime and participants. The state recognized loyal organizations such as Ararat and in turn used their participation to project its own image of power. It coveted loyal religious minorities and benefited from the unique Armenian Iranian scouting program, which suited its goal of developing Western-oriented secular youth organizations and weaning the public back to the reinstitution of Iranian Pishahangi.

Simultaneously, Ararat members and Armenian Iranians benefited from the recognition of their organization and equal status as religious minorities. The annual event, particularly in the turning point year 1953, facilitated an unspoken process of colegitimization between elites and nonelites as well as between the regime and corporate and regional groups. It is irrelevant that Mohammad Reza Shah was a dictator and that the groups "invited" to participate in the parade did not have the option to decline. The celebration of the shah and his power was an interactive, collaborative gathering that produced assorted meanings and various pleasures for its participants. The shah's power was effective because, to paraphrase Foucault, it said yes more often than it said no. This is why the nation appealed to and could resonate with "the masses."

Dialogic interactions and multiple interpretations of the meaning of language, culture, and ethnicity in such an event can motivate and enable a sublime sense of nationalism among diverse participants, for whom its symbolism and rituals resonate variously.[5]

Social biography illustrates the complex role of culture of origin and ethnicity in this event—the culture of the state and the majority of the event's participants was Persian Islamic, whereas that of the Ararat scouts was Armenian and Christian. Because Ararat was treated equally yet organized and recognized distinctly under the banner of the most overtly nationalist Armenian symbol (Mount Ararat), the conception of a broad and inclusive national community and the development and maintenance of a compound national identity were enabled for the Armenian Iranian participants. Here language operates in a much more complex manner than suggested by the theories addressed in chapter 1. The dominant language of culture and the state, Persian, was used to organize the rally alphabetically and was the only language used in song, on banners, and in speeches and announcement of the sports exhibition to follow the parade. However, the allowance of Armenian uniform script and symbols in conjunction with Persian is what rendered the dominant language and society especially appealing and inclusive to Sevak Saginian and Nejde Hagobian.

Having pledged allegiance in Armenian to "Astsous, azgis yev hyrenikis" (My god, my nation, and my homeland), Armenian scouts could individually interpret their loyalties and the orientation of their oath, as opposed to the more specific Persian military and *pishahang* formulation "Khoda, Shah, Mehan" (God, King, and Country), which was never required of Ararat members. The objective display and mutual recognition of Persian and Armenian languages and a sufficient amount of ambiguity allowed for variant, subjective interpretations and suggest a dialogic, collaborational relationship between the regime and its Armenian Iranian citizens central to the shaping and sustaining of nationalism and national identity. As in Anthony Smith's point, the premodern *ethnie*, or ethnic community, was in fact critical to both the Armenian and Persian participants and spectators, yet exactly which *ethnie* was being recognized remained ambiguous. This is what allowed the event's participants a sense of community and patriotism. No violent secular millennialism was required to rally them; no appeals to dark gods and traditional rites by elite political chiliasts were necessary to imbue the event with further meaning and emotional appeal. Inclusion, recognition, and pageantry sufficed to move its participants, who derived different interpretations and sentiments while engaging in the collective activity. Grouped by their ethnoreligious heritage as a troop under the name of Armenia's national icon, they were enabled rather than forced by Iranian elites to embrace the broader Iranian national community. The message of the national elites here resonated because it did not preclude the scouts' Armenian ethnicity and compound Armenian Iranian identity. Sublime feelings were motivated by the acceptance and recognition of their linguistic and religious diversity by the dominant body politic.

But where and how do European colonialism, Orientalist epistemological hegemony, and indigenous elite imitation of European secular nationalism come into play? Mostafa Vaziri's and Elie Kedourie's theories suggest that external influence and indigenous imitation and adaptation are critical factors in the evolution of Iranian nationalism. If Vaziri is correct in his interpretation based on textual analysis, the whole of the Iranian national imagining is a monologically imposed forgery based on Orientalist knowledge, which reified a bogus concept of an ancient and enduring Persian nation and monarchy to a receptive indigenous elite. Kedourie's theory affords us a view of Armenians and the diverse people's of the Iranian plateau as "pulverized" collectivities in need of societal and economic glue after the revolutions, wars, and ethnic conflicts that pervaded Iran and the Caucasus, ready to accept unquestioningly European scholarship, nationalist ideology, and doctrine purveyed by marginalized Iranian elites.[6]

Consider the examples of successive generations of Saginian and Setkhanian families in Iran during the nineteenth and early twentieth centuries. We observe remarkable stability in their social and economic status and in their relationships to the Qajar regime—not pulverization and displacement. Despite these similarities, we see significant differences in the interests, attitudes, and perceptions of contemporaries Iskandar Khan Setkhanian and Zohrab Saginian. Whereas Iskandar Khan's foreign education in Russia yielded an infatuation with military science, allegiance to czarist Russia, and a belief in the concept of monarchy that led him to fight as a general of the Persian Cossacks against the constitutionalist movement, Zohrab's foreign education in Switzerland produced an interest in European legal methods and political institutions that motivated him to join with the nationalist *fedayi*s under Yeprem Khan Davidian to defend the Constitution and Majles against the Qajars and the Cossacks. Both men held strong convictions about Iran's political leadership while maintaining complex amalgamated identities and external allegiances—Iskandar Khan to Russia and the Cossacks; Zohrab to Armenia and the Dashnaks. Both men later found themselves in a tenuous position vis-à-vis Reza Shah and their external alliances, and both negotiated and navigated separate paths to survive and support their families while maintaining divergent interpretations of Iranian nationalism. Although both can be considered strong Iranian nationalists, their conceptions of their nation were widely divergent, and both were personally conflicted by Reza Shah's attempt to impose the Orientalist Aryan–Pahlavi vision of Iran on the country's diverse population.

The biographical explorations in part I demonstrate that the effectiveness of the nationalist message had much more to do with how it accommodated diversity and multiple interpretations rather than with the attempt to monologically impose a forged concept of identity by either Orientalists or Iranian elites. Although Vaziri's study *Iran as Imagined Nation* offers sufficient evidence to link aspects of the modern Persian nationalist conception of the Iranian nation to European scholarship, social biography and oral history are the keys to determining how the perceptions, attitudes, and sentiments of minorities and nonelites interact with the political elites' nationalist message and what they had to do with the development of Iranian nationalism and national identity. Social biographical research suggests that there is a dialogic relationship of power between minority communities and the state as well as between elites and nonelites, who derive different meanings and uses from the nationalist message, however shaped or tainted by Orientalist knowledge that message may be. The details that social biographical and oral historical research provide also highlight the intricacies and fluidity of the process and the uniqueness of individual experiences and family histories, while enabling refinement of theoretical accounts.

The requirement in 1927 that Iskandar Khan wear the Kolah-e Pahlavi, the decreed Iranian nationalist headgear, in public and in a portrait could be interpreted as a purely monologic, juridical imposition of Western norms by Reza Shah, who no doubt possessed the authority and the will to jail or otherwise punish those who refused his mandates. One might imagine Iskandar Khan chafing as he posed for his portrait in the Pahlavi Hat. After all, he had been a commanding officer above Reza Khan in the Cossack Brigade, a diehard supporter of the Qajars, and an avid Russophile. However, in another light, Iskandar Khan's wearing of the Pahlavi Hat in the official portrait can also be interpreted as a demonstration of the dialogic relationship of power between Reza Shah and his former superior in the Cossack Brigade. Such a view is possible when we consider what both Reza Shah and Iskandar Khan gained from the latter's participation in Reza Shah's project to impose a certain form of Western dress, uniformity, and a semblance of loyalty to the regime, according to their individual needs at the time.

In 1927, Reza Shah was seeking to eliminate opposition, acquire legitimacy, and, wherever possible, generate loyalty to his nascent regime. Although he possessed the military power and brutality to arrest, torture, and seize the property of rivals real and imagined and on occasion demonstrated his capacity to do all of these things, it was far preferable to acquire the open acquiescence and tacit approval of a variety of influential societal groups, whether they be members of the ulama, leading bazaaris, large landowners, guild heads, or former Qajar loyalists such as Iskandar Khan. By having Iskandar Khan appear in public wearing the Pahlavi Hat, Reza Shah got another former Qajar supporter and Cossack general to publicly demonstrate his break with the past, allegiance to the new regime, and acceptance of modern, Western styles. As Iskandar Khan spent leisure time in his retirement visiting with the Russian legation, walking around Tehran, hunting in the South, and fishing on the Caspian in his Pahlavi Hat, he was a mobile advertisement declaring Reza Shah's ubiquitous authority and the break with the ancien régime. But again, who rides whom? It is true that Iskandar Khan could not legally don his cherished Cossack headgear while engaging in these activities, but he engaged in these elite leisure activities nonetheless as an essentially carefree retiree when he could easily have been another victim of Reza Shah's vicious purges.

In 1927, Iskandar Khan was settling into a peaceful retirement and seeking to sustain his family's wealth and status. His biography tells the story of a man who was a deft navigator of the political waters (as well as the possessor of a substantial amount of sheer luck) and who was able to survive the Constitutional Revolution, the invasions and occupation of Iran during World War I, and the changeover to a different political and social order in the demise of the Qajars and the rise of the Pahlavi regime, all with his extensive property and good reputation intact in an Armenian Iranian community that had almost unanimously supported the Constitutional Movement he had fought against.[7] When one considers what Iskandar Khan had to gain from his tacit show of subservience and allegiance to the Pahlavi regime through his portrait and public appearance in the Kolah-e Pahlavi, it seems that the price of maintaining his status, property, and lifestyle was negligible, suggesting a negotiated, dialogic, and collaborational relationship of power.

The constructed concept of the Iranian nation as a homogeneous, organic Persian–Aryan entity—the conglomeration of "low cultures" of the plateau in the creation of a single "high culture"—as it is explained in the theoretical discourse is supposed to appeal to diverse, alienated masses thrown together by the forces of urbanization and industrialization and to function as societal cement to bind them together. But the attempt to impose such a concept monologically and juridically is abortive owing to the fact that when nationalism is so imposed, it is alienating rather than providing the intended remedy for alienation and feelings of shared community.

Like the dress codes of the late 1920s and 1930s, the closure of the foreign-language schools in 1938 can also be interpreted as a purely monologic and juridical step by the Iranian political elite toward the implementation of a Western-inspired program of secular nationalism based on fabricated concepts of an Iranian–Aryan nation. Linguistic minorities such as the Armenians and Azeris were not offered any say in the matter, and minority Majles deputies such as Zohrab Saginian found that there was no dialogue in which to be engaged with the state. Here we see the application of power that just says no. And this is why it miserably failed. The height of tension between the diverse citizens of Iran and Reza Shah occurred in the last several years of his rule as he attempted to wield authoritarian power to force a concept of a unified secular Persian community on the population to create Iranians. The monologic act of closing the foreign-language schools worked against Iranian nationalism, unity, and cohesion, not for it. For the Armenians of Iran, it weakened rather than strengthened the appeal of the dominant society that the elites were attempting to develop.

Zohrab Saginian's biography illustrates how the closing of the foreign-language schools also had the unintended effect of weakening anti-Communist Armenian Iranian groups such as the Dashnaks and strengthening Iranian Communist groups. Armenians who had supported Reza Shah, such as Zohrab and the Dashnaks, came under scrutiny and lost credibility among the Armenian Iranian population. Soon after Reza Shah's exile, both the Tudeh and Zohrab Saginian called for the opening of the Armenian schools. But whereas Zohrab and the Dashnaks had been discredited by their early support for Reza Shah and Zohrab was not reelected in the new open political milieu, the Tudeh gained popularity as a political movement that recognized the equality and linguistic freedoms of Iranian minorities and had attempted to combat Reza Shah's draconian policies. Reza Shah's attempt to force a single concept of unity turned many against the regime and remains the most memorable offense to the Armenians of Iran in the twentieth century under any Iranian regime. In the final analysis, it worked against Iranian nationalism, against the Dashnaks, and for the Tudeh Party.

In contrast to the situation faced by Zohrab Saginian while working as Majles member under Reza Shah, we observe their sons, Sevak Saginian and Mohammad Reza Pahlavi, working in a dialogic, collaborative, negotiated relationship that was successful at simultaneously inculcating Iranian nationalism and sustaining Armenian cultural identity and awareness. In their interactions, we witness how the ability to negotiate, compromise, and work with ambiguity on both sides allowed an ethnically diverse society to function and enabled national community to exist and flourish. Take, for example, the negotiations regarding the certification of Armenian secondary schools and the effort to expand Armenian education at the university level. Mohammad Reza Shah and Sevak Saginian were eventually able to strike a balance that satisfied the needs and concerns of both the state and the Armenian Iranian community. The interactions of Dr. Banai and Sevak over the integration of the Ararat scouts into the Pishahangi-ye Iran are also indicative of a dialogic relationship and an effective process of negotiation facilitated through ambiguity and multiple interpretations. This dialogic, negotiated relationship enabled Sevak to play an important and complex role as an elite facilitating Iranian nationalism and loyalty to the Pahlavi regime through the Armenian organization Ararat—which in turn promoted Armenian social interaction, culture, and identity perhaps more than any other institution or organization in Iran outside of the Armenian Church.

In an oral interview in June 1997, I asked Sevak Saginian if he thought that participation in Ararat worked more among its members to develop a sense of Armenian nationalism or Iranian nationalism. He responded, "It ended up working more to serve Iranian nationalism. It's kind of like in the United States. Here people have freedom to express their original culture and language. But they feel American and like being American."

In response to another question in which I asked when he thought Iranian nationalism first developed among Armenian Iranians, he responded:

> Under the Qajars, Armenians weren't supposed to walk in the rain. We were considered *najis* [unclean] by Iranians. They [the Armenians] were not feeling very Iranian then. We were second-class citizens. Under *mashruteh* [the Constitutional Revolution], things began to change. Armenians were involved. Yeprem Khan was one of its heroes. He was interested in democracy for Iran and for helping Armenia. Then, under Reza Shah, there is alienation, but also secularization and inclusion. If anyone bothered Armenian neighborhoods or caused problems, they would be arrested, unlike before. Reza Shah gave people the freedom, by protecting them, to leave the Armenian quarters and to be equal, yet you had to lose your language to a certain extent. It's complex. But we were the best-treated religious minority and still are.

But weren't the positive experiences of Armenian Iranians in Pahlavi Iran the result of the imposition of standardized mass education, which was used to inculcate the values of secular nationalism? Clearly, Lucik Moradiance, Sevak Saginian, and Nejde Hagobian developed their Persian-language skills in the Iranian education system—all owing in no small part to Reza Shah's nationalizing of the foreign-language and missionary schools—and while in attendance at school were exposed to the tainted Pahlavi history that Vaziri exposes in his study. If Ernest Gellner is correct, it is exosocialization—this experience in standardized, mass public education of learning the constructed nationalist history and acquiring a common language—that instills the political principles of nationalism and sentiments of unity. Is public education a primary vehicle through which receptivity to nationalism and a "high culture" is cultivated?

The biographies presented in part I suggest that public education can facilitate the receptivity to the concept of the Iranian nation and the social integration of religious and linguistic minorities, but that it is not an essential factor. Rather, social experiences, personal background, ethnicity, and a dialogic power relationship with the state combine to allow nationalism to develop in the Armenian Iranian individuals spotlighted in this study. For example, Sevak Saginian excelled in Iranian public education. Having acquired the status of national valedictorian and excellent skills in the dominant language, no doubt shaped and honed through his educational experiences, he was able to enter more easily into a position translating between the Iranian government and the clergy. Certainly language skills gained in public education played some role in his initial interactions with the government and eventual rise to the position of minority Majles deputy. But Sevak Saginian's portrait demonstrates that it was aggregated experiences, family history, personal interests and initiative, and the state's flexibility in relation to issues of Armenian cultural and linguistic freedoms that progressively generated his strong feelings of Iranian nationalism and compound identity. Education was but one of many component factors.

Nejde Hagobian's life story also shows in-depth how a complex compound national identity developed and nationalist sentiment was inculcated and shaped through the conglomeration of childhood experiences, family upbringing and values, education in Iranian schools, participation in Ararat and the scouts, and what could be considered a form of grassroots political activity when he was a young adult. Invented traditions such as Lord Baden Powell's Boy Scout activities and rituals translated into Armenian and adapted by the Ararat scouts as well as the Fourth of Aban parade at Amjadieh Stadium were effective in molding Nejde Hagobian's nationalist sentiments, values, and attachments to both Iran and Armenia.[8] College education in the United States, funded in part by the Iranian government, had the effect of strengthening further the bonds Hagobian had with Iran and the responsibility he felt in returning to serve it and was, interestingly, a factor in the antiforeign sentiments he felt as an aspiring Iranian professional working for the Plan Organization. His life experiences congealed to produce a durable, compound Armenian Iranian identity and affinity for the nation of Iran.

Of the five biographies presented in part I, Lucik Moradiance's comes the closest to confirming Gellner's hypothesis. Like Sevak Saginian, Lucik excelled in Iranian public education. In addition to mastering the dominant language (Persian) in primary school, which was a base prerequisite for her later career as an engineering professional, public school was also the vehicle through which Lucik first acquired the understanding that she was considered Iranian, basic (although certainly Orientalist-tinged) knowledge of the nation's history and geography, and shared positive experiences with other "Iranians" of mixed ethnic and religious heritage. The public education system enabled her to pursue her specific educational interests in secondary school and to enter the nation's top university. The state-subsidized university degree she was awarded led directly to an internship and job offer at the core of the country's petrochemical industry and eventually to a technical job in state infrastructural and technological development. Indeed, Lucik Moradiance's "exosocialization" was central to her acquisition of a compound Armenian Iranian national identity and to her career opportunities and successes. Those successes and her resultant professional experiences working on large-scale industrial projects and assessing national resources in turn further strengthened her sense of Iranian nationalism.

Yet to attribute Lucik's sense of national identity solely to mass public education would be overly simplistic and skirt important nuances her story presents. In conjunction with Reza Shah's educational reforms and nationalization, the Women's Awakening of 1936–41 set the stage for the entry of Iranian women into the professional workplace in the 1950s and 1960s and tied the legitimacy of the Iranian state to the principle of women's progress.[9] Iran's rentier economy, breakneck development plans, and social reform agenda under Muhammad Reza Pahlavi are other critical variables. Had Lucik's public education and the ideals that it instilled not been validated by subsequent career opportunities and experiences, she would not likely have been able to cultivate the same level of involvement with and knowledge of national development projects, nor would she have likely experienced the collegial mixed-gender working environment or daily interaction with fellow Iranians of diverse heritage that manifest the knowledge and ideology inculcated in public school through direct adult experience. Moreover, despite personal ambivalence about the monarchy that had enabled these opportunities, the responsibilities and oversight with which Lucik was entrusted, particularly being asked to serve with male colleagues as the NIOC or NIPC representative at foreign conferences—which she proudly felt she was selected for precisely because she was a woman and a Christian—further bolstered her Iranian identity and national allegiance, as did the middle-class status she attained. The Iranian state's investment yielded an indigenous, dedicated female professional who would serve the government for decades through her work and represent the regime's modern, secular character, while Lucik Moradiance acquired the stability and economic opportunity her ancestors so desperately struggled for. Historian Camron Amin sums up the broader implications of this dialogic relationship for the Iranian state, Iranian women, and the women's movement:

> The Pahlavi effort to engage the woman question was enduring and successful in one respect: The legitimacy of the modern state was tied to the principle of women's progress. The state did no more to co-opt and coerce the women's movement in the 1930s than did the various intellectual and political causes that preceded and succeeded the Women's Awakening. However, through its enforcement of laws, its control over and expansion of education, and its domination of communication and the economy in general, the Pahlavi state created a more Foucauldian discourse on gender for Iranian society. The Women's Awakening of 1936–41 was not mere propaganda. With its sheer power over Iranian society, the Pahlavi state could dispense real benefits to those who accepted its synthesis of modern Iranian womanhood as well as real punishment for those who did not. The "co-optation and circumscription" of the women's movement, thus, had its collaborators.[10]

Clearly, Lucik Moradiance's access to and experiences in public education were central to the development of her compound Armenian Iranian national identity, but here too social biographical investigation reveals that the critical factor in her acquisition of a strong sense of Iranian nationalism was the dialogic, collaborational nature of her relationship with the state and her fellow Iranians. In an oral interview with her conducted in 2001, I asked, "While living in Iran, would you say you considered yourself an Iranian, an Armenian, or both?" Lucik replied:

> Politically we Armenians considered ourselves as Iranians, but socially we were Armenian. Going to church, attending only Armenian organizations and clubs like Ararat, the Armenian Club, and the Armenian

> Graduates Club. So close social contact with Persians was infrequent and usually at work. But I never lived in Armenia. I grew up and lived in Iran. So I was thinking of myself as Armenian Iranian. We had all the freedoms, all the privileges, so how could you say, "I am not an Iranian"?

Truck driver Hagob Hagobian had no formal education to speak of and for all practical purposes remained thoroughly oblivious to Orientalist or indigenous-elite conceptions of Iranian history and nationalism throughout his long life. Yet of all of the individual subjects introduced in this study, Hagob Hagobian acquired perhaps the most pronounced attachment to Iran, which was cultivated through a tremendous amount of experiential knowledge and deep understanding of its various regions, climates, terrains, and peoples. As a long-distance truck driver for four decades, Hagobian was almost constantly in the process of traversing the nation and interacting with members of its diverse population while making a living. On his grinding journeys to and from Tehran and the Persian Gulf ports as well as between the capital and Mashḥad, Tabriz, or Yazd, Hagobian experienced the particular sights, sounds, smells, ruts, and dust of Iran. To him and his fellow Armenian and Assyrian truck drivers, Iran was not an "imagined" nation, but a diverse, bordered physical and cultural landscape that they became intimately familiar with and personally connected to through their daily travels and social interactions.

Despite his lack of formal education and exposure to Orientalist history and concepts, the idea of a powerful, omnipotent Persian monarchy appealed to Hagob Hagobian on a practical level—stemming from Reza Shah's ability to provide security and thereby facilitate commerce and travel within the nation's bordered domains. In short, Reza Shah's policies to improve roads and increase security to eliminate tribal raiding made Hagob Hagobian's job safer, easier, and more profitable. Unaware that his career and livelihood came at the expense of regional autonomy, nomadic ways of life, cultural diversity, and the overall health of Iranian guilds and handcraft industries, and not unduly concerned over the closure of Armenian schools, Hagob Hagobian perceived Reza Shah as a paternalistic savior whose rise and fall coincided directly with Hagob's own entry into the trade and his loss of livelihood when Iran's borders were violated by the Allied invasion in 1941. It wasn't elite imaginings, invented traditions, or monologic power that motivated Hagob to affix with pride a small photo of Reza Shah to his truck's dashboard, but rather personal, practical life experience.

Both theory and social biography have explanatory power and illustrative capacity. Theories of nationalism offer compelling hypotheses that enable us to consider global patterns, broad forces, and external influences, while generating subtle questions about how nationalism develops and operates and what functions it serves. Social biography offers details about the lives and experiences of individuals that can be used to respond to the questions about meaning, receptivity, feelings, participation, and agency generated by the theoretical discourse and can itself be framed and analyzed in a more complex manner using theory. I hope that this analysis demonstrates that these two distinct methods of approaching the subject of nationalism and national identity are most effective when they are brought together and used conjunctively.

In addition to the unique insight the social biographies of Iskandar Khan Setkhanian, Sevak Saginian, Hagob Hagobian, Lucik Moradiance, and Nejde Hagobian provide into various aspects of Iranian society, politics, military, economy, and culture under the Qajar and Pahlavi regimes, they yield a substantial amount of detail and critical personal perspective regarding the development of nationalism and national identity among Armenian ethnoreligious minorities in Iran and the attendant complexities of layered allegiances and compound identities. While illustrating how individuals encounter and use nationalism in the course of their lives and detailing the various roles and projects of the state and of religious minorities as well as of elites and nonelites in the development of Iranian nationalism, the five social biographies exhibit the multiple loci of power in this dialogic process. As demonstrated earlier, social biographical research can also be used effectively to respond to lingering questions about function, receptivity, personal meaning, and the role of language and *ethnie* raised by the theoretical discourse on nationalism and national identity.

However, the life stories of this handful of individuals clearly demonstrate that Armenian Iranian economic and social status, career paths, political opinions, and activities were diverse. Indeed, as we have seen, some contemporaries bitterly and even violently opposed each other.

Iskandar Khan of the Persian Cossacks opposed Yeprem Kahn and the *fedayi* in battle, while Zohrab Saginian and the underground Dashnaks were loathed by Ardashir Ovanissian and Tudeh supporters. Other contemporaries held dramatically different political views. Lucik Moradiance was sickened and distraught about the killing of pro-Tudeh student demonstrators at Tehran University in December 1953, whereas Nejde Hagobian and his pro-shah friends at Ararat reveled that Communists had received their just desserts. Taking these contrasting examples into account, it is clear that more oral historical and social biographical research will be necessary before we can determine to what extent accurate generalizations can be made about the Armenian Iranian experience with and role in the development of Iranian nationalism. It must also be recognized that the focus here on one religious minority group under the Qajar and Pahlavi regimes warrants qualified conclusions pertaining to the evolution of national identity within the nation's Persian Muslim majority and within Iran's other linguistic and religious minorities. Although I will restate my contention that, of all Iranian ethnic and religious groups to investigate, Armenians enable the widest applicability of the study's theoretical findings and best underscore the effectiveness of sustained social biographical investigation and that there are strong similarities between the Armenians of Iran and the country's other linguistic and religious minority groups in terms of their relationship with the state and its programs to inculcate a sense of national identity and loyalty, each group needs to be researched on a case-by-case basis to obtain an accurate assessment of its experience. Certainly biographies of individual subjects in other groups would yield different details, experiences, feelings, and memories, especially in relation to their personal senses of nationalism and identity vis-à-vis Iran.[11] Thus, we need to engage broadly and energetically in social biographical research if we are to understand Iranian nationalism in all its manifold complexity and to ascertain how it has evolved over time. These caveats notwithstanding, I hope that this chapter has demonstrated that persistent questions about nationalism and its development in Iran and elsewhere can be effectively answered through an approach that combines social biographical and theoretical methods.

Conclusion

SEVAK SAGINIAN, Hagob Hagobian, Lucik Moradiance, Nejde Hagobian, and the descendants of Iskandar Khan Setkhanian all eventually emigrated with their families from Iran to the United States. After leaving friends and relatives behind in Iran, in addition to all of their possessions and savings, Sevak Saginian and his family were granted political asylum in the United States in 1979 and began life anew in the large Armenian community of Glendale, California.[1] In addition to the substantial number of Armenian Iranian friends living in Glendale and the greater Los Angeles area who assisted in the Saginians' transition, Sevak found comfort and purpose as an active member of the Glendale branch of Homenetmen Ararat, which sponsored and organized many of the activities the Iranian Ararat organization provided to perpetuate Armenian cultural heritage within the diaspora.[2] From 1983 to 1991, he served as a member of the executive board for the Verdugo Hills Scouting Council, which oversaw Glendale-area Boy Scouts of America troops—including the roughly four hundred Armenian scouts of Homenetmen Ararat. In 1993, he was honored with a reception for his nearly forty years of dedication to Ararat. At the reception and in the publication compiled to mark the occasion, his contributions to Armenians in Iran and Glendale were recognized by Armenian community leaders and clergy as well as by Los Angeles County and California state officials.[3] Sevak Saginian passed away in 2003, and his wife, Nella, in 2006.

Hagob and Arshalous Hagobian moved to the United States from Tehran in 1975 after separation from their family members in the United States became unbearable for the couple. Although they settled into a

76. Nella and Sevak Saginian, Glendale, California, 1995. Unknown photographer. Courtesy of Sevak and Nella Saginian.

comfortable retirement in Glendale, where they were close to their family, the Hagobians continued to maintain savings in Iran and returned periodically to visit friends and relatives in Tehran. With the death of Hagob's brother, Aram, in 1988 and their advancing ages making it increasingly difficult to travel, the Hagobians liquidated their savings and left Iran for the last time in 1989. Although Hagob made many good friends among the scores of Armenian retirees in their Glendale neighborhood, life in the United States was not easy for him because he spoke but a few words of English and was unable to adapt to the culture and pace of Los Angeles. Increasingly idealizing life in Iran and periodically becoming fed up with one or another aspect of life in the United States, Hagob would routinely complain about how things were better and easier there and on more than one occasion physically packed his bags for his return "home to Iran."[4] Hagob Hagobian died in January 1992. Arshalous passed away in 2005. They are buried among other Armenian Iranian and Persian Iranian immigrants in Los Angeles and are survived by their children, Nejde and Rima, their grandchildren, and great-grandchildren.

The Moradiance–Melikian family immigrated to the United States in 1981 after the difficulties and liabilities involved in sustaining Levon's law practice in the Islamic Republic began to mount and the majority of his clients had either fled the country or ceased doing business there. Relocating to southern California after leaving their property and savings

77. Hagob Hagobian and Arshak Gorjian, Glendale, California, 1990. Photograph by author.

behind in Tehran, Lucik Moradiance decided to reenter the job market but soon found that many prospective employers deemed her Iranian Foq License (the equivalent of a master's degree) and credentials insufficient. Undeterred, she applied and was accepted for graduate study at the University of Southern California and in 1988 acquired a master's in environmental engineering. With her freshly minted degree to supplement years of hands-on laboratory experience, Moradiance was hired by the Southern California Department of Water and Power in 1989. Soon promoted to environmental associate, she found a niche in landfill, groundwater protection, and groundwater cleanup research. Lucik retired from the department in 2005, and Levon began to dismantle his law practice in 2006. They currently reside in Sherman Oaks, California.

After opening the Tehran office of the American engineering firm Dames and Moore in 1966 and serving as general manager, Nejde Hagobian was transferred to Los Angeles in 1968 to oversee the firm's operations in the Middle East and North Africa. Shortly thereafter, he became a partner of Dames and Moore and settled with his American wife, Lynn, and their two children in the Los Angeles suburb of Sherman Oaks. In 1972, Nejde acquired citizenship in the United States and in a short period of time cultivated a strong sense of American nationalism and patriotism, which became another layer to further complicate his compound Armenian Iranian identity. Throughout the 1970s, Hagobian made frequent trips to Iran and the Middle East, usually to oversee natural-gas and petroleum-related engineering projects. Because Dames and Moore's Iran operations were closed following the revolution in 1979, he has not had the opportunity to travel to Iran, although he plans on returning to visit the country someday. Nejde Hagobian currently resides in Toluca Lake, California, where he develops seismic isolation systems for the protection of museum antiquities.

Events since the Iranian Islamic Revolution of 1979, in which there has been a radical reorientation of Iranian nationalism toward Iran's Shiʿa Muslim history, traditions, and culture, new research into the status of Iran's religious minorities in the Islamic Republic further underscores the

78. Nejde Hagobian with his wife, Lynn, and children, Christina and David, Sherman Oaks, California, 1970. Courtesy of author.

necessity for social biographical research investigating the experiences of members of the Armenian Iranian community in Iran to answer newly emerging questions and to provide an even deeper understanding of how Iranian nationalism functions and is shaped over time. After the Islamic Revolution, there was naturally a rejection of the symbolism of the Pahlavi dynasty and secular Iranian nationalism by the new government and by the large majority of the population who supported the shah's overthrow. Eliz Sanasarian's book *Religious Minorities in Iran* (2006) examines the relationship between non-Muslim religious minorities and the government from the time of the Iranian Revolution through 1999. Sanasarian's research suggests that although Iran's roughly 220,000 Armenian Iranians remain among the best treated of the nation's ethnic minority groups, the challenges they face in sustaining their linguistic and cultural heritage and distinctiveness are similar to those they experienced under the Pahlavi regime.[5] As a result, the tactics employed in negotiations and relations with the government of the Islamic Republic are virtually identical, albeit articulated using the buzzwords of the contemporary Iranian political milieu and appealing to the symbolism invoked by the new regime.

Despite Article 13 of the Constitution of the Islamic Republic of Iran, which recognizes the rights of Zoroastrians, Jews, and Christians to practice their religion and pursue religious education freely,[6] the period 1981–85 saw an increase in the intrusion of the state in the affairs of religious minorities and open job discrimination.[7] In these four years, the state exerted a substantial amount of pressure to get minorities to conform culturally to the new Islamic orientation of society and, remarkably, to conform linguistically to Persian.[8] In 1982, the Majles representatives of the religious minorities were called to a meeting with Mortaza Hosseini, "the prosecutor of courts in charge of combating vice (dadsetan-e dadgahaye mobarezeh ba monkerat)," in which they were informed of their constituents' need to publicly observe Islamic laws as prescribed by the state, especially *hejab*.[9] Referring specifically to the Ararat sports complex in Vanak as a public place, Hosseini emphasized the need for proper segregation of men and women in such settings, suggesting that the office had been thus far too lenient.[10] Several incidents at Ararat, which included forced segregation of males and females at the sports stadium and the arrest of an Ararat organizer and three-day closure of Ararat for the failure to enforce proper *hejab* at a group meeting, demonstrated the government's increasing inflexibility during this period.[11] By 1983, Armenian Iranians faced the same threats to Armenian linguistic education from the new government that had been such a volatile issue prior to the revolution and especially during the reign of Reza Shah.

Required appointment of Muslim principals and teachers, which had been an occasional occurrence under the Pahlavis, was a minor issue, but the proposed ban on the teaching of the Armenian language in Armenian schools that followed was an outrage in Armenian communities across the nation.[12] After a sweeping and unexpected Ministry of Education prohibition on the teaching of the Armenian language in Armenian schools in 1981 erupted into a heated exchange of letters and verbal opinions and resulted in the noncompliance of schools nationwide throughout 1982, by 1983 the situation looked grim for the future of Armenian-language education in Iran. A final directive from the Ministry of Education stipulated that all religious education be taught in Persian from a single, state-sanctioned textbook and that Armenian-language instruction be limited to a maximum of two hours per week.[13] Owing to the continued obstinacy of Armenian teachers and administrators, the conflict peaked in 1984 with the closing of more than a dozen Armenian schools in Tehran alone.[14] Despite Armenian Iranians' despair regarding this issue, Armenian Church and community leaders were highly suspicious and quick to criticize any thought of external support or interference when the Western media picked up on the story. They reiterated Armenian Iranian support for the Islamic Revolution and in the war against Iraq, and their determination to solve the problem through direct negotiations with their own government.[15] Through persistent negotiation in the following years, Armenian-language instruction was first increased to three hours and eventually five hours per week.[16]

While Armenian Majles members and church and community leaders were fighting for Armenian linguistic and cultural rights, young Armenians were fighting and dying on the front lines of the Iran-Iraq War in large numbers proportional to their population.[17] In their interactions with the government, interviews, and newspaper articles, Armenian Majles members and community leaders took every public opportunity presented to them to point out this fact and to emphasize the community's efforts to support the Islamic Republic in its time of need.[18] Cosroe Chaqueri describes several such occurrences. At a ceremony to honor fallen Armenian Iranian soldiers, which was attended by Hujjat al-Islam Karroubi, the chair of the Martyr Foundation, Archbishop Artak Manoukian gave a speech in which he proclaimed that "Armenians, an inseparable part of the Iranian nation," struggled equally with Iranian forces on the battlefield, thus "restrengthening their bonds with their Muslim brothers," with whom they had lived together in "mutual respect and unblemished feelings for hundreds of years."[19]

79. Headstone of an Armenian martyr of the Iran-Iraq War: "MARTYR SOOREN KHANLARIAN 1959–1982," Noor Boorestan cemetery, Tehran, 2005. Photograph by the author.

In April 1985, Armenian Majles representative Vartan Vartanian revealed in an interview with the Tehran daily *Ettela'at* that "the imperialist designs to sow the seeds of dissention among Iranians had failed to break up Iran's unity and defeat the revolution—in part by the participation of Armenian soldiers in the war effort."[20]

The fact that Armenian public figures found the need to repeatedly reiterate the loyalty and sacrifices of Armenian Iranians alongside their fellow Muslim Iranians is indicative of the feelings of marginalization and trepidation within the community following a crackdown on their cultural and linguistic freedoms and in the face of a brutal war with Iraq in which life for all Iranians was strained and degraded and governmental paranoia justifiably heightened. Yet the details Chaqueri and Sanasarian bring to bear suggest that the Armenians of Iran never stopped pushing the limits of the system to legitimate their presence and role in society while pursuing their own agenda. The ways in which the Armenians of Iran made the most of Ayatollah Khomeini's disdain for the Turkish republican government and ongoing tensions between Tehran and Ankara to protest Turkish massacre of Armenians during World War I are but one example. Sanasarian cites a statement by southern Armenian Majles representative Artavaz Baghoomian in 1985 in which he rejected a comment by the US secretary of state regarding minority rights in Iran, while assailing the Reagan administration for "its refusal to accept the Armenian genocide in order to maintain good relations with Turkey."[21] Chaqueri notes several instances where the Islamic Republic's concerns were melded with the contemporary Armenian Iranian political agenda. Armenian Majles member from the North Vartan Vartanian gave a speech in the assembly in 1991 in which he praised the armed forces for the defense of the nation against Iraq, discussed past pan-Turkish imperialist designs to control Iranian territory, and recalled the massacres of Armenians early in the century. In closing, Vartanian "asked for the sympathy of the IRI [Islamic Republic of Iran] as the regime supporting the oppressed of the world during the planned demonstrations on 24 April against the massacre of Armenians by the Turks."[22] In 1989, the daily *Resalat* quoted Armenians from Urmia who simultaneously condemned "the plot of world arrogance against the Islamic Republic" while asking "to bring to justice those responsible for the massacre of one million Armenians in Turkey during World War I."[23] On April 24, 1989, as thousands of Armenian Iranians took to the streets of Tehran bearing portraits of Ayatollah Khomeini and flags of the Islamic Republic to protest the Armenian Genocide, others conducted a vigil in front of the United Nations office, where they condemned Salman Rushdie's novel *Satanic Verses* in addition to recent anti-Armenian violence in Soviet Azerbaijan.[24] At an April 1992 demonstration, Armenian Iranians of Tehran formulated a resolution denouncing the government of Turkey for illegally detaining an Iranian ship in a Turkish port as well as the massacres perpetrated in 1915.[25]

In Sanasarian's final assessment, the Armenians of Iran, like the other recognized religious minorities in the Islamic Republic,

> have mastered the art of accommodation so well that they often appear in sync with the regime, any regime. They take on the coloring of the state ideology whether the system is Islamic theocracy or autocratic monarchy, and within its framework press for their communal autonomy. The state ideology may change, as it has changed several times in twentieth century Iran. What helps in this process of adjustment techniques is the overall connection that the minorities feel they have with the country. Since each in its own way has a special affinity to the land and the culture of Persia, consciously or unconsciously, the loyalty to the (nation-)state [*sic*] becomes a natural extension of that affinity, regardless of ideological filtering.[26]

Although Chaqueri takes a dimmer view of the situation facing the Armenians in Iran during the 1990s and the prospects for their future in the country, suggesting a trend toward emigration from Iran,[27] population statistics indicate stability, if not a rise, in the Armenian Iranian population, and recent trends in Iranian politics, foreign policy, and economy suggest the possibility that the best times for Armenian Iranians have yet to come. As Sanasarian notes, the breakup of the Soviet Union in 1989–90 and the establishment of diplomatic relations between a free Armenian Republic and the Islamic Republic of Iran in 1992 opened a new chapter in the history of Armenian–Iranian relations. Within four years, Iran had become Armenia's biggest partner in trade, and policies to facilitate business interaction included the opening of Iranian businesses in Armenia and the employment of Armenian nationals in Iran.[28] The election of reformist president Mohammad Khatami in 1997 and an overwhelming victory of reformist representatives in the Majles elections of February 2000 led to further improvement in relations between the religious minorities and the state, which was reflected in the increasingly warm public interaction between Armenian politicians, Armenian Iranian community leaders, and the leadership of the Islamic Republic. A brief consideration of speeches and events involving the Armenian Iranian community that were reported in the Iranian press during Khatami's first presidential term (1997–2001) allows a final point about dialogic power relationships, the ongoing development of Iranian nationalism, and importance of social biography.

On July 1, 1999, President Khatami gave a speech at a reception in Tehran honoring the nation's top athletes. As the Islamic Republic News Agency (IRNA) reported,

> Khatami Wednesday evening paid glowing tribute to the country's champion athletes, saying sports is a sign of youthful happiness in Iran. The president who was receiving athletes and national champions also dwelt on the topic of dialogue among civilizations saying all well-wishing personalities in the world had welcomed Iran's proposition for dialog among civilizations. He also told the national champions that their behavior and their life style are very much likely to be copied by the youth of the nation and therefore reminded them of their moral responsibility to be models of virtue. The president called on the administrators of sports programs to come to the aid of Ararat club (of the Armenian Christian community) so that the club, which has had brilliant records in the past, would be able to survive.[29]

Following the September 8, 1999, release of a US State Department report criticizing Iran's respect for religious freedom, Foreign Ministry spokesman Hamid Reza Asefi issued a vehement denial, asserting that "the U.S. State Department has circulated a biased and unjust view on the status of religious minorities in the Islamic Republic of Iran, an indication of its ignorance of human rights in this country. Furthermore, the

United States has been exploiting human rights issues for political gains and ends."[30] Over the next several weeks, daily statements by political and community leaders of the recognized religious minorities and Iranian political elites both explicitly and implicitly addressing the issue of religious minorities' standing were reported in the Iranian press.[31] In a meeting with Danish Social Democratic Party officials to promote trade on September 14, 1999, Armenian Majles representative Vartan Vartanian and Jewish deputy Manouchehr Eliasi stated that they enjoyed equal rights with their Muslim colleagues.[32] Vartanian explained that the Armenians, like all religious minorities, "enjoy religious and civil freedoms and are active in the social political and economic arenas along with their Muslim compatriots." Eliasi concurred: "The Jewish community also enjoys civil and religious freedoms like other religious minorities in Iran."[33]

On September 21, 1999, it was reported that a representative from the Armenian Prelacy Council met with legal experts and representatives from the Majles and various Iranian ministries to report on the situation of the Armenians of Iran and to discuss ways to upgrade the rights of Iranian religious minorities through better enforcement of the Constitution. Secretary of the Islamic Human Rights Commission Mohammad Hassan Ziyaee "welcomed the positive measures adopted [by the committee] to promote minority rights and underlined the need to speed up the process."[34] Also on September 21, 1999, the Iranian press reported that Armenian Iranians would be marking Imam Khomeini's one hundredth birthday anniversary on September 26 by tolling church bells across the nation and organizing a visit to Khomeini's mausoleum to pay their respects. In addition, it was reported that the Armenian Prelacy Council "is to hold a great cultural and artistic festival at Ararat club in Tehran Friday afternoon to mark the occasion. Along with their Muslim compatriots Iranian Armenians have arranged different cultural, art, sports exhibitions during the week to mark the occasion."[35] Zoroastrians in Yazd also marked the occasion of Khomeini's birth anniversary with a ceremony at the Zoroastrian Youth club Qasemabad, where they "recited their holy book of 'Avesta' and prayed for the health of the leader of the Islamic revolution Ayatollah Seyyed Ali Khamenei as well as for the success of the Islamic Revolution."[36] One Zoroastrian in Kerman celebrating the event "described the late Imam as 'the legend of the century' and expressed delight over the fact that Zoroastrians in Iran enjoyed good social rights within the constitution in present Iranian society and lead a free life in the country."[37]

This flurry of statements by religious minority leaders and the Iranian government regarding the freedoms and position of religious minorities culminated on September 28, the sixth day of national celebrations for the anniversary of the Imam's birth, when representatives from each of the recognized religious minorities were invited to attend a reception with President Khatami and Ayatollah Khomeini's grandson Hasan at the imam's mausoleum to celebrate what was named "Followers of Divine Religions Day." In his speech before the Zoroastrian, Armenian, Assyrian, and Jewish leaders from around the country in attendance, President Khatami first expounded on his concept of Dialogue among Civilizations as a remedy for wars and chaos. As reported in the *Iran Daily*, Khatami then told the group that the Jewish, Zoroastrian, Christian, and Assyrian Iranians, similar to the Iranian Muslims, had developed a strong sense of self-consciousness after the victory of the Islamic Revolution in 1979. "They all reached the conclusion that they can express themselves in this world by virtue of relying on religious values," he said, stressing that the country and the Islamic system belong to all Iranians, regardless of their religion.[38]

Khatami also took the opportunity to recognize the religious minorities' contributions in the Sacred Defense (Iran–Iraq War), reminding the audience that "large numbers of Jewish, Zoroastrian, Assyrian and Armenian compatriots selflessly fought in the Iraqi imposed war." The president added, "They are shining stars in the history of this great nation." Shifting the topic to the conflict between the Israelis and Palestinians, Khatami queried, "Fascism and Nazism are by products of the West and not the East. Why should Palestinians pay for their brutal behavior?" Comparing the religious strife in the Levant to a harmonious Iran, Khatami concluded, "Today we also wish to see Palestinian Jews, Muslims, and Christians coexist peacefully in their land."[39] After he was applauded at length by the minority religious representatives, one member from each group took to the podium to reiterate the freedoms they enjoyed in the Islamic Republic and their commitment to the ideals of the late Imam

Khomeini, as demonstrated by their participation and sacrifices in the nation's defense during the imposed war.[40]

In February 2000, the IRNA website featured photographs of Armenian Iranian men and women voting in the elections for the Majles (no photographs of other Iranians of any religious background were presented), an interview with head Armenian Iranian bishop Sepuh Sarkissian after his tour of the polling facilities, and man-on-the-street interviews with Armenian Iranians who had cast ballots. According to this report, one citizen in Tehran, "Jorik Timash, an Armenian Christian, who voted in an Armenian church, told IRNA that in no other country in the world have religious minorities such freedoms for self-determination."[41]

Later that year, at a reception for visiting Armenian Catholicos of Cilicia Archbishop Aram Keshishian, President Khatami thanked Keshishian for his support of the Islamic Republic, and, after describing how dialogue between religions is a cornerstone of his concept of Dialogue among Civilizations, he noted that "[Keshishian's] presence in Iran indicates the active presence of Armenians in the country and the experience of coexistence among Muslims, Armenians, and other religions." Explaining that "Islamic civilization is indebted to thinkers and scholars of Islam and other religions" and that disputes between religious groups are "rooted in ignorant prejudices or in political issues imposed from outside," President Khatami stated, "I am proud of being president of all Iranians, including the dear Armenians, and of defending the rights of them all; I hope that problems, if any, would be eliminated gradually." Keshishian, in his turn, praised Khatami's effort to create a dialogue among civilizations and observed that "the community of Armenians in Iran enjoy all civil and political rights and are well-organized," adding that "the community has always been a source of pride for the community of Armenians worldwide. Armenians in Iran play a grave role among the world Armenians and are ambassadors of Iran in the world community of Armenians."[42]

During his three-week visit to Iran in which he met with dozens of Iranian officials, toured Armenian communities and churches across the country, and attended a celebration with more than ten thousand Armenian Iranians at the Ararat Sports Complex for the 1700 anniversary of Armenian Christianity,[43] Archbishop Keshishian made several more strong statements underscoring the freedom and stability of the Armenians in Iran. While visiting Isfahan and New Julfa, he "spoke highly of what he termed 'the goodwill of the Iranian officials towards Armenian Iranians' and stressed that people of his faith in Iran are considered as Iranian citizens rather than a religious minority."[44] In a meeting with Isfahan's governor General Seyed Jafar Mousavi, the archbishop thanked president Khatami and other officials of the Islamic Republic "for their kindly behavior towards the Armenian community in Iran and said that in his trip to different areas of the country, he has heard no complaint from the Armenian communities living in those areas. He also said Iran pursues the policy of establishing good relations between religious minorities and that Isfahan is a blatant example of dialog between religions."[45]

Two days later, Leader's Representative and Friday prayer leader of Isfahan Ayatollah Sayed Jalaleddin Taheri spoke at another reception for Keshishian, explaining that "Muslims and followers of Christianity, including Armenians, enjoy bonds of amity, affection and mutual friendship which has also been mentioned in the Holy Quran." Ayatollah Taheri went on to point out that "the Holy Quran refers to 'Nasara' and introduces them as the friends of Islam, [and] in the divine book hands of friendship have been extended to the followers of Christianity so that in light of the shared elements between the two religions, they both form a unified front vis-à-vis enemies of religion and God." He remarked further that "Muslims are living beside their Armenian fellow countrymen in Isfahan and that an atmosphere of amity, friendship, and affection is governing among followers of both the divine religions." In Archbishop Keshishian's speech, he agreed that "the Bible and the Quran enjoy common points in moral principles, adding that greater endeavor should be made to bolster ethical principles."[46]

In yet another publicized meeting, this time with Iranian Majles Speaker of the House Hujjat al-Islam Karroubi on July 24, 2000, Archbishop Keshishian stressed that "Armenian Iranians form an inseparable part of the Iranian nation and . . . that people of his faith in Iran are not really a religious minority." He went on to explain how all nationals in Iran, regardless of their religion, enjoy full and equal rights as citizens. After thanking Iran's religious leadership for the freedom of Armenians to worship and lauding Iran's national progress, Keshishian expressed hope that Armenians would contribute to that progress on the side of their Iranian fellow citizens. He also called for the help of the Iranian government for Armenian schools in Iran. Karroubi, in response, underscored Armenians' contribution to the development of the country in all areas and promised to work on Keshishian's request.[47]

In Eliz Sanasarian's interpretation, almost all of the events and exchanges described here are transparent in their motivation. As a defensive tactic employed by the recognized religious minorities to distance themselves from outside concern and interference, "Every time a human rights violation report on Iran is issued, all recognized religious minorities, and particularly Armenians, hold a press conference . . . and publicly recant and criticize the report."[48] The government of the Islamic Republic, in Sanasarian's view, utilizes three defensive strategies to deflect such criticism of its policies concerning religious minorities, all of which can be seen in the examples provided: (1) the invitation of foreign religious figures to Iran, where they receive extended press coverage as they make statements as to the well-being of Iranian religious minorities; (2) public denial of the charges in speeches detailing the freedoms religious minorities enjoy; and (3) obfuscation of issues by employing "linguistic verbiage" in the discussion of abstract concepts such as "civil society" and "dialogue among civilizations."[49] Sanasarian concludes that the necessity for the religious minorities to employ such defensive tactics to protect their freedoms, culture, and reputation is indicative of their perilous position as collectivities and individuals at the margins of a society whose government still has far to go in assuring equitable treatment of all its citizens.[50]

One cannot deny the accuracy of Sanasarian's observations about the public interactions and tactical statements of both Armenian Iranian community leaders and Islamic Republic officials in regard to the freedoms and standing that religious minorities enjoy in Iran, which as of 2013 continue to grace news headlines.[51] Yet, in light of the discussion of the dynamics of power relationships in the previous chapter, the dialogue produced in these interactions can also be interpreted as indicative of an ongoing, dynamic dialogic power relationship between the Iranian political elites and the Armenian Iranian community, each of which derives benefits and both subtly and not so subtly integrates and pursues various agendas through its statements—which are intended for both internal and external audiences.

Through these interactions, representatives of the Armenian community pursue as their primary agenda the same issues that they pursued under the Pahlavi regime—expansion of Armenian education and the maintenance of religious and cultural freedoms. Their requests are legitimated by solidifying a reputation as a distinct yet integral part of the Iranian national fabric who rose to the call of the nation's defense and remain steadfast in their loyalty, while distancing themselves from and criticizing foreign sources of concern over the status of Iranian religious minorities. In addition, whenever possible, Armenian Iranian elites and nonelites manipulate the zeitgeist of the Islamic Revolution and take advantage of the poor state of Tehran–Ankara relations in their attempt to gain Turkey's recognition of the early-twentieth-century Armenian massacres.[52]

80. March to commemorate Armenian Genocide is led by Armenian clergy, community leaders, and Ararat scouts, Tehran, April 24, 2006. Photograph by Vigen Mouradian.

Elites of the Islamic Republic also simultaneously pursue a number of agendas in their statements and interactions with Armenian Iranian elites and visiting dignitaries. On one level, they seek to deflect foreign criticism over human rights in Iran and to obtain recognition of both the just laws of the Islamic government and the justice inherent in Islam. Furthermore, they seek to utilize the memory of the Sacred Defense to bolster national pride and unity, expound on concepts such as dialogue of civilizations and Iranian civil society, strengthen Armeno-Iranian relations,[53] and glorify Iran's cultural diversity and recognition of this diversity by the Islamic government and Constitution. Iranian political elites seize every opportunity to shape their points about the positive relationship between the Iranian state and Iranian religious minorities around criticism of Israel's treatment of Palestinians and the continued settlement and occupation of Palestinian territory.

Once again, exactly who rides whom in these various interactions is unclear because the power relationship is dialogic and collaborative. Both the Armenians and the political elite of the Islamic Republic shape their own image and independently benefit from the strategic, public dialogue and negotiation. In the dialogic process, Armenian Iranian identity—like the symbolism, emphasis, and meaning of Iranian nationalism—continues to evolve.[54]

Because Iranian minority groups face unique challenges in the twenty-first century as they struggle to maintain their cultural and religious heritages, and because of the diversity of opinion and action within each group, it is difficult to predict or to generalize about contemporary political views, voting patterns, and hot-button issues.[55] For example, in the summer of 2005 I was surprised by the high hopes held by the majority of my Armenian Iranian friends and acquaintances in Tehran for the recently elected president Mahmoud Ahmadinejad and to learn that most of them had voted for him in the election that June. Although several noted his status as a professor and political outsider (in contrast to the *nomenklatura* that included former president Hashemi Rafsanjani and reformist candidates perceived to be inert), anecdotal evidence suggests that it was his strong support of the Ararat organization and facilities while he served as Tehran's mayor that secured their votes. Different Iranian minorities undoubtedly went to the polls with their own unique considerations and circumstances in mind, some certainly sharing the frustration felt by their Iranian compatriots of all ethnicities and religions concerning the vetted pool of presidential candidates. Yet, though disenchantment with the quasi-democratic political system spans Iran's diverse ethnic and religious landscape, and Iranian minorities (like most minority populations in Western nations) remain equally concerned with group and national issues, the chances of mass antigovernment separatist activity, ethnic insurgency, or, as has been proposed, a US-sponsored "fifth column" of minorities are slight.[56] By maintaining the "inclusive" form of Iranian nationalism and dialogic relationships developed during the reign of Muhammad Reza Pahlavi while providing wide political and press freedoms relative to the Pahlavi era, the government of the Islamic Republic has been able to avert ethnic and sectarian discord analogous to that experienced in Lebanon, Syria, Turkey, and neighboring Iraq and Afghanistan.

Today in Iran, Armenian Iranian truck drivers traverse the nation with distinct crosses carved on the panels of their vehicles to proudly indicate their religious affiliation.[57] Ararat scouts continue to march at the Armenian sports stadium in Vanak bearing both the flag of the nation and the flag of their cultural organization and again enjoy the freedom to use the Armenian alphabet on their uniforms and badges.[58] Armenian Iranian youth serve in the armed forces alongside their fellow Muslim Iranian soldiers. The Armenian Majles deputies persist in their efforts to work within the system in the interests of the Armenian Iranian community, and the Armenian Iranian man on the street lauds the political system of the Islamic Republic for the freedoms it provides.[59] This study, I hope, has demonstrated that if we seek a complex understanding of how these activities, images, speeches, testimonials, and headlines relate to the ongoing process of the development of nationalism and national identity in Iran and elsewhere and of how the agendas and projects of elites impact and intersect with the lives of ordinary individuals who collectively constitute and shape the nation, social biographical research must be a primary component of our inquiry.

Notes

Bibliography

Index

Notes

Preface

1. Quoted in Seymour M. Hersh, "Preparing the Battlefield: The Bush Administration Steps Up Its Secret Moves against Iran," *The New Yorker*, July 7 and 14, 2008: 61–67. Vali Nasr is now dean of the Johns Hopkins School of Advanced International Studies.

2. Graeme Wood similarly dismissed the idea, noting differences between Iran and its neighbors, and concluding that "the regime change desired by the White House is quite unlikely to come about as the result of minority unrest" ("Iran: A Minority Report," *Atlantic Monthly* 298, no. 5 [2006]: 46–47; see also Reese Erlich, *The Iran Agenda* [Boulder, CO: Paradigm, 2007], 145–46, and closing comments by Nikki Keddie in *Modern Iran: Roots and Results of Revolution. An Interpretive History of Modern Iran* [New Haven, CT: Yale Univ. Press, 2006], 314–15). Although the incoming Obama administration struck a conciliatory tone in regards to foreign policy in the Islamic world, covert programs to destabilize Iran have continued. See Mark Mazzetti, "U.S. Said to Expand Secret Military Acts in Mideast Region," *New York Times*, May 24, 2010. See also David Sanger, "The Larger Game: Iran," *New York Times*, Apr. 3, 2011; Roger Cohen, "The Making of an Iran Policy," *New York Times*, July 30, 2009; Salar Seifoddini, "Wooden Leg of US Interventions in Middle East Region," *Iran Review*, Sept. 12, 2012, at http://www.iranreview.org/content/Documents/Wooden-Leg-of-US-Interventions-in-Middle-East-Region.htm, accessed Oct. 27, 2012.

3. See Sussan Siavoshi, "Cottam, Richard," in *Encyclopaedia Iranica*, online edition (New York: Columbia Univ., 1996), at http://www.iranicaonline.org/articles/cottam-richard-1, accessed Jan. 26, 2014, and the obituary by Mark Gasiorowski, "Richard W. Cottam (1924–1997)," *Iranian Studies* 30, nos. 3–4 (1997): 415–17. See also Richard Cottam, *Nationalism in Iran* (Pittsburgh: Univ. of Pittsburgh Press, 1964).

4. For a description of the "Cottam channel" pursued by the Carter administration in 1979 to obtain the release of the hostages, see David Houghton, *US Foreign Policy and the Iran Hostage Crisis* (Cambridge: Cambridge Univ. Press, 2001), 106–8. See also Clarke Thomas, "Pitt Professor Tells of Role in Hostage Talks," *Pittsburgh Post-Gazette*, July 25, 1984.

5. Richard Cottam, *Nationalism in Iran: Updated through 1978* (Pittsburgh: Univ. of Pittsburgh Press, 1979), 76; subsequent citations are to this edition unless otherwise noted.

6. Ibid., 81.

Introduction

1. Mostafa Vaziri, *Iran as Imagined Nation: The Construction of National Identity* (New York: Paragon House, 1993), 196.

2. For meta-analyses of theories and interpretations of nationalism, see Anthony D. Smith, *Nationalism and Modernism* (London: Routledge, 1998), and Paul James, *Nation Formation: Toward a Theory of Abstract Community* (London: Sage, 1996). These two works are considered in chapter 1. For brief introductions to nationalism and some of the problems the phenomenon poses to researchers, see Umut Ozkirimli, *Theories of Nationalism: A Critical Introduction*, 2nd ed. (London: Palgrave Macmillan, 2010); Peter Alter, *Nationalism*, 2nd ed. (London: Hodder Education, 1994); Craig Calhoun, *Nationalism* (Minneapolis: Univ. of Minnesota Press, 1997); Philip Spencer and Howard Wollman, eds., *Nations and Nationalism: A Reader* (New Brunswick, NJ: Rutgers Univ. Press, 2005); Jocelyne Couture, Kai Nielsen, and Michel Seymour, eds., *Rethinking Nationalism* (Calgary: Univ. of Calgary Press, 1998); Anthony D. Smith, *Nationalism: Theory, Ideology, History* (2001; reprint, London: Polity, 2005).

3. What Michael Billig refers to as "banal nationalism." Billig takes issue with theories of nationalism that focus on extreme or "hot" expressions of nationalism, such as war and ethnic cleansing, and instead focuses attention on familiar, everyday forms of nationalism expressed in the media, which he argues are a primary feature of national identity (*Banal Nationalism* [London: Sage, 1995]).

4. Richard Handler critiques twentieth-century scholarly uses of the term *identity*, problematizing its usage to denote either primordial or constructed cultural essences. Handler instead stresses the fluid and situational nature of perceptions and expressions of identity and the role of individual memory in its maintenance ("Is 'Identity' a Useful Concept?" in *Commemorations: The Politics of National Identity*, edited by John Gillis, 27–40 [Princeton, NJ: Princeton Univ. Press, 1994]). Craig Calhoun takes perhaps the most tenable approach to the definition of nationalism, arguing that it is "what Michel Foucault . . . called a 'discursive formation,' a way of speaking that shapes our consciousness, but also is problematic enough that it keeps generating more issues and questions, keeps propelling us into further talk, keeps producing debates over how to think about it" (*Nationalism*, 3, citations omitted; see also Craig Calhoun, *Nations Matter: Culture, History, and the Cosmopolitan Dream* [London: Routledge, 2007], 27–41).

5. Ozkirimli, *Theories of Nationalism*, 218–19; Smith, *Nationalism and Modernism*, 94, and *Ethno-symbolism and Nationalism: A Cultural Approach* (New York: Routledge, 2009), 134; Vaziri, *Iran as Imagined Nation*, 216–18; James, *Nation Formation* (198–200); Firoozeh Kashani-Sabet, *Frontier Fictions: Shaping the Iranian Nation, 1804–1946* (Princeton, NJ: Princeton Univ. Press, 1999), 13–14. These works are discussed at length in chapter 1.

6. See Alter, *Nationalism*, 5. Alter does not reject the term *nationalism* or the subject as an area of scholarly inquiry but rather prefers to speak of nationalisms plural owing to the variety of its manifestations. Other scholars have attempted to limit their definitions and analysis of the phenomenon to a single aspect of its manifestation to alleviate the possibility of imprecision in analyzing something so multifaceted and subjective. For example, John Breuilly focuses on nationalism as a form of politics, bypassing issues of national identity, culture, and communal impulses, which he sees as operating "beyond rational analysis and . . . the explanatory powers of the historian" (*Nationalism and the State* [Chicago: Univ. of Chicago Press, 1994], 401; see also 1–40).

7. For the kind of study I am advocating here, see Edmund Burke III, ed., *Struggle and Survival in the Modern Middle East* (Berkeley: Univ. of California Press, 1993), the first English-language social biographical collection to focus on the lives of ordinary Middle Easterners. It uses the term *social biography* "to refer to the use of biography to explore the complex ways in which individuals navigate amidst social structures, processes, and cultural interactions" ("Middle Eastern Societies and Ordinary People's Lives," 6). Social biography is unlike literary biography in that the latter tends to focus more on the inner psychology of the subject and its role in shaping his or her life rather than on broader external forces and interactions (4–9). Definitions of social biography and explanations for its many uses are explored in chapter 1.

8. By the term *dialogic*, I mean a collaborative, two-way exchange of power and knowledge between Iranian elites and nonelites as well as between Europe and the rest of the world. This initial operating definition of the Bakhtinian term is further developed in chapter 1.

9. This is but a partial list of Iranian linguistic and religious groups. Ervand Abrahamian's *Iran between Two Revolutions* (Princeton, NJ: Princeton Univ. Press, 1982) contains a chart providing a demographic breakdown with estimated population statistics for 1850 and 1956 (12).

10. Because the history of Armenians in Iran is outlined in the biographical section of the study, no independent summary is provided in this introduction. For a detailed look at the history of Armenians in Iran, see Cosroe Chaqueri, ed., *The Armenians of Iran: The Paradoxical Role of a Minority in a Dominant Culture* (Cambridge, MA: Harvard Univ. Press, 1998). See also the introduction to Houri Berberian, *"The Love for Freedom Has No Fatherland": Armenians and the Iranian Constitutional Revolution of 1905–1911* (Boulder, CO: Westview, 2001). Although dated and somewhat cursory, Isma'il Ra'in's *Iraniyan-i Armani* (Iranian Armenians) (Tehran: Amir Kabir, 1977) contains some useful information, documents, and photographs pertaining to elite Armenian Iranians of the nineteenth and early twentieth centuries. For a look at Armenian life in nineteenth-century Anatolia and the Caucasus, see Susie Hoogasian Villa, *Armenian Village Life before 1914* (Detroit: Wayne State Univ. Press, 1982).

11. Vartan Gregorian, "Minorities of Isfahan: The Armenian Community of Isfahan, 1587–1722," in Chaqueri, ed., *The Armenians of Iran*, 27–53. This well-known action served

the combined purposes of depopulating the frontier against the Ottomans, diversifying the ranks of Abbas's military slave corps, and adding merchants and artisans to his grand project, Isfahan.

12. George A. Bournoutian, "Armenians in Nineteenth-Century Iran," in Chaqueri, ed., *The Armenians of Iran*, 55. The population statistics for Armenians in Iran provided in this volume vary considerably. Editor Cosroe Chaqueri provides low estimates for Iran's Armenian population in the introduction to his collection, drawn from British Foreign Office documents. He claims that the estimated population was 43,000 Armenians in 1884, growing to some 64,000 by 1917, and topping out at 108,400 by 1971, using UNESCO's *Iranshahr* as his source (Cosroe Chaqueri, "Introduction to *The Armenians of Iran*: A Historical Perusal," in Chaqueri, ed., *The Armenians of Iran*, 11). George Bournoutian's chapter "Armenians in Nineteenth-Century Iran" in Chaqueri's volume estimates the population of Armenians in Iran at a stable 100,000 throughout the nineteenth century, down from 400,000 as a result of the fall of the Safavids and Afghan occupation (55). Bournoutian's estimates are more in line with those of other sources on the subject. Ervand Abrahamian puts the number at 110,000 in 1850 and 190,000 in 1956, using Iranian census data (*Iran between Two Revolutions*, 12). In *Nationalism in Iran*, Richard Cottam, using Richard Frye as a reference, sets the number at 60,000 in 1953 (76). See also "Armenia and Iran," in *Encyclopaedia Iranica*, edited by Ehsan Yarshater (London: Routledge & Kegan Paul, 1982), 2:476.

13. "Armenia and Iran," 2:477.

14. Although there were some random and infrequent instances of anti-Armenian violence in the nineteenth century, Armenians were for the most part a remarkably well-treated minority group who attained a status and received opportunities and protections beyond those of any other ethnic, tribal, or religious minority in the region throughout the nineteenth and twentieth centuries.

15. Labeled an "entropy-resistant" people with a "sacred" language and identity that bind them to their nation, Armenians are often cited with Jews as an "archetypal" diaspora community facing insuperable moral barriers to their assimilation and inclusion in their host societies. See Smith, *Nationalism and Modernism*, 35, 231. Compare Ernest Gellner *Nations and Nationalism* (Ithaca, NY: Cornell Univ. Press, 1983), 70–73, 184; John A. Armstrong, *Nations before Nationalism* (1982; reprint, Chapel Hill: Univ. of North Carolina Press, 2011), chap. 7;. and, more recently, Smith, *Ethno-symbolism and Nationalism*, 10, 45, 94, 110. For recent works on the history of Iranian Jews, see David Yeroushalmi, *The Jews of Iran in the Nineteenth Century: Aspects of History, Community, and Culture* (Boston: Brill, 2009), and Houman Sarshar, *Esther's Children: A Portrait of Iranian Jews* (Beverly Hills, CA: Center for Iranian Jewish Oral History, 2002).

16. As introduced in the preface and detailed in chapter 1, Cottam's analysis of Armenian political affiliation and loyalty in Iran appears in *Nationalism in Iran: Updated through 1978*, 80–81.

17. Two works have guided my approach to the subject of Iranian nationalism and demonstrate the viability and applicability of social biography and oral evidence in the field of Middle Eastern history. Burke's 1993 edited volume *Struggle and Survival in the Modern Middle East* (with a second edition, which I edited along with Burke, issued in 2006) offers a collection of various historical biographies that span the nineteenth through the twenty-first centuries. In it, we witness how large-scale and abstract historical forces affected the lives of Middle Eastern peoples and can locate their own involvement and agency. Concepts such as the world economy are more tangible when we read about the challenges and struggles of journeyman textile weavers in Syria during the nineteenth century. Modernity becomes palpable when seen in the context of the changing realities in the life of a Damascus gang leader in the 1920s, as does the impact of industrialization and the petroleum industry when seen through the story of a Kuwaiti pearl diver in the 1930s and 1940s. Another work of social biography, Roy Mottahedeh's *Mantle of the Prophet* (New York: One World, 2008) details the century-long struggle that ultimately culminated in an ulama victory over the Pahlavis in the Iranian Revolution. By focusing on the life of a single participant in the revolution, Mottahedeh provides a comprehensible account of this event that is one of the most engaging and illuminating texts on the subject to date. Such social biographical works are simultaneously of use in undergraduate survey courses and advanced research because they provide supplementary details and real-life examples that political narrative and theoretical analyses generally lack.

18. Janet Afary's *The Iranian Constitutional Revolution, 1906–1911: Grassroots Democracy, Social Democracy, and the Origins of Feminism* (New York: Columbia Univ. Press, 1996) explores the role of corporate groups that participated in the Constitutional Revolution. Chaqueri's edited volume *The Armenians of Iran* is heavily concentrated on the contributions and role of Armenians in the Constitutional Revolution and Armenian political parties active in Iran at the turn of the twentieth century. Houri Berberian's *"The Love for Freedom Has No Fatherland"* details the role of Armenians, and, in particular, the Dashnaksutiun, the most active Armenian political party to contribute in the struggle for the Constitution and the Majles.

19. An example of how the Iranian experience has been useful in testing theories put forward by observers of large-scale historical/political phenomena is the well-known dialogue between Theda Skocpol, Nikki Keddie, Eqbal Ahmad, and Walter Goldfrank concerning the Iranian Revolution. See Theda Skocpol, "Rentier State and Shi'a Islam in the Iranian Revolution," and Nikki Keddie, Eqbal Ahmad, and Walter Goldfrank, "Comments on Skocpol" *Theory and Society* 2, no. 3 (1982): 265–83 and 285–92. Although the economic and religious complexities of the Iranian Revolution of 1978–79 challenged existing theories, it also generated this scholarly dialogue that enhanced both our understanding of Iranian history and broader understanding of the role of religion, economics, and political structure in revolutions. This dialogue has been extended to interpretations of causation in

the Constitutional Revolution of 1905–11. See, for example, Afary, *The Iranian Constitutional Revolution*, 8–9.

20. Although Iskandar Khan Setkhanian died in 1953, the majority of his descendants currently reside in and around Los Angeles.

1. Nationalism, Theory, and Social Biography

1. This common theme of rethinking or reframing nationalism is evident in recent works on nationalism in the form of short monographs (Calhoun, *Nationalism* and *Nations Matter*; Alter, *Nationalism*), readers containing passages from seminal studies (John Hutchinson and Anthony D. Smith, *Nationalism* [New York: Oxford Univ. Press, 1994]), edited collections of articles and essays (Gerard Delanty and Krishan Kumar, eds., *The Sage Handbook of Nations and Nationalism* [London: Sage, 2006]; Couture, Nielsen, and Seymour, eds., *Rethinking Nationalism*); Spencer and Howard, eds., *Nations and Nationalism*); and textual critique of theories and theoretical introductions and overviews (Ozkirimli, *Theories of Nationalism*; Smith, *Nationalism and Modernism* and *Nationalism*; James, *Nation Formation*; Ernest Gellner, *Encounters with Nationalism* [Oxford: Blackwell, 1994]). See also Rogers Brubaker, *Nationalism Reframed: Nationhood and the National Question in the New Europe*. (Cambridge: Cambridge Univ. Press, 1996).

2. Ozkirimli, *Theories of Nationalism*, 1–7; Monserrat Guibernau and John Hutchinson, "Introduction: History and National Destiny," in *History and National Destiny: Ethnosymbolism and Its Critics*, edited by Monserrat Guibernau and John Hutchinson (Oxford: Blackwell, 2004), 1–44; James, *Nation Formation*, xi–xv, 1–17; Smith, *Nationalism and Modernism*, x–xiv, 1–7; Brubaker, *Nationalism Reframed*, 1–7; Benedict R. Anderson, *Imagined Communities: Reflections on the Origin and Spread of Nationalism* (New York: Verso, 2006), xi–xv; Elie Kedourie, *Nationalism*, 4th ed. (Oxford: Blackwell, 1993), xi–xviii; Smith and Hutchinson, *Nationalism*, 1–13; Anthony D. Smith, *National Identity* (Reno: Univ. of Nevada Press, 1991), 1–17; Smith, *Nationalism*, 1–4; Calhoun, *Nationalism*, 1–8. Reference to the unexpected and tumultuous dissolution of the Soviet Union and Yugoslavia and the continuing emergence of new nations and national conflicts remains a common point of departure in recent books on nationalism, such as Smith, *Nationalism*, 1–3; Delanty and Kumar, eds., *Sage Handbook of Nations and Nationalism* (see the introduction in the latter, 1–3). More recently, Ozkirimli has argued that this still-common point of departure for texts on nationalism needs qualification insofar as the global proliferation of nationalist conflicts has declined since the early 1990s (*Theories of Nationalism*, 1).

3. Calhoun, *Nations Matter*, introduction and chap. 2.

4. Smith, *Nationalism and Modernism*, 4; James, *Nation Formation*. See also Yael Tamir, "Theoretical Difficulties in the Study of Nationalism," in Couture, Nielsen, and Seymour, eds., *Rethinking Nationalism*, 65–92.

5. For sweeping critical analyses that survey the theoretical contributions of different schools, see James, *Nation Formation*; Smith, *Nationalism and Modernism*; Ozkirimli, *Theories of Nationalism*.

6. Ozkirimli, *Theories of Nationalism*, 219. In the first edition of *Theories of Nationalism* (London: Palgrave-Macmillan, 2000), Ozkirimli cites Fred Halliday as the wellspring of this observation, which was expanded and refined further in the second edition, albeit with the reference to Halliday removed. As Halliday originally wrote in 1997, "My own, summary view of the debate is that it has in some ways reached an impasse: an array of *general* theories is offset against a mass of *individual* accounts with relatively little interaction between the two. . . . What we need instead are comparative, individual histories that are both written in the light of these general theories and that, critically, test them against the historical record" ("The Formation of Yemeni Nationalism: Initial Reflections," in *Rethinking Nationalism in the Middle East*, edited by James Jankowski and Israel Gershoni [New York: Columbia Univ. Press, 1997], 26–27).

7. I am not suggesting that this small set (or any grouping) of explanatory theories of nationalism should be expected to explain what is going on in this historical snapshot. Nor am I unaware of the fact that a different photograph or event would yield different results when integrated with different theoretical interpretations than the ones considered here. The photograph of the shah's birthday rally is interjected as a way to illustrate the practical applications of these theories in a historical context apropos to the present study.

8. Smith, *Ethno-symbolism and Nationalism: A Cultural Approach*; Guibernau and Hutchinson, eds., *History and National Destiny*; Athena Leoussi and Steven Grosby, eds., *Nationalism and Ethnosymbolism: History, Culture, and Ethnicity in the Formation of Nations* (Edinburgh: Edinburgh Univ. Press, 2007)

9. By the term *dialogic*, I mean of or pertaining to a collaborative, two-way exchange of power and knowledge, in this case between Europe and the rest of the world as well as between Iranian elites and nonelites. The term *monologic* is used here to imply a one-way imposition of power and knowledge from the Orientalist Europeans to the whole of Africa and Asia as well as through Orientalist-influenced indigenous elites to nonelites.

10. In his concluding remarks and qualifications, Gellner describes the abuses he anticipated with such a cursory and speculative account (*Nations and Nationalism*, 137). These concerns were realized in the scores of books and articles that invoke his definitions of the state and nation to add a theoretical component to their analysis—tacitly accepting his definitions as proven and his general theoretical observations as empirical research.

11. Ibid., 35–38.

12. Ibid., 50–52.

13. Ibid., 72–73. Making a similar point in reference to twentieth-century Somali integration, Gellner explains that "in most cases, the appeal of the new, educationally-transmitted ethnicity comes from both push and pull; the attraction of the new employment opportunities and the repulsion arising from the erosion of the old security-giving kin groupings" (86).

14. Ibid., 40–46, 55.

15. Ibid., 49, 55–58.

16. Breuilly, *Nationalism and the State*, x.

17. Ibid., 2.

18. Ibid., 1–2.

19. Ibid., 5; Smith, *Nationalism and Modernism*, 84.

20. Breuilly, *Nationalism and the State*, 401; see also Smith, *Nationalism and Modernism*, 89.

21. Breuilly, *Nationalism and the State*, 2.

22. Ibid., 9–10; see also Smith, *Nationalism and Modernism*, 84–85.

23. Breuilly, *Nationalism and the State*, 398–99, 401; see also Smith, *Nationalism and Modernism*, 88–89.

24. Elie Kedourie, "Introduction," in *Nationalism in Asia and Africa*, edited by Elie Kedourie (New York: New American Library, 1970), 84–85. Kedourie's theme of the rejection of the colonial subject in educational and civil service milieus is similar to the failed "pilgrimages" Benedict Anderson describes in *Imagined Communities* (113–16, 140).

25. Kedourie, "Introduction," 86–89.

26. Ibid., 27–29.

27. Ibid., 28.

28. Ibid., 31–35.

29. Ibid., 37.

30. Ibid., 92.

31. Ibid., 97–105. With this new gospel of love and brotherhood comes the implicit call for destruction of "all social and political institutions; they must, as Tseng Kuo-Fan put it, 'depose sovereigns and degrade officials'" (ibid., 102). To illustrate the "stern logic" and "tender mercilessness" of this new revolutionary-nationalist love, which must direct its violence at both internal and external enemies, Kedourie quotes Michel Aflaq, who, in expanding on his definition of nationalism as love and the physical guidance fellow citizens needed to feel it, explains that "our mercilessness has for its object to bring them back to their true selves which they ignore, to their hidden will which they have not clearly discerned and which is with us, even though our swords are raised against them" (quoted in ibid., 137). Kedourie underscores the point by reminding us that the Mau Mau movement killed more than 2,000 fellow Africans, but only 32 Europeans died as a result (ibid., 135).

32. Demonstrating how Gandhi generated a concept of a virtuous, backward Indian civilization to contrast to a "satanic" Europe by drawing from the works of European Orientalists, Kedourie anticipates the theory of "cultural rebounding" advanced by Richard Fox in *Gandhian Utopia* (Boston: Beacon Press, 1989). Beyond the picture Kedourie sketches of Orientalism spun by indigenous nationalists as an anti-European tool, Fox provides a framework for understanding agency. Cultural rebounding is a dialogic process involving multiple "authors," whose concepts and ideology are at once shaped and then reshaped by the proverbial Other. Fox's extension allows us to view the process of the development of nationalism in India as a dialogic, collaborative event involving agents/agency on the side of both Europeans and Indians.

33. Kedourie, "Introduction," 147. Indeed, paraphrasing one of the authors in his collected volume, Kedourie asserts that it is a violence-inducing "opiate of the masses" (147).

34. Smith, *Nations and Nationalism*, 107. Here Smith argues forcefully that diffusionism is theoretically inadequate because "it can never account for the *reception* of ideas that are transmitted from one centre to another" (original emphasis).

35. Eric J. Hobsbawm and Terence Ranger, eds., *The Invention of Tradition* (London: Cambridge Univ. Press, 1983); Eric J. Hobsbawm, *Nations and Nationalism since 1780: Programme, Myth, Reality* (New York: Cambridge Univ. Press, 1990).

36. Eric Hobsbawm, "Introduction: Inventing Traditions," in Hobsbawm and Ranger, eds., *The Invention of Tradition*, 1–2.

37. Ibid., 2–3.

38. Ibid., 4.

39. Ibid., 4. Hobsbawm argues that invented traditions are evident throughout history, but that the invention of tradition happens more frequently when societies undergo rapid change that destabilizes the existing social order; thus, the process is most noticeable in the past two hundred years (5).

40. Hobsbawm specifically cites changes in supply and demand; thus, the formalization of traditions is most noticeable in the past two hundred years (ibid., 5).

41. Ibid., 8.

42. Ibid., 5–6.

43. Ibid., 9; see also Smith, *Nationalism and Modernism*, 119.

44. Hobsbawm, "Introduction," 13–14.

45. Ibid., 14. The six historical essays in Hobsbawm and Ranger's volume offer case studies that explore topics such as the recent evolution of the Highland traditions of tartan and kilt as symbols of Scottish national identity, representations of authority in Victorian India, the advent of British coronation souvenirs, scouting rituals, and the impact of invented traditions in colonial Africa. Although the six essays, one of which was contributed by Hobsbawm himself, generally support his thesis of the modernity of European national and monarchial traditions, the fact that they attribute the resonance and appeal of invented traditions to their having drawn from older, preexisting traditions problematizes Hobsbawm's modernist argument somewhat. See Smith, *Nationalism and Modernism*, 120.

46. Paraphrased from Hobsbawm, "Introduction," 9.

47. Hobsbawm, *Nations and Nationalism since 1780*, 11.

48. Ibid.

49. Ibid.

50. In the most recent edition of *Imagined Communities* (2006), Anderson describes at length the process by which the book has come to be published in twenty-nine languages and speculates regarding its widespread use and ongoing popularity as a pedagogical tool (226–27).

51. Ibid., 5–6.

52. Ibid., 12.

53. Ibid., 36.

54. Ibid., 12–19.

55. Ibid., 23.

56. Ibid., 26–36.

57. Ibid., 12.

58. Ibid., 37–41.

59. Ibid., 44.

60. Ibid., 46.

61. Ibid., 77–82.

62. Ibid., 88; see also Hugh Seton-Watson, *Nations and States: An Enquiry into the Origins of Nations and the Politics of Nationalism* (Boulder, CO: Westview, 1977), 148.

63. Anderson, *Imagined Communities*, 87.

64. Ibid., 135, 140.

65. Ibid., 141.

66. Ibid.

67. Ibid., 144.

68. Ibid., 143. Hence the term *naturalization* for the process that those not born into the nation but who wish to become a part of it must go through (ibid., 145).

69. Ibid., 144.

70. Ibid., 154.

71. Smith, *Nationalism and Modernism*, 140.

72. On ethnosymbolism, see Smith, *Ethno-symbolism and Nationalism*, 1–2; Smith, *Nationalism*, 60–61.

73. Smith's most recent work on ethnosymbolism, which is primarily a summary and refinement of his past work on the subject, is *Ethno-symbolism and Nationalism*. For a detached perspective, Daniele Conversi summarizes the modernist, perennialist, and primordialist theoretical paradigms and locates ethnosymbolism in the context of existing literature on nations and nationalism in "Mapping the Field: Theories of Nationalism and the Ethnosymbolic Approach," in Leoussi and Grosby, eds., *Nationalism and Ethnosymbolism*, 15–30. Another recent edited volume on ethnosymbolism is Guibernau and Hutchinson, eds., *History and National Destiny*, which includes a closing chapter of responses and clarifications by Anthony D. Smith.

74. Smith, *Nationalism*, 57; Smith, *Ethno-symbolism and Nationalism*, 134.

75. Smith, *Ethno-symbolism and Nationalism*, 16.

76. Ibid., 58. For a detailed overview of ethnosymbolism, see Ozkirimli, *Theories of Nationalism*, 143–68.

77. Smith, *Ethno-symbolism and Nationalism*, 13–14, 18, 24–25, 60; Smith, *Nationalism*, 57.

78. Smith, *Nationalism*, 57.

79. See Smith, *Ethno-symbolism and Nationalism,* 19, 32–33. Here Smith distinguishes between new "micronationalist" studies that focus on popular, mass expressions and manifestations of nationalism, explaining that ethnosymbolists are relatively "less concerned with studying everyday, popular national practices for their own sakes than in exploring how popular beliefs, memories, and cultures have influenced the views and actions of the elites as they first propose and then promote the idea of the nation; and conversely, how far the various ideas and proposals of nationalist elites have struck a chord among the different strata of the designated populations whom they seek to mobilise and empower" (19).

80. Although several articles indirectly related to the subject of the development of Iranian nationalism are of note, the scarcity of English-language materials on the subject is made painfully obvious by this nearly comprehensive listing: Ervand Abrahamian, "Kasravi: The Integrative Nationalist of Iran," *Middle Eastern Studies* 9, no. 3 (1973): 271–95; Reza M. Ghods, "Iranian Nationalism and Reza Shah," *Middle Eastern Studies* 27, no. 1 (1991): 35–45; Homayoun Katouzian, "Nationalist Trends in Iran, 1921–1926," *International Journal of Middle East Studies* 10, no. 4 (1979): 533–51; Nikki R. Keddie, "Religion and Irreligion in Early Iranian Nationalism," *Comparative Studies in Society and History* 4, no. 3 (1962): 265–95; Mehrdad Kia, "Nationalism, Modernism, and Islam in the Writings of Talibov-i-Tabrizi," *Middle Eastern Studies* 30, no. 2 (1994): 201–23; Jan Weryho, "The Persian Language and Shia as Nationalist Symbols: A Historical Survey," *Canadian Review of Studies in Nationalism* 13, no. 1 (1986): 49–55; Firoozeh Kashani-Sabet, "Fragile Frontiers: The Diminishing Domains of Qajar Iran," *International Journal of Middle East Studies* 29, no. 2 (1997): 205–34; and Mehrzad Boroujerdi, "Contesting Nationalist Constructions of Iranian Identity," *Critique,* no. 12 (Spring 1998): 43–56. Sussan Siavoshi's *Liberal Nationalism in Iran: The Failure of a Movement* (Boulder, CO: Westview, 1990) focuses on the failure rather than the development of liberal nationalism in Iran. The two other book-length manuscripts on the subject are considered later in this chapter: Kashani-Sabet, *Frontier Fictions,* and Afshin Marashi, *Nationalizing Iran: Culture, Power, and the State, 1870–1940* (Seattle: Univ. of Washington Press, 2008). As I was preparing my book for publication, Ali Ansari's *The Politics of Nationalism in Iran* (Cambridge: Cambridge Univ. Press, 2012) was published. Whether this welcome contribution to the field stands "as the first book-length study of Iranian nationalism in nearly five decades" (advertising abstract) is arguable in light of the works previously mentioned, there can be no doubt that it joins a small handful at most.

81. For exaltation of the Pahlavis, see Donald Wilber, *Riza Shah Pahlavi: The Resurrection and Reconstruction of Iran* (Hicksville, NY: Exposition Press, 1975); Peter Avery, *Modern Iran* (New York: Praeger, 1967); James A. Bill, *The Politics of Iran: Groups, Classes, and Modernization* (Columbus, OH: Merrill, 1972); George Baldwin, *Planning and Development in Iran* (Baltimore: Johns Hopkins Univ. Press, 1967); Amin Banani, *The Modernization of Iran, 1921–1941* (Stanford, CA: Stanford Univ. Press, 1961); and especially Roger Savory, "Social Development in Iran during the Pahlavi Era," in *Iran under the Pahlavis,* edited by George Lenczowski, 85–127 (Stanford, CA: Hoover Institution Press, 1978).

82. Examples are Marvin Zonis, *The Political Elite of Iran* (Princeton, NJ: Princeton Univ. Press, 1971); Bill, *Politics of Iran;* and Lenczowski, ed., *Iran under the Pahlavis.* These studies tended to vastly overgeneralize based on their observations of the privileged Tehrani elite, failed to recognize the fragmentation of the nation, and ignored the strong Islamic influences in Iran in favor of analyzing Communist activities and leading figures from the political left.

83. For interpretations of the developments leading to the Iranian Islamic Revolution, see Abrahamian, *Iran between Two Revolutions;* Said Amir Arjomand, *The Turban for the Crown: The Islamic Revolution in Iran* (New York: Oxford Univ. Press, 1988); and Keddie, *Modern Iran.*

84. Cottam's path from Fulbright scholar to service with the CIA in Tehran in early 1953 is described in the preface. For additional details, see Siavoshi, "Cottam, Richard," and the obituary by Gasiorowski, "Richard W. Cottam (1924–1997)."

85. Cottam, *Nationalism in Iran,* 10–11. Cottam explains that events before 1890 are outside of the scope of the study and his area of expertise, so he does not attempt to explain the origins or development of Iranian national identity, but rather the impact of the spread of Iranian nationalism since 1890.

86. Concerns about separatism, irredentism, and the Cold War through which Cottam viewed Iranian nationalism are best illustrated in his coverage of Iranian Kurds, Armenians, Jews, and Assyrians (ibid., 73–83).

87. Cottam does not articulate this formula as a strict rule, but as an analytic theme within each section covering Iran's linguistic and religious minorities. See, for example, ibid., 67–68, 75–77, 81–90.

88. Ibid., 288. In addition to applying the terms *dictatorial* and *totalitarianism* to the Pahlavi regime, here Cottam describes SAVAK, the shah's secret police, as "the Iranian equivalent of the Gestapo." When published in 1964, such strong condemnation of Muhammad Reza Pahlavi from within American academia was exceedingly rare.

89. As Sussan Siavoshi describes in her *Encyclopaedia Iranica* essay on Richard Cottam, "[*Nationalism in Iran*] became a classic reference for all subsequent students of Iranian politics." Although Cottam's formula for plotting minority allegiances would not stand the test of time, his predictions regarding Iranian political stability under Pahlavi dictatorship were revealed by the Iranian Revolution to be spot on, enhancing Cottam's reputation and that of *Nationalism in Iran.*

90. Vaziri, *Iran as Imagined Nation,* 3.

91. Ibid., 189. The portion of Cottam's sentence quoted by Vaziri was itself paraphrased from an interview Cottam conducted in Tabriz in 1952, which Cottam explained in *Nationalism in Iran* as "the bald face assertion by two American missionaries" and then juxtaposed with a commonly expressed nationalist view in a letter to the editor of *The Near East,* July 26, 1912, that "the poorest Persian lad gloats over the history of the conquest of India by Nader Shah or over the doings of the old heroes of Ferdowsi" (quoted in Cottam, *Nationalism in*

Iran, 26–27). Although Cottam does not make a definitive statement one way or the other in absence of a relevant study on the subject, he concludes that it cannot be expected that illiterate Iranians would have deep knowledge of or interest in Iran's national status or history, but he cites the appeal of Ferdowsi's epic *Shahname* as a suitable delivery vehicle for the "rapid infection with genuine nationalism" (27).

92. Vaziri, *Iran as Imagined Nation*, 189.

93. Ibid., 190.

94. Ibid., 191.

95. Vaziri briefly treats the secular nationalist and reformist vision of Armenian Iranian Muslim Malkum Khan in ibid., 180–83. For a detailed account of Malkum Khan's life and contributions to Iranian national development (on which much of Vaziri's account is based), see Hamid Algar, *Mirza Malkum Khan: A Study in the History of Iranian Modernism* (Berkeley: Univ. of California Press, 1973).

96. Vaziri, *Iran as Imagined Nation*, 3; see also 101, 154–55, 192.

97. Ibid., 3–5.

98. Ibid., 5. Aside from Edward Said's *Orientalism* (New York: Vintage Books, 1978) and Benedict Anderson's *Imagined Communities*, Vaziri also draws from Ernest Gellner's *Nations and Nationalism* in the formation of his approach. Vaziri's adaptation of Gellner's theoretical positions and frameworks to Iran is relatively straightforward: the state creates the nation, not the other way around; thus, Iranian nationalism and national identity are modern phenomena (34–35, 192). Mass public education is the state's tool for the creation of a cohesive and loyal citizenry (195–96). The book also draws from the work of Anderson and Hobsbawm in regard to the importance of the concurrent rise of vernacular languages and the emergence of print capitalism in the spread of nationalism in Europe and the rest of the world (13–48).

99. Michel Foucault's applicable works are *Archaeology of Knowledge and the Discourse of Language*, translated by A. M. Sheridan Smith and Rupert Sawyer (New York: Pantheon Books, 1972); *The Birth of the Clinic: An Archaeology of Medical Perception* (New York: Pantheon Books, 1973); *Discipline and Punish: The Birth of the Prison* (New York: Vintage Books, 1975); *Power/Knowledge: Selected Interviews and Other Writings* (Sussex, UK: Harvester Press, 1980); *Archaeology of Knowledge and the Discourse of Language*, translated by A. M. Sheridan Smith and Rupert Sawyer (New York: Pantheon Books, 1972); and *The Order of Things: An Archaeology of the Human Sciences* (New York: Pantheon Books, 1970).

100. Antonio Gramsci, *Prison Notebooks* (New York: Columbia Univ. Press, 1992), see esp. 56–61.

101. Said, *Orientalism*, 5–6, original emphasis.

102. Foucault, *Power/Knowledge*, 119. To make this theory of power relevant to authoritarian states and the unlimited possibilities of physical power in a dictatorship, Foucault recognizes the juridical power of the state over its subjects: "Slavery is not a power relationship when man is in chains. . . . In this game freedom may well appear as the condition

for the exercise of power (at the same time its precondition, since freedom must exist for power to be exerted, and also its permanent support, since without the possibility of recalcitrance, power would be equivalent to physical determination)" (quoted in Hubert Dreyfus and Paul Rabinow, *Michel Foucault: Beyond Structuralism and Hermeneutics* [Chicago: Univ. of Chicago Press, 1982], 221). Power for Foucault, then, has a very technical meaning, which requires juridical freedom as its precondition. On one level, for scholars dealing with states where such freedom does not exist, Foucault thus gives permission to never have to hear his name again. However, Reza Shah's Iran, though autocratic and repressive, does not fit this broad category.

103. Foucault, *Power/Knowledge*, 97–99.

104. For a Lacanian interpretation that suggests the pleasures and "enjoyment" that produce and are produced by nations and nationalism, see Slavoj Žižek's chapter "Enjoy Your Nation as Yourself!" in his book *Tarrying with the Negative: Kant, Hegel, and the Critique of Ideology*, 200–238 (Durham, NC: Duke Univ. Press, 1993).

105. Eugene F. Irschick, *Dialog and History: Constructing South India, 1795–1895* (Berkeley: Univ. of California Press, 1994), 8. Irschick applies Bakhtin's concepts of "heteroglossia" and "dialogism" to help explain how there is a constant interaction between meanings, all of which have the ability and potential to condition the others: "This dialogic imperative, mandated by the pre-existence of the language world relative to any of its current inhabitants, insures [*sic*] that there can be no monologue" (Michel M. Bakhtin, *The Dialogic Imagination: Four Essays*, translated by Caryl Emerson, edited by Michael Holquist [Austin: Univ. of Texas Press, 1981], 426).

106. Irschick, *Dialogue and History*, 11–12.

107. Another study of Indian identity and sociopolitical developments that demonstrates the dialectics in power relationships and the interpretation of knowledge between elites and nonelites is Shahid Amin, "Gandhi as Mahatma: Gorakhpur District, Eastern UP, 1921–2," in *Selected Subaltern Studies*, edited by Ranajit Guha and Gayatri Spivak, 288–342 (New York: Oxford Univ. Press, 1988). By juxtaposing Gandhi's intentions and actions as he toured the district of Gorakhpur to spread a political message with the concerns of the region's peasants during and after his visit, Amin shows how nonelites can use and manipulate the knowledge and power of elites to fulfill their own interests, needs, and desires (288–342). It is with this theoretical understanding of power relationships and agency that I have approached the subject of Iranian nationalism and researched the various roles and projects of individuals in its development, in contrast to textual analyses such as those by Said and Vaziri, which forward monologic interpretations of relationships between nations and citizens, between elites and nonelites, and between Iran and the West in the evolution of national identity.

108. Irschick's work is not cited in Kashani-Sabet's book *Frontier Fictions*, so there appears to be no direct relationship. Similarly, one review of *Frontier Fictions* noted the "unmistakable influence" and echoes of the work of other South and East Asian historians

such as Partha Chatterjee, Prasenjit Duara, and Gyan Prakash (see Afshin Marashi's review of *Frontier Fictions* in *Iranian Studies* 33, nos. 3–4 [2000]: 486–88).

109. Kashani-Sabet, *Frontier Fictions*, 7.

110. Ibid., 7, and Anderson, *Imagined Communities*, 7.

111. Kashani-Sabet, *Frontier Fictions*, 5.

112. Ibid., 6.

113. Ibid., 10.

114. Ibid. 8, 14.

115. Ibid., 14,

116. For example, Turkey, Iraq, and Afghanistan. Turkey is still devoted to ethnic nationalism, and the civic nationalisms of Iraq and Afghanistan have failed to create national unity. In a brief summary denoting the basic essences of ethnic and civic nationalisms, Smith emphasizes the distinction between civic nationalisms, which can be marginally accommodating to minorities but generally demand assimilation, and plural nationalism, which celebrates multiculturalism and diversity (*Nationalism*, 40–42).

117. Kashani-Sabet, *Frontier Fictions*, 213–14, 220.

118. Ibid., 213.

119. Marashi, *Nationalizing Iran*, 4–11.

120. Ibid., 6, emphasis in original.

121. Ibid. 8.

122. Ibid. 8–10. Marashi steers clear of the contemporary debate between the ethno-symbolists and modernists, taking essentially a straight modernist approach. Like Anderson, he argues that the "style of imagination" enabled by the large-scale structural changes is key to understanding nationalism, and he does not take a stand one way or another on the historical depth, veracity, or origins (i.e., Orientalist or indigenous) of the content. Marashi also pursues a "top-down" approach to the subject matter, keeping with the methods of the modernist paradigm that informs his book.

123. Marashi uses the fascinating example of the ceremonies and festivals welcoming writer and poet Rabindranath Tagore from India in 1932 (ibid., 114–24).

124. Hobsbawm, "Introduction," 11. Hobsbawm credits social historians with the methods and capacity to illuminate this view from below.

125. See Edmund Burke III and David N. Yaghoubian, "Middle Eastern Societies and Ordinary People's Lives," in *Struggle and Survival in the Modern Middle East*, 2nd ed., edited by Edmund Burke III and David N. Yaghoubian (Berkeley: Univ. of California Press, 2006), 6.

126. Ibid., 6. The quote comes from the introduction to the second edition of *Struggle and Survival in the Modern Middle East*, but Burke alone should be credited with the ideas. Moshe Behar laments the "ghettoization" of the scholarship on nationalism in the Middle East and limitations imposed by the parallel efforts of historians and theorists, suggesting ways to enable meaningful comparative research ("Do Comparative and Regional Studies of Nationalism Intersect?" *International Journal of Middle East Studies* 37 [2005]: 587–612). It

is of note that Behar draws from the enduring theories of Anderson, Gellner, Breuilly, and Kedourie to illustrate.

127. Burke and Yaghoubian, "Middle Eastern Societies," 15–16.

128. Ibid., 2.

129. By mentioning nonelites and minorities in the same context, I do not intend to imply commonalities other than that biographical studies of individuals belonging to these categories are few and far between. Indeed, as the biographies in the present study demonstrate, minorities can certainly become a part of the elite.

130. The Harvard Iranian Oral History Project is located at http://www.fas.harvard.edu/~iohp/. Two noteworthy exceptions are the Iranian Left Oral History Project (1920s–1990s), directed by Hamid Ahmadi and completed in 1996, which features videotaped interviews with forty Iranian political activists who reminisce about their childhood and talk about everyday life in prison and their relationships with guards and fellow political prisoners (http://www.iranian-l-o-history.com/index.htm); and the Center for Iranian Jewish Oral History, which was established in 1995 by Homa Sarshar to record and archive oral testimony of Iranian Jews (http://www.cijoh.org).

131. Harvard Iranian Oral History Project director Habib Ladjavardi describes at length the problems he had persuading subjects to allow taped interviews and eliciting detailed responses and why this problem is acute when researching Iranian lives. Because the project focuses on political elites, Ladjavardi had a particularly challenging job convincing subjects that talking about the past would not adversely affect their future or that of their families. See the introduction to the first published transcription of the project: Habib Ladjavardi, ed., *Khaterat-e Ali Amini, nakhost vazir-e Iran (1340–41)* (Memoirs of Ali Amini, prime minister of Iran [1961–62]), 1–15 (Cambridge, MA: Harvard Iranian Oral History Project, 1995)–.

132. The methods and process by which the narrator and oral historian participate in the joint construction of narrative intended for publication is detailed by Rebecca Jones in "Blended Voices: Crafting a Narrative from Oral History Interviews," *Oral History Review* 31, no. 1 (2004): 23–42. Virginia Aksan and Cynthia Nelson reflect on the relationship between subject and historian, imagination, memory, and historicism in the process of writing biographies in "The Question of Writing Biography in the Premodern Middle East" and "Writing Culture, Writing Lives: Fictional Boundaries," respectively, in *Auto/Biography and the Construction of Identity and Community in the Middle East*, edited by Mary Ann Fay, 191–200, 201–14 (New York: Palgrave, 2001). For a discussion of the ethical considerations and human subjects protocol oral historians must utilize, see the Oral History Association's *Principles and Best Practices for Oral History* (2009), at http://www.oralhistory.org/about/principles-and-practices/, accessed Jan. 30, 2014.

133. If the researcher's goal is to use the stories of individuals to study broader historical developments and processes rather than to create a subject-specific public archive or to give "voice" through direct quotation, one can be very successful in integrating oral

evidence. For an example of social biographies created entirely without the use of oral interviews, see David G. Sweet and Gary Nash, eds., *Struggle and Survival in Colonial America* (Berkeley: Univ. of California Press, 1981).

134. For a recent overview of the forms, uses, and limitations of social biography, see the introduction to Mark LeVine and Gershon Shafir, eds., *Struggle and Survival in Palestine/Israel* (Berkeley: Univ. of California Press, 2012). In the introduction to *Struggle and Survival in Colonial America,* editors David Sweet and Gary Nash describe the benefits and challenges of social biographical research and locate the study of "ordinary lives" within the broader field of social history (1–13). A primary inspiration for the later volume focusing on the modern Middle East, *Struggle and Survival in Colonial America* features twenty-one social biographical portraits of various women and men that represent ways in which ordinary individuals lived in New World colonies and details some of the strategies they employed to survive and even flourish despite the obstacles colonial life presented (5). For a general overview of the evolution of social historians' methods and focus, see Alice Kessler-Harris's introductory essay in *Social History* (Washington, DC: American Historical Association, 1997). Kessler-Harris comments, "While some scholars fear that social history set in the framework of politics will return us to traditional ways of seeing, the need remains to seek some relationship between everyday life, the values and behavior of ordinary people and the larger mechanisms of change. Attempts to understand the relationship between political mobilization or action and the values of ordinary people lie at the heart of the new social history" (19).

135. Ehud Toledano's social biographical portrait of Shemsigul, a nineteenth-century Circassian slave in Egypt, is based entirely on a single legal report combined with secondary sources ("Shemsugul: A Circassian Slave in Mid-Nineteenth-Century Cairo," in Burke and Yaghoubian, eds., *Struggle and Survival in the Modern Middle East,* 48–63). See also several of the chapters in Fay, ed., *Auto/Biography.*

136. See Lila Abu-Lughod's portrait "Migdim: Egyptian Bedouin Matriarch," in Burke and Yaghoubian, eds., *Struggle and Survival in the Modern Middle East,* 205–22.

137. Alice Hoffman, "Reliability and Validity in Oral History," in *Oral History: An Interdisciplinary Anthology,* edited by David K. Dunaway and Willa K. Baum, 87–93 (London: Sage, 1996). Because the written form of social biography does not rely on the direct quotation of the research subject, it is an effective style when developing a biography of a subject who refuses to be recorded or directly quoted. This issue is pursued in chapter 2.

138. For a thorough consideration of the challenges that the elicitation and interpretation of oral evidence pose to the researcher and of issues of reliability and validity concerning research subjects' historical memory, see Paul Thompson, *The Voice of the Past: Oral History,* 3rd ed. (Oxford: Oxford Univ. Press, 2000), esp. 118–89. See also Dennis Tedlock, *The Spoken Word and the Work of Interpretation* (Philadelphia: Univ. of Pennsylvania Press, 1983); Valerie Yow, *Recording Oral History: A Guide for the Humanities and Social Sciences,* 2d ed. (Lanham, MD: Altamira Press, 2005), 35–67; and Valerie Yow, "'Do I Like Them Too

Much?' Effects of the Oral History Interview on the Interviewer and Vice Versa," in *The Oral History Reader*, 2nd ed., edited by Robert Perks and Alastair Thompson, 54–72 (New York: Routledge, 2006).

139. Dunaway and Baum, eds., *Oral History*; David Henige, *Oral Historiography* (London: Longman, 1982); Yow, *Recording Oral History*; Perks and Thompson, eds., *The Oral History Reader*, esp. 25–72, 177–83, 310–21.

140. Alice Hoffman reminds us that oral evidence is no less challenging to interpret than documentary evidence. "Archives are replete with self-serving documents, with edited and doctored diaries and memoranda written 'for the record.' In fact, when undertaken in the most professional way, oral histories may be superior to many written records in that there is always a knowledgeable interviewer present actively seeking to promote the best record obtainable" ("Reliability and Validity in Oral History," 92). For an illustration of the importance of oral evidence as a source to use in conjunction with government documents, which includes an analysis that weighs the strengths and weaknesses of each source type, see Max Paul Friedman, "Private Memory, Public Records, and Contested Terrain: Weighing Oral Testimony in the Deportation of Germans from Latin America during World War II," *Oral History Review* 27, no. 1 (2000): 1–16.

2. Iskandar Khan Setkhanian

1. Iskandar Khan's funeral coincided with the period of intense political turmoil that immediately preceded the CIA-engineered coup d'état of August 1953 that overthrew Prime Minister Mohammad Mossadegh and brought an end to the nationalization movement.

2. Obituary for Iskandar Khan Setkhanian in the daily Armenian newspaper *Alik* (Tehran), "The Setkhanian Dynasty," Apr. 10, 1953.

3. It is possible to study the events in Iskandar Khan's life and his service to the Qajar regime because of the diligence and perseverance of his granddaughter, Mara Setkhanian-Martin. After the Islamic Revolution of 1979, she dutifully gathered documents and memorabilia relating to her ancestors from the family home in Tehran and transferred them by ingenious means to safety in the United States. I am indebted to the Setkhanian family for their trust and invaluable cooperation and wish to thank them sincerely. My thanks also to Ali Sadrpour for his work decrypting and transcribing the script of the Setkhanian *farmans* and to Ilya Vinkovetsky for translating the Russian documents within the Setkhanian archive.

4. Information about Set Khan Astvatsatourian was derived from an article in *Alik* by Andranik Hovouyan, "The Setkhanian or Saeedkhanian Family," Mar. 23, 1994; Ra'in, *Iraniyan-i Armani*; and oral interviews with Mara Setkhanian-Martin in July and November 1995, Encino, California, and with Alexander Setkhanian in September 1995, Encino, California.

5. "The Setkhanian or Saeedkhanian Family." For a comprehensive history of the Armenian trade diaspora and merchants of New Julfa, see Sebouh Aslanian, *From the Indian*

Ocean to the Mediterranean: The Global Trade Networks of Armenian Merchants from New Julfa (Berkeley: Univ. of California Press, 2011).

6. "The Setkhanian Dynasty."

7. Ra'in, *Iraniyan-i Armani*, 57.

8. Ibid.

9. "The Setkhanian or Saeedkhanian Family"; Ra'in, *Iraniyan-i Armani*, 57.

10. "The Setkhanian or Saeedkhanian Family."

11. Ibid.

12. Husayn Mahbubi Ardakani, *Tarikh-i mu'assasat-i tamadduni-i jadid dar Iran* (The history of the institutions of the new civilization in Iran) (Tehran: Anjuman-i Danishjuyan-i Danishgah-i Tehran, 1354/1975), 199, my translation.

13. Jahangir Qa'im Maqami, *Tarikh-i tahavvulat-i siyasi-yi nizam-i Iran* (History of the political transformation of Iran's military) (Tehran: Ali Akhbar, 1326/1947), chap. 5.

14. *Qa'em maqam* is a title for the chief minister advising the crown prince in Azerbaijan, and, like many Iranian notables, the man in this position was known and remembered by his title as "Qa'em Maqam" rather than by his familial name (Keddie, *Modern Iran*, 40). The Persian system of naming created difficulties for American financial adviser to Iran (1910–11) Morgan Shuster, who criticized the practice and its stylistic traits by making fun of it for the American reader: "Imagine a gentleman in American political life deciding he would adopt and wear the title of 'Marshal of the Marshals,' or 'Unique One of the Kingdom,' or 'Fortune of the State.' Having duly taken such a title, and obtained some form of parchment certifying to his ownership, he drops his real name and thereafter is known by his high-sounding title" (*The Strangling of Persia: Story of the European Diplomacy and Oriental Intrigue That Resulted in the Denationalization of Twelve Million Mohammedans. A Personal Narrative* [New York: Century, 1912], xvi). This practice will be important for the reader to keep in mind because the collection of Setkhanian *farman*s (the "parchment" Shuster derides) from the late nineteenth and early twentieth centuries contains the stamps of other "Qa'em Maqams" who are different individuals. Common titles that frequently occur in conjunction with names are *mulk* (kingdom), *dawla* (state), *saltana* (sovereignty), *sultan* (sovereign), hence the names "Nasr al-Mulk" (Helper of the Kingdom) and "Naib al-Saltana" (Assistant to the Sovereignty). For a lengthy explanation of the complexities of Persian names and the challenges they pose to students of the Constitutional Revolution, see Edward Granville Browne, *The Persian Revolution of 1905–1909* (1910; reprint, Washington, DC: Mage, 2006), xxiv.

15. Like contemporary Middle Eastern reformers in the Ottoman Empire and Egypt who faced similar challenges, the Qajars were concerned mainly with military reforms in the first part of the nineteenth century. It would be almost a century before the concept of reform included large-scale political, legal, and social reforms in addition to military ones.

16. The development of a modern army generated opposition from many traditional interest groups such as the ulama, who were for the most part against foreign military

advisers and Western uniforms. Hamid Algar comments that, like contemporary Ottoman reformers, Abbas Mirza presented the Nezam-e Jedid as not only compatible with the sharia (forms of Islamic law), but as a forgotten and neglected practice of the Prophet Muhammad (*Religion and State in Iran, 1785–1906: The Role of the Ulama in the Qajar Period* [Berkeley: Univ. of California Press, 1969], 76). Abbas Mirza was able to find cooperative ulama who rationalized these innovations as essential to protecting the abode of Islam (Keddie, *Modern Iran*, 27).

17. Firuz Kazemzadeh, "The Origin and Early Development of the Persian Cossack Brigade," *American Slavic and East European Review* 15, no. 3 (1956): 351–63.

18. The Persian government's efforts to establish a domestic technical military school in Tehran in 1851, the Dar al-Fonun, met with mixed results after the attempts by Austrian, Italian, French, Austrian, and Prussian missions had failed owing to funding problems, low enrollment, and even lower graduation rates. See Kazemzadeh, "Persian Cossack Brigade," 352, citing page 243 of Lieutenant Colonel H. P. Picot's report "Military Organization of the Persian Army in 1899," in *British Documents on Foreign Affairs–Reports and Papers from the Foreign Office Confidential Print: From the Mid–Nineteenth Century to the First World War*, vol. 13: *The Near and Middle East, 1856–1914* (Bethesda, MD: Univ. Publications of America, 1986). The practice of sending elite children abroad for their education was an increasing trend that would later have important implications for the development of the ideology and motivation behind the Constitutional Revolution.

19. We don't know much about Zizi Khanom (Lady Zizi), and we are lucky to know her name at all. In nineteenth-century Iran, men did not usually refer to their wives by their names or even by the terms *wife* or *woman*, but rather as "the mother of the children" (*madar-e bache-ha*) or even as "the house" (*manzel*: for example, saying, "Manzel marizeh," "The house is sick"). In general, however, Armenians spoke more freely about women in the family than did their Muslim neighbors.

20. Algar, *Religion and State in Iran*, 73–81. Algar details Abbas Mirza's Nezam-e Jedid, his close relationships with Christians and foreigners, and his poor relationship with the ulama in Tabriz. He points out that there is no evidence of specific objections by the ulama to Western military uniforms, although objections were likely voiced in private (78). Indeed, some members of the ulama were critical of both Abbas Mirza and Western influences, but they were simultaneously concerned about the regime's weakness to defend itself. Voicing their opposition to the DeReuter concession in 1872, the Iranian ulama would cement their financial and political ties to the bazaaris and guilds and show their opposition to Western military influence and political interference increasingly through the events of the Tobacco Revolt in 1892 and the Constitutional Revolution in 1905. It should be noted that although the ulama were anti-Western in many ways, they supported and in fact helped lead the movement to adopt Western institutions (constitution and parliament) to help fend off Western interference.

21. "The Setkhanian or Saeedkhanian Family"; Ra'in, *Iraniyan-i Armani*, 57.

22. Abbas Mirza's son Muhammad Mirza would become shah after the death of his grandfather, Fath Ali Shah, in 1834 (Avery, *Modern Iran*, 29).

23. According to Setkhanian family lore, the image of Set Khan holding his Ottoman jeweled sword has been immortalized in stone within the "Asia Group" statuary at the Prince Albert Memorial in London's Hyde Park, a statue that has physical characteristics similar to Set Khan's. Interviews with Setkhanian family members, July 1995 and Sept. 1995, Encino, California.

24. Kazemzadeh, "Persian Cossack Brigade," 352.

25. Qa'im Maqami, *Tarikh-i tahavvulat-i siyasi-yi nizam-i Iran*. Qa'im Maqami details various unsuccessful attempts by German, Swiss, Austrian, and Russian governments to attempt to establish effective military advisement in Iran between 1828 and 1878. See especially chapters 6–10.

26. Keddie, *Modern Iran*, 28.

27. Oral interview, Mara Setkhanian-Martin, July 1995.

28. I was informed that Bishop Vartan Demurjian has written a book on the Orders of Sattur Khan and Set Khan and on correspondence between them and church officials at the Etchmiadzin, but as of this writing I haven't located this source.

29. This story is composed from oral interviews with Setkhanian family members who had heard the story transmitted orally to them, including Mara Setkhanian-Martin, interviewed July 1995. Although it is known that Sattur Khan's children went to Russian schools, who paid their tuition and how this was arranged cannot be confirmed.

30. Hagob Nagash Hovnatanian (1806–81) painted Nasir al-Din Shah's portrait numerous times as a painter of the Qajar court. A large oil painting is displayed and interpreted by B. W. Robinson in "Persian Royal Portraiture and the Qajars," in *Qajar Iran: Political, Social, and Cultural Change, 1800–1925*, edited by Edmund Bosworth and Carole Hillenbrand, 291–310 (Edinburgh: Edinburgh Univ. Press, 1983). More information about Hagob Hovnatanian and prints of two more royal portraits (of Nasir al-Din Shah and Muzaffar al-Din as crown prince, both on horseback) can be found in M. Kazarian, *Khudozhniki Ovnatanian* (Moscow: n.p., 1968). The Russian filmmaker Sergey Paradjanov made a short film about the work of Hagob Hovnatanian, entitled *Hakob Hovnatanian* (Moscow, 1963).

31. As identified in the certificate of birth in Armenian and Russian written for Iskandar Setkhanian in 1878, before he was sent to military school in Georgia (Setkhanian Collection, Encino, California).

32. Reza Ra'iss Tousi, "The Persian Army 1880–1907," *Middle Eastern Studies* 24, no. 2 (1988): 208–9.

33. Kazemzadeh, "Persian Cossack Brigade," 352.

34. To overgeneralize a bit, in this era preceding the discovery and need for Iranian oil the Russians' basic goal was to gain influence in Iran with hopes of attaining the prize of a warm-water port on the Persian Gulf or through Afghanistan, and the British were concerned primarily with using Iran as a buffer to keep Russia away from its goal and thus

away from Britain's most important colonial holding: India and the Indian Ocean trade. For a detailed account of this struggle, see Firuz Kazemzadeh, *Russia and Britain in Persia, 1864–1914: A Study in Imperialism* (New Haven, CT: Yale Univ. Press, 1968). For a broader historical perspective on these developments, see Rouhollah K. Ramazani, *The Foreign Policy of Iran: 1500–1941* (Charlottesville: Univ. Press of Virginia, 1966).

35. Although there was a branch of the Dar al-Fonun, the Persian technical military school, in Tabriz, it was underfunded most years and, like the Tehran school, received no funding in the years 1896–99; Nasir al-Din Shah and his successor, Mozaffar al-Din Shah, squandered the Dar al-Fonun's 37,000-tuman annual allocation (Picot, "Military Organization of the Persian Army in 1899," 243–44; Qa'im Maqami, *Tarikh-i tahavvulat-i siyasi-yi nizam-i Iran*).

36. Sattur Khan is remembered as a very progressive and open-minded father for those times who was remarkably supportive of his daughters' education. He once came into the house to find his daughter Liza doing needlepoint instead of studying, for which he scolded her. Liza attended the Gymnasia in Tiblisi and later moved to Paris, where she spent most of her life. Oral interview, Mara Setkhanian-Martin, Nov. 1995.

37. A *farman* reinstating Iskandar Khan to rank of *sarhang* (colonel) states his father Sattur Khan's rank at that time as *sarhang kargozari* (staff officer), Ramadan, 1307/1888. A *hokm* assigning Iskandar Khan to rank of adjutant states Sattur Khan's rank as *sartip* (brigadier general), Jamadi 1310/1892; both in the Setkhanian Collection.

38. "The Setkhanian Dynasty."

39. Certificate of birth in Armenian and Russian, 1878, Setkhanian Collection.

40. Notarized form in Russian in Armenian and Russian, 1878, Setkhanian Collection.

41. Kazemzadeh, "Persian Cossack Brigade," 352. Picot's report describes how the shah was most concerned with the uniforms rather than with things that one would normally take into account in creating an effective fighting force ("Military Organization of the Persian Army in 1899," 211, 247).

42. Ibid. Kazemzadeh's 1956 article is one of the only secondary summaries (in any language) dealing specifically with the Cossack Brigade. Kazemzadeh relied mostly on the diaries of the first (Domantovich) and fifth (Kosogovskii) commanders of the brigade: Vladimir Andreevich Kosogovskii [Kosagovskij], "Persija v Kontse XIX veka" (Persia at the end of the 19th century), *Novyj Vostok* 3 (1923): 446–69, and "Ocherk razvitija Persidskoj Kazach'ej Brigady" (Essay on the development of the Persian Cossack Brigade), *Novyj Vostok* 4 (1923): 390–402; A. I. Domantovich, "Vospominanija o prebyvanii pervoj russkoj voennoj missii v Persii" (Memoirs about the first Russian military mission in Persia), *Russkaia starina* 133, no. 2 (1908): 331–40; no. 3: 575–83; no. 4: 211–16. The only recent effort to expand on this work is Tousi, "The Persian Army." Owing to the scarcity of secondary sources on the Persian military, this article is helpful, although it is a repetition of Kazemzadeh's article "Persian Cossack Brigade" and its sources, with the addition of information taken verbatim from Picot's report to the British Foreign Office in 1899. One of the few Iranian sources to discuss the origins of the

brigade is Qa'im Maqami, *Tarikh-i tahavvulat-i siyasi-yi nizam-i Iran*. The information on the Cossack Brigade in these papers comes from essentially three primary sources: Picot, "Military Organization of the Persian Army in 1899"; other Foreign Office correspondence; and the diary of Colonel Kosogovski, a fascinating source on the intrigues of the Qajar court in the decade preceding the Constitutional Revolution. See Vladimir Andreevich Kosogovskii, *Iz tegeranskogo dnevnika polkovnika V. A. Kosogovskogo* (Tehran diary of Colonel V. A. Kosogovskogo) (Moscow: Izd-vo Vostochnoi Lit-ry, 1960), and, in Farsi, *Khatirat-i Kolonel Kasagofski: Tarjumah-i 'Abbas-quli Jalli. Chap-i duvvum* (Memoirs of Colonel Kasagofski: Translation of 'Abbas-quli Jalli. Second edition) (Tehran: Kitab-ha-yi Simurgh, 1976).

43. As well as coinciding with Nasir al-Din's trip to Europe, 1878 is also the year Reza Khan was born in Mazandaran to parents who were Transcaucasian *mohajer*s. See Wilber, *Riza Shah Pahlavi*, 3.

44. Kazemzadeh, "Persian Cossack Brigade," 355; Picot, "Military Organization of the Persian Army in 1899," 226; Tousi, "The Persian Army," 219.

45. Because no Russian Cossack commanders would take orders from the shah without first consulting with their Russian superiors, Russian orders and concerns assumed top priority.

46. Kazemzadeh, *Russia and Britain in Persia*, 166–67. Although this information has been greatly summarized for this chapter, see Kazemzadeh's book for a complex and sustained account of the diplomatic agreements and individual actors in this and other political developments that relate to the two superpowers' involvement in Iran during this time.

47. This battery was a gift from Czar Alexander III, who was informed by Charkovskij that the shah had desired one after it was described to him from a photograph (Kosogovskii, "Ocherk razvitija Persidskoj Kazach'ej Brigady," 392).

48. "The Setkhanian Dynasty."

49. Russian citizenship document, 1888, Setkhanian Collection.

50. The word *poddantsvo* also translates as "citizenship."

51. This transfer of citizenship was not uncommon for Cossack officers and was not necessarily seen as a problem or as limiting one's rights in Persia; Prince Darab Mirza was a naturalized Russian and still attempted to seize the throne in 1910. See Shuster, *The Strangling of Persia*, lii.

52. Russian citizenship document, 1888, Setkhanian Collection.

53. *Farman* reinstating Iskandar Khan to rank of *sarhang* (colonel), Ramadan, 1307/1888, Setkhanian Collection. It should be noted that at age twenty-three Iskandar Khan was entering into service at the same rank of his father, who had served the government and military for some twenty-five years. Although this high rank might make sense in light of the education and type of training Iskandar Khan received, there are also numerous examples of ranks given away to individuals for reasons of nepotism and whim. For instance, Nasir al-Din Shah assigned the rank of *sartip* (brigadier general) to his eight-year-old nephew Malijak Aziz al-Sultan, which drove both the Royalists and the opposition mad and was

even mentioned by Mirza Riza Kermani (who assassinated Nasir al-Din) as a reason for his hatred of the shah and the shah's absurd practices. See Ehsan Yarshater, "Observations on Nasir al-Din Shah," in Bosworth and Hillenbrand, eds., *Qajar Iran*, 9. Colonel Kosogovski abolished these practices within the brigade in 1896 and expelled many *mohajer*s.

54. The British Foreign Office did a remarkable job keeping track of the Persian military, its ranks, members, strengths, and armaments. See, for example, Picot, "Military Organization of the Persian Army in 1899," 200–250.

55. *Hokm* assigning Iskandar Khan to rank of adjutant, Jamadi 1310/1892, Setkhanian Collection. The orthographic and stylistic features of a *farman* (royal edict) and *hokm* (edict issued by a lesser official) are nearly identical.

56. Kazemzadeh, "Persian Cossack Brigade," 357.

57. Colonel Shneur decided to leave his drunk and disorderly Cossacks at the *aazzaqkhane* (Cossack headquarters) to be with his wife, who was upset about the unrest in the city. See Kosogovskii, *Iz tegeranskogo*, 124–25.

58. See illustration 6, correspondence from Colonel Shneur to Iranian ambassador in Russia on Cossack Brigade letterhead. The letter states, "In service to Mr. A'alah ol-Mulk, special Minister and Ambassador at large in the great Russian Empire it is hereby stated that although there are [already] too many officers in the Cossack Cavalry Brigade of His Highness, the magnificently powerful, holy, royal King of Kings and that I, this servant, have begged for the writing of the glorious order that forbids completely entrance of new officers in the Brigade. But with all this, some of the youths you find, that from their presence produce general benefits for the Cossack Cavalry, include Iskandar Khan Sarhang, who for years has been in Russian military schools learning military sciences and tactics, and he can have beneficial service to the Brigade. Because now I have no possibility of instating him as included in [as] part of the Brigade, and meanwhile do not want to violate the meaning and intent of the glorious royal order, Iskandar Khan Sarhang, from sources [funds] outside the Brigade, can [perhaps] be considered in something like a temporary candidacy in the Cossack Cavalry Brigade, and become busy doing his army service as soon as the first opportunity and possibility for him to become part of the Brigade completely, in compliance with your order, Sir. Commander of the Cossack Cavalry Brigade Colonel Shneur," signed "*Colonel Schneaur*." Dated Sha'ban 8, 1310/1893, Setkhanian Collection.

59. Kazemzadeh, "Persian Cossack Brigade," 357.

60. See notes 53 and 55 for this chapter.

61. The summary of Kosogovski's observations on the state of the Persian military and brigade has been gleaned from his memoirs in Russian, *Iz tegeranskogo*, and in Farsi, *Khatirat-i Kolonel Kasagofski*.

62. Kosogovskii, *Iz tegeranskogo*, 56.

63. Colonel Kosogovski watched as the *sarbazan* (soldiers) and their commanding officers broke rank while on military escort duty for the shah and ruined some fruit trees foraging for snacks (*Iz tegeranskogo*, 56). In his memoirs, he also outlines the army's weekly

schedule, which was shaped to allow maximum time for personal and business activities and minimal time for training, which occurred at most once a week, and comments on the irregularity of pay (ibid., 63).

64. Ibid., 73.

65. Tousi, "The Persian Army," 219.

66. Nasir al-Din Shah, who was fond of the *mohajer*s and saw them as defenders of Islam, rewarded rather than punished those who deserted when they returned, saying to Kosogovski upon his complaints, "But the mohajers run away from you precisely because you do not sufficiently appreciate them" (quoted in Kosogovskii, "Ocherk razvitija Persidskoj Kazach'ej Brigady," 397; see also Kosogovskii, *Iz tegeranskogo*, 97–99).

67. One of the late shah's favorite sons, Kamran Mirza Naib al-Saltaneh, the war minister and governor of Tehran, was in a much better position than Tabriz-based Mozaffar al-Din to inherit the crown. Kosogovski was able to exploit the enmity between Kamran Mirza and the Sadr-i Azam Amin al-Sultan to maintain a balance of power until the crown prince arrived on June 7, 1896, in Tehran. The *mohr*, or seals of Naib al-Saltaneh and Sadr-i Azam, appear on three of Iskandar Khan's awards and promotions: the 1313/1896 *farman* awarding the Order of Lion and Sun of the Third Rank; the 1324/1905 *farman* promoting him to *sartip* of the first rank and the title *amir panj* (general); and the 1325/1907 *farman* awarding a "foreign" gold medal of the first rank.

68. Kosogovskii, "Persija v Kontse XIX veka," 448.

69. *Farman* awarding Iskandar Khan the Order of Lion and Sun of the Third Rank, dated Jamadi 1, 1313/1896, Setkhanian Collection. Like the Ottoman star and crescent, the Lion and the Sun was the symbol of the Qajar dynasty.

70. *Farman* promoting Iskandar Khan to *sartip* of the third rank, Ramadan 1314/1896, Setkhanian Collection.

71. Kazemzadeh, *Russia and Britain in Persia*, 410–13. Even the Persian government agreed, when pressed by the British, that the goal of this quarantine effort "was not so much the exclusion of the plague as the placing of every conceivable obstacle in the way of commercial intercourse between India and Khorasan" (Smith to Trench, Mashad, May 1902, FO correspondence).

72. *Farman* awarding the Bukhara Star of the Second Degree–Gold to Iskandar Khan Setkhanian, 1317/1897, Setkhanian Collection.

73. *Farman* promoting Iskandar Khan to *sartip* of the second rank and awarding him a sash, Zihijeh 1318/1900, Setkhanian Collection.

74. Award of Order of St. Stanislaus of the Second Degree, 1317/1900, Setkhanian Collection.

75. Iskandar Khan and Maryam are identified as the parents in the certification of the 1896 birth of Hovannes Setkhanian handwritten in Armenian and Russian, copied and notarized from the "Metric Book," or church register of births, deaths, and baptisms, in 1333/1915, Setkhanian Collection.

76. "The Setkhanian Dynasty."

77. Sevak Saginian recalled that all guests at Iskandar Khan's bathhouse were given a piece of soap and a red-checkered loincloth called a *ghadife*. The items were given away to bathers rather than shared or recycled owing to fear of disease. Visitors were also given free bread on occasion, which was cooked in the estate's brick *tannouri* (bread oven) (oral interview, Oct. 6, 1997, Glendale, California).

78. One of Iskandar Khan's servants at the estate thought it unbecoming of the patriarchal Iskandar Khan to have fathered even one daughter, an opinion proclaimed in mock amazement (oral interview, Mara Setkhanian-Martin, July 1995).

79. Wilber, *Riza Shah Pahlavi*, 9.

80. *Hokm* ordering Iskandar Khan Setkhanian to clear land for development, signed by General Kosogovski, dated Sept. 9, 1901, Setkhanian Collection.

81. Land deed as gift for service specifying outer boundaries of the property in relation to existing roads and properties, Shawwal 1320/1902, Setkhanian Collection.

82. *Farman* awarding Iskandar Khan the Order of the Lion and Sun of the Second Rank, Ramadan 1321/1903, Setkhanian Collection.

83. Tousi, "The Persian Army," 222.

84. *Farman* promoting Iskandar Khan to *sartip* of the first rank and *amir panj*, Muharram 1324/1905, Setkhanian Collection.

85. Homa Katouzian explains that the word used in the movement for a constitution, *mashruteh*, means "constrained," "conditioned," or "qualified." The central demand of the "revolution" was thus for a constrained or qualified monarchy—in other words, a limitation of the arbitrary power of the shah, who was taking out large foreign loans and was perceived widely to be selling out to the interests of foreigners. Radical political, social, or economic change was not on the agenda of the majority of revolutionaries as they rallied in support for the movement (*The Political Economy of Modern Iran: Despotism and Pseudo-modernism, 1926–1979* [New York: New York Univ. Press, 1981], 156; see also Katouzian, "Nationalist Trends in Iran").

86. See Browne, *The Persian Revolution of 1905–1909*. Browne's classic work is a unique and noteworthy source for its attention to substantiated detail and for its analysis of British newspaper coverage of the Persian Revolution—one of the first serious critiques of the bias in Western media coverage of Iran. See also Shuster, *The Strangling of Persia*. Shuster, the American financial adviser brought in as treasurer general in Persia from 1910 to 1911 used as one of his introductory images a photograph showing the Cossack Brigade from around 1909. Iskandar Khan stands next to the Russian colonel Liakhov and the nine-year-old Ahmad Shah Qajar (xxxviii). See illustrations 13a and 13b. For more recent scholarship on the Constitutional Revolution, see Afary, *The Iranian Constitutional Revolution*, and Houshang Chehabi and Vanessa Martin, eds., *Iran's Constitutional Revolution: Popular Politics, Cultural Transformations, and Transnational Connections* (New York: I. B. Tauris, 2010). Houri Berberian provides insight into the activities and motivations of

the Armenian Dashnak, Hunchak, and Social Democrat Parties, which contributed to the revolution, in *"The Love for Freedom Has No Fatherland."* Berberian's work, which is focused entirely on Armenian participation in the revolution, is based primarily on original Armenian-language archival sources and remains the most comprehensive on the subject to date. On the subject of Armenian Iranian identity during the constitutional period, see Houri Berberian, "Traversing Boundaries and Selves: Iranian Armenian Identities during the Iranian Constitutional Revolution," *Comparative Studies of South Asia, Africa, and the Middle East* 25, no. 2 (2005): 279–96, and "History, Memory, and Iranian-Armenian Memoirs of the Iranian Constitutional Revolution," *Critique: Critical Middle Eastern Studies* 17, no. 3 (2008): 261–92. The role of Armenians in the struggle is also considered in Chaqueri, ed., *The Armenians of Iran*.

87. Morgan Shuster's description of the shah was harsh but seems to have been a commonly held view: "Muhammad Ali-Shah Qajar was perhaps the most perverted, cowardly and vice-sodden monster that had disgraced the throne of Persia in many generations. He hated and despised his subjects from the beginning of his career, and from having a notorious scoundrel for his Russian tutor, he easily became the avowed tool and satrap of the Russian Government and its agent in Persia for stamping out the rights of the people" (*The Strangling of Persia*, xxi).

88. Tousi, "The Persian Army," 223. Although it is not within the scope of this work to detail the impact of the Anglo-Russian Agreement, it is important to mention this pact because the members of the constitutional movement were incensed by the fact that Russia and Britain had signed an agreement officially dividing their country up into spheres of influence (Russia in the North with its Cossack Brigade and Britain in the South with its newly formed militia, the South Persian Rifles, under British general Percy Sykes). For a detailed look at this agreement and the developments that led to its creation, see Kazemzadeh, *Russia and Britain in Persia*. Shuster reprinted the entire text to the agreement in his introduction to stress the point that the documents claimed to assure the sovereignty of Persia, but the powers that signed them engaged in activity to undermine it instead (*The Strangling of Persia*, xxvii–xxxiii).

89. Grant Duff to Gray, no. 101, Confidential, Apr. 22, 1906, P.O. 371/109, in Kazemzadeh, *Russia and Britain in Persia*, 496.

90. Kazemzadeh, *Russia and Britain in Persia*, 496.

91. Pension allotment of deceased Marteros Khan spelled out in Cyrillic type, 1324/1906, Setkhanian Collection.

92. Pension allotment of Marteros Khan, disputed, spelled out in Cyrillic type, 1335/1917, Setkhenian Collection. To distinguish between the two Iskandars, both of whom were in the Cossack Brigade, fellow soldiers and family members would refer to Iskandar Khan Setkhanian, who was older and of a higher rank, as "Iskandar-e Bozorg" (Big Iskandar Khan) and Marteros Khan's son as "Iskandar-e Kuchek" (Little Iskandar Khan) (oral interview, Mara Setkhanian-Martin, July 1995). The fact that the Russian official who wrote

the decision on the disputed pension in 1917 did not employ these nicknames and that both Iskandar Khans are referred to as *sartip* (Iskandar-e Bozorg being a *sartip* when the 1906 decision was made, and Iskandar-e Kuchek being a *sartip* when the complaint was filed) made the deciphering of this document almost impossible without the details provided in oral interviews.

93. Kazemzadeh, *Russia and Britain in Persia*, 496.

94. Award from the Russian government to Iskandar Khan, the Order of St. Anne of the Second Degree, May 10, 1906, Setkhanian Collection.

95. *Hokm* awarding Iskandar Khan a gold medal of the first rank from the Ministry of Education, 1324/1906, Setkhanian Collection.

96. Award from the Austrian government to Iskandar Khan, Order of Ritterkreuz, Feb. 27, 1906, in German, signed and issued in Vienna. Further research is needed to determine why this Austrian order and the Romanian orders were given because the documentation available only mentions a failed attempt to bring Austrian advisers to train the regular army in 1906. See Tousi, "The Persian Army," 223–24.

97. *Farman* awarding Iskandar Khan a "foreign" gold medal of the first rank, Zihijeh 24, 1325/1907, Setkhanian Collection. Soon after Iskandar Khan received the Foreign Medal, he was issued an award from the Romanian government (Apr. 28, 1907), the Order of the Crown of Romania (Setkhanian Collection), further distinguishing him and his service in the interests of the brigade.

98. Shuster, *Strangling of Persia*, xxxv.

99. Browne provides the complete text in Russian and English of "Colonel Liakhoff's Secret Reports," correspondence (of questionable authenticity) between the Russian General Staff of the Military in the Caucasus and Liakhov, which would (if genuine) provide proof that Liakhov was acting under direct orders of the Russian government during the attack on the Majles and in establishing martial law in Tehran the following year (*The Persian Revolution of 1905–1909*, 220–32). In addition, Browne provides the complete text to Liakhov's statement to the people of Tehran after the imposition of martial law on June 24, 1908 (ibid., 210–12), and the full text of the original 1882 contract and budget developed for the Cossack Brigade, which was published in one of the many Persian newspapers to emerge during the brief period of free speech before the events of June 23, 1908 (ibid., 230–32).

100. Kazemzadeh, *Russia and Britain in Persia*, 523.

101. Browne, *The Persian Revolution of 1905–1909*, 205–9; Qa'im Maqami, *Tarikh-i tahavvulat-i siyasi-yi nizam-i Iran*, chap. 9.

102. Although Iskandar Khan and other high-ranking officers gave orders to fire on the Baharistan and Majles members, only Hussein Pasha Khan (Amir Bahador Jang) receives credit in Farsi, Russian, and English history books and newspapers for leadership during the siege. This would prove to be a stroke of luck for Iskandar Khan, who received a promotion for his services during the siege but was not associated with it in written accounts of the battle.

103. Hearing of these events, Lenin wrote, "Shamefully defeated by the Japanese, the armies of the Russian czar are taking their revenge by zealously serving the counter-revolution. The exploits of the Cossacks in mass-shootings, punitive expeditions, manhandling and pillage in Russia are followed by their exploits in suppressing the revolution in Persia" (Aug. 8, 1908, Vladimir Il'ich Lenin, *Collected works of V. I. Lenin* [New York: International Publishers, 1927], 15, 182).

104. When asked why he participated in this event, which is one of the most infamous in modern Iranian history, Iskandar Khan would always say, "I am a soldier, not a politician. I took my orders from the shah. To serve the brigade. Period" (oral interview, Mara Setkhanian-Martin, July 5, 1995).

105. For a detailed description, black-and-white reprint, and English-language translation of this *farman*, see David Yaghoubian, "Armenian-Iranian Promoted to Amir Tuman of the Persian Cossack Brigade: Farman of Muhammad Ali Shah Qajar, 1908," in *The Modern Middle East: A Sourcebook*, edited by Camron M. Amin, Benjamin Fortna, and Elizabeth Frierson, 53–56 (Oxford: Oxford Univ. Press, 2006).

106. Nationalist forces in Tabriz were constituted mainly of Persians, Armenians, Turks, and Kurds. Bakhtiaris were the main backers of the movement in Isfahan. Browne chastises the British press for not recognizing the diversity of Nationalist forces, who in his opinion were characterized as Armenians, Turks, and Arabs because of a negative bias by the authors toward Persians. For a detailed account of the siege of Tabriz by Royalist forces and the city's eventual liberation by Russian forces in 1909, see Browne, *The Persian Revolution of 1905–1909*, 233–91.

107. The terms *mujahedin* and *fedayin*, which mean literally "those who sacrifice themselves" or "devotees," are general terms used to describe the Nationalist military forces fighting for the Constitution (Keddie, *Modern Iran*, 70).

108. This speech has been reprinted in its complete form in Browne, *The Persian Revolution of 1905–1909*, 256–58, original emphasis. Browne speculated that the "Hidden Hand" could refer either to God or to Russia, although the last words of the sentence suggest that it denotes the latter. Ervand Abrahamian explores the origins of the complex Iranian political vocabulary concerning foreign intervention, covert action, and spying in *Khomeinism: Essays on the Islamic Republic* (Berkeley: Univ. of California Press, 1993); see especially chapter 5, "The Paranoid Style in Iranian Politics," 111–31.

109. *Hokm* awarding a pay increase to Iskandar Khan, Safar 1327/1909, Setkhanian Collection.

110. In an interview on May 10, 1909, Colonel Liakhov told a *Times* correspondent that the 750 Cossacks would be supported by 5,000 regular army troops and that he was confident that they could defend the city against the constitutionalists.

111. A 21.5-by-35-centimeter document, handwritten in Farsi and Russian on Russian consulate letterhead, Setkhenian Collection.

112. *Times*, July 6, 1909, cited in Browne, *Persian Revolution*, 309–10.

113. *Times*, July 5, 1909, and *Daily News*, July 5, 1905, cited in Browne, *The Persian Revolution for 1905–1909*, 308–9. Browne provides a thorough critique of British newspaper reports on the Constitutional Revolution. He scolds the correspondent who wrote the description of the body-tearing incident for interpreting it as a manifestation of the revolutionaries' "loyalty" rather than as a demonstration of their brutality (308–9).

114. Browne, *The Persian Revolution for 1905–1909*, 309.

115. Ibid., 318.

116. Ibid., 319.

117. This incident was the result of the shooting of a sayyid by a Cossack soldier as the sayyid rushed up to curse the brigade negotiating team arriving to meet its mujahedin escort (*Times*, July 17, 1909, cited in ibid., 321). Iskandar Khan was senior translator of the brigade during these events (per his duties and title described in his 1909 pay increase), although it has not yet been confirmed whether he was the translator for these negotiations and the subsequent chaos after the sayyid was shot (ibid., 321).

118. Ibid.

119. Ibid. See also Afary, *Iranian Constitutional Revolution*, 252.

120. Browne, *The Persian Revolution of 1905–1909*, 329.

121. Wilber mentions combined efforts by the Cossack Brigade and the Nationalists to suppress tribal rebellion in 1910 (perhaps the only common threat to the interests of the Russians, the British, the Royalists, and the Nationalists alike) (*Riza Shah Pahlavi*, 9). On Yeprem Khan and Armenians' evolving and often conflicting allegiances during the constitutional period, see Berberian, "Traversing Boundaries and Selves."

122. Kazemzadeh, *Russia and Britain in Persia*, 605.

123. Ibid., 628; Qa'im Maqami, *Tarikh-i tahavvulat-i siyasi-yi nizam-i Iran*, chap. 13.

124. Kazemzadeh, *Russia and Britain in Persia*, 599; Shuster, *The Strangling of Persia*, 135. Wilber's book *Riza Shah Pahlavi* is the only source to mention the use of Cossacks against the forces of Muhammad Ali Shah (9). He devotes half of a sentence to the 1911 use of Cossack forces against a brother of the shah who was assembling outside Hamadan, but it isn't clear whose interests they were defending.

125. "Treasury Gendarmes" were being trained by four American military officers (Shuster, *The Strangling of Persia*, 190).

126. Kazemzadeh, *Russia and Britain in Persia*, 644.

127. Keddie, *Modern Iran*, 70–71.

128. *Farman* awarding regalia to Iskandar Khan, diamond-studded epaulets of the second rank, Rabi ul-Sani, 1330/1912; *farman* awarding of regalia and pendant with picture of late shah, Ramadan 1332/1914, Setkhanian Collection.

129. *Hokm* awarding a pay increase to Iskandar Khan with handwritten addendum, 1331/1913, Setkhanian Collection.

130. Military leave pass on General Vadbolski's personal Cossack Brigade letterhead, formatted and typed in Cyrillic, Oct. 3, 1913, Setkhanian Collection.

131. Wilber, *Riza Shah Pahlavi*, 8.

132. A military leave pass dated October 6, 1916, states, "The possessor of this document, the Head of the headquarters of the Persian Cossack Brigade of His Majesty the Shah, Sardar/General Iskandar Khan is given by me a leave into all cities of the Russian Empire, for a period of time from the date stated above for two months, that is until the 6th of October, which I attest to by the attachment of the official stamp" (Setkhanian Collection). See also "The Setkhanian Dynasty."

133. For the most detailed and candid account of the early life and rise of Reza Khan through the Cossack Brigade, see Wilber, *Riza Shah Pahlavi*. Although Wilber was a somewhat biased observer as an avowed fan of the Pahlavis who openly acknowledged the help of the late Shah Muhammad Reza in writing the story of his father's life, his work is more detailed than Persian sources produced during the Pahlavi era, which do not describe thoroughly Reza Khan's rise through the brigade. It seems that they were unable to write about any of his commanding officers (such as Iskandar Khan in 1915–16) because it would imply that someone else had been giving orders to Reza Shah. For a survey that considers the rise of the Pahlavi regime in broad historical context, see Nikki R. Keddie, *Qajar Iran and the Rise of Reza Khan, 1796–1925* (Costa Mesa, CA: Mazda, 1999).

134. Russia, Britain, Germany, and Turkey invaded Iran at one time or another during World War I, although the Russian and British military presence had been established the previous century.

135. The seal of the Moscow Police, which was required by those traveling to the city, suggests his primary destination, although the reason for this trip was not stipulated, as it had been in the previous leave/visa issued in 1913.

136. Summary of decision rendered on May 15, 1917, in dispute over Marteros Khan's original pension allotment, Setkhanian Collection.

137. Wilber, *Riza Shah Pahlavi*, 11–12.

138. For a more detailed account of the development of Reza Khan's relationship to the British after World War I, see Keddie, *Modern Iran*, 80–85.

139. R. H. Ullman, *Anglo-Soviet Relations 1917–1921* (Princeton, NJ: Princeton Univ. Press, 1972). Chapter 9 provides details of General Ironside's role in Reza Khan's decision to undertake a coup.

140. This report comes from Jahangir Setkhanian as told to Alexander Setkhanian (interviewed Sept. 1995, Encino, California).

141. Ibid.

142. In his autobiography *Blood and Oil: Memoirs of a Persian Prince*, written with Roxane Farmanfarmaian (New York: Random House, 1997), Manucher Farmanfarmaian vividly describes his dismay upon his return to Tehran in 1941 after studying abroad when he realized that almost all of the family property in Tehran had been seized: "I must have stood there for several seconds before I could shake myself from the reverie of what was clearly gone. Vaguely I remembered my mother having written that Reza Shah had seized

the land of the compound and literally thrown the family into the street. They'd been informed of the move by the construction workers who had shown up to break a road through Masumeh Khanoum's living room. I recalled that the Shah had taken our property of Doulab too, where the train station now stood" (108). In contrast, Iskandar Khan retained possession of the Setkhanian compound throughout Reza Shah's reign, and the family sold it after his death in 1953. The property became the offices of the Point Four program in Iran, which moved into its buildings in 1954. In a later passage commenting on the Point Four program and its problems with corruption, Farmanfarmaian comments: "Point Four (later USAID) occupied offices in a series of large buildings that looked like a good-sized ministry" (315–16), shedding light on the scope of the property Iskandar Khan Setkhanian was able to keep.

143. The Kolah-e Pahlavi was a brimmed headgear, similar to a French *kepi*, and was made mandatory dress in December 1928. The changing over to the Pahlavi Hat was sometimes accompanied by a ceremony, where individuals would hand in their old-style headgear and be presented with their new hats on trays. For an account of the Pahlavi attempt to Westernize the dress of Iranian citizens, see H. E. Chehabi, "Staging the Emperor's New Clothes: Dress Codes and Nation-Building under Reza Shah," *Iranian Studies* 26 (Summer–Fall 1993): 209–33. Specifically on the Pahlavi Hat and its eventual replacement with the bowler, see Homa Katouzian, *The Persians: Ancient, Medieval, and Modern Iran* (New Haven, CT: Yale Univ. Press, 2010), 218.

144. The mixed Western and traditional dress depicted in the hunting and fishing photographs shown in this chapter illustrate the beginnings of the transformation that Pahlavi rule was to impose on Iranians of all ethnicities and religious beliefs.

145. Sevak Saginian, a distant relative of Iskandar Khan who is the subject of chapter 4, recalled how during family visits at the Setkhanians' home Iskandar Khan would stand stiffly and oversee the children while they ate, as if they were a small regiment, barking out orders such as "Don't eat so fast! It is a health hazard! You must chew all of your food completely!" (oral interview, Oct. 6, 1997).

146. In 1938, Iskandar Khan was invited by letter to attend the opening of a new Armenian church in Tehran by the Organization of Armenian Churches in Iran; it also thanked him for a generous donation he had made to the church (1357/1938, Setkhanian Collection).

3. Hagob Hagobian

1. This chapter has been compiled from two previously published essays on the life and truck-driving activities of Hagob Hagobian: David Yaghoubian, "Hagob Hagobian, an Armenian Truck Driver in Iran," in Burke and Yaghoubian, eds., *Struggle and Survival in the Modern Middle East*, 178–86, and "Shifting Gears in the Desert: Trucks, Guilds, and National Development in Iran, 1921–1941," *Jusur* 13 (1997): 1–36. Information about Hagobian's life and the Armenian-Assyrian truck drivers' guild is based on oral interviews with Hagob Hagobian conducted between March and June 1989, Glendale, California, and an oral

interview with Arshak Gorjian—Hagob's best friend, *kavor* (best man), and fellow truck driver—conducted on May 14, 1995, Glendale, California.

2. Such attacks were common in Urmia and surrounding villages between 1907 and 1918, as detailed in Arianne Ishaya, "From Contributions to Diaspora: Assyrians in the History of Urmia, Iran," *Journal of Assyrian Academic Studies* 16, no. 1 (2002): 25–41. As Ishaya explains before illustrating with primary accounts, "A more serious problem was the Kurdish marauders who descended upon the villages during the harvest season and not only plundered the crops, but also took away the livestock and robbed the people of their personal possessions, including the clothes they were wearing. The Persian government was too weak to protect its citizens" (32). With the occupation of Urmia by Turkish and Kurdish forces in the spring of 1915 and subsequent commencement of massacres and ethnic cleansing of Armenians and Assyrians on May 24, a three-year period of "holocaust" was initiated that decimated the region's Christian population and villages.

3. For eyewitness accounts of the Armenian Genocide, see Donald Miller and Laura Touryan Miller, *Survivors: An Oral History of the Armenian Genocide* (Berkeley: Univ. of California Press, 1999). Vahakn Dadrian's *The History of the Armenian Genocide: Ethnic Conflict from the Balkans to Anatolia to the Caucasus*, 4th ed. (New York: Berghahn Books, 2003), offers an unparalleled historical overview. For recent works exploring the controversy regarding operative terminology and its broader implications, see Guenter Lewy, *The Armenian Massacres in Ottoman Turkey: A Disputed Genocide* (Salt Lake City: Univ. of Utah Press, 2007). See also Ronald G. Suny, Fatma M. Göçek, and Norman M. Naimark, eds., *A Question of Genocide: Armenians and Turks at the End of the Ottoman Empire* (New York: Oxford Univ. Press, 2011), and Vahakn Dadrian and Taner Akcam, *Judgment at Istanbul: The Armenian Genocide Trials* (New York: Berghahn Books, 2011). Timothy Pytell provides an introduction to issues raised by the Armenian experience in the field of comparative genocide in "Weighing Genocide," in *Hate Crimes: Understanding and Defining Hate Crime*, edited by Barbara Perry and Brian Levin, 205–20 (Westport, CT: Praeger, 2009).

4. On the history of Presbyterian missionary activity in Iran and implications for subsequent Iran–US relations, see Michael Zirinsky, "Onward Christian Soldiers: Presbyterian Missionaries and the Ambiguous Origins of American Relations with Iran," in *Altruism and Imperialism: Western Cultural and Religious Missions in the Middle East*, edited by Reeva S. Simon and Eleanor H. Tejirian, 236–52 (New York: Columbia Univ. Press, 2002).

5. By 1928, the Iranian government required a driver's test for licenses. The test consisted of a series of tight maneuvers in forward gear. Arshak Gorjian's test, taken in 1927 before this licensing was developed, was given by his *arbab* (master), who spontaneously gave him the wheel on the road between Rasht and Tehran and required him to negotiate the streets and *koutche*s all the way to the Tehran bazaar. He knew he had passed the test when they arrived and he had not hit or killed anything (oral interview, Arshak Gorjian, May 14, 1995). This process needs further research because it is not clear how much power a guild had over an individual who independently passed the driver's test and acquired a

vehicle or how the licensing procedure was adapted to or became a part of the process of apprenticeship and promotion within the guild after 1928.

6. The Iranian government provided the license, and the guild provided the pin. The representation of one's trade through pins, hats, colored cloth, and types of garments was a feature common in Iranian and other Middle Eastern guilds. Mohammed Reza Afshari describes the practice of trade and status differentiation through dress in his article "The *Pishivaran* and Merchants in Precapitalist Iranian Society: An Essay on the Background and Causes of the Constitutional Revolution," *International Journal of Middle East Studies* 15 (1983): 136.

7. For a social biographical portrait of another Iranian who worked as a truck driver during the same period, see Fakhreddin Azimi, "Amir Agha: An Iranian Worker," in Burke, ed., *Struggle and Survival in the Modern Middle East*, 290–304.

8. Katouzian, *The Political Economy of Modern Iran*, 64; Avery, *Modern Iran*, 285. After the abdication of Reza Shah in 1941, various tribes took again to nomadism from their forced settlements and continued the practice of truck caravan raiding.

9. Arjomand, *The Turban for the Crown*, 67.

10. Moustafa Khan Fateh, *The Economic Position of Persia* (London: King & Son, 1926), 56; Arthur Chester Millspaugh, *The Financial and Economic Situation of Persia, 1926* (New York: Imperial Persian Government, Persian Society, 1926), 15; Julian Bharier, *Economic Development in Iran, 1900–1970* (New York: Oxford Univ. Press, 1971), 196.

11. Details about truck driving and the truck drivers' guild in Iran were obtained through oral interviews with Hagob Hagobian and Arshak Gorjian conducted between 1989 and 1995.

12. See Richard W. Bulliet, *The Camel and the Wheel* (New York: Columbia Univ. Press, 1990). In this study, Bulliet demonstrates how the difficulty of road upkeep and the benefits of camel transport accounted for the fifth-century abandonment of wheeled transport in Iran. The advent of the internal combustion engine at the end of the nineteenth century and its proliferation in the twentieth century made possible the efficient use of wheeled vehicles, which returned to replace the camel after a fifteen-hundred-year period of disuse (259–68).

13. Michael Fischer provides commentary on the persistence of ethnic divisions of labor in the Iranian bazaar, noting that whereas the Jews, Turks, and Persians often formed subgroups within the bazaar, Assyrians were important in the trucking industry, and Armenians in the delicatessen business ("Persian Society, Transformation and Strain," in *Twentieth Century Iran*, edited by Hossein Amirsadeghi [New York: Holmes & Meier, 1977], 180, 268). Fischer does not mention how or if this ethnic grouping related to guild structures, but I have not yet seen evidence that specific guilds ever consisted of exclusive ethnicities.

14. Most sectors of traditional handcraft production—the primary producer of goods in Iran—would suffer from inclusion in the expanding world economy, which would, in Wallerstinian terminology, peripheralize Iran. Immanuel Wallerstein explains the

dynamics of core–periphery relations in *The Modern World-System* (New York: Academic Press, 1974), 301.

15. Willem Floor, "The Guilds in Iran—an Overview from the Earliest Beginnings till 1972," *Zeitschrift der Deutschen Morgenlandischen Gesellschaft* 125, no. 1 (1975): 104.

16. It would not be accurate to say that Iran did not have *any* rail because both the Millspaugh and Fateh economic assessments mention a few scattered and limited rail developments that existed in the 1920s. The Tabriz–Julfa Railroad, owned and operated by the Persian government, spanned a distance of eighty miles and had a thirty-mile branch to Lake Urmiah from Sofian. A number of independent narrow-gauge lines existed, as well as a forty-three-mile stretch of line in northwestern Iran that was in disuse owing to its poor condition. See Millspaugh, *The Financial and Economic Situation of Persia*, 16–17.

17. Charles Philip Issawi, "Transport: Distance, Time, and Costs," in *The Economic History of Iran, 1800–1914*, edited by Charles Philip Issawi (Chicago: Univ. of Chicago Press, 1971), 195.

18. Issawi includes H. W. MacLean's "Report on the Conditions and Prospects of British Trade in Persia" in his collection *The Economic History of Iran*, 196–99; MacLean's report was published in 1904.

19. A British source on trade in Bushire commented that before the Constitutional Revolution, about £40,000 was paid for annual transport hire on the 185-mile route between Bushire and Shiraz, but during the subsequent years of disorder as much as £70,000 to £80,000 had to be paid annually for the same service (ibid., 196).

20. The dynamics of Russian and British interests and activities during this period are detailed in George Lenczowski, *Russia and the West in Iran, 1918–1948* (Ithaca, NY: Cornell Univ. Press, 1949). The Anglo-Russian Entente of 1907 that led to the creation of the spheres of influence is described on pages 40–45.

21. Persian Transport Company, unpublished report, July 8, 1914, in Issawi, ed., *The Economic History of Iran, 1800–1914*, 202.

22. From Issawi's analysis in ibid., 202.

23. Avery, *Modern Iran*, 241.

24. Fateh, *The Economic Position of Persia*, 56.

25. Ibid., 94. It wasn't until 1938 that the rail link from the Caspian Sea to the Persian Gulf (870 miles of line with more than 4,700 bridges and 224 tunnels) was finished. Wilfred Knapp explains that during and after its completion, economists criticized the railway as a waste of resources. They argued that the construction of roads would have used a significantly greater proportion of indigenous skill and materials and that powerful trucks were better suited to carry heavy loads over Iran's steep mountain passes. Also, for some unknown reason, the railway missed all major urban centers except for Ahwaz and Tehran ("1921–1941: The Period of Riza Shah," in Amirsadeghi, ed., *Twentieth Century Iran*, 36).

26. Millspaugh, *Financial and Economic Situation of Persia*, 16. The League of Nations' *International Statistical Yearbook 1926 and 1927* estimated that the number of automobiles in

Iran was 4,450, whereas Egypt had 17,740 and Turkey 7,500. In terms of rail in 1926–27, Iran possessed some 250 miles of disjointed track, whereas Egypt and Turkey each had roughly 4,600 miles (Charles Issawi, "The Iranian Economy 1925–1975: Fifty Years of Economic Development," in *Iran under the Pahlavis,* edited by George Lenczowski [Stanford, CA: Hoover Institution Press, 1978], 130; Issawi includes some of the chart/stats from the *Yearbook*).

27. Banani, *The Modernization of Iran,* 135; Millspaugh, *The Financial and Economic Situation of Persia,* 15.

28. Avery, *Modern Iran,* 271. Avery comments on how these developments impacted the bazaar. "Fortunes were amassed by men ready to enter import trade in fields new and unfamiliar to the established merchants of the bazaar; machinery, motor vehicles spare parts . . . things which the older type of tea, sugar and cloth merchants was slow to adopt" (273).

29. Millspaugh, *Financial and Economic Situation of Persia,* 16. Millspaugh also noted, "After the harvest of 1926, it is proposed to use these trucks, not only to insure [*sic*] the bread supply to the central region, but to transport as well passengers, merchandise and mail all over the principal roads" (16).

30. Avery, *Modern Iran,* 306.

31. Floor argues that the ideal of mutual assistance prevailed more strongly in guilds comprising a single ethnic group ("The Guilds in Iran," 102).

32. Arshak Gorjian remembers that in below-freezing conditions, the drivers figured out how to mix diesel fuel with kerosene and use it like a stove to prime their truck engines from below, until the engine oil became warm enough so that the truck could be safely started. Trial, error, and word of mouth refined the technique after flame consumed several trucks (oral interview, May 14, 1995).

33. In addition to trade-specific information, guild members helped each other keep families informed about the progress of their trips by relaying messages and transporting personal letters back to Tehran (oral interview, Hagob Hagobian, Mar. 1989).

34. Especially as motorized vehicles and the quickly developing technology of the machine gun were blended.

35. For a look at the Iranian craft guilds from the sixteenth to the eighteenth centuries, see Mehdi Keyvani, *Artisans and Guild Life in the Later Safavid Period* (Berlin: Klaus Schwarz, 1982).

36. Afshari, "The *Pishivaran* and Merchants in Precapitalist Iranian Society," 148. Certain craft production sectors, most notably cloth spinners and weavers, were beginning to feel the effects of the dumping of machine-processed textiles from Europe in the 1850s and 1860s. A few trades, such as metalsmiths and luxury carpet weavers expanded their production during this period. This issue is pursued in detail later in this chapter in the discussion of the impact of trucking on craft industry in Iran.

37. Jakob Polak, *Persien das Land und seine Bewohner* (Persia: The land and its inhabitants) (Leipzig: n.p., 1865), 2:165–90, excerpted in Issawi, ed., *The Economic History of Iran,* 277; Floor, "The Guilds in Iran," 100–107.

38. Willem M. Floor, "Guilds and *Futuvvat* in Iran," *Zeitschrift der Deutschen Morgenlandischen Gesellschaft* 134, no. 1 (1984): 109–110.

39. To my knowledge, women's craft production was not organized into a guild structure.

40. N. A. Kuznetzova, "Materialy k kharakteristike remeslennogo proizvodzta v iranskom gorode" (Materials and features of handcraft production in the Iranian city), in Issawi, ed., *The Economic History of Iran*, 289; Floor, "The Guilds in Iran," 108. For descriptions of this process within different Iranian guilds, see Afshari, "The *Pishivaran* and Merchants in Precapitalist Iranian Society," and Yaghoubian, "Shifting Gears in the Desert."

41. Kuznetzova, "Materialy k kharakteristike," 289.

42. Afshari, "The *Pishivaran* and Merchants in Precapitalist Iranian Society," 135; N. A. Kuznetzova, "Materialy k kharakteristike," 288. Both of these sources rely on *Jughrafiayi Isfahan* (The geography of Isfahan) (Tehran: n.p., 1963), 66–127, as does Floor, "The Guilds in Iran," 108–9, for much of their data on nineteenth-century Iranian guilds.

43. Floor, "The Guilds in Iran," 108.

44. Ibid., 101.

45. Ibid., 105.

46. Afshari, "The *Pishivaran* and Merchants in Precapitalist Iranian Society," 136.

47. See Jaleh Pirnazar, "Political Movements and Organizations in Iran, 1890–1953," PhD diss., Univ. of California, Berkeley, 1980, 49.

48. Afshari, "The *Pishivaran* and Merchants in Precapitalist Iranian Society," 144.

49. On the scope and agenda of the movement for *mashruteh* to constrain the power of the shah, see Katouzian, *The Political Economy of Modern Iran*, 156.

50. This would set the number of Tehrani guild members at the time at about 40,000.

51. Floor, "The Guilds in Iran," 109; Floor, "Guilds and *Futuvvat* in Iran," 111; Ervand Abrahamian, "The Crowd in Iranian Politics, 1905–1953," *Past and Present* 41 (1968): 193–94.

52. By the time of the Second Majlis in 1909, the dynamics of the constitutional movement had changed, and the guilds and *pishivaran* began to lose their influence. The new electoral laws left them with virtually no representation in the Second Majlis, which, Afshari concludes, "removed the *pishivaran* and merchants from the political scene, and made them worried observers of the political deterioration of the country" ("The *Pishivaran* and Merchants in Precapitalist Iranian Society," 152). Afshari attributes their low representation in the Second Majlis to the entrance of traditional Iranian political interest groups into the movement, such as the Bakhtiaris and other tribal confederations, and the polarization of the movement between conservative (ulama, tribes) and radical (secular, nationalist, Communist) groups.

53. Although Reza Khan did not become Reza Shah until 1925, after deposing Ahmad Shah Qajar and establishing the Pahlavi dynasty, he had increasing influence over governmental policy after the 1921 coup d'état that made him war minister (*sardar-i sepah*) (Katouzian, "Nationalist Trends in Iran," 540–43). The text of an open letter from Iranian guilds

members stating the reasons for their support of Reza Khan in 1922 appears in Reza M. Ghods, *Iran in the Twentieth Century: A Political History* (Boulder, CO: Lynne Rienner, 1989), 93. After 1922, demonstrations and protest movements were suppressed.

54. Gideon Sjoberg, *The Preindustrial City: Past and Present* (New York: Free Press, 1960), 188–89. Sjoberg also describes the guilds of China and India as being very similar in organization and activities.

55. These factors lead Baer to conclude, "Therefore, Muhammad Ali could have hardly wished to suppress the corporative system. It is, indeed, mainly for this reason that the guilds survived throughout the nineteenth century. Since the government was unable to replace them by a new modern administrative system, it had to keep them intact to fulfill a number of important public functions" (*Egyptian Guilds in Modern Times* [Jerusalem: Israel Oriental Society, 1964], 133).

56. Wallerstein provides a summary of his theories of the world-system and explains the difference between "strong core" and "periphery" areas and the implications for each (*The Modern World-System*, 347–57).

57. Gabriel Baer, "Guilds in Middle Eastern History," in *Studies in the Economic History of the Middle East: From the Rise of Islam to the Present Day*, edited by M. A. Cook (London: Oxford Univ. Press, 1970), 26; Baer, *Egyptian Guilds in Modern Times*, 138–9. Baer remarks that the complete change of Egypt's commercial system in the nineteenth century affected merchant guilds in the same ways (*Egyptian Guilds in Modern Times*, 139).

58. Baer, *Egyptian Guilds in Modern Times*, 148–49.

59. This situation was replicated in Iran with the advent of motorized transport and the unique persistence of guild structures.

60. "It is clear that throughout most of the 19th century the guilds in Turkey comprised the whole urban gainfully-employed population" (Baer, "Guilds in Middle Eastern History," 23).

61. The only difference (though a noteworthy one for the conclusions in this chapter) between the Ottoman guilds and their Egyptian and Iranian counterparts is that the Ottoman guilds were shown not to have had consistent fiscal-administrative functions (ibid., 11–30).

62. Syrian guilds were sporadically taxed but, like the Ottoman guilds, were not the most important units of taxation. Citing the work of Ilyas Qudsi on Damascene guilds, Baer contrasts fiscal administration in Egypt and Syria, revealing that, unlike Egyptian traditions of guild tax collection, the Syrian urban quarter was "at least as important a unit of taxation as the guild" (ibid., 22).

63. Abraham Marcus, *The Middle East on the Eve of Modernity* (New York: Columbia Univ. Press, 1989), 78, 172–73. The only noteworthy difference between the Aleppine guilds as described by Marcus and the Iranian guilds as analyzed by Floor lie in the two authors' conclusions about guild hierarchy in each of the regions. Marcus's view of Aleppo's guilds as promoters of economic hierarchy (ibid., 175) conflict with Floor's impression of solidarity

within Iranian guild ranks ("The Guilds in Iran," 100–116). This important issue is taken up in this chapter's conclusion.

64. Baer, "Guilds in Middle Eastern History." These conclusions are based entirely on Baer's interpretations of al-Qudsi's work on Syrian guilds.

65. Ibid., 23. Floor has good evidence to argue against a transference to labor unions in Iran, which calls into question Baer's conclusions on this matter, which were admittedly based on sparse evidence ("The Guilds in Iran"). Further research into the guilds of all Middle Eastern countries in the twentieth century seems to be in need.

66. Hashemite Sharif Hussein declared Hijazi independence from the Ottoman Empire in 1916.

67. Mordechai Abir, "The Consolidation of the Ruling Class and the New Elites in Saudi Arabia," *Middle Eastern Studies* 23, no. 2 (1987): 152. It is important to note that prior to World War I, Arabian politics were for the most part removed from long-term colonial interests and activities, in contrast to politics in Iran, Egypt, Iraq, and the Levant.

68. Kiren Aziz Chaudhry, *The Price of Wealth: Economies and Institutions in the Middle East* (Ithaca, NY: Cornell Univ. Press, 1997). Chaudhry's analysis of Saudi and Yemeni economies and institutions provides a relevant study to use for comparison because it includes an extensive examination of the role of guilds during the development of taxation and the creation of a national market (43–100).

69. Between 1926 and 1952, the Hijaz provided the bulk of state revenues, and most of this revenue was extracted by guild tax farming (ibid., 59, 70).

70. Chaudhry explains, "There was some direct taxation in Jeddah, Tayf, and several other districts, but in Mecca and Medina, as before, the guilds continued to tax and administer the urban economy. Indeed, the guilds became a remarkable facility for the new government, undertaking a variety of state functions with great alacrity and at little expense. The largest revenue generator in the whole kingdom was the *'ayn al-zubaydah*, a water carriers' guild that collected the head tax on pilgrims, the religious trusts and buildings tax, and the charitable donations [that] merchants were assessed. In 1935 the *'ayn al-zubaydah* had dozens of permanent employees, a training program, and the largest independent police force in the Hijaz" (ibid., 59).

71. Ibid., 60.

72. Ibid.

73. Ibid., 61–65. Although the guilds were thus eliminated as a political force, it wasn't until 1964 that they were eliminated as an organizational entity (ibid., 89–90).

74. Ibid., 74.

75. Ibid., 89–90.

76. How the Iranian guilds coped with the challenges brought by Pahlavi modernization efforts is an important subject that has not yet been adequately pursued. Although the guilds' societal position and their economic role under the Qajar government in the nineteenth century has been sufficiently covered in a number of useful English-language works,

a view of the twentieth-century situation remains more elusive and necessitates a piecing together of the fragmentary evidence that is available. Besides Issawi, ed., *The Economic History of Iran*, see Floor, "Guilds and *Futuvvat* in Iran"; Afshari, "The *Pishivaran* and Merchants in Precapitalist Iranian Society"; and Hans E. Wulff, *The Traditional Crafts of Persia: Their Development, Technology, and Influence on Eastern and Western Civilizations* (Cambridge, MA: MIT Press, 1966). The problem of sources leaves me to rely mainly on Willem Floor's work on Iranian guilds for many of my interpretations in the next section in this chapter—that is, until I can engage in more primary research on the subject. See especially Floor, "The Guilds in Iran," 100.

77. Reza Shah's efforts to modernize and industrialize Iran have been referred to as a "big push" effort because of Iran's lack of development and the rapid agenda for reforms (Issawi, "Iranian Economy 1925–1975," 131).

78. Willem Floor, *Industrialization in Iran, 1900–1941* (Durham, UK: Univ. of Durham, 1984), 1.

79. Floor compares this effort and its social and economic costs to two of the other Middle Eastern cases I have examined: "It is true that the gap with countries like Egypt and Turkey had not been closed, but a big leap forward had been made. Although the cost for this big leap had been high, both in economic and social terms, it is difficult to see how Iran could have made such progress at a lower price. The burden of this price had to be borne by the mass of the population, a burden which could not be off-set by the great number of new jobs that had been created" (ibid., 35).

80. Floor, "The Guilds in Iran," 109; *Mudhakarat-i majlis shurai milli* (Memoirs of the National House of Parliament), 4th Majlis, pp. 121–24, cited in a note by editor Issawi in Kuznetsova, "Materialy k kharakteristike," 285. Issawi states that he owes this reference to Ervand Abrahamian (*Iran between Two Revolutions*, 151–52).

81. Child employment was especially prominent in the new industrial carpet factories (Willem Floor, *Labour Unions, Law, and Conditions in Iran, 1900–1941* [Durham, UK: Univ. of Durham, 1985], 60).

82. S. Simmonds, *Economic Conditions in Iran* (London: HMSO, 1935), 37.

83. Keddie, *Modern Iran*, 77–78.

84. Floor, *Labour Unions, Law, and Conditions in Iran*, 1.

85. Ibid., 34.

86. Floor thereby denies the grassroots or popular origins of guilds ("The Guilds in Iran," 101). Baer provides a similar assessment of Egyptian and Ottoman guilds and of governmental interests in them ("Guilds in Middle Eastern History," 29). Abraham Marcus concludes the same about state interest in the Syrian guilds (*The Middle East on the Eve of Modernity*, 78, 172–73.

87. Abrahamian, "The Crowd in Iranian Politics," 193–94.

88. Floor, "The Guilds in Iran," 116. Floor's points seem feasible but need to be tested with new research.

89. Floor, *Labour Unions, Law, and Conditions in Iran*, 33–34.

90. Ann Lambton, *Islamic Society in Persia* (Oxford: Oxford Univ. Press, 1954), 30.

91. The period 1926–31 is particularly dim. We know nothing about how the guilds reacted to the law that abolished their fiscal-administrative duties. Floor's speculation that "some sort of deal" between the guilds and the government to arrange for the collection of taxes until the laws of 1931 were passed is obviously insufficient (Floor, "The Guilds in Iran," 116). To augment our understanding of reasons behind the lack of a strong trade union movement in the period 1918–25, explication on class dynamics within the ranks of the Iranian guild members is necessary.

92. Floor, "The Guilds in Iran," 110.

93. Ibid.

94. Lambton, *Islamic Society in Persia*, 24. In the interpretive structure employed by Floor and Baer, the 1926 Law on the Abolition of the Guild Taxes marks the end of the Iranian guilds as they lost their fiscal-administrative responsibilities. Projecting onto Iran Baer's depiction of the demise of Egyptian and Ottoman guilds, we can guess that it would have been a matter only of years before they would wither and die, provided that Iranian development followed the developmental course of the other Middle Eastern nations (Floor, "The Guilds in Iran," 110). Using the case of the truck drivers' guild in Iran during the 1920s and 1930s as a demonstration of continuity and the fact that in 1948 the fiscal-administrative responsibilities of taxation were returned to the Iranian craft guilds, I would argue that fiscal administration is not the critical or defining function of a guild. In 1958, the Iranian craft guilds were given legal status and continued to organize taxes for guild members in the 1960s and 1970s, which were paid in one lump sum by the guild after negotiation. Government "supervision" of guild-head elections and confirmations of all high posts during this time limited their freedom; however, they were still vocal about pricing and tax rates (Floor, "The Guilds in Iran," 111). Evidence that the Anatolian and Levantine guilds of the Ottoman Empire did not have important fiscal-administrative functions further problematizes their attempt to create a structural paradigm applicable to Middle Eastern guilds and supports my position on this issue. See note 63.

95. Keddie, *Modern Iran*, 93; Donald Wilber, *Iran, Past and Present* (Princeton, NJ: Princeton Univ. Press, 1948), 143–44; R. N. Gupta, *Iran, an Economic Study* (New Dehli: Indian Institute of International Affairs, 1947); Bharier, *Economic Development in Iran*, 194–98.

96. Millspaugh, *The Financial and Economic Situation of Persia*, 16.

97. Knapp, "1921–1941," 33–34.

98. Ibid., 35. Knapp comments that the road guards' low pay and insufficient supplies made them ineffective and led some to rob rather than to protect.

99. Recall that Baer attributed the demise of the Egyptian guilds primarily to their inclusion in (or exposure to) the world economy, which weakened them and readied them for the final blow of legal restriction. Charles Issawi provides a similar assessment that underscores the impact of roads on Egyptian and Ottoman/Turkish craft industries in his

general survey "De-industrialization and Re-industrialization in the Middle East since 1800," *International Journal of Middle East Studies* 12 (1980): 469–79. Issawi describes the "catastrophic" effects that the development of roads had on textile trade in the Middle East and Iran (470–71). In another work on the same subject, he conversely cites poor transportation as having saved handcrafts in inland areas of the Middle East (Turkey, Iran, Egypt, and Syria) from import competition in the late nineteenth century (*An Economic History of the Middle East and North Africa* [New York: Columbia Univ. Press, 1982], 152).

100. By 1948, the Iranian guilds were again taxed as a corporate body by the government (Floor, "The Guilds in Iran," 110). Floor's work, the only secondary English-language scholarship to follow the history of Iranian guilds through the 1950s, 1960s, and 1970s, offers proof that the guilds survived the challenges of this era and continued to be vital agents of labor organizing and fiscal-administrative responsibility. But there is still much work to be done to enhance our understanding of the guilds in twentieth-century Iran. Floor called for more research in 1975 when he wrote his general survey of the Iranian guilds, but his call was not met with any enthusiasm from political scientists and historians. No complex study has been attempted since his last article on the subject in 1984 ("Guilds and *Futuvvat* in Iran").

101. For a social biography describing the life of an Iranian truck driver whose career benefited from the Allied occupation, see Azimi, "Amir Agha," 290–304.

102. Hagob Hagobian's political convictions were simplistic and a product of his personal experiences. Hagob was a strong supporter of Reza Shah, admiring his ability to deal decisively with the tribes and make the trucking profession safer. A subscriber to *Alik* (Wave), a daily Armenian Iranian cultural and community newspaper sponsored by the Dashnak Party, he was sympathetic to the Dashnaks and accordingly developed a dislike for the Soviet Union and communism because of the Soviet grip on Armenia. His dislike for the Soviet Union turned to hatred after the Red Army commandeered his truck in 1941, and he was unable to obtain compensation after years of correspondence and dealing with an obstinate bureaucracy (oral interview, Nejde Hagobian, Sept. 2000, Toluca Lake, California).

4. Sevak Saginian

1. This chapter is based primarily on oral interviews with Sevak Saginian conducted between 1996 and 2000 in Glendale, California. In addition, Sevak was kind enough to provide extended written memoirs and responses to specific questions, access to documents, photographs, and books that detail the long history of the Saginian family in Iranian politics and culture and that trace his own career as Armenian Iranian community leader and parliamentary representative. Although Sevak passed away in 2003 and his wife, Nella in 2006, I would nevertheless like to express my sincere gratitude to both for their participation, assistance, hospitality, and patience as I conducted this research.

2. Sevak Saginain, written memoirs (in Farsi, clarified and elaborated on in English during oral interviews), copy in my files; oral interview, Sevak Saginian, July 12, 1997.

3. Of the martial arts skills the gang attempted to acquire, jujitsu was one of the most coveted. Sevak Saginian, written memoirs.

4. Ibid. In an oral interview conducted on April 28, 1998, I asked Sevak to elaborate on the nature of such meetings. He responded, "Religious officials like the Arch Diocese would seek to obtain a permit or talk to the prime minister, and I would go and translate. At the time, very few of the Armenian religious officials spoke good Farsi, so I was there to clarify things for both sides."

5. David Khan Saginian was born in Tiblisi in 1790. In nineteenth-century Iran, the title *khan* was applied loosely to refer to tribal chiefs, military commanders, and political notables (Muriel Atkin, *Russia and Iran 1780–1828* [Minneapolis: Univ. of Minnesota Press, 1980], 13).

6. Isma'il Ra'in's *Iraniyan-i Armani* contains a painting of Sartip David Khan Saginian in full military dress, with the caption "Sartip David Khan Sakinian, who was commander of Iranian armed forces [*farmandeh-ye qoshun-e Iran*] in the provinces of Shiraz and Isfahan during the reign of Fath Ali Shah, and who died at age 78" (47).

7. Observations on Abbas Mirza's treatment of Christians and his rebuke of the ulama of Tabriz can be found in Myr-Davoud-Zadour de Melek Schahnazar, Envoye de Perse en France, *Notice sur l'etat actuel de la Perse* (Paris, 1818), 13–19, excerpts of which are given as "Armenians and the State of Persia (1818)" in Chaqueri, ed., *The Armenians of Iran*, 351–56; see also Chaqueri, "Introduction to *The Armenians of Iran*," 8–9.

8. For a general description of Abbas Mirza's military reforms, see Abrahamian, *Iran between Two Revolutions*, 52–53. For an in-depth treatment of the Caucasian wars with a political-military focus, see Atkin, *Russia and Iran*.

9. In oral interviews, Sevak Saginian repeatedly commented that the title *sarperast-e Aramane* gave David Khan Saginian *total* authority in all matters concerning Armenians, yet beyond several sources that mention the title itself, I have not found corroborating evidence to support or refute this point. Ra'in's *Iraniyan-i Armani* contains a single *farman* issued by Fath Ali Shah in 1832 that decrees special care for the Armenians of Isfahan by the governor and that their disputes be handled by their religious leaders (119). Sevak's full response when I queried him a second time was, "All courts were governed by the military. And since he [Sartip David Khan Saginian] was a governor of a large region and military commander, he had the final say over what happened to Armenians and Christian minorities in the courts. If there were any rulings against the Armenians, he would intervene and protect them. This included Armenians, Assyrians, and any European Christians in the region (such as technical workers, consultants, and medical experts). This position was given to him by the shah. His territory in this position covered Azerbaijan, Urmia, Shiraz, and Bushire" (oral interview, June 15, 1997). In July 1997, I asked Sevak to tell me anything else he knew of Sartip David Khan Saginian's role as *sarperast-e Aramane*. He stated that "David Khan's office was in his house. From here he would issue judgments on any Christian–Muslim conflicts. I believe his decision was binding." Asked to compare his perception of the power of the *sarperast* with that of a twentieth-century Majles member, Sevak

replied, "This power was beyond that of Majles members. [In the Majles,] there were grievance committees for arbitration but not a binding decision like [a] *sarperast*'s issued under the Qajars" (oral interview, July 12, 1997).

10. David Khan Saginian died in 1867 and is buried in the Saginian mausoleum and church in Tabriz known as Surb Astvatsatsin.

11. Solayman Khan was also buried in Tabriz in the Saginian family mausoleum at Surb Astvatsatsin.

12. Zohrab Saginian traveled to Europe with his friend Alex Aghayan, who decided to study in Belgium instead of Switzerland. Under Reza Shah, Alex Aghayan became the Armenian Majles representative for the South, while Zohrab assumed the deputyship for the North (Sevak Saginian, written memoirs; oral interview, Sevak Saginian, Oct. 6, 1997).

13. Sevak Saginian, written memoirs. Saginian explains that his father, Zohrab, was a proponent of the Latinization of the Persian alphabet because he thought that the lack of vowels in the Persian/Arabic script made it necessary for a reader to be familiar with a word and its context before being able to correctly read and comprehend it.

14. Cosroe Chaqueri, "Armenian-Iranians and the Birth of Iranian Socialism, 1905 to 1911," in Chaqueri, ed., *The Armenians of Iran*, 78. Members of the Dashnak Party included local Armenians recruited by the party and Armenian revolutionaries seeking refuge from the Ottoman and czarist governments, both of which had sought to eliminate Armenian revolutionaries in the 1890s (George Bournoutian, *A History of the Armenian People*, vol. 2: *1500 A.D. to the Present* [Costa Mesa, CA: Mazda, 1993], 184). See also Berberian, *"The Love for Freedom Has No Fatherland,"* 59; Berberian describes a Dashnak arms factory in Tabriz that operated between 1891 and 1906, employing up to thirty-six workers (86).

15. Berberian, *"The Love for Freedom Has No Fatherland,"* 11. Berberian cites three primary factors to explain Armenian participation in the Iranian Constitutional Revolution: (1) the influence of the intellectual and revolutionary milieu of the Caucasus on the historically rooted Armenian Iranian community; (2) the political Left's desire to counter communal violence between Caucasian Armenians and Muslims through collaboration in the Iranian political movement; and (3) a "fluidity of identities" that allowed for participation in a revolutionary movement outside of historical Armenian territory (9). Berberian also elaborates on the subject of Armenian Iranian identity and allegiances in her article "Traversing Boundaries and Selves."

16. Czar Nicholas II confiscated all church properties external to ritual practices and put Armenian schools under government jurisdiction (Berberian, *"The Love for Freedom Has No Fatherland,"* 94.

17. Abrahamian, *Iran between Two Revolutions*, 105. The Hnchakists' intellectual contributions to the Constitutional Revolution and the party's activities and attitudes in Iran during the early twentieth century are pursued at length in Chaqueri's edited volume *The Armenians of Iran*. See in particular Chaqueri, "Armenian-Iranians and the Birth of Iranian Socialism," 77–118, and Aram Arkun, "Grigor Yaghikian: Writer and Journalist," 162–89.

Berberian illustrates how and why the Hnchakists's ended up collaborating with the movement despite their ambivalence ("Traversing Boundaries and Selves").

18. Kazemzadeh, *Russia and Britain in Persia*, 541, 644.

19. Although not described by Sevak Saginian in oral interviews or written memoirs, secondary sources suggest the possibility that Yeprem Khan died while attempting to aid Zohrab Saginian, who was wounded in the engagement. Berberian writes, "Yeprem's army faced that of Salar al-Dowleh in the village of Surjeh, where Yeprem Khan was killed instantly while attempting to reach his wounded friend, Dr. Zohrab Khan" (*"The Love for Freedom Has No Fatherland,"* 274 and especially chapter 2 on Yeprem Khan and Iskandar Khan Setkhanian; see also Berberian, "Traversing Boundaries and Selves").

20. Afary, *Iranian Constitutional Revolution*, 302. Afary cites Mahdi Malikzadah, *Tarikh-i inqilab-i mashrutiyat-i Iran*, 7 vols. (Tehran: 'Ilmi Press, 1984), 6:1350–54. On the vulnerability of the Dashnaks of Iran following the death of Yeprem Khan and the reasons for the party's withdrawal from Iranian politics, see Berberian, *"The Love for Freedom Has No Fatherland,"* 275–280.

21. Oral interview, Sevak Saginian, Apr. 28, 1998; A. Amurian and M. Kasheff, "Armenians of Modern Iran," in *Encyclopaedia Iranica* (New York: Columbia Univ., 1986), 2:479; for an online version of this entry updated in 2011, see *Encyclopaedia Iranica*, online edition (1996), available at http://www.iranicaonline.org/articles/armenians-of-modern-iran, accessed January 26, 2014.

Although *Encyclopaedia Iranica* credits Alex Saginian with the opening of the first movie house in Iran, Sevak Saginian insists that his mother's father, Ardashir Khan Badmagurian, had brought the first motion pictures to Tehran two years earlier, in 1914, showing the films at a theater he opened and named "Khorshid." When asked to clarify in an oral interview on May 28, 1998, Sevak explained, "Ardashir Khan opened a silent picture house in Tehran in 1914 called 'Khorshid.' It showed European films only as nothing else was available. It was open six days of the week for men and on Fridays for women. It was on Al-ol Dawleh, which later became Ferdowsi Avenue. It was closed when Ardashir Khan died. The one in Tabriz, Soleil, was my uncle's. That one came later. It was open for about five years but then closed due to lack of money."

22. Elections for the Fourth Majles lasted from 1917 to 1921. In June 1921, the Majles met for the first time in more than five years (Ramazani, *The Foreign Policy of Iran*, 184).

23. For a brief overview of the independent Armenian Republic (1918–21), see Bournoutian, *History of the Armenian People*, 2:131–49. For an in-depth treatment, see Richard Hovannisian, *The Republic of Armenia*, 4 vols. (Berkeley: Univ. of California Press, 1971–96).

24. On the effects of the harsh winter of 1918–19 following independence, Bournoutian comments, "Lack of bread, fuel, medicine, and shelter caused riots, epidemics and famine. People ate grass, dead animals, and boiled leather; cases of cannibalism were reported as well. By the time it was over some 200,000 people had died from hunger, frost and typhus" (*History of the Armenian People*, 2:135).

25. Major Edward S. Kennedy, "Military Attaché Report, Iran, Military Intelligence Division, WDGS," June 26, 1944, Report no. 312, IG no. 2020, reprinted as "The Armenian Minority in Iran: An American Military Intelligence Report (1944)" in Chaqueri, ed., *The Armenians of Iran*, 382.

26. Abrahamian, *Iran between Two Revolutions*, 113–15.

27. Armenian participation in the Gilan Soviet Socialist Republic is briefly discussed in Abrahamian's *Iran between Two Revolutions*, 116. It is of note that Kuchek Khan himself had participated in expeditions under Dashnak revolutionary Yeprem Khan in 1908. The two major Armenian revolutionary parties (the Hnchaks and Dashnaks) entered into an alliance with the Ettehad-e Islam (Islamic Union) and supported the Gilan Republic. See V. Vasakuni (a.k.a. Grigor Yaghikian, an Armenian socialist writer of the Social Democratic Hnchakian Party), "Kuchek Khan and His Work," in Chaqueri, ed. *The Armenians of Iran*, 247–93.

28. Abrahamian, *Iran between Two Revolutions*, 129–32.

29. Ibid., 130.

30. Lenczowski, *Russia and the West in Iran*, 108–16. As an example, Lenczowski mentions the "bribing of Dr. Gazarian, ex-member of the Dashnak Central Committee, who was persuaded to edit in Tehran an Armenian newspaper, *Gaghapar* (Opinion), in which he was to praise the Soviet Union" (116). Another example is the attempt to influence the choosing of the Armenian Catholicos in 1929. Nerses, an Armenian archbishop of Tabriz, was the top candidate, and he was a Dashnak supporter. Armenian Cheka agents went to great lengths in an attempt to remove Nerses from his position in Tabriz and replace him with Kitchian—a Communist church functionary (115).

31. Ibid., 108.

32. Sevak Saginian, written memoirs; oral interview, Sevak Saginian, Oct. 6, 1997. According to Rouhollah Ramazani, the elections for the Fifth Majles were not controlled directly by Reza Khan, although his utilization of martial law, newspaper closures, and arrests of opponents had the effect of creating a Majles that he could control (*The Foreign Policy of Iran*, 183–86).

33. On the reforms Reza Khan enacted through the Fifth Majles, see Abrahamian, *Iran between Two Revolutions*, 130–33.

34. Abrahamian describes the vetting process in detail (ibid., 138) and quotes a British minister who reported in 1926, "The Persian Majles cannot be taken seriously. The deputies are not free agents, any more than the elections to the Majles are free. When the Shah wants a measure, it is passed. When he is opposed, it is withdrawn. When he is indifferent, a great deal of aimless discussion takes place" (British minister to the Foreign Office, "Annual Report for 1927," FO 371/Persia 1928/34-13069, quoted in ibid., 138).

35. Iskandar Khan Setkhanian (see chapter 2) and Zohrab Saginian were related through Zohrab's wife Sandokht Badmaguryan's family. Ardashir Khan Badmaguryan's other daughter, Sandokht's sister, was married to Iskandar Khan's wife Maryam's brother (oral interview, Sevak Saginian, June 15, 1997).

36. Because of the realities of the Majles's ceremonial status, the record of Zohrab's voting patterns would not demonstrate anything but support for Reza Shah. This conclusion has been drawn entirely from oral interviews of Sevak Saginian.

37. The CCFTU was banned along with all other trade unions in 1927; between 1927 and 1932, it and the CPI were ruthlessly pursued by the Pahlavi regime (Abrahamian, *Iran between Two Revolutions*, 139).

38. Sevak Saginian, written memoirs.

39. In "Report to the Honorable Secretary of State, Washington, D.C.," filed February 2, 1932, American diplomat Charles Hart comments that suspicions surrounding the Dashnak Party's involvement in the murder of an Armenian Soviet spy were "entirely justifiable, for it is well known that the Dashnak Party has recognized and frequently resorted to terrorism as a necessary means to gaining its ends." He continues in a footnote to that passage, "I am told that Dro, one of the party's best-known terrorists, is reputed to have committed about 30 political murders. He is now said to be in Berlin" (USNA, 860 J.00/32, retitled "Political Attitudes and Affiliations of Persian Armenians: An American Diplomatic Report" in Chaqueri, ed., *The Armenians of Iran*, 375, 378 n. 7).

40. Sevak Saginian, who was nine at the time, remembered that the men assigned to surveillance on the Saginian residence were not at all covert in their activities. Rather, they were treated like members of the family, sharing meals with them and sleeping on cots in the foyer. They often walked the Saginian children home from school (oral interview, Apr. 28, 1998).

41. Mohammad Goli Majd, *Great Britain and Reza Shah: The Plunder of Iran, 1921–1941* (Gainesville: Univ. of Florida Press, 2001), 168–71.

42. Abrahamian, *Iran between Two Revolutions*, 163; Eliz Sanasarian, *Religious Minorities in Iran* (Cambridge: Cambridge Univ. Press, 2006), 180 n. 61.

43. The account of this event is detailed by American embassy staff member Charles Hart in his two-page report of April 4, 1931, titled "Armenians of Persia Suspected of Bolshevik Activity" (USNA 891.00B/48), reprinted in Chaqueri, ed., *The Armenians of Iran*, 361–62). Hart concluded his report by stating, "The Persian government has shown the usual hysteria in making wholesale arrests without evidence, I am informed, and has made it dangerous for Persians even to discuss the crime. A few days ago three Persians overheard talking about the crime in the bazaar were arrested on the spot and taken to jail, according to information which seems reliable." Unfortunately, Hart did not reveal his sources of information concerning this event.

44. Hart, "Report to the Honorable Secretary of State"/"Political Attitudes and Affiliations of Persian Armenians," 378. In regard to Mirzayantz, Hart continues, "The latter, is, of course, well known to the Department because of his helpful association with American archaeological work in this country" (378 n. 6).

45. Ibid., 375.

46. On Reza Shah's emulation of Atatürk's reforms, see Keddie, *Modern Iran*, 88–104.

47. Cosroe Chaqueri, "The Armenian-Iranian Intelligentsia and Non-Armenian-Iranian Elites in Modern Times: Reciprocal Outlooks," in Chaqueri, ed., *The Armenians of Iran*, 133.

48. Abrahamian explains that the Armenian schools were first forced to eliminate European-language classes and then closed altogether in 1938 with the revoking of their licenses (*Iran between Two Revolutions*, 163). This perhaps explains why sources cite both 1936 and 1938 as the date of the school closures (see "Armenians of Modern Iran," *Encyclopaedia Iranica*, 2:478; Chaqueri, "The Armenian-Iranian Intelligentsia," 136). It is important to note that Reza Shah also shut down American, French, and Russian schools in 1938.

49. Abrahamian, *Iran between Two Revolutions*, 163.

50. Sevak Saginian, written memoirs. Sevak commented that although schools within church compounds remained unmolested, several of those separate from churches were requisitioned by the government and turned into public schools under Persian Muslim administrators. Fears of government seizure of other types of property were not unsubstantiated. Reza Shah confiscated an entire electrical plant from the wealthy Toumaniantz family without warning or compensation (oral interview, Sevak Saginian, June 15, 1997; see also Chaqueri, "The Armenian-Iranian Intelligentsia," 136).

51. As well as an Iranian nationalist, Zohrab was in a sense an Armenian nationalist. Although secondary to his commitment to supporting Armenian Iranians in his own country, the cause of the Armenian nation's liberation was a primary feature of his thinking and activities as member of the Dashnak Party (Sevak Saginian, written memoirs; oral interview, Sevak Saginian, July 12, 1997).

52. In early 1939, Reza Shah extended his efforts to inculcate Iranian nationalism through propaganda by creating the Sazeman Pervaresh-e Afkar (Society to Guide Public Opinion), which focused on shaping public opinion to support government reforms and to instill patriotism (Donald Wilber, *Contemporary Iran* [New York: Praeger, 1963], 76).

53. Sevak Saginian, written memoirs.

54. Although Reza Shah had been exiled to South Africa, the deck had already been stacked for the Thirteenth Majles elections in November of that year, so there was little change of deputies (Abrahamian, *Iran between Two Revolutions*, 177).

55. Ibid., 387.

56. Kennedy, "Military Attache Report"/"The Armenian Minority in Iran," 382.

57. Ibid., 384.

58. Abrahamian describes the Fourteenth Majles elections, which took a full six months to complete, as "the most prolonged, the most competitive, and hence, the most meaningful of all elections in Modern Iran" (*Iran between Two Revolutions*, 186). Although more research will be needed to determine the primary cause of Zohrab's loss, we can conclude preliminarily that the conjunction of Reza Shah's ouster (and thus influence in choosing Majles *nomenklatura* and power over local landlords) and the presence of Soviet troops combined to make it virtually impossible for Zohrab to win his tenth seat in the Majles.

59. *Azhir* article reprinted in Chaqueri, ed., *The Armenians of Iran,* 130. Chaqueri notes that the article in *Azhir* raised the criticism that Dr. Aghayan had served as a defense attorney to Reza Shah's infamous police chief Rokneddin Mokhtari while failing to mention Aghayan's advocacy for several of the pro-Communist Group of Fifty-three who were arrested and tried in 1938.

60. Lenczowski, *Russia and the West,* 182–83.

61. After retiring from Iranian politics in 1944, Zohrab Saginian became superintendent at the telegraph school and later inspector-general of the school until his death in 1970. He also taught courses in political science at the Dar al-Fonun in the section known as *madraseh siyasi* (oral interview, Sevak Saginian, Oct. 6, 1997). See also the unpublished *Ararat* booklet honoring the lifetime work of Sevak Saginian in Ararat, titled *Sevak Saginian* (Homenetmen Ararat Glendale Chapter, 1993), 12, copy on file with the author.

62. Chaqueri, "The Armenian-Iranian Intelligentsia," 141. Chaqueri details Armenian Iranian involvement in the Iranian-Azerbaijani Communist movements and immigration to Soviet Armenia following World War II and analyzes at length the impact of this activity on the perception of Iranian Armenians by the government (139–44).

63. Sevak Saginian, written memoirs. Sevak explained that the term the officers used for "brother" was the Armenian *akhper,* which he and fellow Armenians would sometimes use to address each other (oral interview, Oct. 6, 1997).

64. Lenczowski notes that during the Allied occupation "the Armenian community in Tehran competed with the Zoroastrians for Soviet favors by organizing fiestas for the Red Army soldiers and gathering funds for Soviet Charitable purposes" (*Russia and the West,* 206). In the oral interview of October 6, 1997, Sevak Saginian recalled how many Armenians of Tabriz had taken to the streets to greet invading Soviet troops with flowers, concluding, "That looked really bad."

65. Abrahamian, *Iran between Two Revolutions,* 385. Abrahamian explains that communism had virtually no appeal within the predominantly Sunni tribes, and the Baha'is generally avoided politics after their nineteenth-century persecution. Zionism attracted most of the Jewish Iranian intellectuals and political radicals, who immigrated to Palestine, leaving mostly families of merchants and traders. Zoroastrians tended to be conservative in this period owing to their identification with Reza Shah's secular nationalist policies and their commercial ties to Britain through the cities of Yazd and Kerman.

66. Abrahamian, *Iran between Two Revolutions,* 386–87. On the leadership roles played by Armenians in the Tudeh Party, see also Sepehr Zabih, *The Communist Movement in Iran* (Berkeley: Univ. of California Press, 1966), 248.

67. Chaqueri, "The Armenian-Iranian Intelligentsia," 138; Abrahamian, *Iran between Two Revolutions,* 386. Both Chaqueri and Abrahamian derive these details from British consular reports from Tabriz covering the years 1943–45, FO 371/Persia.

68. Abrahamian, *Iran between Two Revolutions,* 387.

69. Ibid. The additional seat for Assyrians was not created until the Twentieth Majles (1960).

70. In the 1920s, the Dashnaks generally supported Reza Shah because of his anti-Communist, antiforeign, secular modernist positions.

71. Abrahamian, *Iran between Two Revolutions*, 388.

72. Lenczowski, *Russia and the West*, 286–87.

73. Ibid., 290–311.

74. On April 28, 1998, I asked Sevak Saginian the following question: "The book *Iran between Two Revolutions* shows that Armenian membership in the Tudeh Party was disproportionately high relative to their percentage of the general population. Why do you think this was the case?" He replied, "It was a suspicion that Armenians were all Communists because of the Soviet grip on Armenia. This wasn't right, because for every Communist there were three or four Dashnaks fighting communism, which was antireligious. Lots of Armenians left Soviet-controlled Armenia in disgust in the 1920s and joined the [anti-Soviet] opposition in Iran. So I disagree that a bigger portion were Communists. I think more were Dashnaks. However, many Western-educated Armenians were liberal, and in this way they were lumped in with the Communists. The Dashnak charter itself is social democrat. Reza Shah used the Dashnaks to solidify his position. Then when he came back from Turkey, he changed his attitude toward the Dashnaks and suppressed them."

75. The publication Hay Meshakoutain Ararat Kazmakerpoutun (Armenian Cultural Ararat Organization), *Himnadroutian yev Gortsneoutian 40 Amyak* (40th Anniversary of Founding and Activities) (Tehran: Bashgahe Varzeshi va Pishahangi Ararat, 1984), celebrating the fortieth anniversary of Ararat, contains a graph denoting the size of Ararat membership as it fluctuated over time. It projects the following figures: 150 in 1945; 500 in 1947; 210 in 1952; 900 in 1955; 300 in 1961; 1,700 in 1968; 1,000 in 1970; 700 in 1977; 2,100 in 1984.

76. The original board members were not elected but chosen informally from the most popular and influential leaders of the informal organization. When asked who the original founding members were, Sevak Saginian remembered, "It was me, Hakopic Garabedian, Sebu Hovanessian, Hilda Arzangolian, Vachik Gharabegian, Norik Stephanian, and Hrair Maroukhian. As the most prominent and active of the thirty or so original members, we were the first executives of the board" (oral interview, July 12, 1997). The book *Himnadroutian yev Gortsneoutian 40 Amyak* lists Sevak Saginian, permit holder; Hagopik Garabedian, president; Noriar Pahlavouni, secretary; and Sebu Hovanissian, Arshak Gregorian, and Hrair Maroukhian. Maroukhian would later go on to head the Dashnak Party from its headquarters in Greece.

77. It is of note that Reza Shah ceded Iranian control of Little Ararat to Turkey as a provision of the 1932 Turco-Iranian Agreement. See Chaqueri, "The Armenian-Iranian Intelligentsia," 136.

78. Sevak Saginian explained that the entire organization did not change its name to "Ararat" until 1950. Between 1946 and 1949, an acronym of the Armenian equivalent

of the official Persian name Hay Patanekan Mshakutayin Miutiun (Armenian Youth Cultural Organization), HPMM, was used, along with the title "Ararat," which was originally reserved for the athletes in the group. Members and the community increasingly began using the name "Ararat" to refer to the whole organization until it was officially changed in 1950 (oral interview, July 12, 1997).

79. Sevak Saginian enjoyed recounting the interaction he had with officials from the Ministry of Culture regarding the play *Othello*. As permit holder for the Ararat organization, he was responsible for applying for a permit for the gathering and, because it was for a play, to provide a translation in Persian for the ministry. When Sevak arrived to pick up the permit, he was told that there were inappropriate parts in the play. Thus, although the play would be allowed to happen, the ministry wanted to meet immediately with the author to inform him of his errors in judgment. With a solid poker face, Sevak told the official that it would not be possible, for the author of the play had passed away (oral interview, July 12, 1997).

80. Saginian did not imply that the officials were ignorant of Mount Ararat or its significance. Rather, they were interested in hearing his explanation as to what it meant before making their decision (oral interview, Sevak Saginian, July 12, 1997).

81. Although it was well known that *Alik* was published by Dashnaks, the weekly did not cover political events or party ideology but instead focused on community news and cultural awareness. See Hart, "Report to the Honorable Secretary of State"/"Political Attitudes and Affiliations of Persian Armenians," 376–77.

82. Oral interviews, Sevak Saginian, Apr. 28, 1998; Nejde Hagobian, Sept. 2000, Toluca Lake, California.

83. Sevak Saginian explained that he was initially a supporter of Mossadegh and was at first elated by the effort to nationalize the Anglo-Iranian Oil Company. However, once the boycott was instituted and the economy crumbled, he became concerned about Mossadegh's weakness in the face of the burgeoning Tudeh, which in his view benefited from the poor economic conditions and boycott. Nevertheless, until Mossadegh "turned against the shah," Sevak perceived his own anti-Tudeh activities as a show of support for both the shah and Prime Minister Mossadegh (oral interview, Apr. 28, 1998).

84. Nejde Hagobian remembers that a favorite weapon of the pro-Tudeh gangs was a thick piece of wood resembling a baseball bat with an odd assortment of rusty nails, screws, and pieces of wire fitted on the end to do the most damage possible in a single swing (oral interview, Feb. 1999, Toluca Lake, California).

85. It will perhaps likely remain a mystery as to whether the pro-Tudeh gangs intended to burn Ararat's meeting hall that July night in 1953, but those who were there like to speculate that the guns were the deterrent that saved the club from destruction (oral interviews, Sevak Saginian, Oct. 6, 1997, and Nejde Hagobian, Sept. 2000).

86. On the role of the CIA in the overthrow of Prime Minister Mohammad Mossadegh, see Moyara De Moraes Ruehsen, "Operation 'Ajax' Revisited: Iran, 1953," *Middle Eastern*

Studies 29, no. 3 (1993): 467–86. For a more detailed analysis of the role of the United States in Iran in supporting the Pahlavi regime during the 1950s, see Mark Gasiorowski, *U.S. Foreign Policy and the Shah: Building a Client State in Iran* (Ithaca, NY: Cornell Univ. Press, 1991). For a study of the international implications that shaped the activities and interests of the United States and Britain in Iran during this period, see Mary Ann Heiss, *Empire and Nationhood: The United States, Great Britain, and Iranian Oil, 1950–1954* (New York: Columbia Univ. Press, 1997).

87. Gasiorowski, *U.S. Foreign Policy and the Shah*, 166–70. See also Abrahamian, *Iran between Two Revolutions*, 420–21.

88. Sevak Saginian, written memoirs; oral interviews, Sevak Saginian, July 12, 1997, and Apr. 28, 1998. I asked Sevak to repeat this story several times to be sure I would recount his memories of the event and interaction correctly.

89. A permit was most probably issued directly from the shah because form permits for gun ownership did not exist, and there was no government ministry in charge of issuing guns to civilians. Because it was so rare for a civilian to have the right to own and wear a sidearm, Sevak at first purposely wore the gun on his hip to meetings and functions (such as translation between the prelates and the government) as an indication of his status as a trusted insider. After noticing how the pistol seemed to make people uncomfortable, he relegated it to its wooden box. Sevak kept his gift firearm as well as the *hokm*/permit until he was forced to flee the country in 1978 following the Iranian Revolution (oral interview, Apr. 28, 1998).

90. In chapter 6, we will see how another recipient of the Neshan-e Rastakhiz utilized the document to his personal advantage in 1953 and 1954.

91. One of Sevak Saginian's 1953 articles in *Alik* was an obituary and tribute to Iskandar Khan Setkhanian, who died in April of that year. Although Setkhanian had been a supporter of the Qajars and had fought against the constitutional movement in 1908–1909, he was honored in this unofficial Dashnak weekly because of his philanthropic activity in the Armenian community. See "The Setkhanian Dynasty."

92. Aside from scheduling, the only real tasks necessary to organize the athletes of the Tabriz branch was to make sure that they had clean uniforms, knew to be extremely polite, and didn't show up late to the event. However, Sevak went a step further and readied the theater group to put on a special performance that included a showing of Ararat members' art, which seemed to greatly impress the shah (oral interview, Sevak Saginian, Apr. 28, 1998).

93. Sevak Saginian, written memoirs; oral interview, Sevak Saginian, Oct. 6, 1997.

94. Sevak Saginian, written memoirs; oral interview, Sevak Saginian, Apr. 28, 1998.

95. On the shah's power over government ministers, the Senate, and the Majles, see Gasiorowski, *U.S. Foreign Policy and the Shah*, 159–60. Gasiorowski comments, "Majles elections were routinely rigged by the security forces after the 1953 coup . . . so no more than a handful of popular candidates served in this body. As the Shah consolidated his control over the state, he was able to control Majles elections more directly and thus ensure that this

body would be personally loyal to him. After the heavily rigged election to the Twenty First Majles in September, 1963, the Majles served as no more than a rubber stamp to approve the Shah's decisions" (160).

96. In the Twentieth Majles (1960–63), Assyrians were granted their own Majles seat. Thus, there were a total of three Christian Majles representatives (two Armenian, one Assyrian), one Jewish representative, and one Zoroastrian. Sevak explained that the loss of Assyrian votes in Tabriz and Iranian Azerbaijan because they had received their own representative favored his would-be opponent Felix Aghayan (son of Zohrab Saginian's fellow Majles deputy Alex Aghayan), who had stronger ties with the Armenians of Tabriz. Thus, Sevak ran for the southern Majles seat in the Twentieth Majles elections, confident he would win out over the incumbent.

97. Sevak Saginian, written memoirs.

98. As well as controlling candidates and elections, the shah also appointed half of the members of the Senate, rendering that institution another of his tools (Gasiorowski, *U.S. Foreign Policy and the Shah*, 160).

99. In his memoirs, which he created in response to a series of written questions I posed, Sevak wrote, "I had met the Shah numerous times before I became a Majles member and he was very kind and affectionate with me, and helped me out with things. Therefore in Majles he would issue orders that I would then carry out." In response to the question "What was your relationship with the shah, and how important was it to your success in getting things accomplished in Majles?" Sevak responded in his memoirs, "Iran had previously 2,500 years of monarchy and the Shah was considered to be divine. As Ferdowsi said, 'Farman-e Shah Farman-e khoda' [the edict of the Shah is the edict of God] and before the Majles was created, the Shah had been the owner of the country and its people. He would declare all of the laws and judgments. He could order someone who is guilty, or even someone who was not to be killed. For example, Nasr al-Din executed Sadr-i Azam. Before I became a Member of Majles I met the Shah and he trusted me. Therefore, if I needed anything for the Armenian community I didn't have a problem. The Shah was my backing and influence." In the oral interview of June 15, 1997, Sevak also stated, "I soon realized [after becoming a member of Majles] that it would take ten to twenty years to get things passed if I only relied on Parliament, so I would just go and ask the shah."

100. "To see the shah, I simply had to file a request for visitation with the minister of court. It would take eight to ten days for the request to be granted and scheduled." Sevak recalled that the only thing uncomfortable about his meetings with the shah was feeling overdressed or underdressed because Mohammad Reza Pahlavi's attire would range from casual civilian clothes to full military regalia without notice. Meetings could also be formal or informal at the shah's whim. Sometimes they would walk around the palace grounds and talk or sit outside drinking tea and smoking cigarettes. At other times, their meetings would occur across the shah's desk with an air of great formality (Sevak Saginian, written memoirs; oral interview, Sevak Saginian, July 12, 1997).

101. Although Zohrab Saginian had obtained permission in the Thirteenth Majles to reopen the Armenian schools, this was done with an agreement pending from the Ministry of Education regarding the percentage of Armenian curriculum allowed. By 1956, this issue was still unresolved, such that a technically Armenian-language curriculum was still not fully legal.

102. It was not the Iranian government that was threatening the Armenian school properties, but rather the individual owners of the property. Sevak Saginian explained that property for schools was often donated by a wealthy local Armenian Iranian philanthropist, whose family would often attempt to sell the property when the individual passed away. Having the property purchased for or donated to the church assured that the property would be protected from future loss or litigation (Sevak Saginian, written memoirs; oral interview, Sevak Saginian, July 12, 1997).

103. The Ararat scouts and their relationship to the Pishahangi-ye Iran are discussed at length in chapter 6.

104. Oral interview, Sevak Saginian, July 12, 1997.

105. The Ararat scouts were exceedingly skilled at this competition because they had developed the event and had been competing between each other in previous years of the Fourth of Aban exhibition when there were no Pishahangi-ye Iran troops to compete against (oral interview, Sevak Saginian, July 12, 1997; oral interviews, Nejde Hagobian, Feb. 1999, Sept. 2000).

106. The Twentieth Majles was dissolved in May 1961 by newly appointed Prime Minister Ali Amini amid vast accusations of election rigging. It was widely perceived that Amini was the choice of the Kennedy administration, which was pressuring the shah to initiate needed land reform, and that he disbanded the Majles owing to the large percentage of landed deputies who would ostensibly oppose reform. After several changes in prime minister by the shah, the Majles was not fully reconvened until 1964 (Sevak Saginian, written memoirs; oral interview, Sevak Saginian, Oct. 6, 1997).

107. In regard to Mohammad Reza Pahlavi's control of the Majles, Donald Wilber observes that, "by 1960, the ruler's domination of the government was so all-embracing that one of his prime ministers announced to the Majles that he could not take a position on an issue because he had not received imperial instructions" (*Contemporary Iran*, 118).

108. Sevak Saginian did not state specifically how much lower the salary was for an instructor without a higher degree, but he likened it to a "driver's wage" (oral interview, July 12, 1997).

109. Although the water and electrical projects for Khoygan were completed in 1977, Sevak Saginian left Iran before the Namagerd electrical project was completed, and construction was halted during the revolution (Sevak Saginian, written memoirs; oral interview, Sevak Saginian, Apr. 28, 1998).

110. See the 1955 American consul report "The Gregorian Armenians of Isfahan," reprinted in Chaqueri, ed., *The Armenians of Iran*, 391.

111. Ibid. In regard to the application of Armenian Church law over Iranian laws, the report states, "For example, under the rules governing Armenian distribution of property, both sons and daughters share alike while according to Iranian law the sons get twice as much as the daughters" (391).

112. Ibid.

113. This story is summarized from two oral interviews with Sevak Saginian, one in which he related the basic story and another in which I asked him to tell it again and in greater detail (Oct. 6, 1997, and Apr. 28, 1998).

114. Oral interviews, Sevak Saginian, July, 12 1997, and Oct. 6, 1997.

115. Oral interview, June 15, 1997. This issue is pursued further in chapter 7.

116. For a brief description of the florescence of Armenian Iranian communities in the 1960s and 1970s, see Bournoutian, *A History of the Armenian People*, 2:185. Bournoutian cites the number of Armenians in Iran in the late 1970s as exceeding 250,000.

117. Sevak Saginian believes the land in Vanak was deeded to the Armenian Church by Nasir al-Din Shah in the 1860s for the building of a church and cemetery (oral interview, July 12, 1997).

118. The Ararat sports complex remains the center of Armenian Iranian life in Tehran. Ararat hosted the Pan-Armenian Sporting Games in September 2000, which featured a large fireworks display to mark the opening ceremony of the week-long event and to celebrate seventeen centuries of Armenian Christianity. The event was simulcast on the Internet via the Islamic Republic News Agency (IRNA) website (http://www.irna.com) and featured announcements in Persian and Armenian. For a recent virtual tour of the Ararat sports complex, see PressTV's report "Ararat Club," which aired October 22, 2012, at http://www.presstv.ir/Program/268120.html, accessed Feb. 2013.

119. Chaqueri, "The Armenian-Iranian Intelligentsia," 144.

120. For a description of Bishop Manoukian's statements and activities to keep the Armenian Iranian population in good standing with the Islamic Republic, see ibid., 146–48.

121. Sevak Saginian, written memoirs; oral interview, Sevak Saginian, Oct. 6, 1997.

122. Sevak Saginian's diplomatic passport was rejected in London, but the family was offered political asylum in the United States.

5. Lucik Moradiance

1. This chapter is based primarily on oral interviews with Lucik Moradiance conducted in August, October, and December 2001; August 2002; April 2003; and February 2006 in Sherman Oaks, California. Oral interviews were supplemented by written correspondence between August 2001 and February 2007.

2. For a brief survey of the history of the petroleum industry in Iran that focuses on Abadan, see Kaveh Ehsani, "Social Engineering and the Contradictions of Modernization in Khuzestan's Oil Company Towns: A Look at Abadan and Masjed-Soleyman," *International Review of Social History* 48 (2003): 361–99. For a broader perspective of the Anglo-Persian Oil

Company and Abadan in petroleum history and global rivalries over petroleum resources, see Daniel Yergin, *The Prize: The Epic Quest for Oil, Money, and Power* (New York: Free Press, 2008).

3. Farmanfarmaian and Farmanfarmaian, *Blood and Oil*, 87.

4. Ibid., 84. Farmanfarmaian observes that the exclusively British residential section of Braim "looked like it had been sliced right out of Birmingham and dropped into Abadan: the flower boxes, postboxes, apron gardenettes, and whitewashed stoops and shutters were all so perfectly English. Even the cars and buses—all English makes—drove on the left. This was a company town top to bottom. Everything here was stamped AIOC" (86).

5. A new consortium had been created to bring Iranian oil back on the world market in the wake of the 1953 CIA/MI6-inspired coup d'état that overthrew Prime Minister Mossadegh and brought the nationalization movement to an end, which gave the United States a 40 percent share in Iranian oil, where it had previously had none (Yergin, *The Prize*, 470–78; Heiss, *Empire and Nationhood*, xx).

6. Manucher Farmanfarmaian remembers from visiting Abadan for the first time in February 1941 on a one-week extended tour of the facilities: "The heat was so intense that the asphalt on the docks was soft as marshmallow. *If it was this hot in February, what would it be like in July?* As it was, the water pipes became so hot under the morning sun that we poured our baths hours before we planned to wash so that the water could cool down" (*Blood and Oil*, 87, 185, emphasis added).

7. Certainly the subject was being discussed privately by workers, staff, and management, but in the post coup climate of repression and as a young temporary intern, Lucik would not have been privy to such conversations or sentiments.

8. Leaving Abadan after his first visit in 1941, Farmanfarmaian lamented the total absence of women at the facility, labeling it a *zamharir* (ice hell) and questioning whether he himself could work in such an environment (*Blood and Oil*, 102–3). Farmanfarmaian's concerns were, of course, the inverse of Lucik's father, if not her father's specific source of consternation.

9. One of the oldest churches in the world, the St. Thaddeus Cathedral (known locally as the Black Church or *ghara kelisa*), is an annual pilgrimage destination for tens of thousands of Armenian Iranians, who camp overnight on the surrounding mountains. The church has been renovated with the financial assistance of the Iranian government and UNESCO and is a candidate to join the list of UNESCO World Heritage Sites in 2008.

10. Ishaya, "From Contributions to Diaspora."

11. The Treaty of Turkmanchai also ended Iran's monopoly on Caspian fisheries, imposed a monetary fine and a variety of economic concessions on the Qajar government, and provided extraterritorial privileges for Russian subjects in Iran (Keddie, *Qajar Iran and the Rise of Reza Khan*, 23).

12. Between 1828 and 1831, more than 45,000 Armenians immigrated to Russian-held Yerevan, with roughly 23,000 arriving from Iran and 22,000 from the Ottoman Empire. Some 4,000 others relocated to Nakhichevan, the vast majority from Iran (George A. Bournoutian,

"The Politics of Demography: Misuse of Sources on the Armenian Population of Mountainous Karabakh," *Journal of the Society for Armenian Studies* 9 [1999]: 99–103; see also George A. Bournoutian, "The Ethnic Composition and Socio-economic Condition of Eastern Armenia in the First Half of the Nineteenth Century," in *Transcaucasia: Nationalism and Social Change*, edited by Ronald G. Suny, 77–79 (Ann Arbor: Univ. of Michigan, 1983).

13. Owing to Reza Shah Pahlavi's increasingly close ties to Nazi Germany and the presence of German advisers, technicians, and spies in Iran, in the late 1930s Iranians in the Soviet Union became suspect of subversive activities. Thousands of uneducated Iranian laborers working in Soviet republics were repatriated (*mohajer*s), and many educated Russians with ties to Iran, especially those such as Lucik's uncle Smbat who were found to possess both Iranian and Soviet passports (illegal under Soviet law), were arrested or simply disappeared.

14. And despite the "Scissor Crisis" of 1923 that caused food prices throughout the Soviet Union to fall.

15. For the history of Armenian education in Iran in the late nineteenth and early twentieth centuries, see Houri Berberian, "Armenian Women in Turn-of-the-Century Iran: Education and Activism," in *Iran and Beyond: Essays in Middle Eastern History in Honor of Nikki R. Keddie*, edited by Rudolph Matthee and Beth Baron, 70–98 (Costa Mesa: Mazda, 2000).

16. Camron Amin asserts that the Christian content of missionary schools was a particular concern: "By 1929 the Iranian government was threatening to conscript students of the American Missionary schools if the schools did not adopt government-mandated curricula. By 1940, all foreign schools except the German school were closed or nationalized. For American Presbyterian missionaries only a school for English-speaking students was allowed" (*The Making of the Modern Iranian Woman: Gender, State Policy, and Popular Culture, 1865–1946* [Gainesville: Univ. of Florida Press, 2002], 150). See also Jasamin Rostam-Kolayi, "From Evangelizing to Modernizing Iranians: The American Presbyterian Mission and Its Iranian Students," *Iranian Studies* 41, no. 2 (2008): 213–39.

17. Armenian history and language instruction was given in homes by private tutors. Lucik and her sister Marianna were tutored three times per week after school by Dashnak leader Hovak Stephanian.

18. Amin, *The Making of the Modern Iranian Woman*, 100, 147.

19. Ibid., 147–48.

20. Ibid., 146; David Menashri, *Education and the Making of Modern Iran* (Ithaca, NY: Cornell Univ. Press, 1992), 118.

21. Amin, *The Making of the Modern Iranian Woman*, 147. See also Jasamin Rostam-Kolayi, "Origins of Iran's Modern Girls' Schools: From Private/National to Public/State," *Journal of Middle East Women's Studies* 4, no. 3 (2008): 58–88.

22. Although the student body was mixed, Armenians and Azeris constituted the majority at Farrokhi Girls' School in the 1930s.

23. Rostam-Kolayi demonstrates how the education policies of the Reza Shah era and the agenda and curriculum of American missionary schools (such as Bethel/Nurbakhsh, which Lucik Moradiance would attend in 1949–50) were complementary in promoting the development of an Iranian middle class and ideals of secular nationalism. "Despite the school's promotion of modern American norms and Christian teachings, the young graduates of Iran Bethel/Nurbakhsh developed a strong sense of loyalty to both Iran and Islam, thus turning an evangelist mission into an important feature of the construction of Iranian nationalism and modernity" ("From Evangelizing to Modernizing Iranians," 213).

24. See, for example, Amin, *The Making of the Modern Iranian Woman*. According to Amin, the Women's Awakening was "a bold and controversial attempt by Reza Shah Pahlavi to radically transform Iranian womanhood" that marked a watershed in the making of modern Iranian society (1).

25. Ibid., 1–4. On the problematics of direct translation of the name "Nahzat-e Banovan" to English, see ibid., 11–12.

26. Amin argues that the violence and coercion of forced unveiling (and associated trauma for Iranian Muslim men and women) created false assumptions that (*a*) women's progress was synonymous with unveiling and (*b*) unveiling was central to the Women's Awakening program (ibid., 80–113).

27. Ibid., 157–58; Menashri, *Education and the Making of Modern Iran*, 109. As Amin describes, government propaganda to announce and sell this decision framed women's higher education as essential to motherhood itself. He quotes an *Ettela'at* article from 1936 that states: "What kind of mother could raise the [educated] woman and the [patriotic and well-raised] child that we have imagined? Is it a mother that sits at home and dons a veil, or a mother who enters the arena of life like a lioness, and who sings them lullabies of patriotism and sacrifice for the homeland while rocking their cradles on long nights?" (*The Making of the Modern Iranian Woman*, 161, quoting "Tarbiyat pas az vorud-e zan beh ejtema" [Cultivation of women after entry to society], *Ettela'at*, 1936, specific date not given).

28. Amin, *The Making of the Modern Iranian Woman*, 158–59.

29. Ibid., 160.

30. Mark H. Lytle, *Origins of the Iranian–American Alliance, 1941–1953* (New York: Holmes and Meier, 1987), 6–13.

31. In Camron Amin's periodization, August 1941 also marks the end of the Women's Awakening project (*The Making of the Modern Iranian Woman*, 4). Yet Amin argues that although the Allied occupation of 1941–46 may have unintentionally ended mandatory unveiling, "it did not reverse the Marriage Laws of 1931 and 1937, the opening of higher education to women, or trends toward greater literacy and professional employment among urban women. It did not change the fact that the Iranian state—no matter who controlled it—now explicitly tied its legitimacy to efforts to improve the status of women in Iranian society" (17).

32. Ibid., 159. The number of female medical students in 1944 dropped to a little more than half that of 1941, and by 1945 no female medical students were enrolled. It would not be until academic year 1947–48 that female medical students would return to study at Tehran University, and in that year only five women were admitted.

33. Despite the clothing and gender segregation policies imposed after the 1979 revolution, Iranian women continued to be admitted to Iranian universities at an increasing rate. By 2000, it was widely reported that the percentage of Iranian women exceeded that of men enrolled, and by 2006 women constituted 60 percent of all Iranian university students ("Women Graduates Challenge Iran," *BBC News*, Sept. 19, 2006).

34. Having served in the Iranian army in Tehran in the summer of 1941, Manucher Farmanfarmaian recalls his experiences and observations in the days following the Soviet invasion (August 25, 1941), shedding light on the Moradiance family's experiences in Azarshahr: "Generals deserted the troops and escaped to their country houses. Soldiers grabbed their guns and headed to the villages. The roads were jammed with trucks and cars. At headquarters I was sent on a wild-goose chase to deliver bread to a regiment I was never able to find. The army's trucks had all disappeared, and after signing for the bread I had to commandeer one in the street. With only vague directions we drove for hours along a dusty road past Kharaj well on toward the city of Qazvin. But as night fell we were forced to turn back, afraid of encountering armed stragglers from the Iranian Army or advancing Russians" (*Blood and Oil*, 140).

35. Although Iranian forces in the North dissolved in the face of Soviet attack, some Iranian forces in the South, in particular the Iranian navy, would not surrender to the British and suffered heavy losses before their quick defeat. For an account of the contrasting situations in the North and South, see Richard A. Stewart, *Sunrise at Abadan: The British and Soviet Invasion of Iran, 1941* (New York: Praeger, 1988).

36. Howard Baskerville was a Princeton-educated teacher for the American Mission in Tehran who was shot and killed in 1909 while fighting against the forces of Muhammad Ali Shah Qajar, which had laid siege to the city after bombarding the Majles and imposing martial law on Tehran. Baskerville's involvement on the side of the constitutionalists went against the strict neutrality maintained by the American Mission (Mehdi Heravi, *Iranian–American Diplomacy* [New York: Theo Gauss, 1969], 20–23). Sattareh Farmanfarmaian describes how the story of Howard Baskerville's sacrifice, told to her by American missionaries at Nurbakhsh Girls High School (which Lucik would attend in 1949–50), moved her to tears and left a lasting impression: "If I, I thought, ever had a chance to fight for our democracy like Mr. Howard Baskerville, I would do just as he had done, and show the world that a woman could do something for her country, too!" (with Donna Munker, *Daughter of Persia: A Woman's Journey from Her Father's Harem through the Islamic Revolution* [1993; reprint, New York: Broadway, 2006], 106). Muhammad Ali Shah's coup and the subsequent events of 1909 are covered in detail in chapter 2 of this volume.

37. Gevork Moradiance died of a heart attack in 1958 at age fifty-seven.

38. Marianna, Hasmik, and their fellow female student graduated in 1953. Marianna Moradiance immigrated to the United States in 1956, completing her internship at Jamaica Hospital in New York and her residency at Queen's General Hospital, where she obtained her Pathology Board. While raising her two daughters, she worked part-time as a pathologist at Queen's General Hospital for four years. Later she moved to New York Medical College in Westchester as associate professor of pathology and director of the Anatomical Pathology Laboratory in Valhalla New York (this information is included in Lucik Moradiance's written memoirs in English, copy in my files). Khanom Dr. Hasmik Haroutunian went on to have a similarly distinguished medical career, ultimately becoming "Iran's first woman plastic surgeon" practicing at Tehran University's Mir Alam Hospital (*Tehran Journal*, Oct. 1968, 78, cited in Lucik's memoirs).

39. The achievement was reported again in *Alik* newspaper (July 1948).

40. Camron Amin's central research subject, Dr. Maryam Tusi, faced the same challenge and found the same solution five years earlier: "Dr. Tusi, one of the first nine women admitted to the University of Tehran Medical School from the ranks of Iranian high school graduates, came to Tehran from Tabriz during World War II to attend Nurbakhsh" (*The Making of the Modern Iranian Woman*, 152). Sattareh Farmanfarmaian attended the American Bethel School before going on to attain a degree in social work from the University of Southern California and establishing the Tehran School of Social Work in 1958 (Farmanfarmaian, *Daughter of Persia*). The Nurbakhsh school also features prominently in Jasamin Rostam-Kolayi's exploration of the relationship between the Iranian government policies, Presbyterian missionary education, and the advancement of secular Iranian nationalism in the 1930s and 1940s ("From Evangelizing to Modernizing Iranians").

41. Lucik was able to visit Tabriz for semester breaks during the first and second years of university (1951 and 1952), but in her third year (1953) she was an intern at the glycerin factory in Tehran, and in her fourth year (1954) she would be interning at the Abadan refinery.

42. These statistics and the names of each student are recorded in *Daneshkade Fanni va fareghotahsilanan, Daneshgah-e Tehran, 1313–1373* (College of Engineering and its graduates, University of Tehran, 1934–1994) (Tehran: University of Tehran, 1994), see esp. 42–43.

43. Interviewed by historian Camron Amin, Dr. Maryam Tusi, who was one of the first female students to attend the University of Tehran Medical School (in 1946), could recall no mistreatment by any of her professors and in fact felt that women had received more respectful treatment, "enjoying the address of *khanom* rather than the curt barking of their last name endured by the men in class and on rounds" (*The Making of the Modern Iranian Woman*, 163).

44. In an interview, I asked Lucik: "Were female students ever bothered or harassed by male students, even in seemingly harmless/trivial ways, in your experience?" Lucik replied, "Yes, sometimes as we would walk across campus, a group of male students—juniors not our classmates—would whistle or call "sh sh sh"—[an] abbreviation [of] *shimi* or 'chemical engineers.' Small things like that."

45. The social biographies of Sevak Saginian and Nejde Hagobian in chapters 4 and 6 deal extensively with the origins and activities of Ararat and the nature of opposition to the Dashnaksutiun from within the Armenian Iranian community.

46. The oil nationalization effort and 1953 coup are detailed in chapters 4 and 6.

47. As well as a public-relations boost for the shah, Nixon's visit concerned emergency economic aid to the Zahedi government (Gasiorowski, *U.S. Foreign Policy and the Shah*, 91–92).

48. Ibid., 91. See also Shirzad Abdollahi, "16 Azar Dar Daneshgahe Tehran Che Gozasht" (What happened at Tehran University on 16 Azar?) *Asre Emrooz*, Dec. 10, 2013. For a photographic re-creation of the aftermath taken by Azadeh Akhlaghi, see Jason Rezaian, "Unique Photography Project Gets Strong Reception in Iran," *Washington Post*, Mar. 7, 2013, at http://www.washingtonpost.com/blogs/worldviews/wp/2013/03/07/unique-photography-project-gets-strong-reception-in-ira/.

49. As Kaveh Ehsani explains, on the eve of nationalization in 1951 the AIOC "had nearly 80 thousand Iranian workers, employees, and contractors on its payroll, which was a very substantial portion of the national industrial labor force at the time." By 1956, "after the fall of the Mossadegh government following the American–British coup d'état of 1953, the establishment of the oil consortium, and the subsequent downsizing and rationalization of the employment structure of the newly established National Iranian Oil Company (NIOC) employment in the oil sector had dropped to 25 thousand, while total national employment in 'modern' large industries (defined as those firms employing more than 12 workers) totaled 60 thousand" ("Social Engineering," 369).

50. A biography of John Mowlem and an overview of the company's evolution and achievements are provided in the brochure *Mowlem 1822–1972* (N.p.: Mowlem Public Relations, 1972).

51. After Lucik had worked at Mowlem for a year, in 1957 Tehran University offered her a position as assistant professor in the College of Engineering, but she turned the offer down. With her father's health failing, Lucik and her family needed the money, and the pay difference between the two positions was dramatic (four hundred tumans per month at Tehran University versus 1,000 tumans per month at Mowlem), but these factors were not the sole determinants in her decision. Nevertheless, she considered the offer a high honor and always kept the letter of invitation, wondering if she had made the right decision.

52. Born in Moscow in 1929, Artavast Melikian (called "Levon" by family and friends) was an active member of the Iranian Bar Association from 1956 to 1980. His legal practice was broad but specialized in legal advice to foreign embassies in Tehran (British, Swedish, Soviet, Czech, Romanian, and Bulgarian) and representation for foreign banks and oil companies, predominantly American. Between 1966 and 1970, Levon obtained a PhD in economics from Tehran University to meet the needs of such clientele, which became the mainstay of his law practice between 1970 and 1979.

53. In 1959, Lucik's younger sister, Anahid, moved to Tehran to attend Nurbakhsh High School and then University of Tehran as Lucik returned from her one-year British

scholarship. Lucik's brother, Garekin (b. 1932), graduated from the University of Tehran first in class in 1957, the same year Lucik's father died. Students who were first in their class were given the opportunity to study abroad, but because of Gevork Moradiance's passing, Garekin returned to Tabriz to deal with the family business and property. Because there was no will, nothing could be sold for two years. In that time, he became depressed and began drinking, neither of which conditions were recognized or treated at the time in Iran. His mother, Vardanoush, wanted to sell the wholesale business, but Garekin wanted to keep it afloat, and thus he stayed in Tabriz while Vardanoush relocated permanently in Tehran. He died in 1965 of a stomach ulcer.

54. Upper management at the Plan Organization consisted of a supervisor and assistant supervisor, to whom engineers handling individual projects reported. Almost the same structure existed at the Plan Organization Industrial and Mines Division and the NIPC.

55. Abadan's industrial workforce numbered 55,000 by 1977 (Ehsani, "Social Engineering," 369).

56. In 1963, Iranian women were granted the right to vote, but the granting of suffrage rights and Iranian elections were neither meaningful nor memorable to Lucik.

57. Lucik feels this trend has continued despite initial setbacks for women after the revolution. She remembers, however, that when she went to the NIPC office to find out about pensions during the presidency of Bani Sadr, she was unable to shake the hands of former male colleagues. This was the same when she returned for visits in 1988 and 1991.

58. Rather than considering carrying their own luggage an equal right or duty in prefeminism Iran, women still customarily allowed men to assist with luggage.

59. For a general history of the Iranian Revolution, see Keddie, *Modern Iran*. On the Rex Theater fire and the Black Friday massacre, see pages 231–32.

60. Ehsani, "Social Engineering," 370.

6. Nejde Hagobian

1. This chapter is based primarily on oral interviews with Nejde Hagobian conducted between 1996 and 2000 in Toluca Lake, California. It is supported by written memoirs, photographs, newspaper articles, secondary sources, as well as the oral testimony of Sevak Saginian, Lilit Marzbetuny, Shahen Askari, and Emil Markarian.

2. Wilhelm Eilers points out that Reza Shah had a particular dislike for the traditional Iranian *zurkhane* (house of strength) because of its strong Islamic orientation and sought to replace it with modern *varzeshkhaneh* (sporting halls) and organizations such as Pishahangi-ye Iran (Scouting of Iran). Although Reza Shah's scouting organization was disbanded during the Allied occupation, the 1940s witnessed a resurgence of the *zurkhane* in Iran ("Educational and Cultural Development in Iran during the Pahlavi Era," in Lenczowski, ed., *Iran under the Pahlavis*, 316–17). On Pahlavi efforts to develop sports and scouting in Iran during the 1920s and 1930s, see Cyrus Schayegh, "Sport, Health, and the Iranian Middle Class in the 1920s and 1930s," *Iranian Studies* 34, no. 4 (2002): 341–69.

3. In making a point about the shah's efforts to boost morale and loyalty in the military, Marvin Zonis commented in 1971 that the shah "frequently appears in full military regalia surrounded by a coterie of important generals—even at totally civilian functions, such as the distribution of land reform deeds or supervising a Boy Scout encampment" (*Political Elite of Iran*, 112).

4. On the role of Dr. Keshavarz in the Tudeh Party and his treatment by the Pahlavi regime, see Abrahamian, *Iran between Two Revolutions*, 287–88, 317–18.

5. Arshalous Hagobian explained that the mothers living in the compound generally did not allow their children to venture away from the cul-de-sac for fear that they would be abducted. Although the streets of Tehran were generally safe for young teens at the time, rumors of child kidnappings and molestation abounded within the Armenian community (oral interview, Nov. 13, 1999, Glendale, California).

6. The term *shahrefarang* literally means "city in Europe," most probably in reference to the type of images predominantly exhibited by the vendor known as "Shahrefarangi." The name "Jegh-jeghe-i" has no literal meaning and is an onomatopoeia adapted from the sound of one of the vendor's noisemakers.

7. A common predicament of automobile drivers in Tehran from 1950s through the present day involves an encounter with the *joub*. In attempting to pull their car as far to the side of the street as possible, drivers inevitably drop a tire into the *joub* up to the axle, which makes driving out impossible. Usually a few passers-by offer literally to lend a hand and physically hoist the car back up onto the street using its bumper. When this method doesn't work, which was frequently in the case of large, American-made cars before the 1979 revolution, jacks have to be used. Whatever the method, the scene always attracts a crowd of onlookers, who never fail to offer conflicting opinions about how best to accomplish the task and argue while others are straining in the background to free the vehicle (Nejde Hagobian, written memoirs in English, copy in my files, and my personal observations).

8. From the reservoir, each tenant would hand-pump the water through a pipe that led to a converted steel oil barrel on the dwelling's roof. Additional piping brought the water from the steel barrel into the house's water closet and kitchen.

9. The girls high school (sister school), Anushiravan-e Dadgar, was located a few miles across town.

10. Hayots Dprots was later divided into separate campuses: the Davidian School for boys and the Maryamian Girls School.

11. Nejde did not remember the exact date in August that the single bomb was dropped. However, Lenczowski and others cite the bombing of Tehran by Soviets as occurring on August 31, 1941 (see, for example, Lenczowski, *Russia and the West*, 168). Vanak, which was incorporated into the sprawl of Tehran in the 1950s and 1960s, was previously divided into two village areas, one Armenian and one Persian Muslim. Each village had its own *khadkhoda* (headman), and a small stream separated the two. The Muslim Vanak had

a few small shops that the Armenians would visit during the day, and the Armenian side offered fresh spring water, which Muslims would carry back to their village.

12. After hearing numerous times Hripsik and Hovannes's favorite story about how they lost their fortune to the Bolsheviks, Nejde could not understand how or why they could still maintain support for the Soviet Union or communism. The story went like this: Because Morkur and Hovannes were childless, they were able to amass a sizeable fortune in early adulthood through the tavern and hotel they ran in Tiblisi. As Bolshevik soldiers advanced on Tiblisi, and despite the fact that the couple supported the Bolsheviks, they decided to withdraw their savings from the bank in the form of gold Romanoff coins. To further protect their life savings, Hovannes cut and hollowed out some tree trunks and large branches, which he then filled with the gold coins and then stacked outside their small house in the firewood pile, thinking that it was a brilliant way to camouflage such riches. By the time the Bolshevik regiments entered the city, it was already winter. When a group of soldiers came to what they thought was another abandoned house to loot it, they were surprised to find the couple inside. The soldiers apologized for bursting into the house and immediately went back outside, but their commander stopped at the door to explain that they were going to camp for the night on the property and thanked them in advance for allowing the soldiers to use the plentiful firewood that was stacked outside the house. In the morning, the soldiers and their life savings were gone, and all that remained outside was a smoking pile of ashes. Broke and hungry, the couple decided to flee to Rasht in Iran, where Morkur labored raising hogs and Hovannes supplemented their income by making women's combs from animal horns obtained from nearby herders. Morkur and Hovannes would take turns telling this tale and would always end the story laughing at their own stupidity rather than blaming the Bolsheviks for stealing their life savings. This made no sense to Nejde or his father, Hagob, who would usually end up quictly shaking his head in disgust each time he heard the tale (Nejde Hagobian, written memoirs).

13. Nejde Hagobian, written memoirs, and oral interview, Sept. 2000. On the Pan-Iranists, see Cottam, *Nationalism in Iran*, 266–67. Cottam explains that "the so-called Pan-Iran Party attracted adherents chiefly from middle and lower-middle-class secondary school students, but it also had an appeal for athletic society toughs. Pan-Iran suffered a series of bewildering splits, each splinter group claiming to be the authentic Pan-Iran party. The most loyal and largest of these groups was headed by Dariush Foruhar, but at its height this group could not have numbered more than a few thousand members and was largely confined to Tehran" (267). On street battles between the Somka and Tudehists in the early 1950s, see Gasiorowski, *U.S. Foreign Policy and the Shah*, 69. The Somka are briefly mentioned in George Lenczowski, "Political Process and Institutions in Iran: The Second Pahlavi Kingship," in Lenczowski, ed., *Iran under the Pahlavis*, 451, with the Pan-Iranists described as a "minor peripheral group."

14. Immediately following the death of Stalin in 1953, the Soviet embassy in Tehran opened its gates to the public for the first time to allow visitors to pay their respects by

signing a large register. Thousands of people lined up and down the street and waited for hours to enter the embassy building to add their names to the register—many, in Nejde's opinion, not out of mourning for Stalin, but simply because they were finally allowed to view the inside of the mysterious compound and embassy building (Nejde Hagobian, written memoirs, and oral interview, Nov. 1998).

15. In his written memoirs, Nejde remembers, "When the US library originally opened there was a large portrait of President Truman on the main wall. In January of 1952 I was there when the staff removed President Truman's portrait and replaced it with that of Ike's. I knew of Eisenhower from the *Movietones* of the war. Since then, he has always been my most favorite American dead or alive. After coming to the United States I registered to vote Republican because of Ike."

16. A possible though surely indirect inspiration for the Ararat Scouts was the Lebanese Armenian scouting organization Homenetmen, which was publicly sponsored by the Dashnak Party in Beirut.

17. Lolo Ohanian passed away in May 2006 as I was working on this manuscript. His memory and contributions to the Ararat organization were honored in a ceremony at the Ararat branch in Glendale, California, which included many former Ararat scouts and athletes.

18. Any similarities between the Ararat scouts and the Pioneers were vehemently denied, and it was widely rumored among the Ararat scouts, who were predominantly the children of Gregorian Dashnaks or Dashnak sympathizers, that a heroine of the Soviet Pioneers was a teen girl who had reported the anti-Communist activities of her family to the authorities (Nejde Hagobian, written memoirs, and oral interview, Sept. 2000). For a description of the origins, ideology, and activities of the Soviet Pioneers, see Peter Kenez, *The Birth of the Propaganda State: Soviet Methods of Mass Mobilization, 1917–1929* (Cambridge: Cambridge Univ. Press, 1985), 190–94.

19. "Astsus, azgis yev hayrenikis" was a purposefully vague formulation that allowed for multiple interpretations. Unlike the oath of the Pishahangi-ye Iran, which pledged allegiance to "Khoda, shah, mehan" (God, king, and country) in the manner of the Iranian army, "Astsus, azgis yev hayrenikis" could be interpreted as being applicable to Iran or Armenia or both (Nejde Hagobian, written memoirs, and oral interview, Nov. 1998; see also Zonis, *Political Elite*, 113).

20. Nejde explains in his memoirs, "The Ararat scouts were organized similarly to the Boy Scouts of America. Each troop consisted of four patrols that had eight scouts, one assistant patrol leader and one patrol leader. The troops were headed by a scoutmaster with two assistants. One assistant to whom the patrol leaders reported. His rank was signified with two and half green lines. The patrol leader had two green lines and his assistant one green line. The scoutmaster was signified by three gold lines and his deputy with two and a half gold lines. A gold star with green background signified one year of service. All scoutmasters reported to a chief scoutmaster who was also a member of the scouting council."

21. Sevak Saginian, written memoirs.

22. The anti-shah, pro-Tudeh stance and activities of some Armenian youth in Isfahan during this period was brought to the attention of American consul Bryant Buckingham, who in his 1955 report "The Gregorian Armenians of Isfahan" wrote, "Two or three days before the 19th of August 1953 (when Mossadegh fell and Zahedi came to power) [i.e., the 1953 coup d'état] during the communist rioting and demonstrations, one evening a group of Armenian youths invaded the Cathedral grounds and demanded entry to the museum, where they took a bust of Reza Shah, dressed it up in a chador, put lipstick with a cigarette in its mouth and paraded it about in the square near the Consulate. The bust later disappeared, and, unlike the statue of Reza Shah, which had been dismantled during that time, it was never found. What these Tudehists or former Tudehists are thinking now we do not know. At least their mouths are stilled." Buckingham's entire report (USNA 888.413/1-2055, Jan. 20, 1955) is reprinted in Chaqueri, ed., *The Armenians of Iran*, 387–94, quote on 393.

23. Mark Gasiorowski's study of the role of the United States and the CIA in the events of 1952–53 concludes that the original crowd that formed for that February pro-shah demonstration had been organized by Abdoul Qassem Kashani, the Somka, and pro-Zahedi military officers with the intent of rallying a huge crowd, marching to Mossadegh's residence, and demanding his dismissal (*U.S. Foreign Policy and the Shah*, 73). Leonard Binder also cites the involvement of the Somka in anti-Tudeh, anti-Mossadegh protests, including the protest riots of Tir 30, 1331 (July 21, 1952) and Esfand 9, 1331 (Feb. 28, 1953). See Binder's brief sketch of the party's origins and history in his book *Iran* (Berkeley: Univ. of California Press, 1961), 216–17.

24. As Mohammad Reza Pahlavi explains, it was because of mass demonstrations of support and loyalty such as this one in February 1953 that he decided to stay in Iran. For the shah's own interpretation of the events of February 1953, see *Mission for My Country* (New York: McGraw-Hill, 1960), 97.

25. Some of Shaban "Bimokh" Jafari's pro-shah exploits between 1951 and 1954 are described in Gasiorowski, *U.S. Foreign Policy and the Shah*, 79, 88. On Jafari's role in the coup d'état of August 19, 1953, see Ruehsen, "Operation 'Ajax' Revisited," 480, and Mark Gasiorowski, "The 1953 Coup d'Etat in Iran," *International Journal of Middle East Studies* 19 (1987): 268. Shaban Jafari died in Los Angeles in August 2006, three months after reuniting with several former Ararat members at a gathering of Armenian and Iranian wrestlers and boxers in Glendale, California, in May 2006.

26. Sevak Saginian, oral interview, Oct. 6, 1997.

27. In addition to genuine demonstrations of support for the Tudeh, Mossadegh, and the shah, the CIA hired a large crowd for the price of $50,000 to march through downtown Tehran on Monday, March 17, yelling Tudeh slogans and waving anti-Pahlavi signs. After gathering a crowd of real pro-Tudeh supporters unaware of the rally's true inspiration, the group tore down statues of Reza Shah and Mohammad Reza Shah and proceeded to attack Reza Shah's mausoleum. Because of this seemingly blatant act of Tudeh lawlessness,

Mossadegh was forced to have the police crack down on Tudeh demonstrators, who were then called off the streets. This had the planned effect of strengthening the hand of Zahedi and the pro-shah forces between August 17 and 19 (Bist-o Hasht-e Mordad) (Gasiorowski, *U.S. Foreign Policy and the Shah*, 78).

28. Nejde was never sure how his activities were brought to the attention of the Iranian government because there was no communication or interaction other than receiving the award (medal and *hokm*) through Sevak Saginian.

29. When submitting forms or applications to government agencies, such as the passport office, Nejde discovered that including a copy of his Neshan-e Rastakhiz certificate always guaranteed instantaneous and trouble-free service in offices that were well known for their inefficiency, irrationality, and backlog of work. In 1954, Nejde got into a fistfight with an adult Persian neighbor who had verbally accosted Arshalous and called her a "dirty Armenian" after he was accidentally hit with water from the Hagobian balcony while walking by on the street. Both Nejde and his neighbor were dragged off to the police station, where they were verbally chastised and told they would have to stay in jail until witnesses to the fight could be called to testify. When asked to produce identification for processing, Nejde revealed his Neshan-e Rastakhiz-e Bist-o Hasht-e Mordad certificate. After a quick glance and then a double-take at the document, the policeman stood up at attention, *saluted*, and, referring to twenty-year-old Nejde as "Agha," apologized for the "mistake," and told him he was free to leave. It is not known what treatment or sentence, if any, the neighbor had to endure (oral interview, Nejde Hagobian, Nov. 13, 1998). This story was also related to me separately by Hagob Hagobian, Arshalous Hagobian, and Rima (Hagobian) Baghdasarian.

30. Until the early 1960s, the Ararat scouts had only Armenian lettering on their uniforms, patches, and badges.

31. With the revival of the Pishahangi-ye Iran under the Ministry of Physical Education and Sports under Dr. Banai after 1954, the Ararat troops would engage in this competition against other Iranian troops rather than against each other. Unlike in 1953, when Nejde Hagobian initiated the competition, national events after 1954 would be initiated by Banai from the stands. This would become a point of contention between Banai and Sevak Saginian because of Saginian's perception that Banai was using the occasion to strip the Ararat scouts of their recognition as an all-Armenian organization and the best-organized Iranian scouting group. See chapter 6.

32. The shah's first wife, Princess Fawzia (King Farouk of Egypt's sister), voluntarily divorced him after she did not produce a male heir to the throne. The shah's second wife, Soraya Esfandiari, of combined Bakhtiari and German parentage, was divorced by the shah in 1958 after they failed to produce children together. He married Farah Diba in 1960, who bore a son in that same year, Crown Prince Reza Pahlavi (Keddie, *Modern Iran*, 141).

33. Pahlavi, *Mission for My Country*, 216; see also page 190.

34. Eilers, "Educational and Cultural Development in Iran during the Pahlavi Era," 317.

35. Sevak Saginian, oral interview, July 12, 1997.

36. "Boland sho, boland kon" literally means "get up and pick up," which in its slang interpretation can imply something having to do with getting an erection or picking up prostitutes or both (oral interview, Nejde Hagobian, Sept. 2000).

37. Nejde Hagobian, written memoirs.

38. The Armenian term *yerets* (senior) was used to refer to the group of senior scouts in general, while a single senior scout of the Ararat Yerets who participated in trips and campouts was called a *sayar* (literally "traveler"), which was the closest Persian-language approximation to the senior British Venturer Scouts or the American Explorers.

39. In the 1950s, Hagob Hagobian temporarily switched from long-distance truck driving to contracting dump trucks around Tehran. See chapter 3.

40. Specifically raising the issue of intermarriage with Americans and Europeans, Shah Mohammad Reza Pahlavi describes his consternation over the failure of many Iranian college students studying abroad in the 1950s to return home to Iran and proposes solutions to alleviate the problem in *Mission for My Country*, 261–64.

41. In 1960, more than 4,000 Iranians were attending American institutions of higher learning, constituting one-third of all Middle Eastern students studying in the United States (Pahlavi, *Mission for My Country*, 262).

42. Writing in the year Nejde Hagobian took his position at the Plan Organization, 1961, Mohammad Reza Pahlavi describes in *Mission for My Country* his intentions in creating the Seven-Year Plan Organization and some of its early challenges and failures up until that point; see especially pages 138–39 and 174–76. In his description of vocational training, higher education, and Iranian scholarship programs, the shah tells his own story of an Iranian student who worked at an automobile plant while attending college in the American Midwest and then returned to Iran to apply his practical skills work for the Plan Organization (260–61). See also pages 262–65 for the shah's discussion of his attitude and intent toward motivating Iranian students studying in the United States at that time and his guesses as to why many Iranian students decided to stay in the United States rather than return to Iran after completing their education. See also chapter 5 of this volume on Lucik Moradiance Melikian's professional career.

43. Expatriates were paid in US dollars or Iranian rials, depending on their preference.

44. Because Iran did not have extensive production facilities for mass quantities of different grades of cement, samples of rock and gravel taken from areas surrounding large construction sites in the North would be brought to the Plan Organization lab, and there a formula would be devised based on the type of construction project that would direct contractors in mixing loads of cement that included both local and trucked-in materials and met the requirements for structural stability (oral interview, Nejde Hagobian, Sept. 2000).

45. This story was related to me on several occasions by Shahen Askari, who explained that the confrontation became part of the Plan Organization lab's lore in the 1960s and 1970s.

46. Both Nejde Hagobian and Shahen Askari maintain that the most competent, professional, and trustworthy Iranian engineer working at the laboratory throughout the Mowlem–Amman and Whitney–Plan Organization transition was Lucik Moradiance Melikian, who is profiled in chapter 5.

47. Some of the major projects Nejde Hagobian worked on through completion in the 1960s and 1970s were the LPG plant in Bandar Mahshar, the B. F. Goodrich Petrochemical Plant in Abadan, the Liquefied Natural Gas terminal in Kangan, the Isfahan Oil refinery, and Ahvaz Airport.

48. Nejde attributes this overestimation of expenses to a blend of greed and lack of knowledge of local conditions. In one large-scale project in 1965, for which Nejde still maintains extensive blueprints, documents, and reports, Fluor Corporation was awarded a $100 million contract by the NIOC to build a 100,000-barrel-per-day refinery for Tehran in Shar-e Ray near the city of Qom. After flying over the proposed refinery site, the Fluor engineers decided that the entire refinery had to be supported on extensive pile foundations, which themselves would cost millions of dollars to install. When Nejde, then temporarily working for the American firm Dames and Moore on a refinery project in Torrance, California, got wind of the proposed Fluor project, he intervened, knowing the job could be done safely without piles. The Iranian government was spared millions in unneeded expenses in this instance and in several other similar circumstances involving large foreign firms, including Parsons, Lamas, and Hochtief (Nejde Hagobian, written memoirs, and oral interview, Sept. 2000).

7. Learning from Theory and Social Biography

1. Oral interview, Nejde Hagobian, Sept. 2000.

2. Oral interview, Sevak Saginian, July 12, 1997.

3. To clarify, I am not arguing that Mohammad Reza Pahlavi would have been able to survive the events of 1951–53 with his throne intact had the CIA not intervened and helped to undermine the will of the majority of the Iranian people. However, I am arguing that the CIA's effort was successful in so short a time and with so little funding owing to the manipulation of genuine political sentiments in support of the regime and against Mossadegh and the Tudeh.

4. Elizabeth Fox-Genovese and Eugene Genovese, "The Political Crisis of Social History: A Marxian Perspective," *Journal of Social History* 10 (Winter 1976): 219. See also Kessler-Harris, *Social History*, 19–20.

5. The qualification needs to be made that it is entirely possible that the Fourth of Aban parade was devoid of higher meaning for some of its participants and spectators. Although the experience of Ararat members and leadership is probably not unique, without further oral historical and social biographical research we cannot discount the potential cynicism, skepticism, and indifference of people compelled or "encouraged" to take part in such events, many of whom may have simply welcomed the parade as a break from

work or school. In addition, as the biographies of Sevak Saginian and Nejde Hagobian demonstrate, Iranian public opinion was sharply divided in 1953. The shah, the National Front, the Tudeh, and an assortment of other political groups retained the loyalties and support of different societal segments, and the coup d'état of August 1953 did not change this fact. Because not all Iranians perceived the Pahlavi regime as the legitimate repository of authority over the nation, and loyalty to the Pahlavis was never coterminous with a sense of Iranian nationhood or Iranian nationalism, the possibility exists that there were participants and spectators who were strong "Iranian nationalists" but who also despised the whole affair and its symbolism.

6. Indeed, both Armenians and Iran can easily be fit into the crude framework proposed by Kedourie for understanding the development of nationalism in Asia and Africa. During the nineteenth century, Iranian elites made educational pilgrimages to European countries (including many Armenians) and often returned as proponents of new, Western ideas, values, and reforms. The Armenians of the Caucasus and many of the diaspora to emerge from the Ottoman Empire in Iran after World War I could be said to have been socially and economically "pulverized" in the process of ethnic cleansing that resulted in their dispersion. Iran could be considered a "pulverized" collectivity, having been divided into separate spheres of economic and military influence by the British and the Russians and then assaulted with Reza Shah's multifaceted plans for social economic and legal reform, infrastructural development—including subjugation of tribal peoples and their integration into the public school system—and universal conscription. Thus, Armenians and the assorted peoples of the Iranian Plateau could in these ways be considered the marginalized, dispossessed, and resentful masses Kedourie describes.

7. Sevak Saginian wrote the obituary for Iskandar Khan that appeared in the Armenian Iranian daily *Alik*. Despite the fact that Iskandar Khan had fought against the constitutional movement (which Sevak's father Zohrab had fought in support of) and that *Alik* was essentially a Dashnak publication, there was no question whether Iskandar Khan would be honored with a lengthy obituary, for his family's standing and reputation within the Armenian community remained high, and his philanthropic activities had been deeply appreciated (oral interview, Sevak Saginian, Apr. 28, 1998). See Iskandar Khan Setkhanian's obituary in *Alik*, "The Setkhanian Dynasty," Apr. 10, 1953.

8. No doubt these invented traditions are imitative, but as the details provided by the social biographies demonstrate, simply asserting their fabricated, constructed nature or Western origins does not explain why invented traditions are appealing or how they function in the lives of ordinary people to produce a sense of national identity.

9. Amin, *The Making of the Modern Iranian Woman*, 251.

10. Ibid.

11. For example, see Lois Beck's portrait of Qashqa'i rebel Rostam, who fought against the forces of both the Pahlavis and the Islamic Republic to sustain Qashqa'i culture and nomadic way of life. ("Rostam: Qashqa'i Rebel," in Burke and Yaghoubian, eds., *Struggle*

and Survival in the Modern Middle East, 223–36). See also the social biography of Persian Muslim truckdriver Amir Agha, whose experience in truck driving and Iranian politics offers numerous points to contrast with the social biography of Hagob Hagobian in the present study. (Fakhreddin Azimi, "Amir Agha: An Iranian Worker," in Burke, ed., *Struggle and Survival in the Modern Middle East*, 290–304).

Conclusion

1. According to the 2000 US Census, approximately 175,000 Armenians live in Los Angeles and adjacent cities such as Glendale and Burbank, making it one of the largest centers of Armenian population (outside of Armenia) in the world (at http://www.census.gov/main/www/cen2000.html). Although the 2000 US Census recorded a total of 338,000 Iranian American respondents, the true number of Iranians living in the United States is likely three or four times greater. Mehdi Bozorgmehr surveys patterns of immigration and population statistics in "From Iranian Studies to Studies of Iranians in the United States," in "Iranians in the United States," special issue of *Iranian Studies* 31, no. 1 (1998): 5–30. See especially pages 8–12 on participation in the 1980 and 1990 censuses and questions of accuracy. See also the public-service announcement featuring Iranian American comedian Maz Jobrani that employs humor in an attempt to motivate Iranian Americans to participate in the 2010 census (at http://youtu.be/kgoLjFJorVg).

2. The Armenian General Athletic Union and Scouts, referred to as "Homenetmen" in Armenian, was founded in 1918 in affiliation with the Dashnak Party. Despite similarities in title and Dashnak political orientation, the Homenetmen Ararat chapter of Glendale, California, and the Iranian Ararat organization based in Tehran were not and are not currently affiliated. However, many Homenetmen Ararat members in the United States are former Iranian Ararat members and Armenian Iranian Dashnaks who have immigrated to the United States and reside in Glendale. Information about the mission and activities of the Homenetmen Ararat chapter, which include scouting, athletics, dance, poetry, and language, can be found online at http://www.ararat.org/.

3. In 1993, Homenetmen Ararat compiled a sixty-page booklet in Armenian entitled *Sevak Saginian*, which includes a short biographical profile, photographs depicting Sevak's activities and involvement in Iran's Ararat and Homenetmen Ararat in the United States, and letters of felicitation from Armenian social, cultural, and professional organizations, newspapers, prelacies, and churches.

4. Author's personal observation and oral interview with Nejde Hagobian, Sept. 2000.

5. Sanasarian, *Religious Minorities in Iran*, 2006, 36–37. At roughly 200,000 in the 1990s, Armenians constituted Iran's largest recognized religious minority group. Sanasarian cites the population of Zoroastrians at 50,000, Jews at 35,000, and Assyrians and Chaldeans at 20,000. Although the Baha'is are not an officially recognized religious minority, their numbers in the 1990s are estimated at between 150,000 and 300,000. In total, Iran's religious minorities constitute barely one percent of the total population of some 65 million Iranians (9). The

Turkic-speaking population of Iran in the 1990s numbered roughly 14 million (some 24 percent of the total population), with some 3–8 million Kurds, or 7 percent of the total (10–14).

6. Sanasarian, *Religious Minorities in Iran*, 58–71. The Constitution of the Islamic Republic was drafted in mid-1979 by an Assembly of Experts, which included one Armenian, one Assyrian, one Jewish, and one Zoroastrian delegate from Majles. In this chapter, Sanasarian details the arguments and objections of religious minority delegates concerning the scope and wording of Article 13 as well as the tactics they employed to work for the agenda of their respective communities throughout the drafting of the Constitution, such as providing lengthy histories of their communities in Iran and their contributions to the country for the unaware or uneducated in the assembly and general public. Baha'is and Iranian converts to Christianity are not legally free to practice their religion in the Islamic Republic, although Article 13 does not specifically address this issue (ibid., 67). See also Chaqueri, "The Armenian-Iranian Intelligentsia," 144–46.

7. On job discrimination, see Sanasarian, *Religious Minorities in Iran*, 84–89, 144. Sanasarian notes several instances when religious minorities were specifically named as ineligible in job advertisements, including listings for the Tehran police force.

8. Ibid., 77; Chaqueri, "The Armenian-Iranian Intelligentsia," 151.

9. Sanasarian, *Religious Minorities in Iran*, 89.

10. Ibid. The Armenian deputy candidly explained how it was a common practice for Armenians to have mixed-gender social gatherings and stated that the community hoped that, "just as we respect all Islamic laws, [our] brothers would have mutual respect for ours." Prosecutor General Musavi Tabrizi's 1983 article clarifying proper conduct and prohibited activities for religious minorities in the Islamic Republic is summarized in ibid., 89–90.

11. Ibid., 90.

12. Ibid., 77.

13. Ibid., 80.

14. Ibid. Sanasarian speculates that the limitation of Armenian-language instruction was owing to government concern that the much larger Arabic- and Turkish-speaking citizens of the nation would demand similar rights. Such a concern, Sanasarian argues, would signify the meeting of distinct ideological agendas—the religious program Islamization or "Shi'ization" with a linguistic policy of Persianization reminiscent of the homogenizing nationalist programs of Reza Shah (81).

15. Ibid., 81.

16. Ibid., 82; Chaqueri, "The Armenian-Iranian Intelligentsia," 151.

17. The memory of Iran's brave and effective self-defense and Iranian citizens' immense personal sacrifices during the Iran-Iraq War of 1980–89 (referred to in Iran as "Jang-e Tahmili," the Imposed War, and "Defae Moqadas," the Sacred Defense) remains a major source of national pride and is frequently utilized by the government in its efforts to inculcate and sustain Iranian nationalism. Sacred Defense Week, an annual series of military industry displays and community gatherings and events commemorating the nation's successful

defense and reminding Iranians to be vigilant of external threats, is one cornerstone of the government's efforts in this regard. During Sacred Defense Week of September 22–28, 1999, for example, the *Tehran Times* (in English) reported that the objectives of one military parade were "to revive the aspiration of the late Imam Khomeini, renew allegiance to the grand leader, strengthen the national will in defending the ideals of Islamic Iran, and display unity among the armed forces" ("Khatami Blasts Presence of Foreign Forces in Persian Gulf." Sept. 23, 1999). In the week prior to the Sacred Defense commemorations, secretary of the National Expediency Council Mohsen Rezaei stated that Iran's victory in the war was the first such victory in more than three hundred years and that "Iran's unwanted engagement in an imposed war with Iraq which lasted for eight years had offered many good lessons to the Iranian nation, which, he said, is a precious cultural treasure" (quoted in IRNA Headlines, "Rezaei on Sacred Defense," Sept. 16, 1999; I had originally located IRNA articles in English at http://www.irna.com, but specific web addresses for the articles cited in the notes are no longer active; copies of all cited articles are on file with author). In an opinion article titled "The Brilliance of the Sacred Defense," published on September 25, 1999, in the English-language newspaper *Iran Daily*, Taher Sajjadi wrote, "The sacred defense of the stalwart warriors of Iran against the Iraqi invaders is one of the most honorable pages in the eventful history of this great land. The message conveyed in this noble action was an ever-strong nation's call for justice. The Sacred Defense serves as an invaluable national asset upon which the cornerstone of a brilliant civil society, wherein human dignity is the focal point, can and should be laid."

18. Sanasarian, *Religious Minorities in Iran*, 143–44; Chaqueri, "The Armenian-Iranian Intelligentsia," 147.

19. Quoted in Chaqueri, "The Armenian-Iranian Intelligentsia," 147. Archbishop Manoukian's death on October 16, 1999, and funeral ceremony on October 19 was reported by IRNA. As well as several photographs of the funeral ceremony that depict Bishop Manoukian's casket flanked by Ararat scouts as various members of the community pay their respects, an obituary noted, "Archbishop Manoukian became religious leader of Tehran's Armenians in 1959 and held the position until his death. Archbishop Manoukian was one of the first dignitaries who, after the return of the late Imam Khomeini to the country and the triumph of the Islamic Revolution in 1979, met the founder of the Islamic Republic and expressed support of the Armenian community for the Iranian Revolution" (Oct. 16, 1999).

20. Quoted in Chaqueri, "The Armenian-Iranian Intelligentsia," 147–48. As Sanasarian puts it succinctly, "Serving the nation but being allowed their own cultural freedom was the behavioral motto of a community which had mastered the art of adaptability" (*Religious Minorities in Iran*, 148).

21. Quoted in Sanasarian, *Religious Minorities in Iran*, 148–49.

22. Quoted in Chaqueri, "The Armenian-Iranian Intelligentsia," 150, citing *Ettela'at*, Apr. 20, 1991.

23. Quoted in ibid., 150.

24. Ibid., citing *Kayhan* (Air Edition), May 3, 1989.

25. Ibid.

26. Sanasarian, *Religious Minorities in Iran*, 153. For a study of institutions and literature promoting Christian–Muslim dialogue in Iran, see Sasan Tavassoli, *Christian Encounters with Iran: Engaging Muslim Thinkers after the Revolution* (London: I. B. Tauris, 2011).

27. Chaqueri, "The Armenian-Iranian Intelligentsia," 152–53.

28. Sanasarian, *Religious Minorities in Iran*, 158.

29. IRNA Headlines, "President Pays Rich Tribute to National Athletic Champions," July 1, 1999.

30. Quoted in IRNA Headlines, "Asefi Refutes Claims on Violation of Religious Minority Rights," Sept. 11, 1999. See also *Iran Daily*, "Asefi Denies Religious Persecution," Oct. 9, 1999.

31. On the same day of the release of the negative report, the Jewish Association of Tehran issued a statement congratulating Iranian Jews on the Hebrew New Year and reiterating that Iranian Jews are free to perform their religious ceremonies. The statement explained, "We have tried to shun opportunists and propagandists for Israel and the US from interfering in Iran's internal affairs . . . but they still seek to fish in troubled waters at opportune moments" (*Iran Daily*, "Jewish Community Issues Statement: Israel, US Propagandists Shunned," Sept. 9, 1999; see also IRNA Headlines, "Iranian Jews Free in Performing Religious, Cultural Ceremonies," Sept. 8, 1999).

32. One wonders to what extent the Danish officials were aware of the subtext that shaped the conversation repeatedly toward minority rights.

33. Quoted in *Iran Daily*, "Religious Minorities Enjoy Equal Rights," Sept. 15, 1999. Although the pressures that minority Majles representatives face must be recognized when interpreting such statements, it is nevertheless a fact that tens of thousands of Iranian Jews continue to live and do business in Iran rather than emigrating. A surprising article in the English-language *Jerusalem Post* describes Iranian Jews who, after immigrating to Israel from Iran, desperately miss their country and Iranian culture—some to the extent that they have returned home to Iran despite the strong anti-Zionist rhetoric of former president Mahmoud Ahmadinejad (Orly Halpern, "Exclusive: Immigrant Moves Back 'Home' to Tehran," *Jerusalem Post*, Nov. 3, 2005). See also the thoughtful op-ed piece by Roya Hakakian, "Reading the Holocaust Cartoons in Tehran," *New York Times*, Sept. 2, 2006.

34. IRNA Headlines, "Avenues to Upgrade Minorities' Rights Examined," Sept. 21, 1999.

35. IRNA Headlines, "Iranian Armenians to Mark Imam Khomeini's 100th Birthday Anniversary," Sept. 21, 1999.

36. IRNA Headlines, "Zoroastrians Celebrate Khomeini's Birth Anniversary in Yazd," Sept. 27, 1999.

37. IRNA Headlines, "Zoroastrians Celebrate Imam's Birth Anniversary," Sept. 29, 1999. The following day the Assyrian community was the subject of an IRNA article

titled "Iranian Minorities Perform Their Religious Rites Freely," in which Wilson Saed, an Assyrian Iranian of Khouzestan Province, "said here Thursday that after the victory of the Islamic Revolution the Iranian minorities feel more at ease. He told IRNA that the Assyrians have no problem and they freely perform their religious rituals and rites." Denouncing the "alien propaganda machinery, which claimed that religious minorities of Iran have been ill-treated," and "baseless allegations," Saed went on to add, "During the eight-year Sacred Defense the Assyrians of Khouzestan actively participated in the frontlines and that four of the young Assyrians attained the rank of martyrdom in their fight against the aggressor Iraqi Ba'athist forces. I also fought for nine months in the frontlines against the Ba'athist aggressors" (Sept. 30, 1999).

38. *Iran Daily*, "Khatami Salutes Iran's Religious Minorities: Fascism, Nazism [Are] Western Products," Sept. 29, 1999. The front-page article includes a color photograph of Khatami shaking the hand of a representative from the Jewish community.

39. Quoted in ibid. The story was also covered by IRNA: IRNA Headlines, "Khatami: Humanity Needs to Rely on Common Ground to Resolve Disputes," Sept. 28, 1999.

40. See *Tehran Times*, "Iranian Religious Minorities Renew Alliance to Islamic Revolution," Sept. 29, 1999; IRNA Headlines, "Zoroastrian Priest Shahrzadi Addresses Followers of Divine Religions," Sept. 29, 1999. The IRNA article stated, "Zoroastrian Priest Shahrzadi gave a report on the eye-catching presence of religious minorities in defending the Islamic Republic of Iran in the 1980s. Shahrzadi said the Iranian religious minorities have offered martyrs and disabled war veterans and prisoners of war to protect the sovereignty and territorial integrity of the country." As Dr. Hamid Algar has pointed out to me, it is of note that service by Iran's religious minorities in the armed forces represents an instance where state policy is not governed by religious law, in that Shi'i (like Sunni) jurisprudence provides for their exemption or exclusion from the military in exchange for payment of the *jizya*. The reasoning is that the wars in which an Islamic state engages constitute jihad, which is by definition an Islamic religious duty. Because these provisions of Islamic law were ignored, the Sacred Defense can be seen as a war in which the themes of Islam were prominently and effectively invoked and a call went out for the defense of a nation in which Christians, Zoroastrians, and Jews were seen as full partners.

41. IRNA Headlines, "Massive Participation of Armenian Christians in Iran's National Elections," Feb. 19, 2000, and "Armenian Religious Leader: Interview," Feb. 18, 2000. Bishop Sepuh Sarkissian replaced Artak Manoukian as the Armenian Iranian archbishop following Manoukian's death in October 1999.

42. IRNA Headlines, "Khatami: Iran Takes Dialogue as Man's Most Humane Aspect," July 17, 2000.

43. Held at the Ararat complex in Vanak to coincide with the Thirty-Third Annual Sports Festival of Armenian Iranians, the opening ceremonies featured speeches by officials of the Islamic Republic and leaders of the Armenian community, followed by the release of doves and an extensive fireworks display. The entire ceremony and many of

the athletic events including male and female athletes were broadcast in streaming video on the IRNA website and advertised as a special feature for two weeks. Narration was in Armenian. Several still photographs depicting Ararat members marching around the sports track bearing the flags of both the Islamic Republic and the Ararat club during the opening ceremony were also posted to the site. See IRNA Headlines, "Film on Armenian Sports Festival on Line," Sept. 19, 2000.

44. IRNA Headlines, "Keshishian Hails Developments in Armenian–Iranian Relations," July 19, 2000. On July 24, 2000, IRNA quoted Keshishian as saying, "Armenians, since the victory of the 1979 Islamic Revolution in Iran, have played an active role in all affairs of their beloved country along with their Muslim brothers" ("Armenians' Leader, Speaker"). The integration of Armenians into the national fabric of other Middle Eastern nations is a fact often recognized by Armenian Church officials such as Keshishian (a native of Lebanon) and by state leadership. Faruq al-Shar, foreign minister of Syria, was quoted as saying, "The Armenian who lives in Syria is Syrian. Many Armenians decided not to go back to Armenia after its independence, as they felt deeply Syrian" (*Armenian International Magazine*, "Quote Unquote," Apr. 2000). In a statement rejecting an Israeli demand for annexation of the Armenian Quarter of Jerusalem, Palestinian Authority chairman Yasser Arafat stated, "The Armenian quarter belongs to us and we and the Armenians are one people." An Armenian Palestinian public-relations officer at Beirzeit University explained that the Armenians were "partners in the struggle for a free and democratic Palestine" (both statements given in IRNA Headlines, "Palestine-Armenian Quarter," Aug. 26, 2000).

45. IRNA Headlines, "Armenian Leader Praises Co-existence of Religions in Isfahan," July 19, 2000. As reported by IRNA, the governor-general welcomed Keshishian to the city and said, "We are happy to live with our Armenian compatriots in this old city and Iranian officials have always tried to create a calm and joyful atmosphere for them."

46. Quoted in IRNA Headlines, "Ayatollah Taheri: Muslims, Christians Enjoy Bonds of Amity," July 21, 2000. For reporting on similar exchanges during Keshishian's visit to Tabriz and Chalderan in West Azerbaijan province, see IRNA Headlines, "Armenian Leader: No Religious Discrimination in Iran," July 31, 2000, and "Archbishop: Religious Freedoms of Minorities Safeguarded in Iran," July 30, 2000.

47. IRNA Headlines, "Archbishop Keshishian Lauds Status of Armenians in Iran," July 23, 2000; see also *Iran Daily* on the Karroubi–Keshishian meeting, July 24, 2000.

48. Sanasarian, *Religious Minorities in Iran*, 158.

49. Ibid., 159.

50. Ibid., 162–63.

51. For example, see the January 31, 2013, IRNA Headlines story "Armenian Bishop Urges World to Take Lesson from Iran for Proper Treatment of Religious Minorities." See the September 26, 2010, *Iran Daily* headline story "Armenians Protest in Tehran Following Insult to Quran," which describes a rally by thousands of Armenians on the anniversary

of the September 11, 2001, attacks to protest the proposed burning of the Quran by Pastor Terry Jones in Gainseville, Florida. See also the April 4, 2010, *Iran Daily* report "MP Lauds Armenian Community" on statements by head of the Majles National Security and Foreign Policy Commission Alaeddin Boroujerdi in a meeting with Archbishop Sebuh Sarkisian that Armenians had an "excellent record when it comes to reflecting the image of the country to the outside world" and that "we have a sense of friendship with the Iranian Armenians because of being compatriots and also because of following a divine faith." After recalling the sacrifices by Armenian "martyrs" of the Iran-Iraq War as well as by those disabled and taken prisoner, he commented that "this of itself shows the determination of the Iranian Armenian community to help protect the sovereignty and territorial integrity of the country." Perhaps most notably, he concluded that "Iranians are a great people, and when we speak about Shi'ites it means we talk about Iranians." See also the February 10, 2007, IRNA Headlines story "Armenian Community to Renew Allegiance to Supreme Leader," which reports the statement from the Archdiocese Council of Armenians that "the Armenian Community of Iran will celebrate the [February 11] anniversary of victory of the Islamic Revolution to renew allegiance to [the] Supreme Leader of the Islamic Revolution." "Once again it is an occasion for [the] anniversary of victory of the Islamic Revolution and the nation are [*sic*] going to admire the achievements of the Islamic Revolution in the past 28 years," the statement said. The statement, signed by Archbishop Sibveh Sarkisyan, explained that the nation has been inspired by the Islamic Revolution and has bright prospects for future. "The late Imam Khomeini led the Islamic Revolution in good faith and commitments to the religious principles, it said. The statement said that the Armenian community of Iran has a history of 2,000 years in Iran and is a good witness to the progress Iran has made in the past 28 years in different fields."

52. The tradition of large street protests against the Turkish government by Iran's Armenian community continued on April 24, 2006. Photographs of thousands of Armenian Iranian demonstrators led by Armenian clergy, community leaders, and uniformed Ararat scouts appeared in the Iranian press and were circulated widely on the Internet. *Iran Daily* noted that the protestors "carried placards in [the] Armenian language that read 'Armenian Martyrs, We Will Continue Your Way,' 'Upholding Justice Is Our Right,' and 'Islamic Republic Is Supporter of Oppressed People'" ("Armenian Rally in Tehran," Apr. 25, 2006).

53. In 1999 and 2000, Armeno-Iranian relations were extended through several high-level diplomatic exchanges, including visits to Iran by President Robert Kocharian and Defense Minister Serzh Sarkisian to discuss a proposed gas pipeline project, regional security, and Iran's role in mediating the conflict in Karabagh. See IRNA Headlines, "Armenian Minister Condemns Intervention of Foreign Forces in Region," Nov. 8, 2000; "Khatami: Expansion of Iran–Armenia Ties Will Strengthen Regional Security," Nov. 8, 2000; and "Iran–Armenia–Greece Cooperation Not against Any Country," July 17, 2000. Regarding the further extension of Armeno-Iranian cooperation with the intensification of economic sanctions against Iran, see Voice of America News, "Iran, Armenian Find Solidarity in

Isolation," Mar. 12, 2013, at http://www.voanews.com/content/iran-armenia-find-solidarity-in-isolation/1619833.html, accessed Mar. 20, 2013.

54. The attempt by the government of the Islamic Republic to perpetuate national identity and pride in the Iranian nation has been expanded to include Iranians living abroad, including the many who left the country following the Islamic Revolution. See IRNA Headlines and *Iran Daily* (same article in both), "Every Iranian Abroad Must Feel Proud of Own Nationality," Aug. 25, 1999, and Aug. 26, 1999, respectively.

55. A complex case in point would be the May 2006 demonstrations in northwestern Iranian cities by ethnic Azeris inflamed over a newspaper cartoon they interpreted as insulting to Azeri ethnicity. As a result of ongoing protests, the newspaper that printed the cartoon was shut down, and its editor as well as the Azeri cartoonist were arrested. See "Iran Azeris Protest over Cartoon" *BBC News*, May 28, 2006, at http://news.bbc.co.uk/2/hi/middle_east/5024550.stm, accessed Aug. 2010.

56. In February 2006, *Financial Times* reported that the intelligence wing of the United States Marines was investigating the "depth and nature of grievances" of various Iranian minority groups to determine their potential use in a ground invasion of Iran and the likelihood of sectarian violence in the wake of a military attack and occupation (Guy Dinmore, "U.S. Marines Probe Tensions among Iran's Minorities," *Financial Times*, Feb. 23, 2006, at http://www.ft.com/cms/s/ed436938-a49d-11da-897c-0000779e2340.html, accessed Apr. 2006).

57. Sanasarian, *Religious Minorities in Iran*, 147.

58. Iran's PressTV profiles the Ararat organization and sports complex in "Ararat Club," which aired October 22, 2012, at http://www.presstv.ir/Program/268120.html, accessed Feb. 2013.

59. IRNA Headlines, "Massive Participation of Armenian Christians in Iran's National Elections," Feb. 19, 2000. Articles focusing on Armenian Iranian voting have become standard fare in the Iranian press during election season. For example, see the December 15, 2006, IRNA Headlines report "Isfahan's Armenians Cast Their Votes," which reminds readers that "the Armenians, like other religious minorities living in the Isfahan province, have always had an active participation in the elections to determine the country's fate." See also PressTV, "Isfahan's Minorities," June 12, 2012, at http://www.presstv.ir/Program/245048.html, accessed June 2012.

Bibliography

Abir, Mordechai. "The Consolidation of the Ruling Class and the New Elites in Saudi Arabia." *Middle Eastern Studies* 23, no. 2 (1987): 150–71.

Abrahamian, Ervand. "The Crowd in Iranian Politics, 1905–1953." *Past and Present* 41 (1968): 193–94.

———. *Iran between Two Revolutions*. Princeton, NJ: Princeton Univ. Press, 1982.

———. "Kasravi: The Integrative Nationalist of Iran." *Middle Eastern Studies* 9, no. 3 (1973): 271–95.

———. *Khomeinism: Essays on the Islamic Republic*. Berkeley: Univ. of California Press, 1993.

Afary, Janet. *The Iranian Constitutional Revolution, 1906–1911: Grassroots Democracy, Social Democracy, and the Origins of Feminism*. New York: Columbia Univ. Press, 1996.

Afshari, Mohammed Reza. "The *Pishivaran* and Merchants in Precapitalist Iranian Society: An Essay on the Background and Causes of the Constitutional Revolution." *International Journal of Middle East Studies* 15 (1983): 133–55.

Ahmad, Ishtiaq. *Anglo-Iranian Relations, 1905–1919*. Bombay: Asia Publishing House, 1975.

Algar, Hamid. *Mirza Malkum Khan: A Study in the History of Iranian Modernism*. Berkeley, Univ. of California Press, 1973.

———. *Religion and State in Iran, 1785–1906: The Role of the Ulama in the Qajar Period*. Berkeley: Univ. of California Press, 1969.

Alter, Peter. *Nationalism*. 2nd ed. London: Hodder Education, 1994.

Amin, Camron M. *The Making of the Modern Iranian Woman: Gender, State Policy, and Popular Culture, 1865–1946*. Gainesville: Univ. of Florida Press, 2002.

Amin, Camron M., Benjamin Fortna, and Elizabeth Frierson, eds. *The Modern Middle East: A Sourcebook*. Oxford: Oxford Univ. Press, 2006.

Amirsadeghi, Hossein, ed. *Twentieth Century Iran*. New York: Holmes & Meier, 1977.

Amuzegar, Jahangir, and M. Ali Fekrat. *Iran: Economic Development under Dualistic Conditions*. Chicago: Univ. of Chicago Press, 1971.

Anderson, Benedict R. *Imagined Communities: Reflections on the Origin and Spread of Nationalism*. New York: Verso, 2006.

Ansari, Ali. *The Politics of Nationalism in Iran*. Cambridge: Cambridge Univ. Press, 2012.

Arjomand, Said Amir. *The Turban for the Crown: The Islamic Revolution in Iran*. New York: Oxford Univ. Press, 1988.

Armstrong, John A. *Nations before Nationalism*. 1982. Reprint. Chapel Hill: Univ. of North Carolina Press, 2011.

Aslanian, Sebouh. *From the Indian Ocean to the Mediterranean: The Global Trade Networks of Armenian Merchants from New Julfa*. Berkeley: Univ. of California Press, 2011.

Atkin, Muriel. *Russia and Iran 1780–1828*. Minneapolis: Univ. of Minnesota Press, 1980.

Avery, Peter. *Modern Iran*. New York: Praeger, 1965.

Baer, Gabriel. *Egyptian Guilds in Modern Times*. Jerusalem: Israel Oriental Society, 1964.

Bahar, Muhammad Taqi. *Tarikh-i mukhtasar-i ahzab-i siyasi-ye Iran, inqiraz-i qajariyah* (A brief history of the political parties of Iran: The Qajar downfall). Tehran: Mu'assasah-i Matbu'ati i Amir Kabir, 1323/1944.

Bakhash, Shaul. *Iran: Monarchy, Bureaucracy, and Reform under the Qajars 1858–1896*. London: Ithaca Press, 1978.

Bakhtin, Michel M. *The Dialogic Imagination: Four Essays*. Translated by Caryl Emerson. Edited by Michael Holquist. Austin: Univ. of Texas Press, 1981.

Baldwin, George. *Planning and Development in Iran*. Baltimore: Johns Hopkins Univ. Press, 1967.

Banani, Amin. *The Modernization of Iran, 1921–1941*. Stanford, CA: Stanford Univ. Press, 1961.

Behar, Moshe. "Do Comparative and Regional Studies of Nationalism Intersect?" *International Journal of Middle East Studies* 37 (2005): 587–612.

Berberian, Houri. "History, Memory, and Iranian-Armenian Memoirs of the Iranian Constitutional Revolution." *Critique: Critical Middle Eastern Studies* 17, no. 3 (2008): 261–92.

———. *"The Love for Freedom Has No Fatherland": Armenians and the Iranian Constitutional Revolution of 1905–1911*. Boulder, CO: Westview, 2001.

———. "Traversing Boundaries and Selves: Iranian Armenian Identities during the Iranian Constitutional Revolution." *Comparative Studies of South Asia, Africa, and the Middle East* 25, no. 2 (2005): 279–96.

Bharier, Julian. *Economic Development in Iran, 1900–1970*. New York: Oxford Univ. Press, 1971.

Bidwell, Robert, ed. *British Documents on Foreign Affairs: Reports and Papers from the Foreign Office*. Frederick, MD: Univ. Publications of America, 1985.

Bill, James A. *The Politics of Iran: Groups, Classes, and Modernization*. Columbus, OH: Merrill, 1972.

Billig, Michael. *Banal Nationalism*. London: Sage, 1995.

Binder, Leonard. *Iran*. Berkeley: Univ. of California Press, 1961.

Bonine, Michael E., and Nikki R. Keddie, eds. *Continuity and Change in Modern Iran*. Albany: State Univ. of New York Press, 1981.

Borgomale, H. L. Rabino di. *Coins, Medals, and Seals of the Shahs of Iran, 1500–1941*. Hertford, UK: Austin and Sons, 1945.

Boroujerdi, Mehrzad. "Contesting Nationalist Constructions of Iranian Identity." *Critique*, no. 12 (Spring 1998): 43–56.

Bosworth, Edmund, and Carole Hillenbrand, eds. *Qajar Iran: Political, Social, and Cultural Change, 1800–1925*. Edinburgh: Edinburgh Univ. Press, 1983.

Bournoutian, George A. *A History of the Armenian People*. Vol. 1: *Prehistory to 1500 AD*. Costa Mesa, CA: Mazda, 1993.

———. *A History of the Armenian People*. Vol. 2: *1500 A.D. to the Present*. Costa Mesa, CA: Mazda, 1993.

———. "The Politics of Demography: Misuse of Sources on the Armenian Population of Mountainous Karabakh." *Journal of the Society for Armenian Studies* 9 (1999): 99–104.

Bozorgmehr, Mehdi. "From Iranian Studies to Studies of Iranians in the United States." In "Iranians in the United States," special issue of *Iranian Studies* 31, no. 1 (1998): 5–30.

Brass, Paul R. *Ethnicity and Nationalism: Theory and Comparison*. New Delhi: Sage, 1991.

Breuilly, John. *Nationalism and the State*. Chicago: Univ. of Chicago Press, 1994.

British Documents on Foreign Affairs–Reports and Papers from the Foreign Office Confidential Print: From the Mid–Nineteenth Century to the First World War. Vol. 13:

The Near and Middle East, 1856–1914. Bethesda, MD: Univ. Publications of America, 1986.

Browne, Edward Granville. *The Persian Revolution of 1905–1909*. 1910. Reprint. Washington, DC: Mage, 2006.

Brubaker, Rogers. *Nationalism Reframed: Nationhood and the National Question in the New Europe*. Cambridge: Cambridge Univ. Press, 1996.

Bulliet, Richard W. *The Camel and the Wheel*. New York: Columbia Univ. Press, 1990.

Burke, Edmund, III, ed. *Struggle and Survival in the Modern Middle East*. Berkeley: Univ. of California Press, 1993.

Burke, Edmund, III, and David N. Yaghoubian, eds. *Struggle and Survival in the Modern Middle East*. 2nd ed. Berkeley: Univ. of California Press, 2006.

Calhoun, Craig. *Nationalism*. Minneapolis: Univ. of Minnesota Press, 1997.

———. *Nations Matter: Culture, History, and the Cosmopolitan Dream*. New York: Routledge, 2007.

Chaudhry, Kiren Aziz. *The Price of Wealth: Economies and Institutions in the Middle East*. Ithaca, NY: Cornell Univ. Press, 1997.

Chaqueri, Cosroe, ed. *The Armenians of Iran: The Paradoxical Role of a Minority in a Dominant Culture*. Cambridge, MA: Harvard Univ. Press, 1998.

Chehabi, Houshang, and Vanessa Martin, eds. *Iran's Constitutional Revolution: Popular Politics, Cultural Transformations, and Transnational Connections*. New York: I. B. Tauris, 2010.

Cook, M. A., ed. *Studies in the Economic History of the Middle East: From the Rise of Islam to the Present Day*. London: Oxford Univ. Press, 1970.

Cottam, Richard W. *Nationalism in Iran*. Pittsburgh: Univ. of Pittsburgh Press, 1964.

———. *Nationalism in Iran: Updated through 1978*. Pittsburgh: Univ. of Pittsburgh Press, 1979.

Couture, Jocelyne, Kai Nielsen, and Michel Seymour, eds. *Rethinking Nationalism*. Calgary: Univ. of Calgary Press, 1998.

Dadrian, Vahakn. *The History of the Armenian Genocide: Ethnic Conflict from the Balkans to Anatolia to the Caucasus*. 4th ed. New York: Berghahn Books, 2003.

Dadrian, Vahakn, and Taner Akcam. *Judgment at Istanbul: The Armenian Genocide Trials*. New York: Berghahn Books, 2011.

Daneshkade Fanni va faregholtahsilan, Daneshgah-e Tehran, 1313–1373 (College of Engineering and its graduates, University of Tehran, 1934–1994). Tehran: University of Tehran, 1994.

Delanty, Gerard, and Krishan Kumar, eds. *The Sage Handbook of Nations and Nationalism.* London: Sage, 2006.

De Moraes Ruehsen, Moyara. "Operation 'Ajax' Revisited: Iran, 1953." *Middle Eastern Studies* 29, no. 3 (1993): 467–86.

Deutsch, Karl. *Nationalism and National Development: An Interdisciplinary Bibliography.* Cambridge, MA: MIT Press, 1970.

Domantovich, A. I. "Vospominanija o prebyvanii pervoj russkoj voennoj missii v Persii" (Memoirs about the first Russian military mission in Persia). *Russkaia Starina* 133, no. 2 (1908): 331–40; no. 3: 575–83; no. 4: 211–16.

Dorman, William A., and Mansour Farhang. *The U.S. Press and Iran: Foreign Policy and the Journalism of Deference.* Berkeley: Univ. of California Press, 1987.

Dreyfus, Hubert, and Paul Rabinow. *Michel Foucault: Beyond Structuralism and Hermeneutics.* Chicago: Univ. of Chicago Press, 1982.

Dunaway, David K., and Willa K. Baum, eds. *Oral History: An Interdisciplinary Anthology.* London: Sage, 1996.

Ehsani, Kaveh. "Social Engineering and the Contradictions of Modernization in Khuzestan's Oil Company Towns: A Look at Abadan and Masjed-Soleyman." *International Review of Social History* 48 (2003): 361–99.

Elwell-Sutton, L. P. *Modern Iran.* London: Routledge, 1942.

Erlich, Reese. *The Iran Agenda.* Boulder, CO: Paradigm, 2007.

Farmanfarmaian, Manucher, and Roxane Farmanfarmaian. *Blood and Oil: Memoirs of a Persian Prince.* New York: Random House, 1997.

Farmanfarmaian, Sattareh, with Donna Munker. *Daughter of Persia: A Woman's Journey from Her Father's Harem through the Islamic Revolution.* 1993. Reprint. New York: Broadway, 2006.

Fasa'i, Hasan ibn Hasan. *History of Persia under Qajar Rule.* Translated from the Persian by Heribert Busse. New York: Columbia Univ. Press, 1972.

Fateh, Moustafa Khan. *The Economic Position of Persia.* London: King & Son, 1926.

Fatemi, Nasrollah S. *Diplomatic History of Persia, 1917–1923: Anglo-Russian Power Politics in Iran.* New York: Russell F. Moore, 1952.

Fay, Mary Ann, ed. *Auto/Biography and the Construction of Identity and Community in the Middle East.* New York: Palgrave, 2001.

Filmer, Henry. *The Pageant of Persia: A Record of Travel by Motor in Persia with an Account of Its Ancient and Modern Ways.* New York: Bobbs-Merrill, 1936.

Floor, Willem M. "Guilds and *Futuvvat* in Iran." *Zeitschrift der Deutschen Morgenlandischen Gesellschaft* 134, no. 1 (1984): 106–14.

———. "The Guilds in Iran—an Overview from the Earliest Beginnings till 1972." *Zeitschrift der Deutschen Morgenlandischen Gesellschaft* 125, no. 1 (1975): 99–116.

———. *Industrialization in Iran, 1900–1941.* Durham, UK: Univ. of Durham, 1984.

———. *Labour Unions, Law, and Conditions in Iran, 1900–1941.* Durham, UK: Univ. of Durham, 1985.

Foucault, Michel. *Archaeology of Knowledge and the Discourse of Language.* Translated by A. M. Sheridan Smith and Rupert Sawyer. New York: Pantheon Books, 1972.

———. *The Birth of the Clinic: An Archaeology of Medical Perception.* New York: Pantheon Books, 1973.

———. *Discipline and Punish: The Birth of the Prison.* New York: Vintage Books, 1975.

———. *The Order of Things: An Archaeology of the Human Sciences.* New York: Pantheon Books, 1970.

———. *Power/Knowledge: Selected Interviews and Other Writings.* Sussex, UK: Harvester Press, 1980.

Fox, Richard. *Gandhian Utopia: Experiments with Culture.* Boston: Beacon Press, 1989.

Fox-Genovese, Elizabeth, and Eugene Genovese. "The Political Crisis of Social History: A Marxian Perspective." *Journal of Social History* 10 (Winter 1976): 205–20.

Friedman, Max Paul. "Private Memory, Public Records, and Contested Terrain: Weighing Oral Testimony in the Deportation of Germans from Latin America during World War II." *Oral History Review* 27, no. 1 (2000): 1–16.

Garthwaite, Gene R. "Bakhtiyari Khans: Tribal Disunity in Iran 1880–1915." PhD diss., Univ. of California, Los Angeles, 1969.

———. *The Persians.* Oxford: Blackwell, 2005.

Gasiorowski, Mark. "The 1953 Coup d'Etat in Iran." *International Journal of Middle East Studies* 19 (1987): 261–86.

———. "Richard W. Cottam (1924–1997)." *Iranian Studies* 30, nos. 3–4 (1997): 415–17.

———. *U.S. Foreign Policy and the Shah: Building a Client State in Iran.* Ithaca, NY: Cornell Univ. Press, 1991.

Gellner, Ernest. *Encounters with Nationalism.* Oxford: Blackwell, 1994.

———. *Nations and Nationalism.* Ithaca, NY: Cornell Univ. Press, 1983.

Ghods, Reza M. "Iranian Nationalism and Reza Shah." *Middle Eastern Studies* 27, no. 1 (1991): 35–45.

———. *Iran in the Twentieth Century: A Political History.* Boulder, CO: Lynne Rienner, 1989.

Giddens, Anthony. *The Nation-State and Violence: Volume Two of a Contemporary Critique of Historical Materialism.* Berkeley: Univ. of California Press, 1987.

Gillis, John, ed. *Commemorations: The Politics of National Identity.* Princeton, NJ: Princeton Univ. Press, 1994.

Goli Majd, Mohammad. *Great Britain and Reza Shah: The Plunder of Iran, 1921–1941.* Gainesville: Univ. of Florida Press, 2001.

Gramsci, Antonio. *Prison Notebooks.* New York: Columbia Univ. Press, 1992.

Guha, Ranajit, and Gayatri Spivak, eds. *Selected Subaltern Studies.* New York: Oxford Univ. Press, 1988.

Guibernau, Monserrat, and John Hutchinson, eds. *History and National Destiny: Ethnosymbolism and Its Critics.* Oxford: Blackwell, 2004.

Gupta, R. N. *Iran, an Economic Study.* New Dehli: Indian Institute of International Affairs, 1947.

Hay Meshakoutain Ararat Kazmakerpoutun (Armenian Cultural Ararat Organization). *Himnadroutian yev gortsneoutian 40 amyak* (40th anniversary of founding and activities). Tehran: Bashgahe Varzeshi va Pishahangi Ararat, 1984.

Heiss, Mary Ann. *Empire and Nationhood: The United States, Great Britain, and Iranian Oil, 1950–1954.* New York: Columbia Univ. Press, 1997.

Henige, David. *Oral Historiography.* London: Longman, 1982.

Heravi, Mehdi. *Iranian–American Diplomacy.* New York: Theo Gauss, 1969.

Hersh, Seymour M. "Preparing the Battlefield: The Bush Administration Steps Up Its Secret Moves against Iran." *The New Yorker,* July 7 and 14, 2008: 61–67.

Hershlag, Zvi Yehuda. *Introduction to the Modern Economic History of the Middle East.* Leiden: E. J. Brill, 1964.

Heyd, Uriel. "Farman." In *Encyclopaedia of Islam,* new ed., 803–6. Leiden: Brill, 1986.

———. *Ottoman Documents on Palestine 1552–1615: A Study of the Firman according to the Muhimme Defteri.* Oxford: Clarendon Press, 1960.

Hobsbawm, Eric J. *Nations and Nationalism since 1780: Programme, Myth, Reality.* New York: Cambridge Univ. Press, 1990.

Hobsbawm, Eric J., and Terence Ranger, eds. *The Invention of Tradition.* London: Cambridge Univ. Press, 1983.

Hoogasian Villa, Susie. *Armenian Village Life before 1914.* Detroit: Wayne State Univ. Press, 1982.

Houghton, David. *US Foreign Policy and the Iran Hostage Crisis.* Cambridge: Cambridge Univ. Press, 2001.

Hovannisian, Richard G., ed. *The Armenian Image in History and Literature.* Malibu, CA: Undena, 1981.

———. *The Republic of Armenia*. 4 vols. Berkeley: Univ. of California Press, 1971–96.

Hutchinson, John, and Anthony D. Smith. *Nationalism*. New York: Oxford Univ. Press, 1994.

International Engineering Company. *Report on Program for the Development of Iran*. San Francisco: International Engineering, 1947.

Irschick, Eugene. *Dialogue and History: Constructing South India, 1795–1895*. Berkeley: Univ. of California Press, 1994.

Ishaya, Arianne. "From Contributions to Diaspora: Assyrians in the History of Urmia, Iran." *Journal of Assyrian Academic Studies* 16, no. 1 (2002): 25–41.

Ishqi Sanati, Khanak. *Junbishha-yi nasyunalisti dar Iran* (Nationalist movements in Iran). Ottawa: Ava-ye Iran, 1985.

Issawi, Charles Philip. "De-industrialization and Re-industrialization in the Middle East since 1800." *International Journal of Middle East Studies* 12 (1980): 469–79.

———, ed. *The Economic History of Iran, 1800–1914*. Chicago: Univ. of Chicago Press, 1971.

———. *An Economic History of the Middle East and North Africa*. New York: Columbia Univ. Press, 1982.

Jacqz, Jane W., ed. *Iran—Past, Present, and Future*. New York: Aspen Institute for Humanistic Studies, 1976.

James, Paul. *Nation Formation: Toward a Theory of Abstract Community*. London: Sage, 1996.

Jankowski, James, and Israel Gershoni, eds. *Rethinking Nationalism in the Middle East*. New York: Columbia Univ. Press, 1997.

Jones, Rebecca. "Blended Voices: Crafting a Narrative from Oral History Interviews." *Oral History Review* 31, no. 1 (2004): 23–42.

Kamrava, Mehran. *The Political History of Modern Iran: From Tribalism to Theocracy*. London: Praeger, 1992.

Kashani-Sabet, Firoozeh, "Fragile Frontiers: The Diminishing Domains of Qajar Iran." *International Journal of Middle East Studies* 29, no. 2 (1997): 205–34.

———. *Frontier Fictions: Shaping the Iranian Nation, 1804–1946*. Princeton, NJ: Princeton Univ. Press, 1999.

Katouzian, Homa. "Nationalist Trends in Iran, 1921–1926." *International Journal of Middle East Studies* 10, no. 4 (1979): 533–51.

———. *The Persians: Ancient, Medieval, and Modern Iran*. New Haven, CT: Yale Univ. Press, 2010.

———. *The Political Economy of Modern Iran: Despotism and Pseudo-modernism, 1926–1979*. New York: New York Univ. Press, 1981.

Kazarian, M. *Khudozhniki Ovnatanian.* Moscow: n.p., 1968.

Kazemzadeh, Firuz. "The Origin and Early Development of the Persian Cossack Brigade." *American Slavic and East European Review* 15, no. 3 (1956): 351–63.

———. *Russia and Britain in Persia, 1864–1914: A Study in Imperialism.* New Haven, CT: Yale Univ. Press, 1968.

Keddie, Nikki R. "The Impact of the West on Iranian Social History." PhD diss., Univ. of California, Berkeley, 1955.

———. *Modern Iran: Roots and Results of Revolution. An Interpretive History of Modern Iran.* New Haven, CT: Yale Univ. Press, 2006.

———. *Qajar Iran and the Rise of Reza Khan, 1796–1925.* Costa Mesa, CA: Mazda, 1999.

———. "Religion and Irreligion in Early Iranian Nationalism." *Comparative Studies in Society and History* 4, no. 3 (1962): 265–95.

Keddie, Nikki R., Eqbal Ahmad, and Walter Goldfrank. "Comments on Skocpol." *Theory and Society* 2, no. 3 (1982): 285–92.

Kedourie, Elie. *Nationalism.* 4th ed. Oxford: Blackwell, 1993.

———, ed. *Nationalism in Asia and Africa.* New York: New American Library, 1970.

Kenez, Peter. *The Birth of the Propaganda State: Soviet Methods of Mass Mobilization, 1917–1929.* Cambridge: Cambridge Univ. Press, 1985.

Kessler-Harris, Alice. *Social History.* Washington, DC: American Historical Association, 1997.

Keyvani, Mehdi. *Artisans and Guild Life in the Later Safavid Period.* Berlin: Klaus Schwarz, 1982.

Khan, Yusuf Husain. *Farmans and Sanads of the Deccan Sultans (1408–1687 A.D.).* Hyderabad, Iran: State Archives, Government of Andhra Pradesh, 1980.

Khan Malik Sasani, Ahmad. *Pusht-i pardah: Dastanhayi az dawrah-i Qajar* (Behind the curtain: Stories from the Qajar era). Tehran: Shabaviz, 1372/1993.

Kia, Mehrdad. "Nationalism, Modernism, and Islam in the Writings of Talibov-i-Tabrizi." *Middle Eastern Studies* 30, no. 2 (1994): 201–23.

Kosogovskii, Vladimir Andreevich. *Khatirat-i Kolonel Kasagofski: Tarjumah-i 'Abbas-quli Jalli. Chap-i Duvvum* (Memoirs of Colonel Kasagofski: Translation of 'Abbas-quli Jalli. Second edition). Tehran: Kitabha-yi Simurgh, 1976.

——— [Kosagovskij]. "Ocherk razvitija Persidskoj Kazach'ej Brigady" (Essay on the development of the Persian Cossack Brigade). *Novyj Vostok* 4 (1923): 390–402.

——— [Kosagovskij]. "Persija v Kontse XIX veka" (Persia at the end of the 19th century). *Novyj Vostok* 3 (1923): 446–69.

———. *Iz tegeranskogo dnevnika polkovnika V. A. Kosogovskogo* (Tehran diary of Colonel V. A. Kosogovskogo). Moscow: Izd-vo Vostochnoi Lit-ry, 1960.

Ladjavardi, Habib, ed. *Khaterat-e Ali Amini, nakhost vazir-e Iran (1340–41)* (Memoirs of Ali Amini, prime minister of Iran [1961–62]). Cambridge, MA: Harvard Iranian Oral History Project, 1995.

Lambton, Ann K. S. *Islamic Society in Persia*. Oxford: Oxford Univ. Press, 1954.

———. *Qajar Persia: Eleven Studies*. Austin: Univ. of Texas Press, 1988.

Lawrence-Archer, James. *The Orders of Chivalry: From the Original Statutes of the Various Orders of Knighthood, and Other Sources of Information*. London: W. H. Allen, 1887.

Lenczowski, George, ed. *Iran under the Pahlavis*. Stanford, CA: Hoover Institution Press, 1978.

———. *Russia and the West in Iran, 1918–1948*. Ithaca, NY: Cornell Univ. Press, 1949.

Lenin, Vladimir Il'ich. *Collected Works of V. I. Lenin*. New York: International Publishers, 1927.

Leoussi, Athena, and Steven Grosby, eds. *Nationalism and Ethnosymbolism: History, Culture, and Ethnicity in the Formation of Nations*. Edinburgh: Edinburgh Univ. Press, 2007.

LeVine, Mark, and Gershon Shafir, eds. *Struggle and Survival in Palestine/Israel*. Berkeley: Univ. of California Press, 2012.

Lewy, Guenter. *The Armenian Massacres in Ottoman Turkey: A Disputed Genocide*. Salt Lake City: Univ. of Utah Press, 2007.

Lytle, Mark H. *Origins of the Iranian–American Alliance, 1941–1953*. New York: Holmes and Meier, 1987.

Madhavy, Hossein. "The Patterns and Problems of Economic Development in Rentier States: The Case of Iran." In *Studies in the Economic History of the Middle East: From the Rise of Islam to the Present Day*, edited by M. A. Cook, 428–67. London: Oxford Univ. Press, 1970.

Mahbubi Ardakani, Husayn. *Tarikh-i mu'assasat-i tamadduni-i jadid dar Iran* (The history of the institutions of the new civilization in Iran). Tehran: Anjuman-i Danishjuyan-i Danishgah-i Tehran, 1354/1975.

Mahdavi, Asghar. "The Significance of Private Archives for the Study of the Economic and Social History of Iran in the late Qajar Period." *Society for Iranian Studies* 16, no. 3 (1983): 243–78.

Malikzadah, Mahdi. *Tarikh-i Inqilab-i Mashrutiyat-i Iran* (History of Iran's Constitutional Revolution). 7 vols. Tehran: 'Ilmi Press, 1984.

Manshur Garakani, M. A. *Siyasat-i Dawlat-i Shawravi dar Iran az 1296 ta 1306* (Policies of the Soviet government in Iran from 1917 to 1928). Tehran: n.p., 1326/1947.

Marashi, Afshin. *Nationalizing Iran: Culture, Power, and the State, 1870–1940*. Seattle: Univ. of Washington Press, 2008.

Marcus, Abraham. *The Middle East on the Eve of Modernity*. New York: Columbia Univ. Press, 1989.

Markham, Clements R. *Tarikh-i Iran dar dawrahi Qajar* (History of Iran during the Qajar era). Tehran: Nashr-i Farhang-i Iran, 1364/1985.

Matthee, Rudolph, and Beth Baron, eds. *Iran and Beyond: Essays in Middle Eastern History in Honor of Nikki R. Keddie*. Costa Mesa, CA: Mazda, 2000.

Menashri, David. *Education and the Making of Modern Iran*. Ithaca, NY: Cornell Univ. Press, 1992.

Michener, Roger, ed. *Nationality, Patriotism, and Nationalism in Liberal Democratic Societies*. St. Paul, MN: Paragon House, 1993.

Miller, Donald, and Laura Touryan Miller. *Survivors: An Oral History of the Armenian Genocide*. Berkeley: Univ. of California Press, 1999.

Millspaugh, Arthur Chester. *Americans in Persia*. Washington, DC: Brookings Institution, 1946.

———. *The Financial and Economic Situation of Persia, 1926*. New York: Imperial Persian Government, Persia Society, 1926.

Mottahedeh, Roy. *Mantle of the Prophet*. New York: One World, 2008.

Muqtadir, Ghulam Husayn. *Tarikh-I nizami-i Iran. Chap-i duvvum* (History of Iran's military. Second edition). Tehran: Chapkhanah-i Farvardin, 1318/1939.

Nisan, Mordechai. *Minorities in the Middle East: A History of Struggle and Self-Expression*. Jefferson, NC: McFarland, 1991.

Okazaki, Shoko. *Bibliography on Qajar Persia*. Osaka, Japan: Univ. of Foreign Studies, 1985.

Ozkirimli, Umut. *Theories of Nationalism: A Critical Introduction*. London: Palgrave-Macmillan, 2000.

———. *Theories of Nationalism: A Critical Introduction*. 2nd ed. London: Palgrave-Macmillan, 2010.

Pahlavi, Mohammad Reza. *Mission for My Country*. New York: McGraw-Hill, 1960.

Perks, Robert, and Alastair Thompson, eds. *The Oral History Reader*. 2nd ed. New York: Routledge, 2006.

Perry, Barbara, and Brian Levin, eds. *Hate Crimes: Understanding and Defining Hate Crime*. Westport, CT: Praeger, 2009.

Pirnazar, Jaleh. "Political Movements and Organizations in Iran, 1890–1953." PhD diss., Univ. of California, Berkeley, 1980.

Qadimi, Zabih Allah Rizvani. *Tarikh-i 25 salah-i Artish Shahanshah-i Iran* (History of 25 years of the Imperial Army of Iran). Tehran: n.p., 1326/1947.

Qa'im Maqami, Jahangir. *Tarikh-i tahavvulat-i siyasi-yi nizam-i Iran* (History of the political transformation of Iran's military). Tehran: Ali Akhbar, 1326/1947.

Ra'in, Isma'il. *Iraniyan-i Armani* (Iranian Armenians). Tehran: Amir Kabir, 1977.

Ramazani, Rouhollah K. *The Foreign Policy of Iran: 1500–1941*. Charlottesville: Univ. Press of Virginia, 1966.

Rostam-Kolayi, Jasamin. "From Evangelizing to Modernizing Iranians: The American Presbyterian Mission and Its Iranian Students." *Iranian Studies* 41, no. 2 (2008): 213–39.

———. "Origins of Iran's Modern Girls' Schools: From Private/National to Public/State." *Journal of Middle East Women's Studies* 4, no. 3 (2008): 58–88.

Said, Edward W. *Orientalism*. New York: Vintage Books, 1978.

Sanasarian, Eliz. *Religious Minorities in Iran*. Cambridge: Cambridge Univ. Press, 2006.

Sarshar, Houman. *Esther's Children: A Portrait of Iranian Jews*. Beverly Hills, CA: Center for Iranian Jewish Oral History, 2002.

Schayegh, Cyrus. "Sport, Health, and the Iranian Middle Class in the 1920s and 1930s." *Iranian Studies* 34, no. 4 (2002): 341–69.

Schulze, Kirsten E., ed. *Nationalism, Minorities, and Diasporas: Identities and Rights in the Middle East*. New York: Tauris Academic Studies, 1996.

Seifoddini, Salar. "Wooden Leg of US Interventions in Middle East Region." *Iran Review*, Sept. 12, 2012. At http://www.iranreview.org/content/Documents/Wooden-Leg-of-US-Interventions-in-Middle-East-Region.htm. Accessed Oct. 27, 2012.

Shuster, W. Morgan. *The Strangling of Persia: Story of the European Diplomacy and Oriental Intrigue That Resulted in the Denationalization of Twelve Million Mohammedans. A Personal Narrative*. New York: Century, 1912.

Siavoshi, Sussan. "Cottam, Richard." In *Encyclopaedia Iranica*, online edition. New York: Columbia Univ., 1996. At http://www.iranicaonline.org/articles/cottam-richard-1. Accessed on January 26, 2014.

———. *Liberal Nationalism in Iran: The Failure of a Movement*. Boulder, CO: Westview Press, 1990.

Simmonds, S. *Economic Conditions in Iran*. London: HMSO, 1935.

Simon, Reeva S., and Eleanor H. Tejirian, eds. *Altruism and Imperialism: Western Cultural and Religious Missions in the Middle East.* New York: Columbia Univ. Press, 2002.

Sjoberg, Gideon. *The Preindustrial City, Past and Present.* New York: Free Press, 1960.

Skocpol, Theda. "Rentier State and Shi'a Islam in the Iranian Revolution." *Theory and Society* 2, no. 3 (1982): 265–83.

Smith, Anthony D. *Ethno-symbolism and Nationalism: A Cultural Approach.* New York: Routledge, 2009.

———. *National Identity.* Reno: Univ. of Nevada Press, 1991.

———. *Nationalism and Modernism.* London: Routledge, 1998.

———. *Nationalism: Theory, Ideology, History.* 2001. Reprint. Cambridge: Cambridge Univ. Press, 2005.

Spencer, Philip, and Howard Wollman, eds. *Nations and Nationalism: A Reader.* New Brunswick, NJ: Rutgers Univ. Press, 2005.

Sprinkler, Michael, ed. *Edward Said: A Critical Reader.* Oxford: Blackwell, 1992.

Srivastava, K. P. *Mughal Farmans (1540 A.D. to 1706 A.D.)* Vol. 1. Lucknow, India: Uttar Pradesh State Archives, 1974.

Stewart, Richard A. *Sunrise at Abadan: The British and Soviet Invasion of Iran, 1941.* New York: Praeger, 1988.

Suny, Ronald G., ed. *Transcaucasia: Nationalism and Social Change.* Ann Arbor: Univ. of Michigan, 1983.

Suny, Ronald G., Fatma M. Göçek, and Norman M. Naimark, eds. *A Question of Genocide: Armenians and Turks at the End of the Ottoman Empire.* New York: Oxford Univ. Press, 2011.

Sweet, David G., and Gary Nash, eds. *Struggle and Survival in Colonial America.* Berkeley: Univ. of California Press, 1981.

Sykes, Sir Percy Molesworth. *A History of Persia.* London: Macmillan, 1930.

Tahvildar, Mirza Husayn Khan. *Jughrafia-yi Isfahan* (Geography of Isfahan). Tehran: University of Tehran, 1963.

Tavassoli, Sasan. *Christian Encounters with Iran: Engaging Muslim Thinkers after the Revolution.* London: I. B. Tauris, 2011.

Tedlock, Dennis. *The Spoken Word and the Work of Interpretation.* Philadelphia: Univ. of Pennsylvania Press, 1983.

Ter-Sarkissian, Pierre. *Photographies armeniennes: Scenes et portraits, 1880–1930.* Paris: Centre de recherches sur la diaspora armenienne, Centre de documentation armenien, 1983.

Thompson, Paul. *The Voice of the Past: Oral History*. 3rd ed. Oxford: Oxford Univ. Press, 2000.

Tousi, Reza Ra'iss. "The Persian Army 1880–1907." *Middle Eastern Studies* 24, no. 2 (1988): 206–29.

Ullman, R. H. *Anglo-Soviet Relations 1917–1921*. Princeton, NJ: Princeton Univ. Press, 1972.

Vassilian, Hamo, ed. *Armenians and Iran: A Comprehensive Bibliography in Armenian, Persian, and the English Languages*. Glendale, CA: Armenian Reference Books, 1991.

Vaziri, Mostafa. *Iran as Imagined Nation: The Construction of National Identity*. New York: Paragon House, 1993.

Vidergar, John J. *The Economic and Social Development of Iran*. Monticello, IL: Council of Planning Librarians, 1977.

Viswanathan, Gauri. *Masks of Conquest: Literary Study and British Rule in India*. New York: Columbia Univ. Press, 1989.

Von Graefe, Axel. *Iran das neue Persien*. Berlin: Atlantis, 1937.

Wallerstein, Immanuel M. *The Modern World-System*. New York: Academic Press, 1974.

Watson, Michael, ed. *Contemporary Minority Nationalism*. New York: Routledge, 1990.

Weryho, Jan. "The Persian Language and Shia as Nationalist Symbols: A Historical Survey." *Canadian Review of Studies in Nationalism* 13, no. 1 (1986): 49–55.

Wilber, Donald Newton. *Contemporary Iran*. New York: Praeger, 1963.

———. *Iran, Past and Present*. Princeton, NJ: Princeton Univ. Press, 1948.

———. *Riza Shah Pahlavi: The Resurrection and Reconstruction of Iran*. Hicksville, NY: Exposition Press, 1975.

Wilson, Sir Arnold Talbot. *Persia, a Political Officer's Diary, 1907–1914*. London: Oxford Univ. Press, 1941.

Wilson, S. G. "The Russian Occupation of Northern Persia." *Muslim World* 3 (1913): 339–49.

Wolf, Eric. *Europe and the People without History*. Berkeley: Univ. of California Press, 1982

Wood, Graeme. "Iran: A Minority Report." *Atlantic Monthly* 298, no. 5 (2006): 46–47.

Wulff, Hans E. *The Traditional Crafts of Persia: Their Development, Technology, and Influence on Eastern and Western Civilizations*. Cambridge, MA: MIT Press, 1966.

Yaghoubian, David. "Shifting Gears in the Desert: Trucks, Guilds, and National Development in Iran, 1921–1941." *Jusur* 13 (1997): 1–36.

Yarshater, Ehsan, ed. *Encyclopaedia Iranica*. London: Routledge & Kegan Paul, 1982.

Yergin, Daniel. *The Prize: The Epic Quest for Oil, Money, and Power*. New York: Free Press, 2008.

Yeroushalmi, David. *The Jews of Iran in the Nineteenth Century: Aspects of History, Community, and Culture*. Boston: Brill, 2009.

———. *Recording Oral History: A Guide for the Humanities and Social Sciences*. 2nd ed. Lanham, MD: Altamira Press, 2005.

Zabih, Sepehr. *The Communist Movement in Iran*. Berkeley: Univ. of California Press, 1966.

Žižek, Slavoj. *Tarrying with the Negative: Kant, Hegel, and the Critique of Ideology*. Durham, NC: Duke Univ. Press, 1993.

Zonis, Marvin. *The Political Elite of Iran*. Princeton, NJ: Princeton Univ. Press, 1971.

Index

Page numbers in italics denote illustrations.